English Sociolinguistics

Covering both traditional topics and innovative approaches, this textbook constitutes a comprehensive introduction to English sociolinguistics. Reflecting the field's breadth and diversity, it guides students through the development of research on language and society over the last sixty years, as well as global trends and related fields such as World Englishes, language politics, language and inequality, and translanguaging. It features practical activities, for both individual work and in-class discussion, as well as vignettes introducing specific case studies, additional information on "out-of-the-box" topics, key terms, and examples from around the world and various social settings. Inspiring, personal, and authoritative interviews with leading sociolinguists conclude the book. Assuming only a basic understanding of the English sound system and its grammar, and supported online by additional activities and selected model answers, this is the ideal text for undergraduates wanting an accessible and modern introduction to the field.

Daniel Schreier is Professor of English Linguistics at the University of Zurich. He has taught and researched in the US, New Zealand, and Germany, and held an Erskine Fellowship at the University of Canterbury (Christchurch, New Zealand). His research interests include varieties of English around the world, language variation and change, contact linguistics, and sociolinguistics. He is author of several books on English in the South Atlantic, editor of books on language change in English, including written sources, has published some eighty articles, co-edited the journal *English World-Wide* (from 2013 to 2019), and is Co-Editor of the *Cambridge Handbook of World Englishes*.

"*English Sociolinguistics: An Introduction* combines a comprehensive overview of the study of English sociolinguistics with accessible and topical examples and practical exercises, making the study of sociolinguistics engaging and fun for undergraduates. The novelty of this book is that it bridges many different subfields of sociolinguistics, connecting both historical and modern perspectives, and addresses global, real-world issues like multilingualism and language rights. I'm looking forward to using examples from this book in my teaching."

Lynn Clark, University of Canterbury

"An indispensable guide to English sociolinguistics, this textbook masterfully explores geographical and social variation, language contact, identity, and globalization. Using clear examples and engaging analysis, it bridges theory and practice, making it an essential resource for students and educators at introductory and intermediate levels alike. Highly recommended!"

Jakob Leimgruber, University of Regensburg

"This exciting new textbook on English sociolinguistics is detailed, comprehensive and up to date, packed with fresh, engaging examples. Its unique focus on English sets it apart from other introductory sociolinguistics books. Written in a clear, vibrant style, it is hands-on and accessible, featuring practical activities, case studies, interviews with top sociolinguists, and key takeaways. Perfect for English enthusiasts and students worldwide."

Erik Schleef, University of Salzburg

"A comprehensive and up-to-date account of English sociolinguistics that is delivered with insight and clarity. Schreier has produced a student-friendly textbook that will boost the study of the English language in universities and colleges worldwide."

Rajend Mesthrie, University of Cape Town

"Schreier provides an up-to-date, comprehensive survey of an expanding field. With its exceptionally broad coverage, the book underscores how sociolinguistics encompasses a diversity of scholarly approaches and intersects with a range of disciplines. Readers will discover how English sociolinguistics has developed in the last half-century and glimpse the many directions it may take in the coming decades."

Matthew Gordon, University of Missouri

"This book offers an extensive guide on sociolinguistics, providing global learners with a wealth of information. Each chapter is meticulously detailed, offering both in-depth explanations and engaging activities. Learners will discover valuable knowledge and practical insights, supported by various examples that foster a deep understanding of the concepts presented."

Nabiha El Khatib, Lebanese International University

"I enthusiastically endorse Schreier's *English Sociolinguistics*! Although I'm now retired, this is exactly the kind of text I would have loved to have when I was introducing students to the field! I particularly like the activities in each chapter and the accompanying website, the book's emphasis on how and why sociolinguistics matters and the perspectives of various sociolinguists at the end."

John R. Rickford, Stanford University

"This textbook is unparalleled in its handling of an astonishingly diverse and evolving subject. The lively narrative will draw in any reader, while also deftly weaving in many of the most exciting theoretical questions in current research. The content is genuinely global, the activities refreshingly original, and the ideas – indeed, the scholars themselves – shine through on every page."

Devyani Sharma, University College London

Cambridge Introductions to the English Language

Cambridge Introductions to the English Language is a series of accessible undergraduate textbooks on the key topics encountered in the study of the English language. Tailored to suit the needs of individual taught course modules, each book is written by an author with extensive experience of teaching the topic to undergraduates. The books assume no prior subject knowledge and present the basic facts in a clear and straightforward manner, making them ideal for beginners. They are designed to be maximally reader-friendly, with chapter summaries, glossaries, and suggestions for further reading. Extensive exercises and discussion questions are included, encouraging students to consolidate and develop their learning, and providing essential homework material. A website accompanies each book, featuring solutions to the exercises and useful additional resources. Set to become the leading introductions to the field, books in this series provide the essential knowledge and skills for those embarking on English Language Studies.

Books in the series

The Sound Structure of English Chris McCully

Old English Jeremy J. Smith

English Words and Sentences Eva Duran Eppler, Gabriel Ozón

Meaning in English Javier Valenzuela

The Emergence and Development of English William A. Kretzschmar, Jr

Linguistics and English Literature H. D. Adamson

English Around the World Edgar W. Schneider

Pragmatics in English Kate Scott

English Sociolinguistics Daniel Schreier

English Sociolinguistics
An Introduction

Daniel Schreier
University of Zurich

Shaftesbury Road, Cambridge CB2 8EA, United Kingdom

One Liberty Plaza, 20th Floor, New York, NY 10006, USA

477 Williamstown Road, Port Melbourne, VIC 3207, Australia

314–321, 3rd Floor, Plot 3, Splendor Forum, Jasola District Centre, New Delhi – 110025, India

103 Penang Road, #05-06/07, Visioncrest Commercial, Singapore 238467

Cambridge University Press is part of Cambridge University Press & Assessment, a department of the University of Cambridge.

We share the University's mission to contribute to society through the pursuit of education, learning and research at the highest international levels of excellence.

www.cambridge.org
Information on this title: www.cambridge.org/highereducation/isbn/9781108834889
DOI: 10.1017/9781108877381

© Daniel Schreier 2025

This publication is in copyright. Subject to statutory exception and to the provisions of relevant collective licensing agreements, no reproduction of any part may take place without the written permission of Cambridge University Press & Assessment.

When citing this work, please include a reference to the DOI 10.1017/9781108877381

First published 2025

A catalogue record for this publication is available from the British Library

A Cataloging-in-Publication data record for this book is available from the Library of Congress

ISBN 978-1-108-83488-9 Hardback
ISBN 978-1-108-79245-5 Paperback

Additional resources for this publication at www.cambridge.org/schreier

Cambridge University Press & Assessment has no responsibility for the persistence or accuracy of URLs for external or third-party internet websites referred to in this publication and does not guarantee that any content on such websites is, or will remain, accurate or appropriate.

For EU product safety concerns, contact us at Calle de José Abascal, 56, 1°, 28003 Madrid, Spain, or email eugpsr@cambridge.org

Contents

List of Figures	*page* xi
List of Tables	xiii
Preface	xv
Acknowledgments	xxiii

1 English Sociolinguistics: Why It Matters	1
1.1 Language as Social Fabric	1
1.2 We Just Can't Leave Our Language Alone	5
1.3 Standard and Nonstandard: Some Dialects Are More Equal	9
1.4 Sociolinguistics: Let's Go!	17
Take-Home Messages	17
Activities	18
Key Terms	18
Further Reading	19
2 From Dialectology to Sociolinguistics: A Short History	20
2.1 Regional Dialectology: A Short Historical Sketch	21
2.2 Researching Dialects in Geographical Space: Methodology	23
2.3 The Sociolinguistic Turn	34
2.4 Researching Dialects in Social Space: Methodology and Some First Findings	39
2.5 Conclusion: From Dialectology to Sociolinguistics	47
Take-Home Messages	49
Activities	50
Key Terms	50
Further Reading	50

3 Individuals, Networks, Communities, Society:
   From Variation to Change 52
   3.1 On Variation: General Issues 53
   3.2 Individual Speakers: Stylistic Variation 62
   3.3 Variation in Social Groups: Social Stratification,
       Social Networks, Communities of Practice 65
   3.4 Linking Variation and Change 74
   3.5 Conclusion 80
   Take-Home Messages 81
   Activities 82
   Key Terms 82
   Further Reading 83

4 English in Contact: From Code-Switching to the
   Birth of New Varieties 84
   4.1 Contact in the History of English: Old and
       Middle English 85
   4.2 Bilingualism and Multilingualism Today 87
   4.3 English Dialect Contact: How New Dialects
       Are Formed 92
   4.4 English in Contact with Other Languages:
       Jargons, Pidgins, and Creoles 97
   4.5 The Global Englishes 105
   4.6 Conclusion 113
   Take-Home Messages 114
   Activities 114
   Key Terms 117
   Further Reading 117

5 English Historical Sociolinguistics 119
   5.1 Historical Sociolinguistics: Projecting Back
       in Time 120
   5.2 Life in England Before 1800 123
   5.3 Language Standardization in Late Modern
       England (1600–1900) 127
   5.4 Literacy and Data 135
   5.5 Tracking Variation and Change in Time 141
   5.6 Conclusion 149
   Take-Home Messages 150
   Activities 151
   Key Terms 152
   Further Reading 153

6 Interactional Sociolinguistics — 154
- 6.1 Sociolinguistic Aspects of Interaction — 155
- 6.2 The Sociolinguistics of Discourse Markers: The Case of *Uhm* — 159
- 6.3 Inferencing, Contextualizing, Indexicality — 163
- 6.4 Losing and Keeping Face — 168
- 6.5 Language in the Workplace — 173
- 6.6 Crossing and Translanguaging — 178
- 6.7 Conclusion — 182
- Take-Home Messages — 184
- Activities — 184
- Key Terms — 185
- Further Reading — 186

7 Applied Sociolinguistics — 187
- 7.1 Applying Sociolinguistic Knowledge — 188
- 7.2 Linguistic Discrimination — 192
- 7.3 Forensic Linguistics — 198
- 7.4 Educational Failure — 203
- 7.5 Language and Social Justice — 211
- 7.6 Conclusion — 215
- Take-Home Messages — 217
- Activities — 217
- Key Terms — 219
- Further Reading — 219

8 Language Planning and the Law — 220
- 8.1 Language Planning: Basic Issues — 221
- 8.2 Language Policies in the US: A Case in Point — 226
- 8.3 Language Obsolescence and Revitalization — 232
- 8.4 Speak Good English in Singapore — 240
- 8.5 Language Rights vs. Language Survival — 244
- 8.6 Conclusion — 247
- Take-Home Messages — 248
- Activities — 249
- Key Terms — 250
- Further Reading — 251

9 The Sociolinguistics of Globalization — 252
- 9.1 Language in a Globalizing World — 253
- 9.2 Mobility and Superdiversity — 253
- 9.3 Sociolinguistics Goes Global — 256

	9.4 The World Language System	259
	9.5 Winners and Losers	264
	9.6 Conclusion	268
	Take-Home Messages	269
	Activities	269
	Key Terms	271
	Further Reading	271
10	A Tribute to Sociolinguist(ic)s	272

Appendix: Phonological Symbols and Lexical Sets	306
Glossary	307
References	316
Index	332

Figures

1.1 Negative dialect attitudes in the UK, rated by pleasantness and prestige	*page* 9
1.2 Example of a hand-drawn dialect map	16
2.1 Regional variation for the word *pfeffer* "pepper" in German, based on Wenker's map	24
2.2 Display map based on the *Survey of English Dialects*	29
2.3 Interpretative map based on the *Survey of English Dialects*	30
2.4 The English Dialect App and selected functions on a smartphone	32
2.5 William Labov	35
2.6 The usage of the word *sociolinguistics* on Ngram Viewer	36
2.7 Centralization of /au/ and /ai/ on Martha's Vineyard distributed by age	42
2.8 Frequency of /r/ in three New York City department stores	45
2.9 Stylistic and social variation in New York City department stores	46
3.1 Hymes' 1974 SPEAKING model.	56
3.2 *Couch, chesterfield*, and *sofa* by age-group in Canadian English	60
3.3 The Lower East Side in New York.	66
3.4 Individuals and social networks	68
3.5 The S-Curve and language change	77
3.6 The progress of TH fronting in British English	78
4.1 A traditional cottage on Tristan da Cunha, where the world's most isolated dialect is spoken	94
4.2 The 1884–85 Berlin Conference	99

4.3	Hypercorrect article usage in a Cyprus shop	107
4.4	Consonant cluster reduction in a Cape Town parking lot	107
4.5	The Welcome to India Arch in the British Raj, ca. 1850	108
4.6	The three-circle model of English as a World Language	111
5.1	Scenes from a London Street in the mid nineteenth century	126
5.2	Book printing in sixteenth-century England	129
5.3	An English classroom in Victorian times	136
5.4	A German farmer stopping work to hear his wife read a letter from the US (nineteenth century)	142
5.5	Multiple negation by social rank and gender	145
6.1	The interdisciplinary character of interactional sociolinguistics	158
6.2	Hesitation phenomena by age-group in the BNC (normalized per 100,000 words)	161
6.3	Graffiti in inner cities	167
6.4	The hierarchy of a small cleaning business in the US	175
7.1	Alfabet ina Jamiekan	209
7.2	Rachel Jeantel testifying in court	214
8.1	Language vitality	234
9.1	The World Language System	259
10.1	David Britain	275
10.2	Jenny Cheshire	279
10.3	Ana Deumert	284
10.4	Lisa Lim	287
10.5	Dennis Preston	290
10.6	John R. Rickford	293
10.7	Sali A. Tagliamonte	296
10.8	Lionel Wee	299
10.9	Walt Wolfram	301

Tables

1.1	4th grade NAEP reading scores in the US, by ethnic group (1992–2019)	page 8
3.1	The (-ng) variable in Norwich, by social class and gender in formal style (%)	61
3.2	Raising and backing of /a/ in Belfast, index scores from 0 to 4	69
4.1	Plural marking in Tok Pisin	103
4.2	Global Englishes, features around the world	106
4.3	Functional specialization of English and Hindi in India	110
5.1	Standardization processes	132
5.2	Social status of informants, (% of running words per gender)	139
5.3	Feature analysis in letters written by Annie Carroll in the 1880s and 1890s	143
5.4	Decline of multiple negation between 1460 and 1599, by social rank	146
5.5	The use of third person pronoun forms in Generation III Paston family members, acting as authors and scribes	148
6.1	Threats to positive and negative face in speakers and addressees	170
7.1	Differences in the text messages written by Jenny Nicholl and her alleged murderer	200
8.1	The language statuses of English around the world	224
8.2	The Hispanic/Latinx population in the US (% of total population by state)	228
8.3	Levels of language endangerment and loss	235
8.4	Language policy and planning goals	248

Preface

Aims of the Book

When Helen Barton approached me to inquire whether I would like to contribute a volume to this series, we quickly decided to go for *English Sociolinguistics*. When thinking about how to set up and compose a textbook for BA students, a first for me in fact, I wanted to produce something that reflected the breadth and astounding diversity of the field. There are excellent introductions to individual topics, such as language variation and change or historical sociolinguistics, but in my view a sociolinguistic macro-perspective, so important in early work, had been lost somewhat over the years. Not everyone will agree with me, but I feel sure that linguistics is strongly rooted in the humanities. So, in my teaching over the last twenty-five years, I have tried to show my students how versatile and interdisciplinary the field is, drawing on sociology, linguistics, politics, educational sciences, and the like. I continue to be surprised by the many ways in which sociolinguists approach language, both theoretically and methodologically, and admit that sometimes I feel a bit overwhelmed by the speed with which all this happens. But the more I discuss sociolinguistics with students, the more firmly I believe that a broad knowledge is important in order to understand how various sub-branches are connected and influence each other. Language and society affect all of us in different ways, from multilingual advertisements to the language of social media, from communities of practice to language minorities and migrant groups, from bilingualism to dialect death – sociolinguistics matters!

So, writing this textbook, I attempted to gently lead into the most important and influential subfields as comprehensively and accessibly as possible. Some knowledge in linguistics may be expected or required here or there, as indicated, and a basic understanding of the International Phonetic Alphabet is certainly helpful. Examples and exercises are provided throughout, relevant quotations from the literature are given, and I hope readers won't mind a few anecdotes and personal experiences here and there as well. The book is primarily designed for undergraduates and BA students of English Language and Linguistics at universities around the world. In addition to presenting key studies in the various branches, I have done my best to ensure that the textbook has didactic qualities and manages to raise students' interest in the field generally. The book is as hands-on an introduction to English sociolinguistics as I could make it: Activities are suggested for individual work or in-class discussions, there are vignettes with additional information on related issues, and there is additional information about "out-of-the-box" topics which I find personally interesting or which have stood the test of time in my own teaching. Wherever possible, connections are made to readers' own language observations, and I have done my best to bring in examples of English in various social settings and from around the world. Concepts are explained in relatively simple terms, using accessible language, connecting research issues with facts and observations from students' firsthand language experiences.

As for the structure of the book, chapters do not have to be read in sequence but can be skipped and cross-read. Given that issues are not restricted to individual fields (e.g. variation or identity are central in many ways), the order of materials and some of the readings can be altered so as to fit instructors' course syllabi and touched on (parallels between fields are pointed out where relevant). The chapters are structured as follows.

After a short introduction to language and social life and the structure and contents of the book in *Chapter 1 – English Sociolinguistics: Why It Matters*, in *Chapter 2 – From Dialectology to Sociolinguistics: A Short History*, I will trace the development of the field from its beginnings to the present day. We will discover that research on language and society has a long tradition. Before the start of sociolinguistics proper in the early 1960s, regional dialectologists had already made considerable efforts to explore the spatial dimension of language, using different methodologies to collect data on regional dialects. The impact of the so-called "sociolinguistic turn" is discussed with reference to Labov's early work (on the island of Martha's Vineyard and in New York City), and first findings and methods are presented. Building up, we will go on to present the subsequent waves of variationist sociolinguistics, social network theory and communities of practice, which saw a shifting focus on individual speakers and their social order and organization, as well as an orientation and affiliation with other speakers in indexical relationships. The chapter concludes with some recent developments and a presentation of current research themes.

In *Chapter 3 – Individuals, Networks, Communities, Society: From Variation to Change*, we will look in more detail at what we have briefly introduced in Chapter 1. Language variation is found on all levels: in the form of accents, different (but semantically equivalent) words, morphosyntactic forms, and also in discourse-oriented patterns (pragmatics, e.g. discourse markers); in other words, what has been called "different ways of saying the same thing." Speakers face alternative choices and these are in part determined by regional and social backgrounds or by the general context of a speech situation. We introduce the concept of the sociolinguistic variable and show that variation is necessarily rule-conditioned and systematic. Building on the origins of sociolinguistics and its relationship with dialectology, we introduce "the envelope of variation": the complex interplay of the social dimension of language usage (via individuals, groups, and communities) with intertwining linguistic and social correlates (region, class, gender, ethnicity, education). The chapter critically assesses notions such as style, identity, and indexicality, looks at the spread of innovative features in English around the world, and theoretically approaches diffusion from individual speakers throughout wider society (via processes known as actuation, diffusion, and embedding).

In *Chapter 4 – English in Contact: From Code-Switching to the Birth of New Varieties*, we introduce the importance of language contact for the sociolinguistic processes that enable change in the first place, all the way from borrowing words to wholesale restructuring of grammar. We illustrate possible outcomes by looking at different contact settings of English around the world, involving both (English) dialects and languages, the emergence of koinés (contact-derived dialects) and jargons, pidgins, and creoles (the product of language contact). Special focus is given to extralinguistic conditions: the historical and social backgrounds that are paramount in shaping the emergence of new varieties of English around the globe. The chapter discusses patterns of language shift and death, bilingualism and multilingualism, and more recent processes such as multiethnolectalization in major European cities, with a focus on London in the UK.

In *Chapter 5 – English Historical Sociolinguistics*, we travel back in time. We focus on the historical dimension of sociolinguistics by showing how it is related to the field of historical linguistics. Variation is seen as ahistoric here in that its mechanisms operate at all times and in all societies. According to the principle of uniformitarianism, "the same mechanisms which operated to produce the large-scale changes of the past may be observed operating in the current changes taking place around us" (Labov 1972a: 161). In other words, we can jump back and forth between centuries and see how variation and change operated in different periods, in possible motivations and outcomes. The chapter demonstrates how sociolinguists conduct their research, quantitatively and empirically, with very different sets of data. We show how their work is applied to historical data and corpora, giving in-depth examples of social-network studies and code-switching processes in the history of English. There is also a discussion of the so-called "alternative histories of English" (Watts & Trudgill 2002) and a brief introduction to English-language ideologies, which are particularly important when we look at standardization.

In *Chapter 6 – Interactional Sociolinguistics*, we concentrate on language usage and interaction and move into the fields of variational pragmatics and discourse analysis. We investigate the conventional patterns speakers use when they construct, participate in, and evaluate discourse at large. The concept of face is important here, namely the self-image of speakers that they wish to maintain and protect via sociolinguistic resources: speech events in the form of narratives, telephone conversations, weblogs, university lectures, and so on. Context effects on sociolinguistic interaction are discussed with examples of turn-taking, power, solidarity and cross-cultural communication, and also with a focus on social hierarchies and language practices in the workplace. We conclude with a discussion of crossing and translanguaging in multilingual contexts.

In *Chapter 7 – Applied Sociolinguistics*, we investigate how sociolinguistics overlaps selected areas of applied linguistics. Topics discussed are: How insights from variation and change can be used to help improve children's reading and writing skills; How our knowledge of English varieties around the world is integrated into schoolbooks; How sociolinguists are involved in activities of dialect maintenance and revival. There are special sections on forensic sociolinguistics, sociophonetics, and legal aspects of language usage, and we present hands-on cases of political issues related to language (multilingualism, education, etc.). A special focus is given to what John R. Rickford has labeled "activist sociolinguistics," that is the involvement of linguists in public issues and court cases, and we look at a case which has received a lot of attention and fundamentally changed the way we examine dialect evidence in the courtroom: the trial of George Zimmerman for the shooting of Trayvon Martin in 2012 which was so instrumental in the #BlackLivesMatter movement.

In *Chapter 8 – Language Planning and the Law*, we continue our discussion of applied dimensions of language usage and look into a range of aspects which are paramount for politics and nation building. One important issue is when, where, and under what circumstances English is adopted as a national or official language, which is a particularly pressing question in postcolonial contexts. We will weigh arguments in favor of and against English serving official functions and ask whether it would not make more sense if a local language (or local languages), accessible to larger sections of a community, were endorsed instead. We will discuss how and to what extent governments plan and orchestrate language-related activities in education and public discourse and language policies, with the US and Ireland (history, socioethnic varieties, bilingualism and multilingualism) serving as examples. We also discuss the impact of governmental bodies on language planning by focusing on the Speak Good English movement in Singapore and present efforts to achieve language revitalization: These issues are particularly important given the increasing rate of language obsolescence and death around the world. We end with a look at language rights in the case of migrant communities.

In *Chapter 9 – The Sociolinguistics of Globalization*, we discuss how language in society has changed in the age of globalization and what consequences this has for our everyday lives. As a result of mobility and medial communication, English is no longer tied to stable, resident communities but has been transported around the globe at increasing speed, in different forms and via different agents, changing form and function during the process. We will look at the role of English in the World Language System and show that the world is no longer a global village but has been turned into a complex web of communities (real and imagined) which are connected by linguistic, materialistic, and symbolic ties. As Blommaert (2010) has argued, we need to fundamentally revise our perception of linguistic communication, reconsider theories of changing language in a changing society, and develop fresh and innovative concepts such as repertoires, competence, and sociolinguistic inequality. One of the central tenets is the role of mobility, which "is the great challenge: it is the dislocation of language and language events from the fixed position in time and space attributed to them by a more traditional linguistics and sociolinguistics" (Blommaert 2010: 21).

In *Chapter 10 – A Tribute to Sociolinguist(ic)s*, we jointly reflect on the various contributions that English sociolinguistics has made to language and society. When I say *jointly*, I include some of my colleagues around the world who generously share their impressions and opinions. I remember very well how much in awe I was as a PhD student at meeting the people whose work I had read and who had influenced me. I thought it would be a good way to end this book, with students working with the text getting to hear firsthand what some of the most eminent sociolinguists of our time have to say. The conclusion is built around their input, and each was sent a set of questions ("How did you become a sociolinguist in the first place?"; "What do you consider your most important contribution to sociolinguistics?"; "What advice would you give students of sociolinguistics today?"; and "How do you think your field will branch out and develop in coming years?") as well as one or two questions relating to their field of experience discussed in the book. The result is a somewhat unusual conclusion (personal, authoritative, and entertaining) in which readers get to know some of the greatest sociolinguists of our time, receive advice, and learn about what could become potential trends in the years to come.

A Note on How to Use the Book

Sociolinguistics courses were among the most popular when I was a student and they still are today. This is no surprise, really, as language in its social context(s) touches on so many aspects of our everyday lives. From the rich world of dialects to multilingualism, language change and educational policies, standardization to language-related inequality, sociolinguistics has never failed to amaze, and I have done my very best to share my experience of curiosity and fascination with those using the book.

Though I hope that the book is read by laypeople with a genuine interest in language in society, I expect that most readers will be students using it as a textbook in a BA course titled "English Sociolinguistics," "Language and Society," or something similar. While I have written several books before, this is the first time I have written a textbook, and my learning curve involved tackling new challenges and demands. From my own experience, the Preface is not the most frequently read part of any book, but let me take this opportunity to say a few things about how the rest of the work is set up and can be used best. (At the least, I'd like to convey what went through my head when I decided to write it the way I did.) First of all, I tried to be as accessible and nontechnical as possible, so there should not be a lot of necessary knowledge students need to bring in. Occasionally, they may find it helpful to know the basics of the English sound system or its grammar, but this is indicated where it occurs and additional reading is pointed out when necessary. The book can be read from cover to cover, but the order of chapters may be reshuffled, or only some of the chapters may be used in courses (which is what some of the anonymous reviewers said they would do when adopting the textbook in class) so as to give instructors and students maximum flexibility.

I found that Edgar W. Schneider's *English Around the World*, published in this series and now in its second edition, provided a perfect model. In agreement with Cambridge University Press's representatives, I adapted some of the features of Edgar's book to make the text as reader-friendly and learner-friendly as possible. Many of them are pedagogic, giving the readers a sense of orientation and direction, including:

- a chapter preview, entitled "In This Chapter …," which provides a roadmap of the materials presented, so readers know what to expect
- a list of all the chapter sections, which structure the content by subtopics
- a summary of the main points at the end of each chapter, which revises what was learned
- various activities to make readers discuss important issues, ask them to think about or share opinions and concerns or to bring in their own language experience or invite them to look at language materials and do some research – there's nothing like working with data firsthand
- a list of "Key Terms" at the end of each chapter, comprising the terms and notions readers should be familiar with and able to apply properly in their discussions and analyses as students of sociolinguistics
- a "Further Reading" section which suggests additional texts on selected contents discussed in the chapter. The selection may have a personal bias, and I am sure no two sociolinguists would suggest an identical set of readings, but these titles include materials I have used in class which were popular with my students
- for the benefit of readers who have little or no familiarity with phonetic transcription, an appendix at the end of the book presenting and illustrating phonological symbols
- a glossary which explains and illustrates technical terms as accessibly as possible
- a references list, which refers to the sociolinguistic work discussed in the chapters, providing a list for further reading to guide readers to alternative sources of further interest
- the index, which will help find materials and topics discussed throughout the book.

Moreover, the book is accompanied by a website: www.cambridge.org/schreier. It provides, among other things:

- a suggestion for additional activities
- links to video and audio files demonstrating the use of English by different speakers in a range of contexts
- links to further interesting materials, especially language-related websites or onsite corpora instructors which readers may want to use for research
- selected model answers for the activities (restricted to use by instructors).

Another important point concerns the sensitivity of some of the topics discussed in this book. Language can create positive vibes and emotions in us, create identity, and serve as social glue, but it has its dark sides also:

discrimination, hate speech, social control, and so on. These topics should not be ignored here, certainly not when we look at recent efforts to make sociolinguistics activist and engaging, but some readers may find them insensitive and upsetting. It is not my intention to shock readers but to show how important scociolinguistic work is in the community.

I hope the combination of textbook and website provides all that is needed for an active and exciting sociolinguistics class, and I am excited to hear whether or not it works. I would be most grateful to hear feedback from instructors and students around the world, so please don't hesitate to contact me. And that's all I needed to say in the Preface, other than …

… When I started to work on this book, I stuck a Post-it note on my computer screen which read: "Always remember to write the book you would have wanted to work with when you were a student." I did my very best to stick to this principle, and now in a way it's strange to realize that the book is no longer mine alone but ours. Let's hope you enjoy working with it, is all I can say – sociolinguistics makes a difference, after all.

Further Reading
For an introduction to English phonetics and phonology:
Davenport, M. & Hannahs, S. J. (2020). *Introducing Phonetics and Phonology*. London: Taylor & Francis.
Roach, P. (2010). *English Phonetics and Phonology: A Practical Course* (4th ed.). Cambridge: Cambridge University Press.

Acknowledgments

First of all, I would like to express my gratitude to a number of colleagues, friends, and institutions for giving me permission to reproduce or use materials in this book. In order of appearance, these include: Chris Montgomery (Figure 1.1), Adrian Leemann (Figure 2.5), Bill Labov (Figure 2.6), Terttu Nevalainen (Figure 3.4), Paul Kerswill (Figure 3.5), Alex Bergs (Figure 5.6), Kellie Gonçalvez (Figure 6.4), David Britain (Figure 10.1), Jenny Cheshire (Figure 10.2), Ana Deumert (Figure 10.3), Lisa Lim (Figure 10.4), Denis Preston (Figure 10.5), John R. Rickford (Figure 10.6), Sali A. Tagliamonte (Figure 10.7), Lionel Wee (Figure 10.8), and Walt Wolfram (Figure 10.9).

My heartfelt thanks go to publishers or institutions for giving me permission to reproduce graphs, tables, maps, and illustrations from previously published sources: Forschungszentrum Deutscher Sprachatlas, Philipps Universität Marburg (Figure 2.1), Cambridge University Press (Figures 2.2 and 2.3), John Benjamins Publishing Company (Figure 3.6), and The Jamaica Language Unit (Figure 7.1). All other sources were adapted or my own. Every effort has been made to secure necessary permissions to reproduce copyright material in this work, though in some cases it has proved impossible to trace or contact copyright holders. If any omissions are brought to our notice, we will be happy to include appropriate acknowledgments on reprinting or in any subsequent edition.

English Sociolinguistics could not have been written without the support and trust of Cambridge University Press. A huge thank you goes to Helen Barton, the General Editor, for originally suggesting I write such a book and for generously supporting me throughout, to Emily Watton, Emma Collison, and Isabel Collins for stylistic and pedagogical advice and their thoughtful and helpful readings, and to Alan McIntosh for his impeccable copyediting.

This book owes much to the input, inspiration, and advice of friends and colleagues around the world. Most of all, my gratitude goes to Peter Trudgill, who supported me in so many ways over the last thirty years and without whose help and encouragement I simply would not have become a sociolinguist. Pete is a genuine sociolinguist, loving what he does, working and reading every day, fascinated by language and society, kind, generous, and supportive, and his input and guidance have been a transformative force in my life; Jenny Cheshire, who convinced me that studying language and society (rather than psycholinguistics) was something worth doing for a living when I was her student in Neuchâtel; Walt Wolfram, who gave me a research fellowship at North Carolina State University and who has provided so much inspiration and camaraderie over the years; Liz Gordon and Jen Hay, with whom I worked as a postdoc in New Zealand and who were kind and helpful at all times; and of course Edgar W. Schneider, who has been a most understanding and nurturing colleague, introducing me to the complex field of World Englishes and the intricacies of German academia. Moreover, I am thankful for long, energizing, and inspiring discussions with colleagues around the world at conferences, summer schools, and other venues: Anita Auer, Dave Britain, Alex d'Arcy, Lynn Clark, Stephanie Hackert, Magnus Huber, Ray Hickey, the late Alex Kautzsch, Bernd Kortmann, Robert McColl Millar, Raj Mesthrie, Lesley Milroy, Terttu Nevalainen, Simone E. Pfenninger, Dennis Preston, John R. Rickford, Erik Schleef, John Singler, Sali Tagliamonte, Erik Thomas, Graeme Trousdale, Bertus van Rooy, Richard Watts, Laura Wright … a list that can be extended at length, so whoever feels offended at having not been mentioned will be offered a glass of wine or a beer. My thanks go as well to the institutions and universities which invited me to lecture, teach, and do research over the years. Of these, most of all: Canterbury University, Christchurch, New Zealand, where I received an Erskine Fellowship; the Historical Sociolinguistics Network (HiSON); and the Deutsche Gesellschaft für Sprachwissenschaft (DGfS). Further, I wish to thank: the truly astounding number of external reviewers who read various drafts of the book and provided so much input and good advice; my former student assistant Sydney Childers, who read through the entire manuscript with a student's eyes and made most helpful suggestions and comments, suggesting additional activities, too; my students, colleagues, and team members at the University of Zurich; my friends, none of whom cares much about sociolinguistics but who are great fun to hang out with and constantly show me there's so much more to life than academia; and, above all, my partner and my wonderful daughters, who make it all worthwhile. Last but not least, I am grateful to the University of Zurich, which awarded me a competitive sabbatical and allowed me to make headway with the manuscript after long years in administration.

CHAPTER 1

English Sociolinguistics: Why It Matters

In This Chapter ...

... we will look at the attitudes and value judgements which speakers and communities have about English dialects and discuss what this means for the social relevance of language in general. We will see that language is not only a means to share information but an essential part of social life which helps us organize ourselves and define our identity. We will discover that there are different levels of usage and that variation has regional, social, and individual dimensions. We start with a short discussion of general attitudes about language varieties, look at social prejudice based on language usage, find out why some varieties are stigmatized whereas others have high prestige, and get a first glance of perceptions about standard and nonstandardized varieties. Looking at examples from English around the world, we take a first look at perceptual dialectology to demonstrate how views toward dialects affect our everyday lives – not forgetting the negative side effects this may have.

1.1	Language as Social Fabric	*page* 1
1.2	We Just Can't Leave Our Language Alone	5
1.3	Standard and Nonstandard: Some Dialects Are More Equal	9
1.4	Sociolinguistics: Let's Go!	17
	Take-Home Messages	17
	Key Terms	18
	Further Reading	19

1.1 Language as Social Fabric

When I ask students in their first year what they think the purpose of language is, they typically tell me that language is a way of communicating information. When we look at sentences such as:

1. Our dog has a bad toothache.
2. Sally bought a bicycle for her grandson.
3. Actually, I am going to the Hebrides for my summer vacation.

then passing on news is certainly important. However, when we engage in some more discussion and look at different examples, it does not take my students long to realize that the communication of news may not be at all central or perhaps even absent entirely. Take for instance:

4. Nice day today, isn't it?
5. Hmmmmm, your accent sounds familiar.
6. Why are you looking so worried?

Saying something new is not the main motivation here; rather, we engage in small talk which does not really have much meaning (sentence 4), comment on something which strikes us as interesting (5), or inquire about someone's well-being (6). In other words, we use language for a range of purposes: to pass on information, sure, but also to ask questions, to complain or entertain, to make statements, to speculate, or simply to pass the time.

This means that language is central in our everyday lives for several reasons: the act of speaking has a social purpose, carrying information about speakers, hearers, or the setting in which the exchange occurs. It is language that helps us build relationships, express solidarity, create social distance, and ultimately define our own identity. Of course, we can discuss at great length how much of the language we use on an ordinary basis strictly serves a social function, and there will be different opinions, but it is important to keep in mind that all of us follow norms and patterns which are part of social behavior. Just think about it: we greet our neighbor on the way to work, ask whether a seat is taken on the bus, have a chat with colleagues about the weekend, and so on, even though none of these activities is really *necessary*. We use language following social and cultural conventions – in fact, it would be considered strange not to return a greeting or impolite not to thank someone for a favour. Language is not only used to communicate or learn something new but also to organize our routine and lives as members of various speech communities. This means it is an important part, some would say the most essential one, of our socialized routines. We are social beings, and language is an essential part of our normal lives, defining what we do and who we are. Language is social by character.

A second characteristic is equally important here: We cannot speak without giving away something about ourselves. Sociolinguists like to point out that the very act of saying something serves as a social expression of the speaker's persona. Sometimes, people say things like "I don't have an accent" or "You have such a funny way of speaking" – but this is not correct: We all have an accent, and the way we speak reveals important information about us. An **accent** refers to the sound-related features of speech, the way we produce sounds (phonetics), and how they build a complex system (phonology) – so when we say just a few words, we immediately create an image of our personal characteristics. Just imagine a situation when you are listening to an unfamiliar voice behind you in the bus or in a queue and you immediately form an opinion about the person – how old they are, where they are from, whether they sound nice or charming or posh, and so on. Perhaps we may even have some sort of mental image of what the person may look like! It is an accent that indicates from what region they are from, either from within the country or elsewhere (if they have a foreign accent), what social class or ethnic group they belong to, how old they are, what education they received, and so on. The very act of speaking gives away all that information, and hearers can make such judgments within a split second, so this is a central function of language.

The term **dialect**, however, is used as a neutral label for the regional and social use of language varieties. The *Longman Dictionary of Contemporary English* defines dialect as "a form of a language which is spoken only in one area, with words or grammar that are slightly different from other forms of the same language." When sociolinguists refer to dialects, they are usually talking about grammatical and morphological patterns and the lexicon. Diversity exists on several levels:

- *geography*, language in space in the form of traditionally well-known dialects
- *social position*, as social groups differ in their way of speaking due to their background and education
- *ethnicity*, as ethnic varieties – such as Indian communities in London or Hispanic (Latino/Latinx)-Americans in San Antonio, Texas – have their own characteristic ways of speaking
- *identity*, who we are and how we use language as a means of expression.

As we will see later, variation is not random: Most differences in pronunciation, grammar, and vocabulary are systematic and rule-governed. Everyone speaks a dialect – or several dialects in different contexts, just as everyone has an accent. Sociolinguistically, it makes sense to distinguish dialect and accent, as speakers can have the same dialect while using a different accent. Speakers from Glasgow and Edinburgh by and large speak the same dialect, Scottish English, but have recognizably different accents.

When we discuss these questions in sociolinguistics courses and reflect on the social function of language, students soon realize that their way of speaking is characteristic and unique. When comparing themselves and the way they speak with people in their immediate social environment (family, friends, other students, or work colleagues) they find that they all speak differently in some way. For instance, they may come from different places and have distinct regional ways of speaking, they may be members of different social classes and speak different **sociolects** (the same goes for ethnic groups), or they may belong to distinct age groups and vary from generation to generation (which we can easily verify by speaking to our grandparents), and of course they may differ because they belong to different gender groups (male, female, or nonbinary).

The way we speak provides information as to where we come from, both regionally and socially, how educated and old we are, and to what gender group we associate ourselves with. Though this may sound a bit romantic, language has been called the "window to the soul" and it is an important resource to create and express our sense of identity. We will see in Chapter 6 that speakers exploit variation in language and conscientiously make use of their **sociolinguistic repertoire** to express identity. This can occur with different forms of one and the same dialect, for example various words, expressions or speech sounds, with different dialects (as when both standard and nonstandardized dialects are used to signal authority or familiarity), and of course with different languages when speakers are bilingual or multilingual.

Importantly, English is used alongside other languages in many parts of the world, and these varieties have different functions for speakers and communities. In Singapore, for instance, it is not unusual for a person to speak Tamil in the family, English at school or work, and Malay with the neighbors. Or consider the following scenario from South Africa, where several languages are used in everyday life. The language experience of a student from Cape Town University is described as follows:

> My father's home language was Swazi, and my mother's home language was Tswana. But as I grew up in a Zulu-speaking area we used mainly Zulu and Swazi at home. But from my mother's side I also learnt Tswana well. In my high school I came into contact with lots of Sotho and Tswana students, so I can speak these two languages well. And of course, I know English and Afrikaans. With my friends I also use Tsotsitaal. (quoted in Mesthrie 2002: 12)

In South Africa and many other settings around the world, **multilingualism** is the norm rather than the exception. While the sociolinguistic repertoire of this particular student consists of as many as seven languages, she stresses that they are not used interchangeably and that knowing *when* to speak a language is just as important as knowing *how* to speak it. Zulu and Swazi are the languages spoken at home in the family, Tsotsitaal is used with peers and friends in and outside school, and English and Afrikaans are the medium of instruction in school. In other words, each of these languages is used domain-specifically; speaking Swazi during a lesson would be just as inappropriate as speaking Afrikaans at home. South Africans, like many other speech communities around the world, are used to living in multilingual environments. They instinctively know when to use what language with whom, and all the languages have a different social meaning as they are spoken in different contexts. We return to this issue in Chapter 4.

To summarize, language is used for many purposes. We cannot exist without language, not only because we need to pass on information, but also because we use language to organize and maintain our social lives. It is the social glue which links individuals and holds speech communities together, which allows us to establish and uphold social relationships, and which expresses our identity and what kind of person we are. Language and social identity are intimately connected; language is our social fabric.

1.2 We Just Can't Leave Our Language Alone

Once students understand that ways of speaking have a social function, it is a small step to realize how much social meaning language carries. Our opinions about language variation are not neutral but are often charged with all sorts of attributes. It is a simple fact that most people hold beliefs and make occasionally strong value judgments based on the way others speak. As language is used to carry information about speakers, we interpret, classify, and develop **stereotypes**: Canadians say "eh" all the time, New Yorkers live on "toydy-toyd" Street (for *thirty-third*), New Zealanders order "feeesh and cheeps" (*fish and chips*), working-class Londoners say "'ammer" for *hammer*, etc. These generalizations may be humoristic and joking but they can also have a dark side, as when they lead to prejudice against dialects as such, that is to say when they are interpreted as an expression of speakers' low intelligence, unfriendliness, or rudeness. This occurs more often than we might think.

In her book *Verbal Hygiene*, Deborah Cameron famously pointed out that speakers constantly create opinions based on the social or attitudinal evaluation of dialects (Cameron 1995). Among other points, she claimed that:

1. People can't leave their language alone.
2. People believe that some languages are better than others.
3. People associate "bad" language with "bad" character.
4. People have "nonlinguistic," "nonlogical" notions about language.

In other words, it is a short step from ideas about how dialects and sociolects sound to forming opinions about the social attributes of their speakers. As Fridland (2020) wrote:

> Of course, recognizing that some language features might indicate someone's gender, age or race itself is not problematic, and, in fact, something we all do. But associating them with generalized negative traits or discriminating against them on the basis of these traits is where the inherent danger lies. And often these negative associations are not overt, and we might not even be aware of doing it, but instead are implicit in how we make decisions about how we are going to interact with or evaluate those we hear.

Let's illustrate this with one of the most distinctive varieties of English in the US: **African American Vernacular English** (**AAVE**; currently called African American Language/AAL in the US). Americans of all ethnic groups are surprisingly good at identifying AAVE/AAL speakers: Within two seconds they can confidently assess whether a voice listened to is African or European American and a study (Purnell, Idsardi & Baugh 1999: 18–21) showed that there was already a 70 percent chance of correct identification after one word (so just by hearing the word "hello," Americans may identify the speaker's ethnic background).

The grammar and sound system of AAVE/AAL have been studied for more than half a century now, making it one of the best-researched varieties of American English. Ever since the 1960s, sociolinguists have tried to use their knowledge to address issues related to linguistic equality, reading failure, equal access opportunities, courtroom discourse, and so on, all of which involve language-related evaluation. Notwithstanding their efforts (see Chapter 7), AAVE/AAL is still viewed negatively throughout the US. For instance, it is denied the status of a proper variety, occasionally referred to as "slang," "street speech," or "broken English." Forms of AAVE/AAL (in fact many, if not all, varieties spoken by ethnic minorities around the world) continue to be openly stigmatized by wider society, and speakers continue to suffer discrimination. The following experience (by Anita Henderson, an African American linguist) is a good example:

> I went to a large apartment complex in Philadelphia to inquire about apartments. I was steered to the most expensive apartment in the building

and told this was the only apartment available for the following month and that no other apartments would be coming available. However, the next day, using my very best Standard American English on the phone and inquiring about an apartment in the same complex, I discovered that, miraculously, several less expensive apartments were immediately available, and I was more than welcome to come and see them. (Henderson 2001: 2–3)

There are many examples of what linguists such as John Baugh have labeled **"linguistic profiling."** Studying footage from body cameras on police officers in Oakland (California), Voigt et al. (2017) found that in routine traffic stops, law enforcers used less respectful language when the driver was African American; and in a widely discussed court case (the trial of George Zimmerman for the shooting of Trayvon Martin in 2012), the attacker was found not guilty in part because the defense lawyer targeted the credibility of the prosecution's key witness as she was a speaker of AAVE/AAL (Rickford & King 2019; see Chapter 7). Language-based prejudice and discrimination are reported in: employment, as a negative evaluation of accents may reduce job opportunities (Spence et al. 2024); education, as children with local accents consistently have a lower success rate in placement tests (Baugh 1996); and also in the judicial system, as nonstandardized dialect speakers are considered less credible as witnesses (Rickford & King 2016).

This has far-reaching implications for language and society. Take for instance the fact that African American schoolchildren typically trail behind European American students of the same age group. The biannual National Assessment of Educational Progress (NAEP) indicates a strong and persistent gap in reading scores between European and African American schoolchildren (Table 1.1). The 2019 report found that, while there had been some progress since the 1990s, African American 4th- and 8th-graders showed the same, stable difference in reading scores. Whereas there was some progress in the 1990s, in other minorities as well, particularly the Asian/Pacific Islander community, African American schoolchildren continued to trail behind European American peers in their reading performance.

All groups (White, Black, Hispanic [Latino/Latinx], and Asian/Pacific Islander students) had higher average scores in 2019 than in 1992 and 1998, yet the 2019 average scores for African American and European American 4th-graders were not significantly different from scores ten years earlier. Despite all educational efforts, a consistent gap had remained for over thirty years.

Table 1.1 *4th grade NAEP reading scores in the US, by ethnic group (1992–2019). Adapted from The Nation's Report Card (2022).*

Average score	2019 score	2019 compared to			
		2017	2009	1998	1992
White	230	↓ 2	♦	↑ 6	↑ 6
Black	204	↓ 3	♦	↑ 11	↑ 12
Hispanic (Latino/Latinx)	209	♦	↑ 4	↑ 16	↑ 12
Asian/Pacific Islander	237	♦	♦	↑ 23	↑ 21
American Indian/Alaska Native	204	♦	♦	n.d.	n.d.
Two or more races	226	♦	♦	n.d.	n.d.

↓ Score decrease, ↑ Score increase, ♦ no significant change, n.d. "no data" (reporting standards not met, insufficient sample size, etc.).

Decades of sociolinguistic and applied linguistic research have shown the complex causes of educational failure in multiethnic contexts. On the one hand, social-class membership, the parents' degree of education, as well as income and place of origin, motivation, the training of teachers, and quality of schools are all factors which influence the success of children in school (Lanehart 2015). However, sociolinguists and educationalists have shown that there was a general lack in knowledge about the children's social backgrounds, and that language-related claims about African American schoolchildren were ill-informed or simply wrong. Notwithstanding, there is still little awareness of AAVE/AAL as a systematic yet different variety of English, and negative perceptions prevail. This has disastrous consequences, as we will see later in the book.

Of course, dialect-based discrimination is not an exclusively American phenomenon. Similar findings are reported throughout the English-speaking world in Australia, Hong Kong, South Africa, and of course also in the UK. There are surveys claiming that 28 percent of the UK population report discrimination based on the regional accent they speak, and attitudes toward accents have remained remarkably stable over half a century (Sharma, Levon & Ye 2022). A 2014 YouGov accent poll showed that, while Received Pronunciation – the accent spoken by the monarchy and the social elite – continues to enjoy high prestige, accents from Liverpool, Glasgow, or Birmingham in particular continue to be heavily stigmatized (Figure 1.1).

Another survey found that 25 percent of adults said their accents had been mocked or criticized at work, while 47 percent of university students and 46 percent of adults said their accents had been ridiculed. Devyani

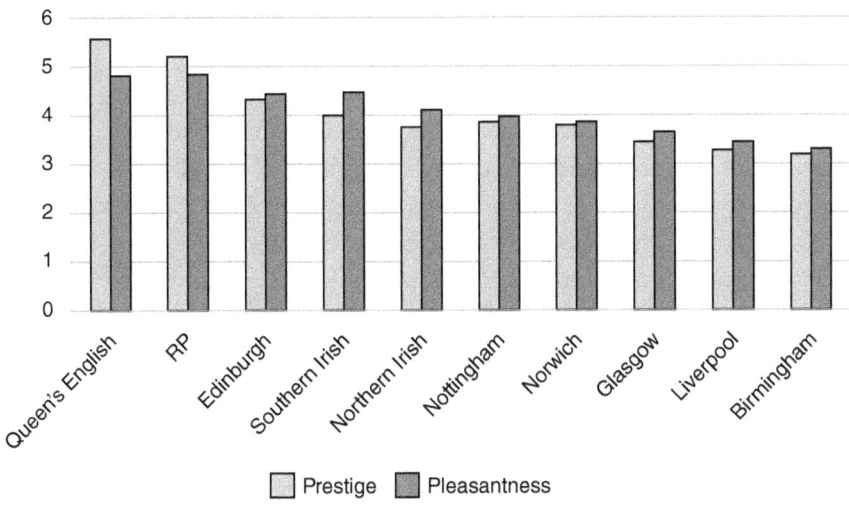

Figure 1.1 Negative dialect attitudes in the UK, rated by pleasantness and prestige. Adapted from Sharma et al. (2022: 145, Figs 1 and 2).

Sharma, one of the researchers involved in the *Accent Bias Report*, was quoted by the *Guardian* in November 2022 as saying that "Accent-based discrimination actively disadvantages certain groups at key junctures for social mobility, such as job interviews … This creates a negative cycle, whereby regional, working-class and minority-ethnic accents are heard less in some careers or positions of authority, reinforcing anxiety and marginalisation for those speakers."

The results of these studies show that views about dialects are widely held by society and that, what's worse, most people do not see any problem here at all. While it is no longer acceptable to hold prejudices based on ethnic group membership, gender categories, or sexual orientation, we still have a long way to go in our efforts to mitigate negative effects of language-based evaluation.

1.3 Standard and Nonstandard: Some Dialects Are More Equal

Speakers have strong views on what is correct (or "good") language usage and what is not, and students at university courses do as well. Though these beliefs have changed over the centuries, and **Standard English** has not always existed (as we shall see in Chapter 5), some dialects of English are valued by the general public whereas others are openly stigmatized. English has a long and persistent **complaint tradition** (Milroy & Milroy 1985) about language in general, and views that English is changing for the worse are strong and century-old.

The interesting thing is that, when you ask people what exactly is wrong with the English language, then you receive few detailed answers. Of course, there are vague complaints about foreign words or ongoing Americanization, or young speakers who can't be bothered to speak English as they should, or foreigners who have a negative influence on the language, and so on. But when pressed to give examples of allegedly "bad" English, then only a handful of grammatical features are singled out, such as:

- "I" or "me" in the phrase "you and I/me"
- split infinitives ("to boldly go" vs. "to go boldly")
- "different to/than" vs. "different from"
- whether or not to end a sentence with a preposition
- "who" or "whom" in sentences such as "Who(m) were you talking to?"
- when to use "shall" and when to use "will"
- incomplete sentences ("Over to John Smith" vs. "I am now passing you over to John Smith").

This is where things don't work out and language complaints become paradoxical. Just think for a second how complex grammar is (in English, or any other language you may know), let alone the sound system, and how many rules there are. There are so many rules, yet there are fewer than a dozen grammatical features that are the subject of complaints. How come there are only a few cases of "bad language," not even frequent ones when you come to think of it? This is strange, isn't it, particularly when we think about the intensity and emotional load of the worries and fears that English is deteriorating? There is a strong mismatch here.

However, when you ask what should be done to address these issues, it is common to hear calls for a language authority to intervene: the Académie française is a case in point. The King's English Society, for instance, was founded in 1972 (as the Queen's English Society) to join the campaign to raise standards in the understanding and use of English at schools and among the general public. On its website, the Society's aims and objectives are described as follows:

> to promote the maintenance, knowledge, understanding, development and appreciation of the English language as used both in speech and in writing; to educate the public in its correct and elegant usage; and to discourage the intrusion of anything detrimental to clarity or euphony. The phrase "the queen's (or king's) English" has been used for centuries

simply to imply spoken or written English which is standard – characterised by grammatical correctness and proper usage of words and expressions. (King's English Society 2022)

These views have a social basis, judging dialects on the basis of sociolinguistic characteristics (working classes, minorities, and rural speakers are particularly frowned upon), but they are not linguistically justified. English sociolinguists have long emphasized that it is impossible to assess levels of correctness in language as these exist in the minds of speakers only, not in the language itself. A standard variety is selected through processes and decisions which are purely social, economic, and cultural, and factors such as logic or internal complexity, historical consistency, expressivity, or systematicity play no role in these attitudes (see Chapter 5).

To equate language usage with correctness and logic is highly problematic, as can easily be shown. Let's look at one of the most prominent complaints about English: the use of double negatives as in "She ain't going nowhere." Some people take issue with such a sentence, saying it is not correct, and their line of argument is always the same and by no means new. Back in 1762, Bishop Lowth, in his influential *Short Introduction to English Grammar*, wrote that "two negatives in English destroy one another, or are equivalent to an affirmative – in English, that is to say, just as in mathematics" (p. 126). Minus and minus equals plus, two negations result in an affirmative, just as we learnt at school; Multiple negatives, it is claimed, cancel each other out and have to be avoided at all costs to keep a sentence clear and concise.

There are several reasons why such an argumentation makes no sense at all. First of all, if multiple negation really posed problems for understanding, then speakers would no longer use it. However, the opposite is the case. Two or more negations in one sentence are found in many varieties of English around the world, from traditional English dialects in Northumberland, second-language varieties in Southeast Asia, all the way to English-based creoles in the Caribbean. Why would a feature that causes serious problems for understanding and logic be so widespread, one wonders? Second, looking at the history of English, we find that these forms abounded in earlier times. Geoffrey Chaucer, one of the greatest poets, used multiple negation. In the General Prologue to his *Canterbury Tales*, written in the late fourteenth century, we find an example of four negatives in a single sentence: "He nevere yet no vileyneye ne sayde in al his lyf unto no manner wight" "He never said any evil, nor, in all his life, did he do any" (*Canterbury Tales*, General Prologue, lines 70–71). And yes, William Shakespeare used them too:

> *This England never did, nor never shall,*
> Lie at the proud foot of a conqueror,
> But when it first did help to wound itself.
> Now these her princes are come home again,
> Come the three corners of the world in arms,
> And we shall shock them. Nought shall make us rue,
> If England to itself do rest but true.
> (*King John*, Act 5, Scene 7, lines 2749–2755; my emphasis)

England "never did, nor never shall" succumb? What is meant here? Certainly not that England is so strong and powerful that it will surrender. Rather, no matter how many *nevers* or *nors* are used here, the character in the play emphasizes that England will not bend down before another nation. So, multiple negatives do not cancel each other out and must have a different meaning. And this leaves only one interpretation: Their function is to *reinforce* negation, not to reverse it. Two negatives emphasize that something is not going to happen, under any circumstances whatsoever, with negatives functioning like other parts of speech (e.g. intensifiers: "This is really really cool" means something is cooler than cool).

Last but not least, if logic were an issue and two negatives really cancel each other out, then some of the world's major languages, including Russian and French, would have an entirely different sense of logic. They allow multiple negation even in their standard varieties – people in Bordeaux or St. Petersburg would certainly be surprised to learn that constructions such as *je ne viens pas* "I am not coming NOT" or Никто не знает, сколько стоят эти бусы "Nobody NOT knows how much these beds cost" should be illogical or an impediment to understanding. So, if multiple negatives express negation in world languages such as French, why should they not do so in English? In other words, it just doesn't make sense.

As a bottom line, we should try not to worry too much about correctness and logic in language. Multiple negation has been traced throughout the history of English, so it simply does not pose problems for the day-to-day usage of the language; it is used by millions of speakers today. There are other problematic issues about language usage, as we will see throughout the book, but multiple negation is not one of them. What we learn here is that, no matter how negatively some individuals view multiple negation (or similarly emotionally charged constructions such as split infinitives, "between you and I" vs. "between you and me," or prepositions at the end of a sentence as in "Whom did you talk to?"), the simple fact is that speakers continue using it. There is a **prescriptivism vs. descriptivism** clash between what we call prescriptivism (strong views on language "correctness," that is how individuals should speak) and descriptivism (the study or observation of how speakers actually speak in their normal lives). Language is not mathematics, and speakers are not mathematicians; likewise, most sociolinguists are interested in how we speak and not how some claim we should speak.

This does not mean we should disregard prescriptive views, as from here it is a short step for people to associate "bad" language with "bad" character. Some dialects are stigmatized strongly, whereas others are valued and associated with high prestige. As George Bernard Shaw famously wrote in his preface to *Pygmalion*: "It is impossible for an Englishman to open his mouth without making some other Englishman hate or despise him." Opinions about dialect diversity form the basis of attitudes about groups and entire speech communities. I have experienced this everywhere I have taught: Dialect diversity is not neutral and perceptions need to be justified and explained somehow. What do you think happens when I ask students about their justification of why they favor some dialects and dislike others? They point to alleged beauty, logic, or expressiveness and claim that some varieties lack these qualities, so that speakers sound uneducated. We have already looked at AAVE/AAL, but there's no shortage of other examples: Alabama English, Spanglish, Cockney, Scouse, **Singlish**, and many other forms of English around the world.

As a result, millions of nonstandardized English-speakers are discriminated against simply because of the way they speak. People write to the media, increasingly complain online, and politicians express these views in public. Singlish, the variety of working-class Singapore English that emerged from contact with Asian languages, for instance, was officially stigmatized as "a handicap we must not wish on Singaporeans" by former prime minister Lee Kuan Yew in a National Day Rally speech back in 1999. He said:

> If we carry on using Singlish, the logical final outcome is that we, too, will develop our own type of pidgin English, spoken only by three million Singaporeans, which the rest of the world will find quaint but incomprehensible. We are already halfway there. Do we want to go all the way? We would be better off sticking to Chinese, Malay or Tamil; then at least some other people in the world can understand us.

In an interview with the *Straits Times* in August 1999, the Prime Minister went a step further by calling for official intervention: "we should ensure that the next generation does not speak Singlish." In other words, the Government should make every effort to eradicate a social dialect from Singapore society – this may sound harsh and shocking, but as we will see in Chapter 5, such calls for official intervention are by no means rare. So the

Government acted by launching the **Speak Good English Movement** and tried to implement the use of Standard English in administration and education. Singlish, the language of the working classes, was considered an impediment to the country on its way to becoming one of the Asian Tiger States; the Government feared that the economy would fail to prosper because millions of Singaporeans did not speak "good" English (Wee 2018). We will discuss this case further in Chapter 8.

Taking all this together, there is an important take-home message: Language stigmatization is socially grounded. It primarily reflects attitudes against speakers and by consequence against their dialects and sociolects, and these are evaluated socially. And in case my students still do not believe this, then I ask them to rate dialects they are not familiar with. (Note the preposition at the end of that last sentence, by the way. Did it bother you or did it prevent you from understanding?) Speakers of American English who know little about sociolinguistic variation in the British Isles rate Cockney just as pleasant as any other dialect, on a par with varieties considered much more prestigious by speakers of British English. In a wonderful study, Giles, Bourhis, Lewis & Trudgill (1974) studied perceptions about varieties of Greek, Athenian and Grecian, which carry high (Athenian) and low (Grecian) prestige for speakers of Greek. Speakers of English, however, not familiar with Greek, rated the varieties similar in terms of correctness, beauty, and social importance – it was all Greek to them in a way. Similarly, speakers unfamiliar with French gave similar ratings to the "prestigious" Paris variety, regional French, or Quebecois dialects (which are perceived very differently in France). So, when speakers lack social knowledge of prestige and stigma of dialects in Greece and France, they rank them the same. Such a study can be easily replicated in English sociolinguistics courses: When I ask my students to listen to and rate samples of a language they do not speak, most of them cannot differentiate between standard, regional, social, and nonstandardized varieties. They just don't carry social meaning for them.

The **Social Connotation Hypothesis** holds that speakers' opinions about languages (and dialects) are largely a function of positive or negative associations with extralinguistic factors. Italian, accordingly, is not perceived to be a beautiful language because of its harmonic vowel system but because it is associated with Italy, popular for holidays, globally known and loved for food, hospitality, *dolce vita*, and *Italianità*. However, languages are stigmatized because of negative associations with nations and speakers, and these may change across time. Take the example of German in the US: By the late nineteenth century, there were millions of native speakers of German and their language was rather neutrally perceived until the Second World War, when sentiment against German changed for political reasons. Again: While such views have no sociolinguistic justification, they are socially powerful and deeply engraved in the minds of speakers (very often passed on via language socialization). This is strong evidence of Cameron's claim that "People believe that some languages are better than others." Attitudes toward "good" or "beautiful" French or Italian, "ugly" or "harsh" German, or "simple" English are social assessments without a linguistic basis, nothing more and nothing less. Negative attitudes are held and perpetuated by the mainstream population at large (Chapter 7). They are often top–down, as higher-status groups impose their opinions on lower-status groups: "Bad" English is spoken in the rural parts of the country by the uneducated and ethnic minorities and often stereotyped ("Everybody from that place speaks like that").

Perceptual dialectology studies nonlinguists' perception of dialects in regional or social space. In one of the methods used, the so-called "draw-a-map" task, participants are asked to draw lines on a map, singling out dialect areas and providing additional comments with information about the speakers. Figure 1.2 illustrates this well. The participant, a 17-year-old female from Presteigne, Wales, singles out dialect areas such as "Scottish," "Northern," "West Country," and "Scouse" but also makes social judgments about the dialect speakers (the Scots are "fast, sometimes angry," East Anglians are "farmers").

To sum up: Speakers differ in how they talk depending on where they come from socially and regionally, what degree of education they have, how old they are, whether they are male, female, or nonbinary, and so on. Most speakers are quick at picking up these differences and evaluating them, so it is perfectly normal to express value judgments such as "good" vs. "bad," "beautiful" vs. "ugly," or "educated" vs. "noneducated." As Cameron observed: "People can't leave their language alone." I have taught entire sociolinguistics courses at various universities only to read in end-of-term papers that some dialects sound "uneducated" – this was not at all what I taught in the course but showed how strong such beliefs are. As sociolinguistically uninformed as attitudes and value judgments of "ugly dialects" may be, they essentially shape, create, and maintain our social evaluation of language and society, and everyone interested in sociolinguistics should be aware of that. The shared experience of speakers causes all sorts of attitudes to develop and be passed on, sometimes supported by unsound explanations, and, sadly, this leads to discrimination against speakers at the social and regional periphery. As the great English sociolinguist Peter Trudgill said:

> Accents aren't inherently attractive or nice or beautiful or ugly, they just are. It is often the association that people have with those accents

1 English Sociolinguistics: Why It Matters

Figure 1.2 Example of a hand-drawn dialect map. From Montgomery (2017: 154).

which can form an opinion … Accents are all good, they're all nice, and they're all attractive, and we shouldn't encourage people to think otherwise. (Bishop 2022)

Linguistically speaking, all dialects are equal; sociologically and perceptually speaking, they are not, and this may have dramatic consequences, particularly in education and on the job market. If linguists, educationalists, and policymakers fail realize to demonstrate how important dialects are, all forms of racial and social prejudice, misinformation, and language-based discrimination will abound.

1.4 Sociolinguistics: Let's Go!

So far, by means of an introduction, we have focused on the social perception of language. Nevertheless, sociolinguistics involves so much more than how language is used and evaluated in different social contexts. One of the chief characteristics of the discipline is that it is very interdisciplinary, and sociolinguistics have worked with – and been inspired by – colleagues from different branches in the humanities: sociology, geography, psychology, to name but a few. Since the 1960s, sociolinguistics has grown and developed into one of the most dynamic and vibrant research fields within general linguistics, and it is also thanks to its inclusive and open character that it has become so popular. The early separation of the "sociolinguistics of language" and the "sociolinguistics of society" (still propagated by Fasold [1984], who actually wrote two textbooks with these titles) is much less rigidly applied today and there has been a fusion of language- and society-related domains in line with recent modeling, statistical analysis, and innovative theoretical approaches (e.g. the sociolinguistics of globalization; Blommaert 2010). From a strong concern with variationist and applied sociolinguistics in early work on the social stratification of English in New York City (Labov 1966) and Norwich (Trudgill 1974), the field has diversified and branched out into subdisciplines as diverse as historical sociolinguistics, translanguaging, indexicality, contact linguistics, multilingualism, language and the law, and so forth. This book is a modest journey through sixty years of sociolinguistics, from its beginnings to its current state, providing an overview of its most important subfields. The ideal starting point is the question of how it all began and where sociolinguistics came from in the first place. So let's go!

Take-Home Messages

- Language carries strong social meaning for speakers and speech communities. It not only transmits information but is also the social glue; a medium to create and maintain social relationships.
- Language carries essential information about speakers (social or regional origins, education, age, ethnic group, sex/gender/non-binary).

> - Speakers have strong views on what is correct (or "good") language usage, and attitudes are transferred from individual speakers to speech communities and dialects/accents. The result is discrimination, social prejudice, and self-denigration.
> - Language is not value-free. Some dialects (and dialect speakers) are stigmatized strongly, whereas others are socially valued. Nonstandardized dialects can also carry positive connotations such as friendliness, warmth, charm, and so on, particularly when they function as carriers of identity in a community.

Activities

1.1 Reflect on differences in (Standard) British and American English and compare with a third variety of English from around the world that you may choose yourself. How do they differ in phonemes, grammatical patterns, and lexical characteristics? List your observations and discuss them in groups. What social evaluations do they carry?

1.2 Watch the Open Office Hours post by Professor John Rickford of Stanford University, where he comments about public views on the linguistics of race and ethnicity in America: www.youtube.com/watch?v=Ig4iwkeLjpA.
   What are the major claims and concerns here and what is the sociolinguistic reaction? List your observations and discuss them in groups.

1.3 Read and discuss the following report: https://accentbiasbritain.org/wp-content/uploads/2020/03/Accent-Bias-Britain-Report-2020.pdf.
   What are the major findings and recommendations to address language-based discrimination in the UK?

Key Terms

accent	linguistic profiling
dialect	Standard English
sociolect	complaint tradition
sociolinguistic repertoire	Singlish
multilingualism	Speak Good English Movement
stereotypes	Social Connotation Hypothesis
African American Vernacular English (AAVE)	perceptual dialectology
	prescriptivism vs. descriptivism

Further Reading

For a detailed account of African American English, read:
Green, L. (2002). *African American English: A Linguistic Introduction*. Cambridge: Cambridge University Press. doi:10.1017/CBO9780511800306.

For a history of the English language, with a focus on standardization:
Horobin, S. (2015). *How English Became English*. Oxford: Oxford University Press.

The following is a concise introduction to attitudes toward language:
Montgomery, C., & Beal, J. (2011). Perceptual Dialectology. In: W. Maguire & A. McMahon, eds., *Analysing Variation in English*. Cambridge: Cambridge University Press, 121–148, doi:10.1017/CBO9780511976360.007.

A good overview of the most important field of sociolinguistics is found in:
Trousdale, G. (2010). *An Introduction to English Sociolinguistics*. Edinburgh: Edinburgh University Press.

CHAPTER **2**

From Dialectology to Sociolinguistics: A Short History

In This Chapter ...

... we trace the development of the field from its beginnings to the present day. Before the start of sociolinguistics proper in the early 1960s, regional dialectologists had already made considerable efforts to explore the spatial dimension of language variation, using different methodologies to collect data on regional dialects. The impact of the so-called sociolinguistic turn is discussed with reference to Labov's early work (on the island of **Martha's Vineyard** and in New York City), and some principal findings and methods of early work in the field are introduced. We will take a first look at the subsequent waves of variationist sociolinguistics, social network theory, and communities of practice, which entail a focus on individual speakers and their social grouping and ordering as well as their orientation and affiliation with other speakers in indexical relationships. The chapter concludes with some recent developments and a presentation of current research themes.

2.1	Regional Dialectology: A Short Historical Sketch	*page* 21
2.2	Researching Dialects in Geographical Space: Methodology	23
	Vignette 2.1: The English Dialect App (EDA)	31
2.3	The Sociolinguistic Turn	34
	Vignette 2.2: William Labov (1927–2024)	35
2.4	Researching Dialects in Social Space: Methodology and Some First Findings	39
	Vignette 2.3: /r/	43
2.5	Conclusion: From Dialectology to Sociolinguistics	47
	Take-Home Messages	49
	Activities	50
	Key Terms	50
	Further Reading	50

2.1 Regional Dialectology: A Short Historical Sketch

Though sociolinguistics properly dates back to the 1960s and is thus a more recent field in the humanities, it is sometimes forgotten that research on language and society (depending on how it was defined, of course) has a more long-standing tradition. As is well-known, it was only in the twentieth century that a synchronic focus emerged in the research canon, and until then the objectives of linguistic inquiry were predominantly diachronic. Linguists worked historically and were interested in finding out the form of Sanskrit and the reconstruction of an Indo-European *Ursprache*. As Sir William Jones famously wrote in 1786:

> The *Sanscrit* language, whatever be its antiquity, is of a wonderful structure; more perfect than the *Greek*, more copious than the *Latin*, and more exquisitely refined than either, yet bearing to both of them a stronger affinity, both in the roots of verbs and the forms of grammar, than could possibly have been produced by accident; so strong indeed, that no philologer could examine them all three, without believing them to have sprung from some common source, which, perhaps, no longer exists; there is a similar reason, though not quite so forcible, for supposing that both the *Gothic* and the *Celtic*, though blended with a very different idiom, had the same origin with the *Sanscrit*; and the old *Persian* might be added to the same family. (Jones 1807; originally printed 1786: xi)

This was common practice before the herald of de Saussure's *Cours de linguistique générale*, the synchronic turn in the early twentieth century. Linguists looked back in time and not at the dialects spoken around them. (As late as 1875, Alexander Ellis ascertained that "Collecting country words is looked upon as an amusement, not as laying a brick in the temple of science.") However, some nineteenth-century publications foreshadowed what was to come: In 1821, Johann Andreas Schmeller (1785–1852) had published *The Dialects of Bavaria* (including a small map classifying local dialects), the first grammar that treated dialects of a particular region and not a historical or geographical account of former stages of the German language.

One of the founding fathers of regional dialectology, the German linguist **Georg Wenker** (1852–1911), wrote his doctoral dissertation on shifts and syllabic effects on consonants in early Germanic before going on to produce the first groundbreaking dialect survey of our time, a milestone in the history of both dialectology and linguistics: the *Sprachatlas des Deutschen Reichs*. For this project, Wenker first surveyed the dialects in his native

Düsseldorf, which was the first empirical study of language usage in a single locality. From 1888 to 1911, he headed the *Forschungsinstitut für Deutsche Sprache* (today: *Deutscher Sprachatlas*) in Marburg. Upon Wenker's premature death, Ferdinand Wrede took over as coordinator and the first volume of the *Deutscher Sprachatlas*, including linguistic maps, was published in 1926.

This paved the way for similar surveys in most European countries. Between 1926 and 1933, projects were carried out in the entire German-speaking area. In France, Jules Gilliéron had already published a linguistic atlas reporting on dialect variation in twenty-five localities south of the Rhône and began a great national survey in the 1880s. The *Atlas Linguistique de France*, compiled under his direction, was published from 1902 to 1912, with thirteen volumes and a stunning number of 1,920 dialect maps. Karl Jaberg and Jakob Jud, influential figures in Italian dialectology, directed a survey of Italian dialects of Italy and southern Switzerland: the *Sprach- und Sachatlas Italiens und der Südschweiz* (1928–40). There was an early European network of dialectologists who met and exchanged ideas: Jaberg, who had studied in Paris and took courses with Gilliéron, recalled their encounter as "the most personal and decisive academic encounter of my life."

It was only a matter of time before there was an interest in the study of English dialects. Immediately after the Second World War, Eugen Dieth, Professor of English Language at the University of Zürich, and Harold Orton from the University of Leeds began work on the **Survey of English Dialects** (SED). Their aim was to compile a linguistic atlas of England with four major regions (North, East, West Midlands, South). They were worried that the rich dialect landscape was disappearing quickly and made every effort to document regional forms of English before it was too late:

> Harold Orton often told us that it was the eleventh hour, that dialect was rapidly disappearing, and that this [the SED] was a last-minute exercise to scoop out the last remaining vestige of dialect before it died out under the pressures of modern movement and communication. (Ellis 1992: 7)

All in all, 313 localities were selected from England, the Isle of Man, and some parts of Wales, and a total of 404,000 items were collected and published in thirteen volumes from the early 1960s onwards.

On the other side of the Atlantic Ocean, the American Dialect Society started publishing a journal in 1889: the "Dialect Notes." Hans Kurath (originally from Villach, Austria) started systematic dialect investigations which were to culminate in the *Linguistic Atlas of New England* (LANE) and the *Linguistic Atlas of the Middle and South Atlantic States* (LAMSAS) in the 1930s. Kurath collaborated with colleagues from Europe, some of whom he hired for the training of fieldworkers, which helped advance the methodology of American dialectology generally.

To conclude, concepts of regional space and physical distance have for a long time been central in dialect research, and the first dialectologists had to establish the field against the common research paradigms based on philology and historical linguistics. By the early twentieth century, the documentation and study of dialects gathered momentum and led to a pan-European development that started in Germany and then took hold in France, Switzerland, Scotland, Denmark, and England. There was close collaboration with dialectologists working in the US, which shows how international research activities were at the time.

2.2 Researching Dialects in Geographical Space: Methodology

In my personal view, it is a bit ironic to talk about "big data" and Large Language Models (LLMs) which have become so fashionable recently. In a sense, working with large amounts of data has been prominent for a long time, though collection and analysis always depended on the technological possibilities available. It is not always considered that in the era before digitalization, the collection and storage of dialect data was a massive undertaking. In one course, I gave my students fifty cards with dialect words and asked them to classify and label them; it took them nearly two hours to do so. The earliest dialectologists did not turn to the libraries to look for language data, as philologists were doing, but went out into villages and cities to find out how people spoke in their everyday lives. By doing so, they started a paradigm shift in data collection, heralded usage-based linguistics, and laid the foundation of modern sociolinguistics which has persisted to the present day. They collected big data at least for their day and age.

How was this done? In the beginning, postal questionnaires were used. When collecting data for the *Sprachatlas des Deutschen Reichs* from 1876 to 1887, Georg Wenker sent out questionnaires to every village in Germany that had a school, a massive number of 40,736 places. Teachers were sent a list with forty sentences, which included the days of the week and numerals. They were asked to translate these from Standard German into the local dialect, using the common alphabet. Sentences were constructed to yield information on the phonetic and phonological characteristics of the regional dialects as well as their syntax. This was adapted from Wenker's earlier study in Düsseldorf, which had shown that local features were represented in questionnaire data. The materials used were collected indirectly, as the questionnaires were filled in and completed by the local authorities (Wenker obviously placed considerable trust in teachers).

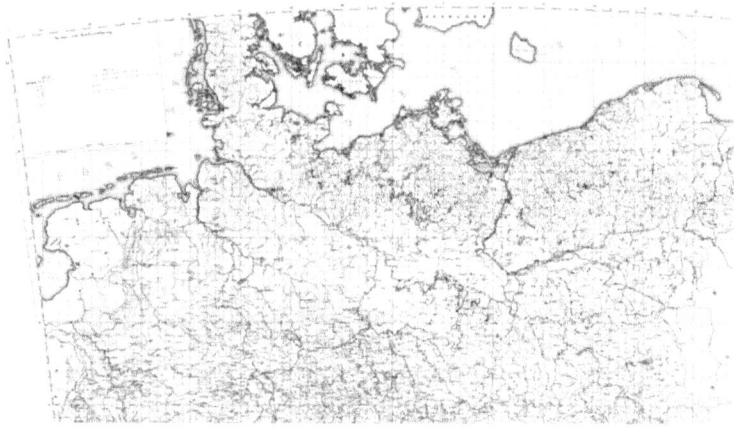

Figure 2.1 Regional variation for the word *pfeffer* "pepper" in German, based on Wenker's map. Reproduced by courtesy of the Forschungszentrum Deutscher Sprachatlas, Marburg/Research Center Deutscher Sprachatlas, Marburg, BY-SA 4.0, http://creativecommons.org/licenses/by-sa/4.0/

This approach yielded an impressive body of data for comparison, with an extraordinary density of places investigated across the German-speaking area, and thus provided an unprecedented macrolevel perspective on language variation in geographical space. The self-reported data provided dialectologists with a first opportunity to identify linguistic differences between regions and to track dialect variation and change spatially.

However, Wenker's method had a couple of disadvantages. For one, it did not allow for cross-checking or double-checking: It remained unclear whether and what adaptations teachers made to render local speech by using the (standard) alphabet, and this makes a detailed phonetic analysis difficult. Teachers were neither linguists nor had they been trained in language transcription. Moreover, metadata were missing: It was not known who the teachers were, how old they were, where they came from, whether they were dialect speakers themselves, whether they filled in the questionnaires alone or whether they sought the advice of locals, and so on. Nobody knows how accurate and trustworthy their transcriptions were.

Moreover, only a small section of the overall population was represented in the sample: those privileged with education and who worked at schools. Of course, this would raise the question of how they perceived local dialects as spoken by uneducated members of the community. If the translation did not tap into their own language repertoire, which was unlikely, then it was unclear whom they asked for advice and where their information had been taken from. It was certainly possible that local informants accommodated to the teachers, perhaps to sound more educated or to avoid unintelligibility. Last but not least, there was little (if any) awareness of individual variation (see Chapter 3), as this was only to come onto the dialectologists' radar in the twentieth century. As there is a continuum from standard to local non standardized varieties, it is problematic that we do not know what stage of the continuum was represented in the responses, or how far-reaching the differences between varieties were in the first place. There is no possibility to establish this now.

Notwithstanding, questionnaires remained popular in traditional dialectology: For the lexical component of the *Survey of Scottish Dialects*, compiled in 1952, Angus McIntosh used a postal questionnaire, and one of the most eminent sociolinguists of our time, Jack K. Chambers, used an online questionnaire for his dialect topography project in the 1990s to collect comparative linguistic data from individual speakers in distinct geographical settings. Chambers considered his online survey as an alternative to traditional dialect geography and found that it had two advantages: representativeness and time-effectiveness:

1. Such a practice was sociolinguistically relevant, as a representative sample allowed the correlation of language variation (see Chapter 3) with independent variables such as age, gender, and ethnic background (by contrast, all of Wenker's informants were educated male teachers).
2. Online surveys provide a more efficient technique for data collection and handling. Dialect atlases took an unduly long time, on occasion more than twenty years, to reach completion and publication. Work on the SED, for instance, was delayed several times due to funding difficulties, and the venerable Institute of Dialect and Folk Life Studies, established by Harold Orton, had to be closed down in 1983 when the University of Leeds no longer provided financial support. In order to be of maximal benefit for the research community, dialect data should be published and made available as quickly as possible, which gives online surveys another advantage.

The *Atlas linguistique de la France* adopted an alternative method of dialect collection. Here, data were collected right away and potential informants were selected and asked to give their responses, which were transcribed directly. For the compilation of dialect data, Jules Gilliéron employed a single fieldworker, the legendary Edmond Edmont. Between 1896 and 1900, Edmont cycled across the countryside of France, southern Belgium, and western Switzerland to conduct 700 interviews at 639 locations, using a standardized questionnaire with over 1,500 items.

Edmont had received training in data transcription and used a phonetic alphabet for his methods of data collection. Being the only fieldworker in the project, it was his single responsibility to select dialect speakers and collect and prepare all the materials. He was instructed to approach mostly elderly, non-mobile, rural males (as was customary in dialect geography), but to also note biographic information (from his notes we know they were aged between 15 and 85, classified as "local intellectuals", "folk speakers," etc.).

Of the total 700 interviews, sixty were conducted with female speakers and about 500 of the consultants had received little or no school education; all the interviews were conducted in rural villages and small towns, larger cities being avoided. As Edmont sent his questionnaires back to Paris regularly (and as these invaluable materials were delivered reliably by the French mail service), Gilliéron was able to start his research and cartographic activities immediately, which allowed him to publish the first volume of the *Atlas* as early as 1902 (in fact, twenty-five years earlier than the *Deutscher Sprachatlas*). As the final, thirteenth volume was published in 1910, it is remarkable that such a monumental study reached completion in less than ten years.

As for the method, Edmont asked direct questions in standard French (e.g. "How do you say *head*?" "What do you call a *cup*?"). He was not familiar with local varieties (or *patois*) of French, so it was certainly possible that the consultants adjusted their speech when speaking to a foreigner in some way, not responding in the manner they would normally have done (e.g. just echoing the words he used). As with Wenker's approach, questions remain about the authenticity of the responses: We do not know how accurate and consistent Edmont's observations were, but direct observation seems more reliable. Moreover, he was the only fieldworker and quickly gained experience in his methods of selection and transcription.

Gilliéron and Edmont's project (they published the *Atlas* jointly, which shows how high was Gilliéron's respect for Edmont's fieldwork and linguistic talent) is a landmark in dialect geography. It stimulated considerable interest in dialect geography in other countries and provided a model for subsequent dialect research elsewhere. Research on dialects of Italian built on the methodology of the *Atlas linguistique*, though Karl Jaberg and Jakob Jud chose a more ethnographic approach when adapting their questionnaires to the local environments so as to reflect varying cultural and linguistic nuances in the speakers' everyday lives.

The situation in England was a bit different. The English Dialect Society had been founded in 1873, and Joseph Wright published his *English Dialect Dictionary* (1898–1905) and the *English Dialect Grammar* (1905) comparatively early. Wright, originally from Yorkshire, was a truly remarkable scholar: As a child, he worked in a Yorkshire factory and taught himself to read and write. At the age of 21, he traveled to Heidelberg (walking all the way from the Atlantic coast), where he enrolled himself as a student and studied languages such as Sanskrit, Gothic, Lithuanian, Russian, and Old English. He earned his PhD in Heidelberg, returned to England and became Professor of Comparative Philology at the University of Oxford, where he worked from 1901 to 1925. Wright had a deep interest in local dialects; his *Dialect Dictionary* comprised more than 5,000 pages and presented materials from glossaries and a variety of philological sources – a truly massive undertaking of "big data" for his day and age.

Inspired by Wenker's methods, Alexander Ellis sent questionnaires mostly to clergymen across the country and asked them to render the sentences "into the idiom and pronunciation of the place" (Ellis 1889: 1). The same caveats apply: The sample was skewed (instructions were given to approach local farmers), responses were incomplete and unbalanced (some questionnaires contained just a handful of local words), and there is no possibility of verifying whether the responses were authentic or whether the informants accommodated to the more standard-like dialects of the vicars.

Fieldwork proper only started much later, when the *Survey of English Dialects* (SED) began in 1948. Data were collected between 1950 and 1961, and the aim was to collect a full range of speech in England and parts of Wales. The original questionnaires included some 800 questions, the first interviews were carried out by nine fieldworkers trained in **International Phonetic Alphabet (IPA)** notation and, a real bonus, from 1953 onward, some audio recordings were made as well. A total of 311 locations were selected across England, and Harold Orton had a clear idea as to the kind of dialect speakers studied:

> ... elderly speakers of sixty years of age or over belonging to the same social class in rural communities ... those who were, or had formerly been, employed in farming, for it is amongst the rural populations that the traditional types of vernacular English are best preserved to-day ... dialect speakers whose residence in the locality had been interrupted by significant absences were constantly regarded with suspicion. (Orton & Dieth 1962: 14–16)

The most authentic dialect speakers were what Chambers & Trudgill (1998: 33) referred to as **NORMs**: non-mobile, older, rural males. The focus was on rural areas, villages, and small towns in the countryside, far away from the major cities, as mobility was considered as having a contaminating effect on dialect usage (or "purity," a rather problematic concept in language). Fieldworkers were instructed to collect the traditional speech of elderly men, aged 60 or over, preferably with a background in farming and little or no school education. Data were collected in the informants' homes (one fieldworker famously recalled he was told to wear old clothes to gain the confidence of elderly villagers), and the fieldworkers were told to act as pupils learning from an expert.

In each of the 311 locations, a questionnaire was used by the eleven fieldworkers (Orton & Dieth 1962: 33). Between three and six informants were interviewed at most sites, on occasion only one or two. The questionnaire contained over 1,300 items, with different domains, and was set up to elicit phonological, grammatical, and lexical forms. Unlike in the *Atlas linguistique de France*, fieldworkers used indirect questions or sentence completion tasks ("What is left in a cornfield after harvesting?", "A hen that wants to sit, you call a …?") and all answers were transcribed using consistent principles of the IPA. The results were published in so-called display maps (Figure 2.2), where all the responses of particular items were entered on a map with symbols, or in interpretative maps (Figure 2.3) which showed the distribution of the responses (Chambers & Trudgill 1998: 28).

All things considered, the sample of speakers who provided material for the compilation of the SED was rather homogeneous, as it exclusively focused on elderly rural men with little education. The assumption was that these speakers would preserve dialects in their archaic and "pure" form and that their speech had to be recorded so as to document the quickly disappearing traditional dialects. While this allowed for a first adequate comparison of speakers and localities, the downside was that this was a mere snapshot of the British population in the mid twentieth century. Moreover, the fieldworkers were not familiar with the informants and their everyday lives, and it remained unclear how they adjusted their speech when speaking to outsiders and strangers. While the fieldworkers had received linguistic training, the transcription of words elicited from a word list or questionnaire could not provide much information about speech in ordinary conversation and community life in general.

In the US, finally, the American Dialect Society had been established in 1889. The systematic study of dialect geography began under the guidance of Hans Kurath. In 1931, he hired Jakob Jud and Paul Scheuermeier, one of his colleagues, to train fieldworkers for the *Linguistic Atlas of the United States and Canada* project and produced the **Linguistic Atlas of New England** (LANE), published in 1939–40, the first large-scale atlas-type

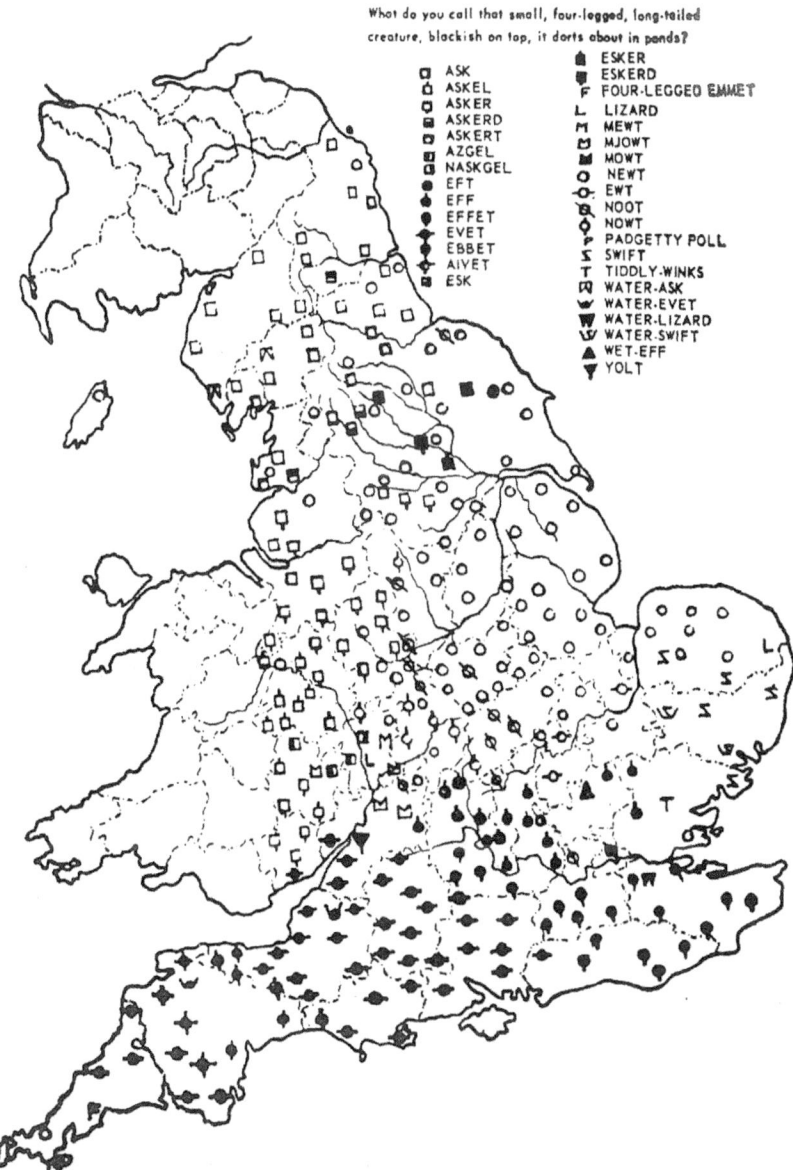

Figure 2.2 Display map based on the *Survey of English Dialects* (Chambers & Trudgill, *Dialectology*). Reproduced with permission of the licensor through PLSclear.

research in American English. The survey of the *Linguistic Atlas of the Middle and South Atlantic States* (LAMSAS) was directed by Guy Lowman and Raven McDavid. For the *Linguistic Atlas of the United States and Canada*, 416 interviews were conducted by nine fieldworkers. Questionnaires were divided into a general and a specific part for each region. Instead of direct questions ("How do you say head?"), words were

2 From Dialectology to Sociolinguistics: A Short History

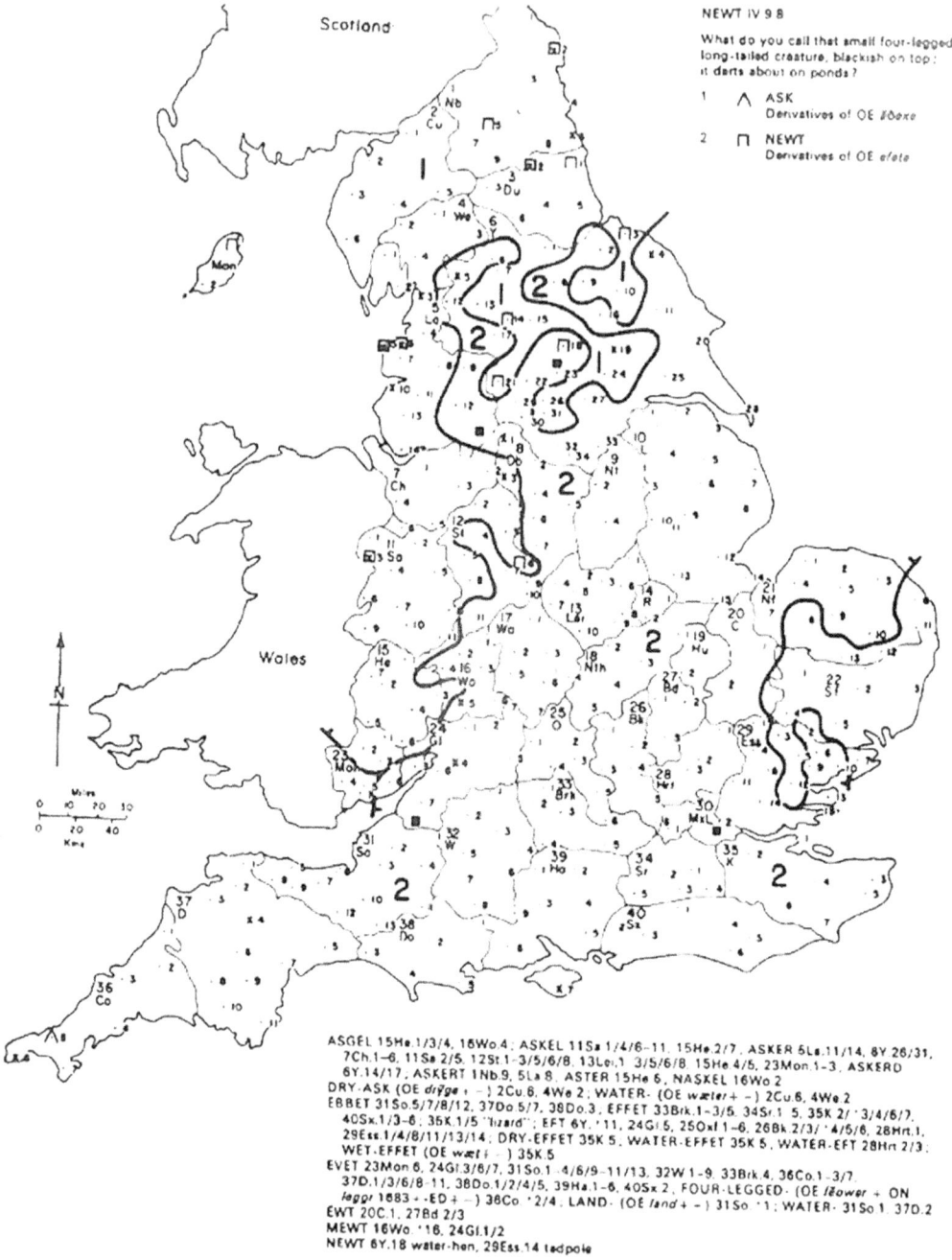

Figure 2.3 Interpretative map based on the *Survey of English Dialects* (Chambers & Trudgill, *Dialectology*). Reproduced with permission of the licensor through PLSclear.

elicited by gestures and questions ("What's this?" pointing to the head) and diagrams and pictures were used so as not to influence the responses. Moreover, fieldworkers took note of spontaneous speech – informants' personal opinions, reminiscences and anecdotes, occupational details, and so forth.

The US provided a different dialect scenario altogether. It had less time depth compared to England, France, and Germany, which meant there were fewer archaic or traditional dialects, and the population was characterized by geographical and social mobility. Kurath adopted the practice of European colleagues in that he instructed fieldworkers to focus on rural communities and to avoid cities and towns. They were to preferably select male speakers from the same social class, aged 60 or over, from communities that had had a more or less stable population of approximately 500 inhabitants for a hundred years or more.

However, Kurath was aware of the challenges. New England was subject to sharp social stratification, and there were differences between social and regional dialects, so LANE also included speakers who did not have the traditional NORM characteristics. Individuals of different ages and backgrounds were interviewed, and Kurath separated different categories of informants, establishing five different types (three categories and two subcategories):

1. Type 1 had little formal education, little reading, and restricted formal contacts.
2. Type 2 had some formal education and usually attended high school. They had some wider reading, and more social contacts.
3. Type 3 had higher education, usually at university level. Speakers were characterized by wider reading and extensive social contacts (this category was subdivided into old-aged and middle-aged speakers).

While Kurath still believed that non-mobile speakers would represent older or more archaic forms, he developed a higher awareness of language differences between different social classes, which would soon become the prime concern of American sociolinguistics.

> VIGNETTE 2.1 The English Dialect App (EDA)
> There has been no national regional dialect survey since the mid twentieth century and the work of Harold Orton, Eugen Dieth, and their associates. Using smartphone technology, the English Dialect App (EDA), developed by Adrian Leemann and David Britain of the

University of Bern, Switzerland, has given a recent boost to regional dialect variation. The EDA is a free iOS and Android smartphone-app-based dialect survey. After downloading the App, users answer 26 questions about their language use, listening to recordings of variants before giving their responses. The EDA aims to gather data on lexical, phonological, and grammatical variables via a dialect quiz which tries to predict users' dialects based on their answers. Twenty-five maps of linguistic variables from the SED serve as the basis. To guess a user's dialect, Leemann's team selected variables with particularly diagnostic geographical distributions to localize the user's dialect as precisely as possible (the lexical variable "splinter," for example, has ten different variants). For the quiz, users indicate which variants of twenty-six words they use and can optionally record a short text. The result, the English Dialect App Corpus (EDAC), includes metadata on mobility, ethnicity, age, educational level, and gender.

Launched in January 2016, the app was immediately commented upon by national newspapers and BBC Radio, and more than 47,000 users from across the UK indicated dialect variants for these twenty-six words. Over 3,500 users provided audio recordings, providing a rich source for dialect research (Figure 2.4). Unfortunately, distributions of age, ethnicity, qualification levels, and other parameters found in the UK

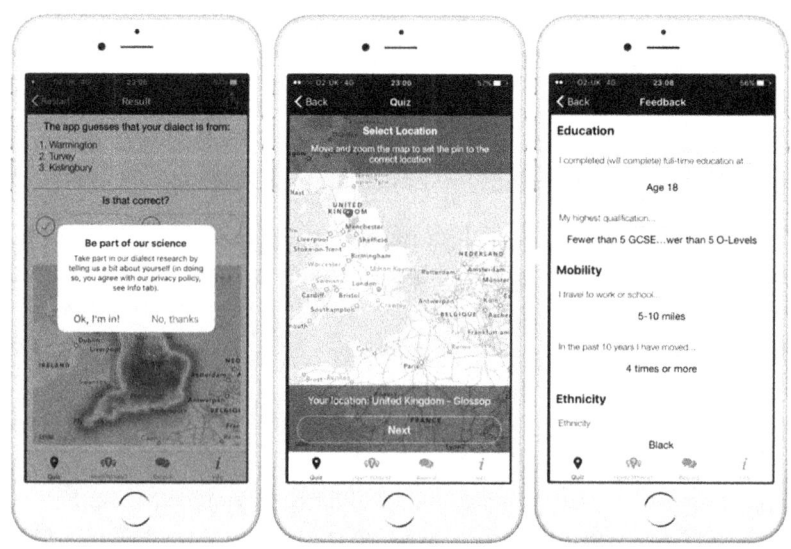

Figure 2.4 The English Dialect App and selected functions on a smartphone. Courtesy of Adrian Leemann.

> population cannot be controlled for and are not evenly balanced (the 16–25 year-old age-group is overrepresented, males and females are not equally balanced, and more than 80 percent of the users are of white ethnicity; Leemann, Kolly & Britain 2018). Smartphone-based research reaches a specific sector of the population, and it remains to be seen whether the sheer mass of big data can remedy this shortcoming. The database will provide much-needed opportunities for researching English regional dialect variation to track change since the traditional dialectologists published their work.

In sum, the work of traditional dialectologists provided invaluable data. A Europewide network connected the early dialectologists, and cooperation and knowledge transfer (between Jules Gilliéron and Karl Jaberg, Harold Orton and Eugen Dieth, Hans Kurath and Jakob Jud) helped refine data-collection methods. From a modern perspective, it would be easy to criticize these projects, but one should never forget the research opportunities and technological possibilities in those days. The completion and analysis of a questionnaire with more than 1,000 single responses was a tedious and cumbersome undertaking; as Orton & Dieth (1962: 17) wrote, "under conditions … each of the nine sections … of the questionnaire took at least two hours to answer … the whole questionnaire could be recorded satisfactorily and conveniently in some four days." This was extremely time-consuming, as data had to be entered and copied by hand.

The two strongest points of criticism concern the sampling of informants and the questionnaires used. The standardized questionnaires used direct questions ("How do you say 'fifty'?") vs. indirect questions ("What is this?" holding up a knife), but not all the researchers took the trouble to adapt the questionnaire to the environments of the speakers they investigated (simply so as to allow consistent comparability). Though indirect questions were favored in almost all surveys, fieldworkers were instructed not to choose freely how to elicit the desired answer. Such an artificial context was not ideal for the extraction of local speech forms, particularly as the researchers were community outsiders. In order words, their elicitation techniques inevitably resulted in relatively formal or careful responses.

The second point concerned the quasi-dogmatic decision to give preference to rural areas and elderly non-mobile speakers: the NORMs. Perhaps due to the philological agenda of the time, there was an extraordinarily persistent view that the allegedly archaic (or "pure") dialects had to be documented in the isolated countryside. The exclusion of mobility was particularly problematic here as, in the age of postindustrialization and out-migration (see Chapter 5), the vast majority of the British population was anything but stable. In some ways, it is ironic that traditional dialectologists fell victim to the myth that the most conservative dialect was necessarily most typical or authentic. But of course, dialectologists are only humans after all, and they have language attitudes as well (see Chapter 1).

Though the SED allowed the comparison of a sample of speakers across the country, it provided a snapshot of the dialects spoken by a small (and perhaps uncharacteristic) section of the overall population. Dialect geographers worked with unbalanced and non-representative samples (we have shockingly little information about the speech of women) and were fully aware of, yet not interested in, dialect variation across society. This has to be kept in mind at all times when working with traditional dialect data.

The 1950s and 1960s saw continuing social changes in the direction of conditions far removed from the world of NORMs. The insistence of de Saussure on synchronic linguistics had become accepted by most scholars, and there was a growing awareness that dialect-geographical data were limited. The time was ripe for a push toward the investigation of language variation in cities, with random and representative samples: The result was a paradigm shift from regional to social dialectology.

2.3 The Sociolinguistic Turn

American dialect geography, most notably that of Hans Kurath, had realized that the social characteristics of speakers needed to be included in some way. There was a growing awareness that dialects were both regional and social forms of language. However, an adequate methodology to investigate the speech of mobile urban speakers was lacking, and there were no data on language variation in metropolitan settings. At the same time, most linguists denied that it was possible to observe ongoing change: "The process of linguistic change has never been directly observed: we shall see that such observations, with our present facilities, are inconceivable" (Bloomfield 1933: 247).

Theories of language change came to be seen as socially grounded, and a methodology for the exploration of change was subsequently developed, thanks to the Labovian revolution in the early 1960s – the so-called **sociolinguistic turn**. William Labov (1927–2024) took on both traditional dialect geography and the then prevailing generativist views by insisting that language change was essentially a social product. Language had to be investigated not as some abstract mental competence, accessed by intuition, but within the community itself, where everyday interaction was a driving force both for variation and change, in all speakers and not only in some NORMs.

> VIGNETTE 2.2 William Labov (1927–2024)
>
> William Labov was born on December 4, 1927 in Rutherford, New Jersey, and studied chemistry at Harvard. He worked as an industrial chemist until 1961, when he started studying linguistics with Uriel Weinreich at Columbia University. In 1970, Labov became Professor of Linguistics at the University of Pennsylvania, where he established the Linguistics Laboratory (Figure 2.5). In his essay "How I got into linguistics, and what I got out of it" (see Further Reading below), written for undergraduates in 1987, he wrote:
>
>> There were (and still are) two major branches of linguistics. One deals with the description of languages as they are now; the other deals with their history, how they came to be. On both sides, I saw that there were some big problems to be solved if linguistics were to make contact with what people said. Linguists wanted to describe languages, like English or French, but their methods only brought them in contact with a few individuals, mostly highly educated. Whenever someone raised a question about the data, they would answer, "I'm talking about *my* dialect." The current theories held that every individual had a different system, and they weren't making much progress in describing the English language and the speech community that owned it. Even more mysterious was the problem of accounting for language change. If language is a system for transmitting information from one person to another, it would work best if it stayed put. How do people manage to understand each other if the language keeps changing under their feet?
>
>
>
> Figure 2.5 William Labov. Photo courtesy of William Labov.

> William Labov established the field of variationist sociolinguistics, both in terms of theory and methodology, and pioneered it for decades. After nearly sixty years in the field and receiving outstanding honors (including about half a dozen honorary PhDs, two Guggenheim Fellowships, and various medals and awards), he officially retired in 2015, continuing to do research and publish. He died in December 2024 at the age of 97 years.

Labov's achievements for sociolinguistic theory were twofold. First and most importantly, he developed both a methodological tool kit and a theoretical framework to empirically investigate social aspects of language usage, particularly in the organization and structuring of a **speech community**. Second, he was the first linguist to emphasize that language variation had to be tackled thoroughly so as to understand and model change, and that the two mechanisms were language-inherent and connected. His credo was that variation in the structural and social fabric of language was not random and unpatterned, as many believed, but socially and historically determined. While language could have variation without change, there could not be change without variation. Without a proper description of the community itself, both were unapproachable. In the early 1960s, sociolinguistics quickly took off and became a highly influential field within general linguistics (Figure 2.6 documents this nicely, displaying the occurrence of the term "sociolinguistics" in Google Books Ngram Viewer).

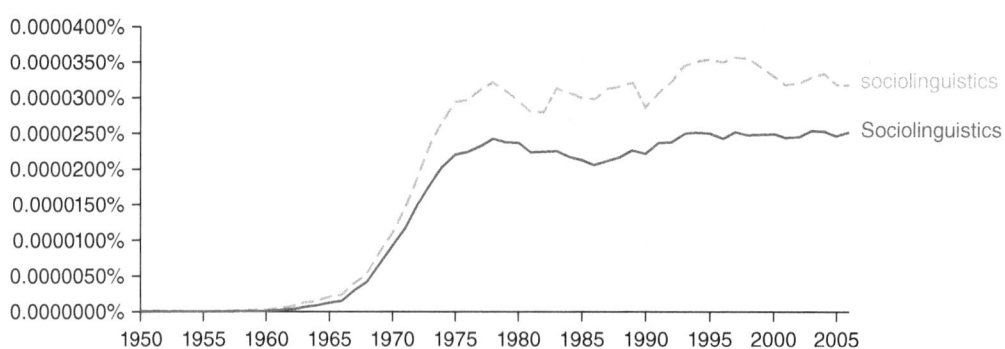

Figure 2.6 The usage of the terms *Sociolinguistics/sociolinguistics* on Ngram Viewer. Data from Google Books Ngram Viewer.

Technological innovations made it possible to record and permanently preserve dialect data, so researchers could listen to interviews over again and double-check their findings. Recording devices had been used before, for instance in the compilation of LANE in the 1930s or in the SED in the early 1950s, but the recordings were of poor quality and devices were costly and heavy. The advent of the tape recorder provided the opportunity to record large samples of speakers, and American sociolinguists pioneered these methodologies in the 1960s. In order to study variation and change, Labov (and other first-wave scholars, such as Ralph Fasold and Walt Wolfram) adopted the technique of selecting and studying linguistic variables that

1. were sensitive to social context, and
2. correlated with social (ethnicity, social class, sex/gender, age), stylistic (casual, careful, formal), and/or linguistic parameters (phonetic environment, etc.).

By pairing up sociolinguistic variables with social criteria, first-wave sociolinguists showed that variation systematically correlated with language-external criteria (such as membership of a particular social class or an ethnic group), and that individuals varied according to the formality of the setting (informal and formal styles). The approach was empirical and according to the principle of accountability, "all occurrences of a given variant are noted, and where it has been possible to define the variable as a closed set of variants, all non-occurrences of the variant in the relative environments" (Labov 1982: 30). For their empirical work, sociolinguists needed to count all cases where a variable could apply in theory (in total, not just where it *was* used) in order to quantify how often and in what contexts a variable was found.

One of the best-researched variables is the variable (-ing) in *"singing"* ([n]). The English progressive *-ing* can be pronounced with a velar nasal /ŋ/ (note that the term "g dropping" is a complete misnomer) or with /n/, which (when written) is symbolized with an apostrophe (e.g. singin' for *singing*). Counting variables in the recordings made it clear that the frequency of (-ing) differed across individuals and social groups; it was not free or random at all. Labov developed a so-called **index score** to indicate the percentages of variables:

$$(-ing) \text{ index} : \frac{\text{number of "-in" forms}}{\text{total number of occurrences of } (-ing)} \times 100$$

By dividing the total number of occurrences by the total number of cases where a variable might have potentially occurred, multiplying by 100, individual speakers were assigned indexes between 0 and 100 to establish the overall frequency of variables, making it possible to compare speakers and communities in how often they had a particular variable.

Sociolinguistic research involves quantitative work with linguistic variables (mostly phonological or morphosyntactic) to establish the frequency with which they occur (all possible cases). These are correlated with social criteria (e.g. social class), allowing the identification of language-internal and language-external constraints. According to Tagliamonte (2012: 8), five steps are involved in the process:

1. Identify linguistic variables.
2. Relate linguistic variables to each other.
3. Correlate independent variables with each other.
4. Correlate linguistic variation as the dependent variable with independent variables.
5. Correlate linguistic variation as the independent variable with dependent variables in society.

Labov insisted on the primacy of spoken language, as "the basis of inter-subjective knowledge in linguistics must be found in speech – language as it is used in everyday life by members of the social order, that vehicle of communication in which they argue with their wives, joke with their friends, and deceive their enemies" (Labov 1972a: xiii). His focus was on the so-called **vernacular**: "the style which is most regular in its structure and in its relation to the evolution of the language is the vernacular, in which the minimal attention is paid to speech" (Labov 1972a: 112) and he developed a sophisticated methodology to elicit precisely these data.

Whereas (Labovian) sociolinguistics was primarily interested in effects of social stratification and style shifting, later work focused on a more ethnographic analysis of individuals and their participation in networks and communities of practice. Eckert (2005) identified three waves of variationist sociolinguistics. First, language variation in socially stratified urban settings, predominant in the 1960s and 1970s, practiced by pioneering sociolinguists such as William Labov, Walt Wolfram, and Peter Trudgill, who interviewed and analyzed the speech of hundreds of individuals. Here social categories were typically predefined by the researchers themselves, who applied rigid formal criteria to classify informants. Categories such as "social class" were defined by criteria such as income, education, housing, and so on, and sex distinguished two categories: "male" and "female." Gradient gender differences, transgender people, homosexuality, sapiosexuality, and so forth were not taken into consideration at the time, neither was the self-definition of the speakers. It was only later that more sociologically refined categories of masculinity and femininity were applied to the concept of gender (Chapter 3). When analyzing stratification effects, social classes were treated as separate units with little permeability. All in all, little attention was given to individuals who could not easily be assigned to a particular category, for example when moving between social strata, and this made the classification of individual speakers somewhat mechanistic – but then again, society was different, less transient, in the 1960s than it is now.

Second-wave sociolinguists concentrated on the individual speaker and the social links they created and maintained. Researchers like James and Lesley Milroy researched the formation and maintenance of identity via linguistic practices, often via **social networks**. They focused on the social ties of individuals in groups (density and multiplexity; cf. Chapter 3), showing that local features served as carriers of identity; these were so strong that they were maintained even when stigmatized by society at large. Third-wave sociolinguists were also interested in local practices yet approached variation via the concept of **communities of practice**. They studied the social meaning of variation in subgroups of communities by approaching language variation as a proactive process, that is as a tool to negotiate the speakers' place in the real world. Some key concepts in their work were **indexicality** (the deliberate projection of identity by symbolic, diagnostic language forms) and **enregisterment** (when "a set of linguistic features that were once not noticed at all, then used and heard primarily as markers of socioeconomic class, have come to be linked increasingly to place and 'enregistered' ... as a dialect," Johnstone, Andrus & Danielson 2006: 78). The latter two approaches meant that a more informed and ethnographic approach to communities was needed, since it was essential to look at local patterns without recourse to large-scale social categories. There was closer focus on individual speakers and their immediate reference groups, and this will be discussed in more detail in Chapter 3.

To sum up, the so-called sociolinguistic turn in the early 1960s saw a true paradigm shift. The focus was on settings that had been neglected up to that point: highly mobile, metropolitan, multiethnic communities distributed in social space. Not only was there a new methodological tool kit to investigate language variation, but language change came to be seen as socially grounded and motivated.

2.4 Researching Dialects in Social Space: Methodology and Some First Findings

We saw above that sampling (the decision about precisely *whose speech* to study) is a central concern. Whereas NORMs were initially preferred, sociolinguists interested in studying language usage in communities at large were less exclusive in their choice of informants as long as there was a representative group of speakers from all strata of society. There is a distinction between random and stratified samples. In the former, individuals are selected so as to adequately reflect the sociological characteristics of an entire speech community (i.e. members of a particular neighborhood, an ethnic group or social class, schoolchildren, etc.).

- Random samples are usually very large, as there is no connection between sample size and population characteristics. Each individual has to have an equal likelihood of selection (which must not be biased in any way so as not to falsify the sample). It is only at a later stage of the project that sociolinguists can assess whether informants meet the necessary requirements (e.g. in terms of age or education) for inclusion in a study. As a result, researchers have to collect more data than they actually need and this is immensely time-consuming. To avoid bias as much as possible, Roger Shuy, Walt Wolfram, and their associates randomly selected and interviewed 702 residents of Detroit from 31 school districts and over 250 families (Shuy 1968). The majority of these recordings have not been studied so far.
- Alternatively, stratified samples are more suitable as only a particular section of the community is selected: Individuals are chosen because they meet predefined requirements; for example, Mexican-Americans aged between 15 and 25. When sampling this way, researchers decide on the categories within a general population *before* starting to collect data. A stratified sample is a small-scale mirror of the community, split into representative groups defined by social class, education level, ethnic group, gender, and so on. Though such a sample is more hands-on, it has the disadvantage that it is to some extent biased; that is, it has been set up in view of the researchers' (possibly preconceived) notions of how a community is structured.

Once selected and agreeing to participate, informants are asked to participate in **sociolinguistic interviews**, where they tell stories and anecdotes (informal styles) but also read passages, word lists, and minimal pairs (formal ones). Labov argued that attention paid to speech, which in his view is central to stylistic variation, has a direct influence on how frequently sociolinguistic variables are used. More standard variants are used in formal settings (such as reading a word list or delivering a speech in public), whereas non standardized ones are typically found in informal contexts (e.g. in casual conversation with friends). Labov insisted on studying the individual speakers' vernacular: the least monitored type of speech.

The identification of styles in a sociolinguistic interview turned out to be a special challenge for research design. Great care was taken to set up structured interviews that would allow the elicitation of different speech styles. Speakers were recorded in casual styles but also asked to do more formal tasks, such as reading a text, word lists, or also minimal pairs, where attention was maximal. These four tasks (note that Labov called them "styles," which was contested later, as we will see in Chapter 3) were: (a) casual speech; (b) careful speech; (c) reading style; (d) reading word lists and minimal pairs. Along with criteria such as income, education, residence, and housing, speakers were lumped together into different social classes (groups numbered 1–9, ranging from the lower- working class (0) to the upper-middle class (9)). Fieldworkers used a set of questions in their interviews, and the most well-known of all sections, the danger of death section, ran as follows:

Q-GEN-II, Module 6 (developed by W. Labov; April 9, 1973 reprinted by courtesy of William Labov)

Danger of Death

1a. Have you ever been in a situation where you were in serious danger of getting killed (where you said to yourself, "This is it!")?
1b. What happened?
2a. Some people say, in a situation like that, "Whatever is going to happen is going to happen."
2b. What do you think?
3a. In most families, there's someone who gets a feeling that something is going to happen, and it <u>does</u> happen.
3b. Is there anybody like that in your family?
3c. Do you remember anything like this that came true?
4a. Was there ever anything that happened when you were growing up that you couldn't explain?
4b. Were there any spooky places you wouldn't go at night?
4c. Does it bother you when people talk about ghosts?
5. Have you ever been somewhere new and know that you've been there before?

One should note that in recent years ethical issues have been raised regarding such kinds of questions. While they can be ideal to elicit spontaneous speech, it always has to be borne in mind that they can bring up serious traumas and sets of emotions that a sociolinguistic interviewer would in fact not want to elicit. The most important point is that interviewees feel at ease during all research activities and fieldworkers should remember this at all times (Schreier 2013).

Structured interviews were first implemented in the study on Martha's Vineyard, an island about three miles off the Massachusetts coast. Labov carried out interviews with sixty-nine residents from all over the island and focused on the variable pronunciation of the diphthongs /au/ (as in *out*, *house, trout*) and /ai/ (as in *while, pie, might*). The first part of the diphthong varies, sounding more like an /a/ (which probably most readers of this book would say) and a more central *schwa*-type /ə/ sound, the last vowel in words such as *sofa* or *letter*. Labov considered the social variables such as age, occupation, place of residence, and attitude to island life. Islanders who had most central *schwa*-type /ə/ sounds were in the group aged 31–45, who worked as fishermen on the rural, western "up island" that had long-term residents and was less touristic. The Chilmark fishermen formed a close-knit group: independent, skillful, physically strong, representing traditional island values, and opposed to the visitors who swarmed Martha's Vineyard in summer.

The study paved the way for sociolinguistics. Labov showed that there was variation between the realizations of the two diphthongs and that this led to language change in the community. Younger speakers had considerably higher frequencies of schwa-sounds than those aged 60 years and over (Figure 2.7).

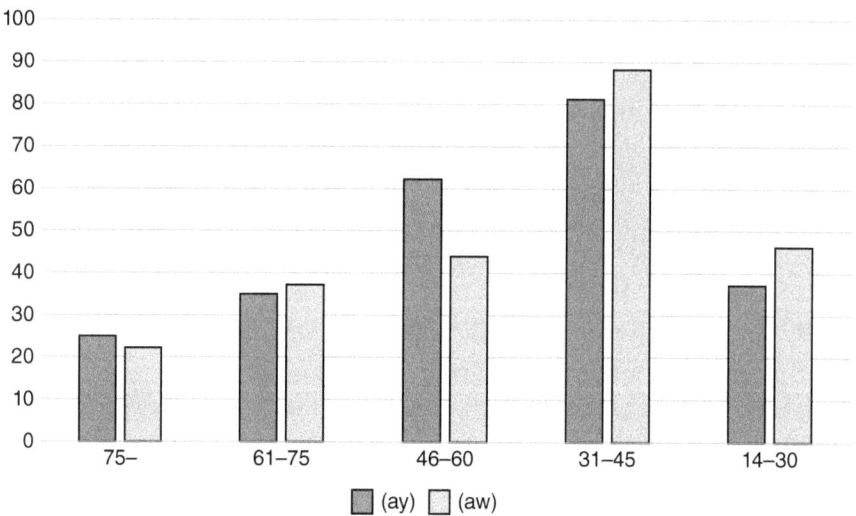

Figure 2.7 Centralization of /au/ and /ai/ on Martha's Vineyard distributed by age. Adapted from Labov (1963: 27).

Moreover, traditional islanders, the middle-aged rural fishermen, had the highest values overall. The usage of this sociolinguistic variable strongly correlated with attitudes to Martha's Vineyard: Those who had a favorable view of the island had considerably higher frequencies than those who did not. In other words, variation indicated different views in the community (which Labov checked against traditional dialect data from the LANE, made in the 1930s). They correlated with attitudes toward island life; the more positive, the higher the frequency of the local vernacular variable. Labov presented his research at the annual meeting of the Linguistic Society of America and wrote in his (1987) essay (see above):

> In those days, there was only a single session, and you practically addressed the entire profession when you advanced to the podium. I had imagined a long and bitter struggle for my ideas, where I would push the social conditioning of language against hopeless odds, and finally win belated recognition as my hair was turning gray. But my romantic imagination was cut short. They ate it up!

Labov went on to research variation in urban settings and developed a different project: the New York **Department Store Study**, in which he carried out rapid anonymous interviews with employees of three stores in Manhattan, all with a different clientele:

- Saks, located at Fifth Avenue, catering for the upper-middle class
- Macy's, at Broadway, for the lower-middle class, and
- S. Klein, on the Lower East Side, mostly frequented by the working-class speakers.

The sociolinguistic variable investigated was postvocalic /r/, which had been subject to variation in New York City for generations.

VIGNETTE 2.3 /r/

Rhoticity, the realization of /r/ in words such as *farm*, *park*, or *car*, is one of the most widely researched sociolinguistic variables. Old English was strongly /r/-ful and /r/ began to be dropped in the early fourteenth century, a change which gained momentum in the seventeenth and eighteenth centuries. Varieties of English vary in rhoticity: It is not found in British Received Pronunciation (but is still common in rural dialects, as well as in Scottish and Irish English) and the major varieties of Southern Hemisphere English, whereas most dialects of American and Canadian English are strongly /r/-ful (with the exception of areas such as New England and ethnic varieties, most notably African American English).

   This can be explained historically. Those American areas that remained in extended contact with Great Britain after Independence picked up the innovation from English English. The outcome was rather complex. In South Carolina, dialect geographers such as Raven McDavid have noticed considerable regional variation, as /r/ was

> brought via the Scotch-Irish, who settled in the mountains. The coastal areas were mostly inhabited by residents with English origins (who thus had less and variable rhoticity), which was also where the large slave-based plantations were situated. McDavid distinguished between a rhotic "hill type" and a non-rhotic "plantation type" and observed that, in South Carolina, rhoticity was associated with older speakers from rural areas and with little education. The /r/-lessness diffused from Charlestown with the plantation system so that the variable was most frequent in former plantation areas that had had an African majority in the nineteenth century. This enhanced the social status of the variable and attests that the work of dialect geographers focused on parameters later attributed to sociolinguistics.
>
> The /r/ remains one of the most widely recognized and commented-on features of American English. It is socially connoted and stereotyped with shibboleths such as "Pahk you Cah in Hahvahd Yahd."

Labov pretended to be a customer and approached employees of the three department stores with an enquiry about which floor to find a particular item on. The question was phrased so that items asked for were always on the fourth floor of the building. When an answer was received, Labov pretended not to have understood and asked again, whereupon the information was repeated with more emphasis. The reason why he asked for a repetition was to elicit a second more careful articulation, that is where speakers showed higher awareness of what they were going to say:

LABOV: "Excuse me, where are the ...?"
EMPLOYEE: "On the fourth floor."
LABOV: "Excuse me?"
EMPLOYEE: "On the fourth floor."

The advantage here was that people were not recorded, which meant that the **observer's paradox** was avoided: "the aim of linguistic research in the community must be to find out how people talk when they are not being systematically observed; yet we can only obtain this data by systematic observation" (Labov 1972a: 209).

Using this design, a total of 264 interviews were carried out (68 in Saks, 125 in Macy's, and 71 in S. Klein). With this short, impromptu and fully anonymous elicitation technique, Labov managed to obtain data from two different styles (one rather casual, the second one more careful) in very little time. Moreover, the variable /r/ features in two different environments – preconsonantal (*fourth*) and word-final (*floor*) – so he collected four variants for each informant, two each in preconsonantal and word-final environments and one in casual and one in more formal speech.

As simple as it was (and in fact, it was merely meant as a pilot study to test some working hypotheses later explored in the Lower East Side study), the Department Store Study presented truly groundbreaking findings. Labov demonstrated that middle and upper-middle class New Yorkers were more likely to pronounce /r/ when compared with working-class speakers. Postvocalic /r/ was most frequent in employees working at Saks (Fifth Avenue) and lowest in the Lower East Side (S. Klein; Figure 2.8). The frequency of a given sociolinguistic variable correlated with class (reflected by store type) and rank of employees (management, sales, shelf-stackers, floorwalkers – note that some of these jobs no longer exist today), so social organization did have an impact on sociolinguistic variation. Moreover, style (defined as attention to speech) was an important factor as well. In the second utterance, when the information was repeated, informants tended to use /r/ more often than in the first response (Figure 2.8). This pattern was identical in all three stores, so /r/ variation in New York English was conditioned by factors such as social class and awareness of speech.

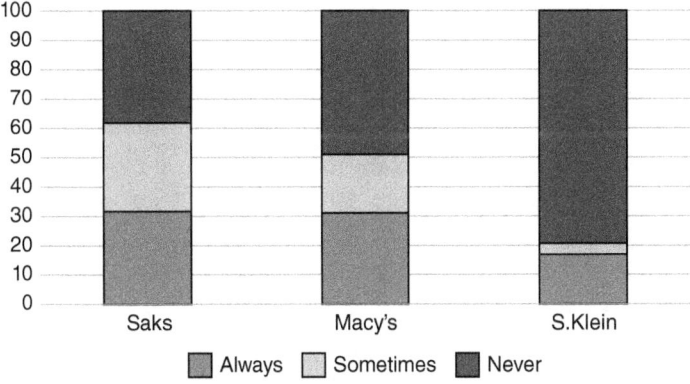

Figure 2.8 Frequency of /r/ in three New York City department stores. Adapted from Labov (1972a: 174).

These findings were integrated into the research design of the first major sociolinguistic study in the early 1960s, with more than 150 interviews of New York residents. As in the Department Store Study, speakers of five social classes showed identical patterns of sensitivity to context and formality. Moreover, the classes differentiated themselves in how often they used the variable, differing (at times significantly) in each of the five tasks. Labov found a crossover pattern, namely that members of the lower-middle class had higher percentages of standard /r/ variants when they showed higher

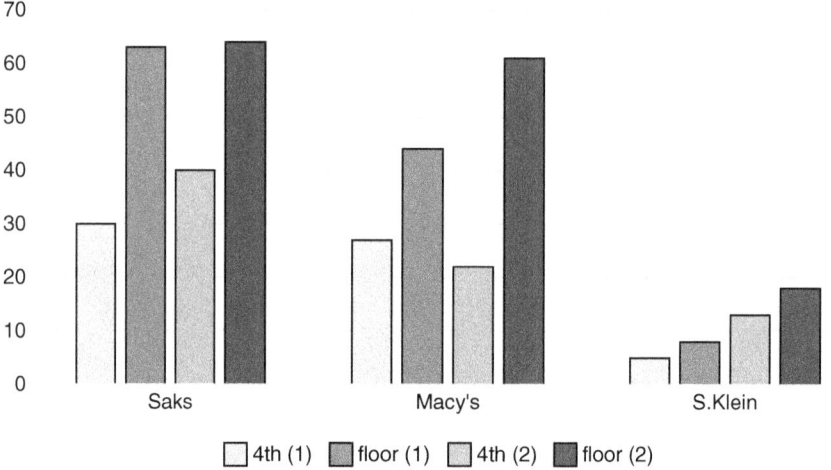

Figure 2.9 Stylistic and social variation in New York City department stores. Adapted from Labov (1972a: 175).

awareness to speech, overtaking the middle-middle and upper-middle class speakers. This was interpreted as evidence that the middle class was instrumental in language change.

For their study on language variation in Belfast (see Chapter 3), James and Lesley Milroy adapted their methodology to the living conditions of Northern Ireland at the time, minimizing the observer's paradox as much as possible by employing the "friend-of-a-friend" technique. They relied on mutual acquaintances to gain access to the communities and made every effort to collect samples of the vernacular by addressing local topics and collecting group interviews. The study consisted of a combination of interviews, reading of word lists, and recording of spontaneous exchanges. The intention was to record in both a formal interview style (Labov's careful style) and in a more spontaneous one (casual style). Sample size was much smaller: For the main study, there were only sixteen Belfast residents, eight middle-aged and eight young people, from three areas of Belfast. In terms of methodology, special precautions were necessary due to what Lesley Milroy later described as a "generally disturbed situation" in Belfast:

> Women were much less likely to be attacked than men, and since male strangers were at the time viewed with considerable suspicion in many parts of Belfast, they were likely to be in some danger if they visited one place over a protracted period. (Milroy 1980: 44)

The political turmoil of Northern Ireland at the time meant that it was too dangerous for men to carry out fieldwork – which meant that Lesley Milroy collected all the data herself for safety reasons.

The Milroys argued that the formation and organization of social networks between speakers were crucial for the way they varied and established the strength of individual social networks according to five criteria:

1. kinship ties with more than one household in the neighborhood
2. same workplace as at least two others in the neighborhood
3. same workplace as at least two others of the same gender
4. regular participation in a territorially based activity (street gangs, bingo games, football teams) and
5. voluntary association with workmates after working hours.

Network strength indexes from 0 (unintegrated) to 5 (highly integrated) helped explain why young women were much more advanced in using innovative language forms, while their male cohorts trailed behind. Different vowel realizations functioned as social markers, signaling group membership; so whether or not to use a local variant was an act of solidarity and local identity, particularly in male speech (a common finding in sociolinguistic theory; see Chambers 2008). The focus shifted away from larger categories such as "social class" or "ethnic group" to the immediate environment of individual speakers. James and Lesley Milroy demonstrated how social networks, or links in the social behavior of individual members of a speech community, influenced variation in different Belfast communities. Their work was instrumental in developing sociolinguistic theory further, as we will see in Chapter 3.

To summarize, early work in sociolinguistics was primarily interested in effects of social stratification and style-shifting, whereas later work adopted a more ethnographic approach, focusing on individuals and interaction patterns in the speakers' immediate social environments. Whereas attention to speech and social-class membership was central in the early days of sociolinguistics, later work concentrated on language variation as a function of social integration. This had far-reaching implications for methodology and principles of data collection.

2.5 Conclusion: From Dialectology to Sociolinguistics

Sociolinguistics in a sense built on traditional dialectology, which had a strong interest in dialect variation in horizontal space. After the sociolinguistic turn, there was a shift from rural areas to urban environments. The focus was no longer on the behavior of individuals per se but on the speech of groups of individuals representative of various categories within society at large. Participants were sampled along a predefined set of criteria so as to represent larger groups within a community. The methodological practices changed, away from collecting data from elderly men who had received little or no education, living in rural settings, to residents of metropolitan cities, from all age categories and ethnic groups with high social mobility. Earlier, single speakers were identified as prime informants in traditional dialectology and their speech was studied with the venerable aim of documenting disappearing traditional dialects. Variationist sociolinguistics established itself as the study of variable language and social structures: social class, gender, age, religion, ethnicity, attitudes. Pioneers such as William Labov, Walt Wolfram, and Peter Trudgill demonstrated that there was a social motivation for variation and showed that language change was systematic and structured. Their pioneering work was a milestone in the history of linguistics.

It would be unfair to disparage the efforts of the dialectologists, however. One should bear in mind how time-consuming and challenging data collection was at the time. Notes were handwritten, stored in libraries and retrieved by hand, and this limited research possibilities considerably. Dialectologists during that period were aware of social issues but were not in a position to carry out systematic research. Louis Gauchat, in his work in the village of Charmey in Switzerland, noted that "variation in pronunciation among members of a single speech community has not been studied systematically, despite its potential for our understanding of language change" (1902: 1) and he was acutely aware of key processes such as generational change and social diffusion:

> In Cerniat the speech of young people diverges from that of old people in the same way and to the same extent as in Charmey. The speech of two old men, one from each village, is more alike than that of two individuals of different generations from the same village. A single phonetic shift is under way in both locations. This is all the more curious in that there is no mixing and little contact between the populations of the two villages. Yet the pronunciation of young people is so consistent, it is as if they had conspired. One can treat the Charmey dialect as unified only by establishing an average among the different generations, selecting for example the middle generation. From the perspective of an exact science, this generation is only roughly representative of the actual speech of Charmey. Observation of the same circumstances elsewhere makes the establishment of a Charmey type even more illusory. Strictly speaking, there is no unity in the speech of Charmey, because the generations do not agree, and unity is even less of a reality because other villages have come to the same point in linguistic evolution. (1902: 47)

Though formulated more than 120 years ago, note how modern these views are. Similarly, in the late nineteenth century, Alexander Ellis had already observed "idiomatic alterations of language" in what he called "the geographical law":

> A series of spoken sounds adopted as the expression of thought by persons living in one locality, when wholly or partly adopted by another community, are also changed, not by insensible degrees, but per saltum, in passing from individual to individual ... the peasantry throughout the country have usually two different pronunciations, one which they use to one another, and this is that which is required; the other which they use to the educated ... is absolutely worthless for the present purpose. (1889: 3–4)

So, long before the sociolinguistic turn, Ellis was fully aware of the observer's paradox; just like William Labov eighty years later, he emphasized the importance of vernacular speech. Looking back, these insights seem truly visionary, and one truly wonders how Gauchat or Ellis would be recognized if they had today's technological possibilities.

To conclude, dialectology probably always carried a sociological element, even though in earlier days this was less erudite. Some attempts at generalization were made, but these mostly served the purpose of identifying dialect areas and their boundaries, since speakers were seen as representative of their respective local communities. Notwithstanding, dialectologists such as Hans Kurath, Harold Orton, and Jakob Jud left an invaluable amount of data which sociolinguists still rely on today. In his study on Martha's Vineyard, for instance, William Labov resorted to the LANE (for which a fieldworker had visited the island in the early 1930s) to show that diphthong realizations with a schwa-type first element were used again when they became indexed as a marker of local identity and good old island values. Very often, researchers benefit from combining different corpora. Sociolinguists readily resorted to earlier resources for their research, as we will see in the chapters which follow.

> **Take-Home Messages**
> - The scholarly interest in regional dialects (and dialectology) goes back to the nineteenth century.
> - There were large-scale studies in Germany, France, England, and other European countries; in the US, the first projects were carried out in the 1920s.
> - Different methodologies were used: Data were mostly elicited via postal questionnaires and fieldwork activities.

- The sociolinguistic turn in the 1960s meant a shift in focus from elderly (mostly male) speakers in rural settings to stratified samples in urban environments.
- The sociolinguistic variable is central in variationist sociolinguistics.
- The structure and organization of social networks was a later development and refinement of sociolinguistic research.

Activities

2.1 Reflect briefly: What sounds right to you and what would you say?
   a) Our house is very different to yours.
   b) Our house is very different from yours.
   Now access the Dialect Topography Website at https://dialect.topography.artsci.utoronto.ca/dt_about.php (the website is a bit dated but still fun to use) and find out which preposition Canadians would use (Interface "View results"). Compare how different regions across Canada vary (e.g. the Golden Horseshoe and the Ottawa Valley). You may want to check out other features, for instance different lexical items in Canadian and American English.

2.2 What do you call a small piece of wood stuck under the skin?
   Read the article on www.cam.ac.uk/research/news/do-you-say-splinter-spool-spile-or-spell-english-dialects-app-tries-to-guess-your-regional-accent and compare this type of methodology with the work of traditional dialectologists.

Key Terms

Department Store Study
indexicality
International Phonetic Alphabet
William Labov
Linguistic Atlas of New England
Martha's Vineyard
NORMs

observer's paradox
sociolinguistic variable
Survey of English Dialects
vernacular, social networks
Georg Wenker

Further Reading
If you are interested in general dialectology, then a somewhat dated but still recommended book is:
Chambers, J. K. & Trudgill, P. (1998). *Dialectology* (2nd ed.). Cambridge: Cambridge University Press.

Labov's lighthearted essay on his career is found at:

Labov, W. (exact date unknown). "How I got into linguistics, and what I got out of it." (www.ling.upenn.edu/~wlabov/HowIgot.html). Accessed November 11, 2024.

The early work on Martha's Vineyard is:

Labov, W. (1963). The social motivation of a sound change. *Word,* 19, 273–309.

The discussion of second-wave variationists, both in theory and methodology, is:

Milroy, L. & Gordon, M. (2003). *Sociolinguistics: Method and Interpretation* (2nd ed.). Oxford: Blackwell Publishing. doi:10.1002/9780470758359.

And if you are interested in principles of data collection and fieldwork, I would recommend:

Schreier, D. (2013). Collecting Ethnographic and Sociolinguistic Data. In: J. Schlüter & M. Krug, eds., *Research Methods in Language Variation and Change* (Studies in English Language Series). Cambridge: Cambridge University Press, 17–39.

The URL for Chambers' dialect topography website is: https://dialect.topography.artsci.utoronto.ca/dt_about.php.

CHAPTER **3**

Individuals, Networks, Communities, Society: From Variation to Change

In This Chapter ...

... we will discover that language variation is a normal characteristic of speech on all language levels: in the sounds of accents, words, in grammar, but also in discourse. When speaking, we always face alternative choices, and these are determined by our regional and social backgrounds and by the context of situation. We will discuss the concept of the sociolinguistic variable in more detail and find that variation is rule-conditioned and systematic. We focus on all actors and factors involved: the social dimension of variation (individuals, groups, communities) and its social correlates (region, class, gender, ethnicity, education). Last but not least, we will look at the spread of innovative features and trace patterns of diffusion from individual speakers, the point of origin of change, throughout wider society (via processes such as actuation, diffusion, and embedding).

3.1	On Variation: General Issues	*page* 53
	Vignette 3.1: "She was *like* 'this is so cool'"	55
3.2	Individual Speakers: Stylistic Variation	62
3.3	Variation in Social Groups: Social Stratification, Social Networks, Communities of Practice	65
	Vignette 3.2: "Pittsburghese"	73
3.4	Linking Variation and Change	74
3.5	Conclusion	80
	Take-Home Messages	81
	Activities	82
	Key Terms	82
	Further Reading	83

3.1 On Variation: General Issues

In Chapter 1, we saw that English has a long history of language complaints, stretching back to the seventeenth century at least. Language variation and change are very much in the public eye, observed, noticed, and nearly always frowned upon. Change is typically seen as an obstacle to mutual understanding, harmful as the language can no longer be read, a sign of sloppiness and laziness (particularly of youngsters and adolescents), or the consequence of inadequate learning (by foreigners). Such views led to prescriptive, norm-embracing attitudes, with linguistic prejudice and sociolinguistic insecurity as side effects. Language attitudes are extremely strong and powerful, but when we look at them more thoroughly, we find that complaints about apparently "bad language" simply do not make sense. We know from observing how people really speak that language change can occur quite quickly.

Let's take the expression *never ever* as a case in point. Is it unusual to you in any way? Crystal (1981: 38) published a language complaint that "way back in 1953 in a broadcast interview with Sir Edmund Hilary on his return from his ascent of Mount Everest, he used the completely ungrammatical phrase *never ever*, and its use has been growing ever since. It means absolutely nothing, being a self-denial of each word of the other." It seems strange to hear that *never ever* should have been infrequent a few decades ago, as today, most English speakers would not hesitate to use it. Or do you find something strange about the saying "Never ever give up!"? This is perfectly commonplace today.

We can only begin to understand how innovations spread and gain acceptability once we accept that variation is the normal state of language. This has been known for some time: "EVERY ONE knows that language is variable. Two individuals of the same generation and locality, speaking precisely the same dialect and moving in the same social circles, are never absolutely at one in their speech habits" (Sapir 1921: 157). Variation exists on all language levels: phonetics/phonology (in the form of different accents), lexicon (semantically equivalent words), morphosyntax (alternative grammatical structures), as well as patterns of discourse (such as greetings or ways to start a conversation). Let us illustrate these with English examples.

In terms of sound variation, speakers may vary according to how they produce /r/ in words such as *bar* or *bark*. For instance, they may have …

- a tap (where the tip of the tongue taps against the alveolar ridge, as in Scottish English)

- a retroflex (where the tip of the tongue is pulled back slightly, as in Indian English)
- or a lateral approximant, where the tongue moves closely to the palate without touching (as in American English).

The vowel in the word GOAT (by the way, this is a system of lexical sets developed by Wells (1982) to illustrate vowel realizations) may be …

- a monophthong /o:/ (as in Scottish English)
- a diphthong with central onset (/əʊ/ as in Received Pronunciation) or
- a diphthong with a fully open onset (/aʊ/ as in UK Midlands English).

Caribbean and African Englishes typically have fewer vowels than North American or British varieties. In Trinidad, for instance, the word pairs *bird-bud*, *body-buddy*, *cut-cot-caught*, *bit-beat*, *harm-ham* are identical (this is a consequence of language and dialect contact, as we discover in Chapter 4).

Variation in lexis may be illustrated by alternative candidates for the term *bread roll*: in British English, we have *barm cake* (in Lancashire), *bread cake* (Yorkshire), *cob* (Derbyshire), *batch* (Coventry and Liverpool), or *bap* (Scotland). All in all, British English alone may have more than twenty terms for *bread roll*. Similarly, the same piece of furniture is called *chesterfield*, *couch*, or *sofa* in Canada, whereas US Americans have several words for carbonated soft drinks (*pop*, *soda*, and *coke*). There is also lexical variation along stylistic dimensions, and intensifiers are a good example here: One can be "very tired," "super tired," or "bloody tired," and the decision about which intensifier to use depends on the formality of the interaction and the degree of familiarity between speakers. We saw in Chapter 2 that regional word variation has been mostly the concern of dialectologists, whereas sociolinguists have focused on phonetics/phonology and morphosyntax. Still, vocabulary differs from features from other levels inasmuch as speakers have a particularly high awareness and very often comment on where words are from and how they are used.

It is in the domains of morphosyntax and syntax that we find some of the best-researched variables in English sociolinguistics:

- past tense be leveling with the pivot form was ("we was happy," "the dogs was barking all night," etc.)
- the dropping of verbs, known as copula absence ("she happy," "the kids going to school")
- negation patterns (such as "I did not see her" or "I never saw her," or "I don't have any money" vs. "I don't have no money"), or
- dative alternation ("she gave the man her keys" vs. "she gave her keys to the man").

There is also variation in the domain of situational context(s), for instance in the field of variational pragmatics (see Schneider and Barron 2008), situated at the interface of pragmatics and dialectology (see Chapter 8). Here one studies variation in speech communities on a pragmatic level. Doing so, the focus is on everyday speech samples, such as discourse markers like "you know," "you see," greetings and apologies, for example, but also intensifiers (*really*) or quotatives ("she was *like* 'this is so cool,'" "I was *all* 'let's do it,'" etc.).

> VIGNETTE 3.1 "She was *like* 'this is so cool'"
> A quotative is a word or grammatical item used to introduce a direct quote in speech. English has quite a few of them: "say," "all," "so," and "like." Examples for the latter are: "I was *like*, 'Give it back'" or "'We're *like* 'Oh, we need more tickets?'" This is a good illustration of grammaticalization: the evolution of grammatical forms (function words, affixes, etc.) out of earlier lexical forms. So-called **quotative "like"** has become one of the fastest-spreading innovations in English today. Whereas earlier research found that it used to be associated with the speech of people in their teenage years and their early 20s, it was later adopted by speakers in their late 20s and early 30s, and is now becoming more frequent in the overall quotative system of different varieties of English.
>
> In their work on Canadian English, Sali Tagliamonte and Alex d'Arcy compiled the 500,000-word corpus of Toronto Youth English (TYE), where they found that "be like" is the most frequent quotative in the TYE corpus, now making up 58 percent of all quotatives used. There are two internal constraints (in the language itself) and one external constraint (outside of the language) that influence whether it is used or not: "be like" is favored for first-person subjects and primarily used to introduce internal thought ("It skinned us. It was *like* 'whoosh,'" "The professor opened his mouth and I was *like*, 'This is bad news for me'"). Traditional forms like "say" ("so he says 'this is bad news'") have become much less frequent, within one generation, and these findings have been replicated from studies of English around the world.

The central question to answer involves what factors influence language variation systematically and how they interact in socially meaningful ways. Dell Hymes, an anthropological linguist, put forward the **SPEAKING model** (Hymes 1974), in which he defined all the parameters that are at play. SPEAKING is an acronym for the key players *Setting/Scene,*

Participants, *Ends*, *Acts/Sequence*, *Key*, *Instrumentalities*, *Norms*, and *Genre* (Figure 3.1).

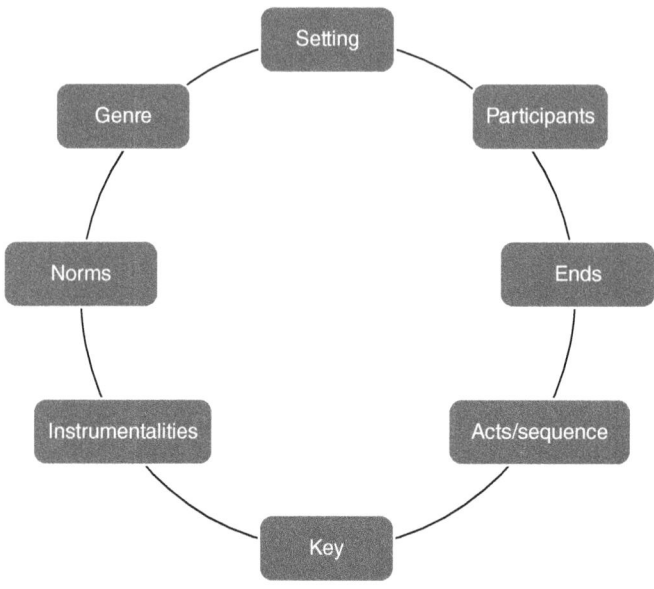

Figure 3.1 Hymes' 1974 SPEAKING model. Adapted from Hymes (1974).

Though a bit dated, this model still includes all the parameters involved in a clear and insightful way. It can be summarized as follows.

- *Setting*: the external environment in which a speech act takes place (the office where a meeting is held, the auditorium where a lecture is given, or the kitchen table where worries are shared), whereas *Scene* provides the background expressed by the formality induced by the participants and the topic (family members may discuss both joyful or serious topics around the dinner table).

Interacting in a particular setting means that we share (typically implicit) knowledge of how we are expected to behave and speak in a particular speech event. For instance, the setting of the speech event that determines who should speak when, what type of speech it is, or when interrupting is acceptable. Speech events in the classroom have specific rules for teachers speaking and students listening, and the formality of words used (which may change in the break or after class). Conversely, different implicit rules and expectations apply at social gatherings and work settings.

- *Participants*: the speaker (participants take turns in adopting this role) and their audience.

An audience may include hearers to whom a speech act is addressed, but there may be others who are not included in this category (the overhearers). For instance, a university professor may tell anecdotes to some colleagues in the cafeteria, and some students, though not directly addressed but sitting at a nearby table, might hear these as well (which can be quite embarrassing from experience). The tacit rules of conversation between participants depend on cultural values. Interruptions are a good example here: What is customary and accepted in some parts of the English-speaking world can be considered aggressive and impolite in others. Cultural norms provide a shared set of expectations of how men address women, how children speak to parents and grandparents, and how employees approach their superiors in the workplace (see Chapter 6). All participants engage in various roles and follow specific rules and expectations, which are part of their sociolinguistic repertoire. For instance, there are cultural conventions as to whether participants are addressed by their first or last name (US exchange students in Germany may find this out the hard way when addressing professors by their first names), or with a title (which is customary in my Asian students).

- *Ends*: the aims, goals, and ultimate outcomes of a speech event. A stand-up comedian will entertain their audience, a lecturer will want to educate the students, a doctor wishes to inform and calm down a patient.

The ends of a speech event may differ for those participating, no matter whether the exchange takes place at a dinner table or in a law firm. An appointment between a lawyer and a client may have the end of receiving advice and information (for the client) and to appear professional and knowledgeable (for the lawyer), and this may prove difficult for the speech event. Similarities and differences in the ends of speech events are important for successful communication as they are culturally defined and vary between speech communities as well.

- *Act Sequence*: the sequence of speech acts that constitute and greatly influence an event.

The initial sequence, for instance, sets the tone for a speech act. "Once upon a time" introduces a fairy tale; "And now, ladies and gentlemen," the beginning of a stage act; "I welcome you to my presentation," the start of a student contribution in my class, etc. It also refers to discursive cues, such as when to do turntaking and interrupt a speaker ("just wait a second," "this reminds me of …"; Chapter 6).

- *Key*: the tone of a speech act, often in connection with the social environment, the participants, and the topic of the conversation.

Different keys are used in different situations, for instance at baby showers, Christmas parties, and funerals. Keys can be lively and engaging (radio hosts), unemotional and monotonous (newsreaders), and provide important information on social norms and expectations of a speech community. There is an overlap with formality as keys can be both formal and informal, which has sociolinguistic consequences (e.g. the use of slang or profanity, which are totally taboo in some keys).

- *Instrumentalities*: The channels via which a speech act is effectuated.

These channels include the method of communication (writing, speaking, or, in the case of Sign Language, signaling), the language selected (in the case of multilingual settings (as the quote from South Africa in Chapter 1 showed; see also Chapter 8), or dialect (e.g. a standard or nonstandardized form) or register (a variety of a language that is used in specific settings). Hymes defined instrumentalities as speech styles and argued that a register may influence the speech event. For example, a patient might address their doctor in a casual register with many dialect features, but if the latter continues the conversation in a more formal register, adopting a standard variety with grammatical norms, then this might be perceived as social distance that seems disruptive.

- *Norms*: The social rules that determine the participants' behavioral patterns and expectations and vary for each (e.g. whether the church audience is expected to participate in a sermon or not).

These norms are important for the topics that can be brought up (e.g. taboo topics such as disease and death, which have to be avoided at all costs), the contribution of participants (who speaks first, and who carries more prestige and has more weight in a speech act), or also whether silence is appropriate or not.

- *Genre*: the kind of speech act or event; fathers might tell a story to their children for entertainment or moral instruction, or a boss might disguise a warning to a colleague as a jocular remark.

To summarize, the combination of these eight categories is instrumental in accounting for variation within speech acts and allows us to account for variation in speakers within a particular exchange. While the SPEAKING model is anthropologically oriented, it is certainly of importance for sociolinguists working on external variables. These can be identified socially (social class, age, ethnic group, social network, etc.) and allow researchers to address variation, study regular patterns of distribution throughout the speech community, or establish correlations with social variables.

3.1 On Variation: General Issues

Variationist sociolinguists are interested in the social factors involved when we are "saying the same thing in different ways." They differentiate between linguistic and sociolinguistic variables: "We refer to features of language ... that essentially offer more than one way of saying 'the same thing' as *variables*. And the study of patterns of use of such variables is referred to as *sociolinguistic variation*" (Eckert and McConnell-Ginet 2003: 269). In his early work, Labov (1972b) suggested a threefold distinction:

- **linguistic norm:** any linguistic feature found regularly in the speech of more than one speaker in the community (in other words, any feature that is not idiosyncratic).
- **linguistic variable:** any linguistic feature realized by more than one form and having several variants (i.e. lexical synonyms such as *pop* or *soda*, pronunciation of the word *economic* with initial [e] or [iː], or the realization of the suffix (-ing) in "talking" as [in] or [iŋ]).
- **sociolinguistic variable:** any linguistic feature that covaries not only with linguistic factors but also with independent nonlinguistic ones, such as social class, ethnicity, gender, age, or contextual style.

Let's illustrate how this works with two well-known studies from sociolinguistics, one on lexical variation in Canadian English and one on stylistic variation in East Anglian (British) English. First, Canadians have several terms for the generic term *sofa*: "couch," "chesterfield," "sofa," "davenport," "settee," "love seat," "lounge," or "divan." A hundred years ago, dialectologists would have collected data to illustrate local usage (in analogy to various terms for carbonated soft drink in the US) and produced dialect maps to show regional variation. Sociolinguists today, however, are interested in finding the social parameters that correlate with how these words are used.

With this aim, the Canadian sociolinguist J. K. Chambers conducted a large-scale postal survey in the so-called Golden Horseshoe around the western tip of Lake Ontario, stretching from Toronto to Niagara Falls, where more than one-sixth of Canada's population live (see Chapter 2). The "Dialect Topography of the Golden Horseshoe" project elicited linguistic responses from a large representative sample in Canada's most populous region, asking specific questions on the usage of dialect words, and more than 1,000 questionnaires were returned (which means this is still a valuable technique of data elicitation, more than 100 years after Wenker began his project). The results were clear: Chambers found that for *sofa*, the 80 American participants indicated using the term "couch" (81.2%), "sofa" (12.5%), "davenport" and "love couch" (2.5% each), with one person returning "love seat." Of the 935 Canadian respondents,

70 indicated that they used more than one term (which none of the US Americans did, interestingly). Based on metadata provided, Chambers (1992) divided the respondents into age-groups according to decades and calculated the percentage for each of the 11 terms in each group. Only three terms (*couch*, *chesterfield*, and *sofa*) occurred in all age-groups, whereas the other terms (*davenport*, *settee*, *love seat*, *love couch*, *lounge*, *divan*, *bank*, and *chair*) were hardly used.

This is socially relevant. The percentages for *couch* declined steadily from the youngest to the oldest speakers, whereas they increased for *chesterfield* in the same age-groups. Younger speakers preferred *couch*, older speakers *chesterfield*. *Sofa*, on the other hand, increased slightly among speakers aged 30–59, so it briefly but unsuccessfully competed with *couch* when *chesterfield* was losing ground (Figure 3.2). As for the other terms, *settee* occurred frequently enough to have the status of a regional variant, but all others were not widespread. Chambers found that variation correlated with age: *chesterfield* was still the most common word for residents of the Golden Horseshoe aged 50 and over. In the 1950s, when the 30–39-year-old participants (at the time of the study) were born, *chesterfield* was in competition with *couch*, the variant that became more frequently used by younger speakers. In the 1970s, when the youngest group included in the study was born, it was so common that *chesterfield* had practically disappeared (in fact, Chambers (1992) reported that some of the younger Canadians had no idea what the word meant). Social dialectology can trace the disappearance of words throughout the overall age pyramid, and this is a first indication of how language change can be observed in real and apparent time (see below).

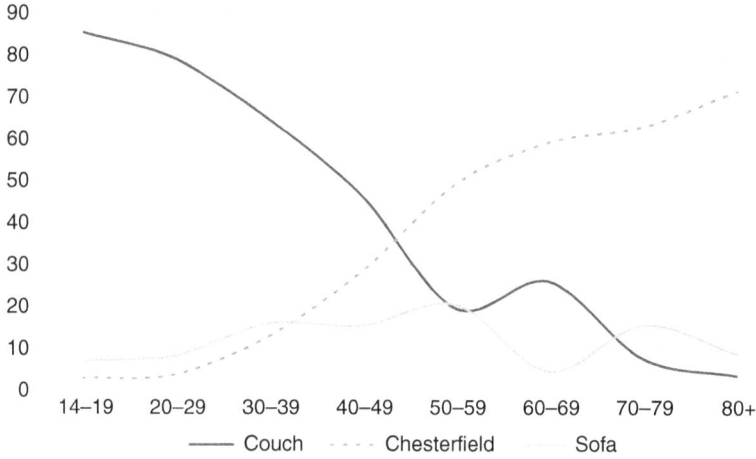

Figure 3.2 *Couch, chesterfield*, and *sofa* by age-group in Canadian English. Adapted from Chambers (1992: 162).

Variation exists across the **stylistic continuum** as well, and evidence here comes from phonetic and phonological studies. Trudgill (1974) adapted Labov's variationist methodology (Chapter 2) and studied social variation in his native Norwich, England. The variable studied was word-final (-ing), which, as we discussed in Chapter 2, may have two variants /ŋ/ or /ɪn/. Trudgill carried out sociolinguistic interviews in Norwich and asked speakers to read word lists and passages and interviewed them in formal and casual contexts (the latter eliciting most local speech). There was a consistent pattern: All social classes behaved similarly in that the more careful their speech was (when reading words), the more likely speakers were to have standard /ŋ/, and middle-class speakers tended to have significantly more /ŋ/ forms than working-class ones. Gender had an effect as well: /ɪn/ was more common in men's than in women's speech (in all social classes; Table 3.1). When Trudgill asked participants to self-report how often they used features, women typically indicated that they used standard /ŋ/ more often than they really did, whereas men reported that they used /ɪn/ more often than they did. Men, in other words, underreported, claiming that they used the informal feature more often, which was exactly the other way around for the women. Men and women show variationist differences but seem to have little awareness of how often they use variants.

Table 3.1 *The (-ng) variable in Norwich, by social class and gender in formal style (%). Adapted from Trudgill (1972).*

Class	Gender	Word List	Reading Passage	Free	Casual
Middle-middle	Male	0	0	04	31
	Female	0	0	0	0
Lower-middle	Male	0	20	27	17
	Female	0	0	03	67
Upper-working	Male	0	18	81	95
	Female	11	13	68	77
Middle-working	Male	24	43	91	97
	Female	20	46	81	88
Lower-working	Male	66	100	100	100
	Female	17	54	97	100

(Style spans Word List, Reading Passage, Free, Casual)

To sum up, variationist sociolinguists, while not ignoring region as an independent variable, include more external factors (social class, gender, style) and study the interaction between factors (e.g. style and gender). Whereas dialectologists are interested in language in geographic space, sociolinguists look into the correlation of linguistic variation with social variables. (Early) variationist approaches drew heavily on **social stratification** of society, producing a quantification of dependent variables in certain speaker groups and different speech styles, "controlled by extra-linguistic factors such as age, sex, social status and geographical location of the speaker. Spontaneous speech appears to be affected earlier than the speech characteristic of more careful styles" (Labov in Milroy and Milroy 1985: 340). These variables, as we shall see now, are crucial indicators and offer possible explanations for variation and change alike, both in individual speakers and speech communities.

3.2 Individual Speakers: Stylistic Variation

Speakers vary depending on whom they are speaking to (Hymes' Participants criterion). Analyzing his Norwich data, Trudgill (1974) found that the frequency of variables in his own speech varied with the frequency of his informants (so as a researcher, he subconsciously adapted his speech to the people whose sociolinguistic behavior he analyzed). Similarly, Coupland (1980) found that a travel agent in Cardiff adapted her speech to customers. The higher the frequency of a particular variable in the customer's speech, the higher it was in her own. The pattern was so consistent that the extent of variable frequency mirrored the status of her clients and served as a predictable indicator of the customers' social class. Coupland's treatment of stylistic variation as a dynamic presentation of the self has resonated in many studies that see linguistic style as a set of cooccurring variables which are used in the active construction of a speaker's identity in relation to social meaning.

An important point here is the so-called **audience design** framework (building on accommodation theory, Bell (1984), see below), according to which speakers vary their speech and shift styles in response to their interlocutors. The rationale is as follows: If someone wishes to sound more like a person they are talking to, then speech converges and styles become more similar (e.g. when people are familiar and get along well). However, speakers may diverge in that their speech becomes less similar, for instance to mark distance, signal authority, or express disagreement, and so on. This may involve accommodation of dialects (standard vs. nonstandard) or entail the switching of languages in given situations (Chapter 7).

Importantly, then, stylistic variation involves all levels of language (phonetic, morphosyntactic, lexical, pragmatic) and involves different types of variation:

- shifts in usage levels for features associated with particular groups of speakers (e.g. in the form of dialects)
- shifts in features associated with particular situations of use (or registers)
- individuals shifting in and out of dialects, sociolects, registers, or genres (ritualized, routinized varieties, often associated with performance).

The big question in this context, and this is one of the major controversies in English sociolinguistics, is precisely how the concept of **style** should be defined. By and large, there are at least three different approaches, reflecting the three waves of sociolinguistic theory (see below). We already saw that a first approach (somewhat mechanistic) was to consider style loosely as a function of attention paid to speech. This is why Labov's early methodology aimed at collecting speech in various contexts (reading word lists and passages, careful and casual conversation). Speakers varied consistently in that vernacular features were used in informal contexts and in that standard ones were more frequent in formal settings (when more attention was paid to speech).

But is style not more complex than that? Some sociolinguists argued that there are at least two problems with this approach. First, shifts are characteristic of any speech repertoire: "an individual ... controls a number of varieties of a language or of two or more varieties" (Wardhaugh 2002: 127). Accordingly, speakers need to have some social knowledge of when and how to shift along a stylistic continuum. However, it is extremely difficult, perhaps even impossible, to methodologically differentiate casual from careful speech in normal conversation (code-switches (Chapter 4) can be quickly identified but the transition from careful to casual speech is not clearly marked). Second, speakers are not mere passive respondents who adjust the way they speak, responding to changes in the external environment (formal vs. informal) or mode (reading vs. speaking). They can also proactively take advantage of stylistic resources for communicative purposes.

A different approach, so-called audience design, was advocated by Allan Bell in the early 1980s. The basic assumption was that speakers style-shift not in response to various amounts of attention but in response to other speakers. The process was to some extent motivated by accommodation, that is the adoption of one's speech in response to others. Bell studied variation in New Zealand radio broadcasters, where there was a practice for radio channels to share broadcasters, which meant it was common for them to read texts on air for different audiences. Crucially, they all varied in frequency as to what social group they were addressing on air so "[v]ariation on the style dimension within the speech of a single speaker derives from and echoes the variation which exists between the speakers on the social dimension" (Bell 1984: 151). Bell suggested that there was a hierarchic relationship of four distinct hearer roles: addressee (known, addressed), auditor (known, ratified), overhearer (known), and eavesdropper (unknown), and that these engaged in different ways during the accommodation process: "at all levels of language variability, people are responding primarily to other people. Speakers are designing their style for their audience" (Bell 1984: 197).

Bell's model was popular but was criticized for having a strong responsive function and for being purely speaker-based. Alternatively, speakers could exploit stylistic variation as a resource to create, present, and reshape their identities: "style-shifting can be a dynamic resource for a speaker, not necessarily the automatic correlate of contextual features" (Coupland 1980: 1), which means it could also exploit language variation proactively via social interaction. Speaker design models emphasized the identity (or, better, identities) individuals wanted to construct via language usage, choosing variables based on the values and social qualities they are associated with. Just as identity was increasingly defined as a fluid, variable construct and difficult to theorize, style-shifting was no longer perceived as static or (pre)defined by fixed social categories (e.g. "white Middle Class male," "older African American female"). Identity-formation was a dynamic process drawing on the resources of speech repertoires:

> A person might be identified as 'a woman', 'a parent', 'a doctor', 'a husband', 'a failure', 'an apprentice', 'a drop-out', 'a lay reader', 'a political activist', 'a senior citizen', 'a *Times* reader', 'a member of the proletariat', 'a respected community leader', or in many other ways. Any of these identities can have consequences for the kind of language we use. Indeed, it is usually language – much more so than clothing, furnishing, or other externals – which is the chief signal of both permanent and transient aspects of our social identity. (Crystal 2003: 364)

To conclude, the interpretation of individual variation in the form of style-shifting has changed considerably since Labov's early work. First, it was seen as responding to various social environments (formal vs. informal, casual vs. careful speech) and subsequently as a consequence of accommodation to other speakers (in Bell's words, "A sociolinguistic variable which is differentiated by certain speaker characteristics (e.g., by class or gender or age) tends to be differentiated in speech to addressees with those same characteristics" (1984: 167)) and a proactive resource to shape, form, and create speaker identity. Therefore, the main question for sociolinguists is whether accommodation is primarily an active or a receptive/responsive process, whether speakers shift style in reaction to elements of the speech situation (formality or audience) or draw on existing resources to use and shape interpersonal relationships or personal identities. As different as they are, these approaches share an important assumption: Speakers are sensitive to their immediate surroundings and aware that variation is a function of interlocutors and contexts (who we are talking to, in which context, and about what), which is where the categories of Hymes' SPEAKING model can be integrated with benefit.

3.3 Variation in Social Groups: Social Stratification, Social Networks, Communities of Practice

Until the sociolinguistic turn, studying language change in progress was considered an impossible mission: "[t]he process of linguistic change has never been directly observed: we shall see that such observations, with our present facilities, are inconceivable" (Bloomfield 1933: 247). As we saw in Chapter 2, Labov shifted the focus away from regional to social variation, from horizontal to vertical space in society, and change in progress correlated with social factors. Research was conducted more and more in high-contact communities and major urban centers, first in North America, later on in Europe, and samples of speech data were collected systematically. Participants included native residents alongside recent arrivals, speakers of diverse sociolinguistic backgrounds (speaking different languages and dialects), members of various ethnic and socially stratified groups, and so on.

Sociolinguistic research in the 1960s, particularly in the US, focused on social stratification along ethnic lines. Labov, Wolfram, and others compared variation in the speech of Anglo Americans and African Americans, adopting a quantitative paradigm and studying the frequency of sociolinguistic variables in the two groups, which was also practiced in research on immigrant groups (e.g. Italians in Australia, Hispanic (Latino/Latinx) Americans in the US, as in the Lower East Side in New York; Figure 3.3). Other independent variables were speaker sex (classified as male or female) and age, which turned out to be particularly important for the study of change in progress. The urban focus is still strong today, for instance in research on **multiethnolectalization** in major European cities (Chapter 4) or the maintenance of heritage languages and emergent multilingualism.

Figure 3.3 The Lower East Side in New York. (Moment/Alexander Spatari/Getty Images.)

The large-scale quantitative studies on social variation were further refined in the 1980s. Whereas Labov and other first-wave variationists defined social and ethnic groups via predefined criteria (housing, income, education, race, etc.), they found considerable variation in each of the predefined cells. This was difficult to account for. As Milroy (1987: 131) put it, "there is a large residue of systematic variation between individuals which cannot be characterized in any clear way by subdividing individuals into further subgroups."

Such an approach was considered to be static, particularly as the 1970s and 1980s saw a gradual opening-up of social barriers; societies became more fluid and open, members of different social classes and ethnic groups interacted more regularly. Similarly, in the workplace, there were fewer restrictions on hiring policies than in the 1950s and 1960s (in some parts of the US, segregation was still practiced years after Labov had carried out his Harlem study), and contacts between members of different ethnic groups increased as well. As a result, early work on social stratification now seems rather rigid, with imposed categories.

An alternative approach to understanding language variation and change was to concentrate on the social relationships that speakers establish on a daily basis. It is important to identify whom they associate with (and talk to), for what purpose and how often, and what influence the organization of groups may have on the frequency of sociolinguistic variables. This means that, instead of imposing predefined social criteria (e.g. income or education) on a sample of speakers, sociolinguists have gradually attempted to study the sociolinguistic criteria of individual speakers as set and experienced in their everyday lives. The **social network**, "one of the most fruitful explanations of linguistic variation in recent years" (Coates 2004: 70), was developed to investigate the effects of social structure in speech communities, effectively replacing the social class as the chief extralinguistic variable. This approach, inspired by sociology and sociometry, was interested in how kinship ties were formed and maintained, and how social relationships of individuals influenced their access to employment and economic resources. Individual members (no matter where they live) are connected via the social networks they form, and these networks can be either loose or tight, depending on how frequently members interact with each other. For instance, a research team observing wildlife in the Arctic for a couple of months will have tight networks, as members interact with each other for various purposes on a daily basis. A lecture at a university course with some 200 students will most likely be a loose network; though meeting on a regular basis (once or twice a week), students may only interact with the instructor and have little or no contact with many of the other participants.

Social networks are not only characterized by interaction frequency but also by the nature of their ties. Members of our Arctic research team might work at the same university, live on the same campus, and meet regularly at social outings of the Department, spending time together (and talking to each other) in a range of situations. They might have a different social relationship with each other than with those team members who just join in on the project. Accordingly, one distinguishes between **uniplex networks** and **multiplex networks**: If networks are uniplex, individuals are linked in one way only (they work together, *or* live in the same street, *or* meet before football games for a chat, etc.). In multiplex networks, however, individuals form more complex social relationships (e.g. they live in the same street, work in the same factory, *and* share leisure activities). Thinking this through, the overall organization of a speech community (including its sociolinguistic repertoires) is in a way a function of the density and manifestation of networks which are constantly formed by speakers. Networks in socially mobile and large cities are often uniplex and of low density (e.g. there are more single-person households), whereas rural village communities and traditional working-class communities typically have multiplex networks of high density (Figure 3.4).

3 Individuals, Networks, Communities, Society: From Variation to Change

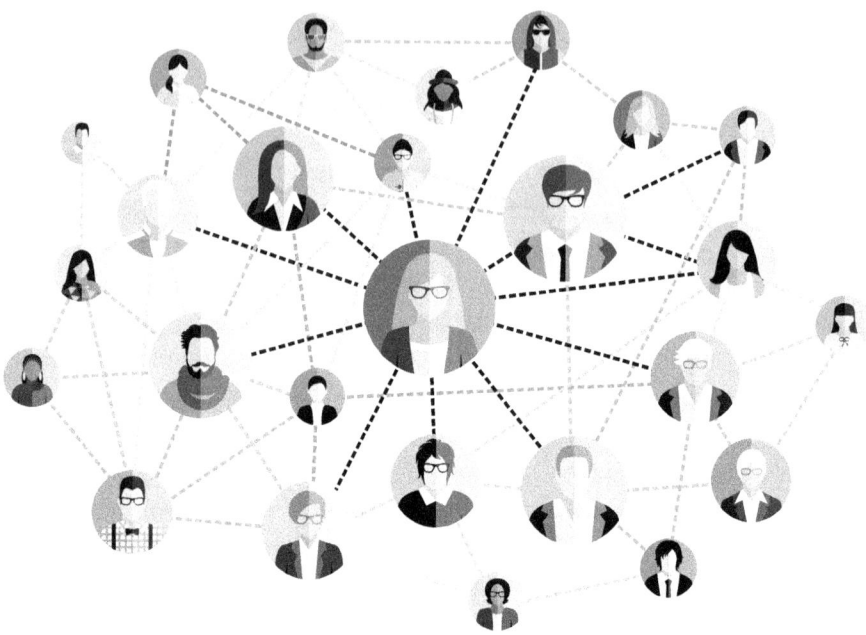

Figure 3.4 Individuals and social networks. (DigitalVision Vectors/aelitta/Getty Images.)

Taking all this into account, closed, high-density networks are those where individuals are familiar with each other and engage in different activities. Open networks are those where an individual's personal contacts tend not to know each other; these have low density. Neighborhoods are a wonderful example here: Some are characterized by tight and multiplex relationships between residents, who have a strong community feeling, whereas other residential areas have loose and at best uniplex networks, resulting in anonymity.

We have already discussed the methodology of James and Lesley Milroy in Chapter 2. Their study on social networks in three working-class communities in Belfast, Northern Ireland, is without doubt one of the most important contributions to English sociolinguistics theory. One of the variables studied was the raising and backing of /a/, which was subject to considerable variation in Belfast Urban Vernacular (BUV; see Chapter 2). This vowel is highly variable and can be realized in several ways:

- /ɛ/, the DRESS vowel, in words like "bag" or "bang"
- /æ/, the TRAP vowel, in "back" or "flash"
- /ɑ/, the LOT vowel, in "bag," "flash," "chap," "hat," "dance," "aunt"
- /a/, the START vowel, in "grass," "bad," "man," "pal," "hand," "can"
- /ɔ/, the THOUGHT vowel, in "bad," "man," "can," "hand."

3.3 Variation in Social Groups: Social Stratification, Social Networks, Communities of Practice

The Milroys noticed how native Belfasters varied a lot in the realizations of this vowel and studied the contribution of social network strength. For each speaker, they set up an index from 0 "no backing, slight fronting" to 4 "fully backed and raised," extracted tokens and calculated average scores for each of the speakers, divided by age and gender (Table 3.2). Male speakers used backed variants (/ɔ/, the FLOOR vowel) more frequently than women, and older speakers did so more than younger ones, with the highest scores coming from among male speakers in East Belfast.

Table 3.2 *Raising and backing of /a/ in Belfast, index scores from 0 to 4. Adapted from Milroy (1985: 357).*

East Belfast (Ballymacarrett)			
Men (40–55)	Women (40–55)	Men (18–25)	Women (18–25)
3.58	2.58	3.43	2.10
West Belfast (Clonard)			
Men (40–55)	Women (40–55)	Men (18–25)	Women (18–25)
2.79	1.85	2.33	2.61

The Milroys focus on three traditional working-class communities: one in East Belfast (Ballymacarrett, a relatively well-off Protestant community), and two in West Belfast (the Clonard (Catholic), and the Hammer (Protestant)). The Clonard and the Hammer were so-called "blighted areas" with high unemployment rates, juvenile crime, and high mortality rates. The political situation at the time was one of segregation and sharp ethnic boundaries along religious lines. While Protestant Ballymacarett was (comparatively) quieter, the social tensions in West Belfast were explosive: The Clonard and the Hammer (one predominantly Protestant, one predominantly Catholic) were only a few hundred yards apart. During the political conflicts which started in the late 1960s and cost more than 3,500 lives (half of whom were civilians), many inhabitants moved out of previously mixed areas. Physical barriers, known as the "Peace Line," separated the two communities and led to sharp social segregation. There was social demarcation, and it was perfectly normal for members of these communities not to interact with residents of "the other side," except in neutral areas such as the city center.

The Milroys found that both gender and age had an effect in BUV /a/ variation. Male speakers used backed variants more frequently than women, and older speakers did so more than younger ones. Backing was the innovation and occurred most frequently among Ballymacarrett men, which was explained via the social conditions of the community. East Belfast was home to the shipyards, where most of the men worked in construction (there were over 30,000 employees in the 1970s). Most of the men in Ballymacarrett were employed in shipbuilding, and these blue-collar, working-class communities were organized in high-density, multiplex networks (the men lived in the same area, worked together, and had strong solidarity). The usage of backed /a/ carried social meaning in East Belfast and encoded informality, social familiarity, class membership, and male identity. The stronger and more multiplex a network, the more pressure there was on individuals to maintain shared forms.

So far, so good, but one of the most unexpected findings was that young Catholic women from West Belfast had high index scores also, which, given the ethnic separation of the two communities, was difficult to account for. Clonard residents had adopted the innovation and backed /a/ had spread to West Belfast, but an approach based on social stratification would have made no sense. The question concerned how a linguistic innovation could have spread from male Protestants to younger Catholic women in a segregated community. Young Ballymacarrett men were unemployed, not leaving their community, whereas women usually had jobs, many of them in a city-center store. This store was on neutral ground and not segregated, frequented by Catholics and Protestants alike. Based on tracking multiplex networks, the Milroys argued that the Clonard women picked up backed /a/ variants when communicating at the workplace with customers from Ballymacarrett, and subsequently introduced them into their closely knit Clonard community. Since high-density, multiplex networks resist external influence (and the adoption of innovations from other groups), more mobile members of a speech community act as agents picking up and transmitting linguistic innovations. The Milroys distinguished between:

- **overt prestige**, when speakers of nonstandardized dialects openly endorse and adopt standard forms, often with a social motivation, in a more or less deliberate attempt to associate with the most prestigious dialect of a community, and
- **covert prestige**, when speakers dissociate themselves from standard varieties and prefer local (typically nonstandardized) variants for reasons of group identification and pressure.

Language change was not seen as a consequence of social stratification but as a product of the speakers' social organization. The weaker a network, the more likely change is passed on; the more mobile individuals are in terms of their networks, the more likely they are to pick up and pass on innovations. Consequently, speakers with multiplex, low-density networks may act as linguistic innovators, and this has nothing to do with their social class. Theoretically, all individuals can start change everywhere, but it is the integration into social structure at large that determines whether or not they are able to pick up and pass on innovations. The concept of social networks is still relevant in sociolinguistic theory today, applied to social media and diachronically in historical sociolinguistics (Chapter 5), where the spread of innovations was approached via a reconstruction of social ties and mobility.

The third wave of variationist sociolinguistics saw a further paradigm shift. In Labovian and Milroyan approaches, variation correlated with external categories and social organization at large. Variationists, such as Penny Eckert, claimed the focus should be on the social meaning speakers constructed via their sociolinguistic repertoires. Formerly rigid social boundaries needed to be reconsidered to account for social permeability and greater mobility of individuals within society at large. As a consequence, sociolinguists needed to respond by focusing on local, negotiated manifestations of language variation and their meaning for the speakers themselves. The community of practice (**CofP**), first developed by the sociologist Etienne Wenger, served as an ideal construct to link local practice and group membership into extralocal categories:

> A community of practice is an aggregate of people who come together around mutual engagement in some common endeavor. Ways of doing things, ways of talking, beliefs, values, power relations – in short, practices – emerge in the course of their joint activity around that endeavor. As a social construct, a community of practice is different from the traditional notion of community, primarily because it is defined simultaneously by its membership and by the practice in which that membership engages. (Eckert & McConnell-Ginet 1992: 95)

A CofP can be defined as a group of speakers who regularly engage in some common sociolinguistic practice. The social meanings of these relationships are brokered and negotiated by the participants. They are indexing the roles of speaker, group, and place in a broader social order and thus provide a setting in which linguistic practice emerges as a function of shared values and interests. Language variation is no longer perceived as a rigid process, a correlation with predefined variables, but is used and renegotiated as a sociolinguistic resource for identity construction; the speech of a white working-class Italian-American woman is not constrained sociolinguistically because she is a member of this particular group but varies because she draws on her everyday experience as a person who combines the categories working-class, Italian-American, and *female* in various situations and with distinct speaker groups (note the overlap with Hymes' ethnographic SPEAKING model discussed above). Linguistic practices are fundamental to develop and negotiate identity, allowing speakers to share the experience of membership in broader social categories which they create themselves.

A central study is Eckert's (2000) analysis of sociolinguistic variation in adolescent students attending "Belten High," a high school in the Detroit suburbs. Penny Eckert carried out long-term ethnographic research in the school, collecting more than a hundred hours of speech via informal notes and recordings, in different contexts and styles. She classified the students into three main groups:

- The so-called *Jocks* included the pupils who aligned with the school and its goals, endorsed the ethos of "Belten High" and participated with great enthusiasm in school and athletic activities. They were cleanly dressed, mostly came from a middle-class background, and aimed to have tertiary education.
- The *Burnouts*, however, were more or less egalitarian, rejected school values, smoked, occasionally consumed drugs, drank alcohol, and skipped class. The Jocks and the Burnouts had dense and multiplex networks (hence the overlap with the Milroys' work) but varied in their attitudes to life and school in general.
- The third group of students, the *In-betweens*, engaged in school-based practices as the Jocks did but had frequent contact with the Burnouts, whose lifestyle and attitudes they held in high esteem.

Given her long-term engagement with the school, Eckert was familiar with all three groups. The ethnographic approach made it possible to observe the social practices of the groups (how they dressed, what music they were listening to, what they thought about life in general, how they spent their weekends, etc.), which she correlated with the individuals' participation in ongoing sound changes involving the Northern Cities Shift (NCS), a rotation of six vowels (*bit, bet, but, caught, cot, cat*; Labov 1994).

The Burnouts were innovative and led the change. They had frequent contacts with the Detroit city center, making them more likely to pick up and maintain innovations (like the Protestant women from the Clonard). Interestingly, the Jocks participated in the change as well, though they resented the Burnouts' lifestyle and social values and there was rivalry between the two groups. So why would they adopt features from a group whose appearance and attitudes they deeply rejected? Eckert suggested that the In-betweens acted as brokers between the two groups and diluted the symbolic "Burnout-ness" of the features, making the innovation acceptable for the socially aspiring Jocks. The In-betweens acted as sociolinguistic couriers between the two groups, taking on a crucial role in transmitting innovations from one adolescent CofP to the other.

Eckert interpreted this as a creative act of using linguistic variation to construct social organization. Participation in one of the three CofPs (Jocks, Burnouts, In-betweens) is central to identity construction, as is the relation of speaking and participating in/constructing the social world. Thus, sociolinguistic variation did not primarily obtain social meaning because of a correlation with larger social structures (such as classes or ethnicities), but because social meaning was embedded in language and actively used as a resource to portray a self-image on a more micro level. Meaning was created via engaging in social practice(s) and conventionalized on the basis of shared experiences.

> VIGNETTE 3.2 "Pittsburghese"
> In third-wave variationist sociolinguistics, dialect variation is actively used as a means to create and maintain identity. This may apply to entire dialects, which come to emblematize local identity. A well-known example is Pittsburghese in the US. Pittsburgh was founded by Scots Irish, Pennsylvania Germans, and Eastern European immigrants. While the dialect participates in ongoing changes such as the Northern Cities Shift, the COT~CAUGHT merger (words such as "cot," "caught," "don," and "dawn" all have the same vowel (/ɔː ~ ɒː/), there are some more local features: "yinz" (from you'ns) as a second-person plural pronoun and /au/ monophthongization, which means that some speakers produce words such as "house" or "sauerkraut" with a long START vowel instead of the more standard diphthong in MOUTH, as evidenced in eye spellings such as *hahs* or *dahntahn*. Dialect words are also prominent (*jag-off* "jerk," *buggy* "shopping cart," *Yinzer* "Pittsburgher," *redd up* "clean," etc.). Some local features have become highly noticeable on T-shirts, coffee mugs, and postcards. Dialect variation is an index of local identity and being a Pittsburgher: The local residents shaped this by drawing on the sociolinguistic repertoire of the local dialect as a resource.

Pittsburghese is an important variety in that it shows how local varieties come to be associated with social meaning, both in terms of places and speakers. We speak of enregisterment as a "process, by which particular linguistic forms become linked with 'social' meaning" (Johnstone 2009: 159), and it can be separated into three stages of indexicality:

- First-order: A "correlation between form and sociodemographic identity or pragmatic function" (Johnstone et al. 2006: 81). Regional variants

mark origin, class, and gender, but socially non-mobile individuals are not aware of the variants. One should note here that gender refers to the characteristics of women, men, girls, and boys that are socially constructed, not, as in earlier research, as biologically given. As such, it is defined to include norms, types of behavior and roles associated with being a woman, man, girl, or boy, as well as relationships with each other. As a social construct, gender varies from society to society and can change over time – this is important theoretically, as we shall see.
- Second-order: "[P]eople begin to use first-order correlations to do social work" (Johnstone et al. 2006: 83). Speakers notice variants, attribute meaning (class, correctness, locality) to them and start using them actively so that the variants are "enregistered."
- Third-order: People realize second-order stylistic variation (some people speak differently), and link this to identity (particularly area of origin); features are often used ironically and are normally highly stylized (potentially leading to what Labov called "stereotypes").

To sum up: The move from first-wave to third-wave variation saw a shift in the relation between language and society. Speakers are no longer understood as passive representatives of dialect variation but agents, tailoring linguistic styles in processes of self-construction and differentiation. Identity is not fixed, depending on social affiliations, but actively constructed via drawing on the resources of language variation in social practice. Patterns of variation do not emerge from the speaker's position in a spectrum of society but reflect the active production of social differentiation (Eckert 2012: 97–98).

The interpretation of the (-ing) variable is an excellent example here. Trudgill (1974: 93), in good old first-wave variationist tradition, finds that "[w]e have shown, then, that the proportion of N to NG suffixes that occurs in speech is a function of the social class of the speaker and of the social context in which he is speaking." Schleef and Flynn (2015: 49), some forty years later, study the same variable in order to "conceptualise social meanings as stances, personal characteristics, personae and social types indexed through the use of linguistic features in specific interactions," focusing on whether and how social meanings are negotiated between age-groups in Manchester. The variable is the same, the theoretical approach fundamentally different.

3.4 Linking Variation and Change

So far, we have pursued two goals: (1) to establish language-external parameters and discuss how the organization of groups and communities within society affects variation on various levels, and (2) to illustrate that social meaning is created by speakers, using their sociolinguistic repertoire as a means to shape and negotiate identity. A central point is missing, however: We need to ask how an innovation, necessarily originating in the speech of individuals, spreads on to peer groups, social networks, and social classes. How can we proceed from variation on an individual to change on a societal level? When, how, and under what conditions does variation give rise to change?

In their Belfast study, the Milroys established links between **innovators** and **early adopters**. Innovators represent the point of origin, the source of an innovation. In terms of social-network structure, they are "marginal to the group adopting the innovation, often being perceived as underconforming to the point of deviance ... weakly linked to the group" (Milroy & Milroy 1985: 367). Innovators may have few contacts or be socially mobile but they typically do not have tight, multiplex ties in their environment.

Early adopters represent a different category. They are "central members of the group, having strong ties within it, and are highly conforming to group norms; they frequently provide a model for other non-innovative members of the group" (Milroy & Milroy 1985: 358). One of the crucial steps in the development from spontaneous (individual) variation to stable (social) change is the spread from peripheral to core-group members. When more central members of social networks pick up a (speaker-based) innovation, new features are much more likely to survive. It is then that they are adopted by an ever-increasing number of speakers who transmit the feature to an ever-increasing number of social networks in the wider society. Milroy and Milroy (1985: 340) argue that "[a]fter its adoption by these central figures (from more marginal persons), an innovation is typically disseminated from the inside outwards with increasing speed, showing an S-curve of adopter distribution through time." They suggest the following trajectory:

- Stage 1: A speaker innovation may fail to diffuse beyond the speaker. Change stops and is not implemented.
- Stage 2: Innovations may be picked up by a social network, where they serve as identity carriers and are noticed, perhaps even stereotyped or enregistered, by other speaker groups. This stage is a necessary requirement for a change to be successful. New features may diffuse into that group only and not on to other communities. They may also stop and go no further.
- Stage 3: An innovation leads to change when it diffuses to further social networks or speech communities which the innovator has no direct ties with. If an innovation is passed on by speakers with weak ties and

carried from one social network to the next by individuals who have no knowledge of where and when the innovation started, then a change is ultimately successful.

An interesting question is how long it would take for a change to be successful. The overall speed and directionality of innovations, or change in progress, follows a so-called **S-curve** pattern (Bailey 1973). Linguistic change is not a linear process (speed does not remain equal over time), and innovations spread through regional and social space(s) in varying stages: initiation, expansion, and termination.

During initiation, an innovation appears in the speech of an individual or a group of individuals who pass it on to others in their peer group (a good example here would be the quotative expression "this is," as in "this is me 'I'm from East London;'" Kerswill et al. 2013: 272). An initiation phase is typically slow, but new features have to occur frequently enough in order to be adopted permanently by a speech community (or at least parts of it). There is no consensus about how many innovations do not pass this threshold only to disappear again or how high the threshold should be in terms of percentage of all the environments where an innovation could apply. Milroy (1992) estimated 5 percent; it would be interesting to find out whether quotative "this is" becomes adopted in London permanently and how it has stabilized or even diffused.

Things change in the expansion phase: The innovation is adopted by an ever-increasing number of speakers and often competes with and replaces older, established variants. According to Labov (1994), in the final stage, termination, the speed rate slows down as the change nears completion. Very often, though, some items are not affected and remain as residue forms.

English plural formation provides a good example. Historically, there was a lot of variation in English plural formation: Until the early modern period, *eyen* was the plural of "eyes," for instance. Then a more regular -s morpheme was adopted more regularly. Even though plural -s was highly successful, ousting earlier forms, some relics of alternative English pluralization mechanisms survive to the present day: *oxen*, *geese*, or *fish*, and so on. Figure 3.5 (courtesy of Terttu Nevalainen) models this development, arguing that the change was slow at first, involving only innovators and early adopters, before picking up speed and being used by the early and late majority of the total population, before slowing down again in the speech of those who lagged behind the change process. The dotted line in Figure 3.5 indicates the speed with which plural is used by the population, whereas the straight line represents the total percentage of each of the five groups (innovators, early adopters, early majority, late majority, laggards) in the speech community.

3.4 Linking Variation and Change

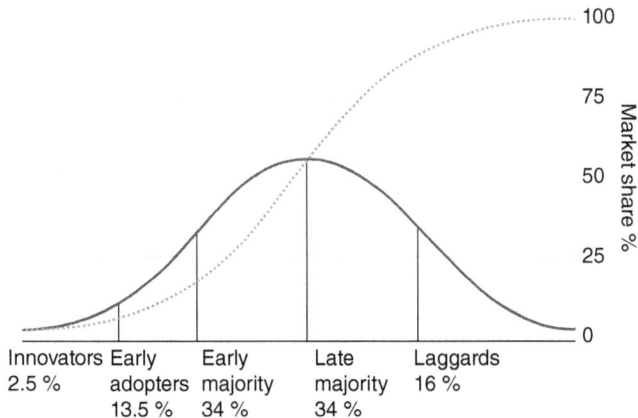

Figure 3.5 The S-Curve and language change. Courtesy of Nevalainen (2015).

Modeling change this way meant that some of the problems of traditional dialectology could be solved. Innovations did not fan out from a point of origin in regular ways (Chambers & Trudgill 1998) but jumped from place to place as speakers traveled and moved. TH fronting in British English, for instance, a classic and well-studied variable where the dental sound in words such as *three* or *this* is pronounced with an /f/ (so *three* sounds like *free*), showed an "extraordinarily rapid spread" and is an ideal example to illustrate this (Trudgill 1986: 54). Speakers within two generations differed significantly in their frequency: Norwich natives born in the 1950s had no or very little TH fronting whereas those born in the late 1960s had adopted the feature quickly and progressively (Trudgill 1983).

Analyzing the progress of this innovation, Kerswill (2003) found that it was first reported in London in the mid nineteenth century, from where it was brought to Bristol (1880s) and then on to other big cities in the second half of the twentieth century. Innovations were transported via human traffic to major towns first, from where they spread into the surroundings and rural hinterlands. This means that TH fronting was found in London and Norwich but not in smaller cities at half-distance (likewise, the NCS in the US involves major cities around the Great Lakes and not smaller rural ones).

New features may thus jump places and be adopted in new localities without making a presence in immediately adjacent regions. The diffusion of innovations is influenced not only by distance but also by population density and human traffic. They are most likely to start in heavily populated places that involve high contact between speakers of different dialects and sociolects (see Chapter 4) and then spread from there to moderately sized cities. It is the highly mobile members with loose network ties who act as transmitters and agents of change. This has been demonstrated by English

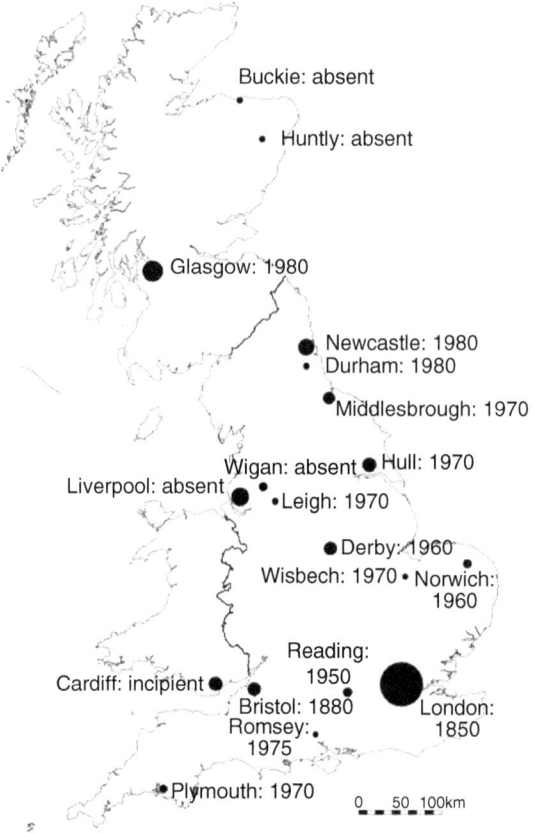

Figure 3.6 The progress of TH fronting in British English (Kerswill 2003). Courtesy of Paul Kerswill and John Benjamins Publishing Company.

historical sociolinguists as well. Bergs (2006: 28), for instance, has argued that patterns of diffusion and spread of innovations from speakers into the wider speech community historically depend on what he refers to as the human thread, "the actual way(s) and path(s) of travelling speakers" (see Chapter 5). Language-internal factors play a role as well, and we can distinguish between:

- **off-the-shelf features** that diffuse quickly through the English-speaking world; globally progressing changes (such as TH fronting, GOOSE fronting, or the spread of quotative "like") are cognitively and linguistically simple (i.e. they can be picked up easily, Chapter 4), they are frequent, salient, and used generally by a community.
- **under-the-counter features** (such as /a/ in Belfast) that are local and restricted to individual speech communities. They are linguistically constrained and structurally complex, typically found in small, close-knit communities (Trudgill 2003).

The biggest challenge, given the intricate social and linguistic complexities of variation, is what a general theory of language change should look like. In a seminal article, Weinreich, Labov, and Herzog (1968) laid the theoretical foundations for quantitative sociolinguistics, sketching out the necessary theoretical cornerstones. Building on Labov's early work, variation was seen as a function of social organization: Members of a speech community share sets of rules, and their social background and upbringing (social class, age, gender, ethnicity, etc.) determine language use, correlating with the frequency of sociolinguistic variables. So, if social parameters are known (e.g. formality of setting, or speaker's class membership), then the patterning of variation should be predictable to some extent (i.e. speakers will use higher percentages of standard features in formal contexts).

The term **orderly heterogeneity** (Weinreich, Labov & Herzog 1968) was essential here. As we saw, change operates when there is intraspeaker variation across contextual styles in a socially stratified sample of speakers. Intraspeaker variation, that is when individual speakers vary in their particular language use, was a function of social awareness and an indicator of change in progress, particularly in change from above (Labov 2001: 86). A good illustration here is the crossover pattern (Labov 2001), when the lower-middle class actually has a higher percentage of prestige variables than the highest-status group. Weinreich, Labov, and Herzog (1968) sketched five theoretical issues that needed to be addressed in any theory of language change.

- First of all, one needs to identify *constraints*: No matter how common changes are (e.g. global "off-the-shelf" features), sociolinguists first have to identify the internal and external parameters that favor or inhibit innovation and variation.
- As changes are gradual, following a series of steps, sociolinguists have to focus on an innovation's *transition* via intermediate stages and the social dimension of change. This allows modeling diffusion through the speech community and explains the acceptance of the innovation by a wider speech community.
- *Embedding* refers to the relationship of the change with other linguistic and social changes (how simultaneously occurring changes affect each other).
- *Evaluation* refers to the effect innovations may have on the linguistic system at large (e.g. vowel realizations), communicative efficiency, and the social standing of speakers (e.g. when incoming features are regarded as prestigious).
- *Actuation*, finally, is the most intriguing and theoretically challenging issue: Why does a change happen when and where it does? Why does it

manifest itself at one particular period in time (and not at another one) and in one particular speech community (but not in another one)? Why does it start in some innovators (but not in others)? In its most radical form, actuation refers to the motivation and spread of changes, from their very beginnings to their diffusion both in the language system and the community, all the way to completion.

Quantitative sociolinguistics has made enormous progress over the last fifty years, both methodologically and theoretically, and we now have a better understanding of constraints and embedding that form the envelope of variation. The quantitative paradigm helps to show how innovations spread within a linguistic system or between individuals via their social organization. Evaluation has been studied in detail, as social stigma and prestige, overt and covert prestige are central issues in sociolinguistic theory (see Chapter 1). There have been advances in explaining diffusion and spread, in how innovations spread from single speakers to networks, how they are carried from one community of practice to the next, and how they diffuse through social classes and across regional areas. The most intricate and complex issue, however, is actuation. Why, where, and when change starts are mysteries still. Any theory on language change must model actuation somehow, but after all these years it remains the biggest challenge in the field.

3.5 Conclusion

We now know a few things about variation and change: The two are intimately connected and shaped by social organization. From single speakers as a place of origin, innovative forms disperse throughout the wider community and may eventually become new norms in society at large. We distinguish between spread as a geographic, social, and an intra-linguistic process. Variationist sociolinguists ask how an innovation diffuses from one place to the next, how it passes from one speech community within the larger social organization to all others, and how it makes its way through the system of a language so as to affect all possible environments, competing with simultaneous change processes.

We discussed the paradigm shift induced by first-wave sociolinguists, who demonstrated that variation correlated with social structures (social stratification); that the frequency with which sociolinguistic variables occurred differed systematically between speaker groups (classified by class, ethnicity, age, etc.); and that all speakers, regardless of positioning and status in their society, shifted along formal settings. Second-wave sociolinguists built on and refined these insights by showing that innovations diffused via social networks, so that the immediate social environment of individuals mattered (density, the connections formed by network members, and multiplexity, the various domains network members engage in). Close-knit networks were norm-enforcing mechanisms, and speakers with weak ties were much more likely to pick up and pass on innovations. In contrast to Labov's views, change was not always led by the middle class, who showed maximal awareness of the social status of language, and there was a separation of covert and overt prestige. Men in close-knit social networks tend to be more sensitive to covert prestige, being more vernacular and local in their speech, whereas women typically lead changes when an innovation is socially evaluated as prestigious. Third-wave variationists, finally, looked at variation and change in groups of speakers who engage in some common endeavor on a regular basis: the communities of practice. Variation was considered as indexical in the presentation and construction of individual identity, essential for any endeavor to investigate the roles of individual, group, and community. Linguistic practice, including enregisterment, emerged as a function of shared values and interests.

Theoretically, one of the greatest challenges in variationist sociolinguistics is finding out how variation leads up to change, how an innovation originates in the speech of individuals and diffuses on to other speakers, groups, and throughout the wider speech community. The task is to find out how individual usage correlates with the social context of an interaction (anticipated by Hymes' SPEAKING model), such as degree of formality, participants, or topic in order to tackle the ultimate challenge of laying out a theoretical basis for language change (constraints, transition, embedding, evaluation, actuation).

> **Take-Home Messages**
> - Language variation is central to any approach to language change (orderly heterogeneity).
> - Individual speakers vary in systematic ways along parameters such as context, topic, and setting of the interaction. The degree of formality was originally seen as quintessential to stylistic variation.
> - The social organization of communities propagates or inhibits change (stratification, social mobility, networks, communities of practice).
> - There is a differentiation between innovators and early adopters.
> - A theory of language change must account for constraints, transition, embedding, evaluation, and ultimately actuation.

Activities

3.1 Visit the website www.bl.uk/british-accents-and-dialects/articles/lexical-variation-across-the-uk and listen to the recording made in Stannington, Northumberland. How many alternative terms for *cowshed* can you hear? Are there any other features which seem unusual to you?

3.2 Americans have dozens of generic words for carbonated soft drinks. "Pop," "soda," "coke" are the most frequent ones, but there are lots of regional terms. Visit https://popvssoda.com/ and establish regional variation by looking into the great "pop vs. soda controversy" first-hand. What are the regional preferences for these terms in the US, what are the most frequently used terms – and why do you think infrequent words with little regional distribution survive?

3.3 Make a list of the people in your close social surroundings (family, friends, relatives) and place them into categories of density and uniplexity vs. multiplexity. Do they find this difficult? Try to make some general assumptions about language variation. Who in your system of social networks would be most likely to accommodate and adopt features from whom?

3.4 Read and discuss the short article "Steel Town Speak" (written by Barbara Johnstone and Scott Kiesling) at www.pbs.org/speak/seatosea/americanvarieties/pittsburghese/. Can you think of other cities where local dialect features have come to signal such a strong sense of identity, and what are these features?

Key Terms

- audience design
- community of practice
- covert prestige
- early adopters
- enregisterment
- indexicality
- innovators
- linguistic norm
- linguistic variable
- multiethnolectalization
- off-the-shelf features
- orderly heterogeneity
- overt prestige
- quotative "like"
- S-curve
- sociolinguistic variable
- social network
- social stratification
- SPEAKING model
- style
- stylistic continuum
- uniplex and multiplex networks
- under-the-counter features

Further Reading

For more information on audience design, read:

Bell, A. (1999). Styling the other to define the self: A study in New Zealand identity making. *Journal of Sociolinguistics*, 3/4: 523–541.

Enregisterment is well explained in:

Johnstone, B. (2016). Enregisterment: How linguistic items become linked with ways of speaking. *Language and Linguistics Compass*, 10: 632–643.

One of the most detailed accounts of sociolinguistics and language change is found in:

Labov, W. (2001). *Principles of Linguistic Change 2: Social Factors*. Oxford: Wiley-Blackwell.

Social network theory is introduced in:

Milroy, J. and Milroy, L. (1985). Linguistic change, social network and speaker innovation. *Journal of Linguistics*, 21: 339–384.

And for a most suitable volume on variationist sociolinguistics, I would suggest:

Tagliamonte, S. A. (2012). *Variationist Sociolinguistics: Change, Observation, Interpretation*. Oxford: Wiley-Blackwell.

CHAPTER **4**

English in Contact: From Code-Switching to the Birth of New Varieties

In This Chapter ...

… we will take a closer look at some of the fundamental principles that operate when social and/or regional varieties of English are in contact with each other or with other languages, often in colonial settings. We begin by taking a historical look at English and explore the various contact settings which have shaped its development, from contact with Old Norse, Latin, and Norman French to the present day. We discuss patterns of bilingualism and multilingualism, that is when speakers use two or more languages in their everyday lives. As the product of migration and colonization, different kinds of English have emerged in different locations around the world. We will learn how new dialects emerge as a product of new-dialect formation or koinéization, and how contact-derived varieties such as pidgins and creoles develop under conditions of language contact, with special emphasis on issues such as different theories of origins and creole exceptionalism. Finally, we will discuss the so-called Global Englishes which have emerged as a product of second-language learning around the world.

4.1	Contact in the History of English: Old and Middle English	*page* 85
4.2	Bilingualism and Multilingualism Today	87
4.3	English Dialect Contact: How New Dialects Are Formed	92
	Vignette 4.1: The Origins of the New Zealand English (ONZE) Project	92
	Vignette 4.2: Tristan da Cunha English	94
4.4	English in Contact with Other Languages: Jargons, Pidgins, and Creoles	97
	Vignette 4.3: The Scramble for Africa	98
4.5	The Global Englishes	105
4.6	Conclusion	113
	Take-Home Messages	114

Activities	114
Key Terms	117
Further Reading	117

4.1 Contact in the history of English: Old and Middle English

From the very start, English has had an extensive contact history. Starting with the migration of Germanic tribes in the fifth century, there was contact between:

- the dialects spoken by Angles, Saxons, Jutes, and other varieties spoken by the arriving groups
- Old English and Old Norse, spoken by Vikings who settled from the eighth century onwards
- Old English and the various Celtic languages spoken by the local populations
- Old and Middle English and Latin, the language of learning and the Church
- Middle English and Norman French, as the social elite was French-speaking following the 1066 Norman invasion.

It has always been part of the cultural history of English for speakers to adopt loanwords from other languages. Whereas it is still debated precisely how much influence the Celtic languages had on the emergent English language, the lexical influence of Latin, the language of education, and French, spoken by the local elite, was significant early on. The contact between English-speaking, Latin-speaking, and French-speaking communities is a good illustration of how **language contact** coincides with cultural contact. For example, the Norse influence on English began in the eighth century and continued well after the Norman Conquest brought a large influx of Norman French to England. Rather ironically, contact with Latin predates the origins of English. The Germanic tribes who arrived in the British Isles had already had contact with Latin-speaking populations on the Continent, bringing borrowings with them, and the Celtic tribes had contact with Latin already. The earliest borrowings from Latin include the so-called popular lexicon, brought to Britain by Roman settlers and soldiers, but the majority of Latin words came during the fifth century as a result of Christianization. The Anglo-Saxons were familiar with Latin words via contact with Roman traders and missionaries on the Continent.

The majority of these words came from the *Vulgata* (Popular Latin), spoken by the general population in their everyday lives. Early borrowings reflected contact in military, administrative, and commercial contexts. These mostly referred to everyday (often military) life: *camp, chest, copper, mile, mint, wall,* and so on. This contrasted with religious words coming in via the Christian missionaries who arrived in the sixth and seventh centuries: *altar, candle, monk, priest, school,* and so forth. The Catholic Church retained its strong influence well into the Middle Ages and the Renaissance, as monasteries were places of teaching and learning. Monks read, produced, and copied Latin texts and Latin remained Europe's preeminent **lingua franca** for centuries. It was only much later, in the fourteenth and fifteenth centuries, that official documents were written in English.

Another important contribution to the early lexicon of English was Old Norse. The Vikings' invasions and subsequent settlement, beginning around 850, brought many Old Norse words into the language, particularly in the North of England. It is debated how linguistically similar Old English and Old Norse were at the time, and whether the varieties were mutually intelligible or not. The Scandinavian and English populations mixed quickly (intermarriages were frequent), as there were social and cultural similarities, and as many of the Norsemen had accepted Christianity early. There were not many loanwords from Scandinavian sources, but some of them replaced frequent Old English (OE) ones (e.g. Old Norse (ON) *take* replaced OE *nemman*), and occasionally both words survived with different meanings or usages (*shirt–skirt, kirk–church*). The impact of Old Norse was particularly strong in toponymy: There are more than 1,000 placenames of Scandinavian origin ending in *-by, -thorpe,* or *-thwaite* in England today.

The total number of French borrowings was much higher. Starting in the twelfth century, thousands of French loanwords were added to the English word stock (which increased lexicon size considerably): Old English (450–1150) probably had about 24,000 common words (an estimated 3 percent of foreign origin), whereas Middle English (1150–1500) had about 100,000 words, about 25 percent of which were borrowed from other languages, ca. 10,000 from French alone.

Language contact was normal: The coexistence of English, Anglo-Norman French, and Latin characterized much of early medieval society. For centuries after the Norman Conquest in 1066, French was used at courts, schools, and universities, Latin in church, and the vast majority of the general population spoke local varieties of English, so English society was in fact trilingual. English kings had close contact with the Continent. Nearly all official business was recorded and conducted in French, the language spoken by the higher social classes, much of the gentry and growing upper-middle class. It took centuries for English to reemerge as a language of official administration.

English thus has a long tradition of dialect and language contact with Germanic and Romance languages. English has been a mixed language from its very beginnings, and this tendency has continued and intensified since the early modern period.

4.2 Bilingualism and Multilingualism Today

Today, it is estimated that English is an official language and serves special purposes of communication in more than eighty countries (Crystal 2009), for example in the Bahamas, Sierra Leone, Papua New Guinea, and the Philippines. However, the situation is rather different to what we saw in medieval times in England. In Asia and Africa, English is not the primary language and coexists alongside many other languages, spoken for all sorts of purposes.

As we saw in Chapter 1, it is normal for students at South African universities to communicate in English in the classroom, to hear Afrikaans on the media, and to speak Zulu and Tswana at home with family and friends. In India, education may be offered in English whereas the home language is Hindi or Telugu; and in Switzerland, English is the second (or for some students, third) foreign language learnt at school, spoken alongside other national languages (French, Italian, or Swiss German) and immigrant languages such as Albanian, Turkish, or Portuguese. The usage of several languages can be approached from an individual or a societal perspective and there is some discrepancy in how the terms **bilingualism** and **multilingualism** are defined. Some sociolinguists prefer to use bilingualism for cases where only two languages are used (e.g. English and French in Canada), whereas others classify cases where two or more languages are used as multilingualism, thus making the term bilingualism redundant. For the sake of simplicity, I suggest using the term multilingualism for individuals and communities where more than two languages are used regularly, and the term bilingualism for specific purposes when there are only two languages.

Speakers are said to be multilingual when they use several languages in their everyday life: either actively (by speaking, writing, or signing) or passively (by listening, reading, or interpreting). Of course, this does not mean that speakers have equal command of all the languages they speak; even if children use two languages from infancy on, it is unlikely that these are both used equally often and for the same purposes. Languages differ in their function. Some are used in the home domain, so speakers tend to be more fluent and informal there, others in educational and official domains, where speakers are more formal. The order and manner of language acquisition is an important criterion as well and one which distinguishes between language(s) that are:

- acquired in childhood, at home and without formal education
- acquired later in life, typically in classroom settings and via processes of second-language (**English as a Second Language (ESL)**) or
- learnt as a foreign language (**English as a Foreign Language (EFL)**) in instructional (classroom) contexts.

Language contact is complex, and the influence of one language on another is not restricted to the lexical level but also extends to phonetics and phonology, morphosyntax and pragmatics. Many multilingual speakers use elements from more than one language when they speak, in a process called **code-switching**. There are several reasons why speakers switch between languages. For one, words are used to fill lexical gaps; when there are no words for certain concepts, then speakers can resort to words from the other language. In Australia, for instance, British settlers were not accustomed to the local flora and fauna, so words were borrowed from Aboriginal languages for animals (*kangooroo*, *kookaburra*), places (*billabong* "lake"), plants (*waratah*, *jarrah* "eucalyptus tree"), and hundreds of placenames (Coonabarabran, Naracoopa, Wollongong).

But there is not always a need to borrow words. As we saw in Chapter 3, mixing linguistic resources is an active process to express group solidarity, building a sense of familiarity and identity perhaps, and this can also be a motivation for code-switching, for instance when immigrant communities have a strong sense of loyalty to more than one cultural group. Mair (2013) studied posts in Nairaland (an internet forum for Nigerian expatriates around the world), where West African English is the default language, but where English (bold) and Nigerian Pidgin (bold and italicized) elements are inserted into Igbo sentences:

oga deeje **sir**. a maghikwa m na i no na **sidelines a watchi ma moves**. biko pres, ma nchi gi ooo, ma azu gi ooo *carrry go,* aka m ukwu m *no dey again oga* m ga azutara m nchi **first thing tomorrow morning**. **pres**, anu nchi gi gbakwa oku dia. **lol** nna **ball**uia dikwa *hard.o* burkwa na emelie CIV m ga alakpu kwa ura.iwe di ha no obi **too much**, mmadu eme kupu m isi.

[English gloss: Boss carry on sir, I don't know why you sideline me and watch all my moves. Please Pres, take away both your bush meat (grasscutter) and your fish, my hands and legs are no more there [I'm no longer interested]. My boss will buy me bush meat first thing tomorrow morning. Pres, to hell with your bush meat. lol. His ball is hard. If they win, my CIV will be asleep. Their heart is full of anger too much; let no one knock off my head.] (adapted from Mair 2013: 319–320).

The writer (note that this comes from an online forum) switches between English and Nigerian Pidgin elements, using local proverbs in English form as well (<my hands and legs are no more there> "I'm no longer interested").

Or let's look at an example from Malaysia. Two lawyers, Chandra and Lee Lian, both from Kuala Lumpur, one of Tamil origin and the other Chinese, have learned English and Malay as additional languages, and their exchange (adapted from Crystal 2003: 166–167) is reported as follows:

CHANDRA: Lee Lian, you were saying you wanted to go shopping, nak pergi tak?
LEE LIAN: Okay, okay, at about twelve, can or not?
CHANDRA: Can lah, no problem one! My case going to be adjourned anyway.
LEE LIAN: What you looking for? Furnitures or kitchenwares? You were saying, that day, you wanted to beli some barang-barang for your new house.
CHANDRA: Yes lah! Might as well go window-shopping a bit at least. No chance to ronda otherwise. My husband, he got no patience one!
LEE LIAN: You mean you actually think husbands got all that patience ah? No chance man! Yes or not?
CHANDRA: Betul juga. No chance at all! But if anything to do with their stuff – golf or snooker or whatever, then dia pun boleh sabar one.
LEE LIAN: Yes lah, what to do? It still is a man's world, in that sense! Anyway, we better go now – so late already – wait traffic jam, then real susah!

This chat contains sentences that are:

- Standard English ("Might as well go window-shopping a bit at least"; "It still is a man's world, in that sense!")
- Malay words or expressions (*betul juga* "True also"), but note that there are various instances where Malay words are inserted into English sentences, as in: "No chance to *ronda* otherwise" [Malay *ronda* "loaf"], then real *susah*! [Malay *susah* "difficult"], You were saying, that day, you wanted to *beli* some *barang-barang*. [Malay "buy … things"], But if

anything to do with their stuff – golf or snooker or whatever, then *dia pun boleh sabar one*. [Malay "he too can be patient"].
- Mixed utterances: "My case going to be adjourned anyway" [auxiliary verb omitted], "wait traffic jam" [preposition and article omitted], "Can lah, no problem one!" ["I can"; lah and one are emphatic particles], "Okay, okay, at about twelve, can or not?" [distinctive tag question in English], "you were saying you wanted to go shopping, nak pergi tak?" [tag question in Malay "Want to go, not?'].

The two Malaysian lawyers use sentences which are grammatically indistinguishable from British or American English alongside those with code-switching, where Malay words and constructions are inserted. They thus engage in **language hybridization**, ranging from the lexical borrowing to wholesale grammatical restructuring. They draw on their linguistic resources to produce mixed sentences, and their language is not a homogeneous English variety with clear-cut boundaries.

Often one hears complaints that such English is "broken" or "incorrect," but importantly, code-switching is not a random process. It is determined by sociolinguistic factors such as interlocutor, situation, and topic, and there is a distinction between **situational and metaphorical switching**:

- Situational code-switching involves change in social setting, for example when university teachers deliver formal lectures in English but switch to the local language during the break.
- Metaphorical code-switching, however, is triggered by changes in topic, so that family-related issues may be discussed in the local language and official ones in the standard one (leading to switching, when the topic is changed).

Code-switching may have a social motivation. In East Africa, for instance, where societal multilingualism is widespread, the usage of English may carry the meaning of "education," "social status," "positive attitudes toward Westernization," whereas local languages signal local and traditional values. Speakers may switch from Kiswahili (the supralocal language) to a more localized language to emphasize group membership and solidarity, or switch from either of these to English. English emphasizes power and distance from the interlocutor. A clerk may start speaking to customers in Kiswahili for some small talk and then switch to English to signal control and authority.

Diglossia (first suggested by Ferguson (1959)) is a rather specialized outcome, as languages are not mixed but functionally specialized to particular domains. There are two languages (not necessarily related): one of high prestige, generally used by the government, the media, and in formal contexts; and one of low prestige, usually spoken at home and in informal contexts. Regional languages or dialects (L) are spoken in informal, usually oral, contexts, while the official language (H) is used in more formal situations. This is found all over the world and Ferguson's original study discussed case studies from Haiti (Kreyol and French), Greece (Katharevousa and Dhimotiki), and Switzerland (Swiss German and High German). His criteria to identify diglossia were, among others:

- Functional specialization of H and L
- H is believed to have higher status than L
- Sizeable body of literature in H, which is held in high esteem by the speech community
- H is chiefly acquired via formal education
- Strong tradition of grammatical study of H
- Social stability over several centuries
- Differences in grammatical structure.

Ferguson stated that diglossia was very common: "It can probably be shown that this combination of circumstances has occurred hundreds of times in the past and has generally resulted in diglossia. Dozens of examples exist today, and it is likely that examples will occur in the future. Diglossia seems to be accepted and not regarded as a 'problem' by the community in which it is in force" (1959: 338). There was a clear case of diglossia in the history of English, namely when English and Norman French were in a diglossic relationship from the eleventh to the early fourteenth century (French being used by the elite, English by members of the middle and working classes).

To sum up, most (if not all) nations are multilingual: "bilingualism is much more widespread than monolingual citizens of countries traditionally dominated by English [...] tend to believe. The idea that monolingualism is the human norm is a myth" (Thomason 2001: 31). Languages coexist, sometimes separately, sometimes they are mixed by speakers in everyday conversation.

As English is a global language, enjoying high prestige in many communities around the world, it will continue to coexist with local varieties. Some may have lower social prestige, but they have the advantage of indicating high solidarity and group membership. For instance, before my courses, I often find myself chatting with students in native Swiss German before switching over to English, the official language of education. These trends will arguably continue as English is adopted as a lingua franca around the world, since there is a strong demand for a common language in international and global collaboration.

4.3 English Dialect Contact: How New Dialects Are Formed

Some 400 years ago, English was just one language among many. It had about 4 million speakers, living in the British Isles, and the language of learning and education was Latin. John Florio said in 1600, "What do you think of this English? ... It is a language that will do you good in England but, pass Dover, it is worth nothing ... It doth not like me at all because it is a language confused, bespieced [spiced] with many tongues." Who would have predicted that English would become the world's most widely spoken language? The reasons for this are historical, social, and cultural. The fifteenth and sixteenth centuries were the age of exploration, and, from the 1620s on, the British Empire began to expand and colonize overseas territories in:

- the Caribbean and North America in the seventeenth century
- Asia in the eighteenth century
- the Southern Hemisphere in the late eighteenth and nineteenth centuries.

Countless dialects came into contact, spoken by people from different areas and social strata in the British Isles. Their dialects formed the pool out of which new local varieties emerged via processes of dialect contact. **New-dialect formation** (or koinéization) occurred in communities with high mobility and sociolinguistic diversity. In order to understand how a "new" dialect is formed, it is helpful to conceptualize a **feature pool** (cf. Mufwene 2001) that hosts all the variants from the varieties brought to a particular place. These features (phonological, morphosyntactic, lexical) compete for permanent selection. Whereas some are adopted, others are dropped and disappear as the localized dialect focuses. Speakers of a fully focused variety are aware of the social significance of language and know that their dialect differs from others on linguistic grounds. Focused varieties often have a "proper" name (e.g. "Australian English") and there may be processes of standardization later (see Chapter 5).

> VIGNETTE 4.1 The Origins of the New Zealand English (ONZE) Project
> From 1946 to 1948, the New Zealand National Broadcasting Service carried out interviews with native New Zealanders to collect pioneer reminiscences and stories from rural parts of the country. Producers and technical assistants traveled the country in a large van, the "Mobile Unit," and interviewed elderly residents in their homes (background noises include ticking clocks, meowing cats, and rattling teacups). The

> microphone was connected to the technical equipment in the bus via long cables, so the interviews could be carried out in familiar environments. Speech was recorded on 16-inch discs (consisting of an acetate coating on an aluminum base), with 10–11 minutes' recording time per side. The earliest recordings were made with islanders born between 1851 and 1910; they vary in their degree of formality, with some speakers reading from notes, others telling anecdotes and stories.
>
> Together with the Intermediate Archive and the Canterbury Corpus, this set of recordings represents a unique opportunity to study and retrace the development of an English dialect. There have been several large-scale projects on the phonetics and phonology of New Zealand English (NZE), with high-profile publications in the finest journals.

Colonial varieties are not unchanged versions of one of the founder varieties (Australian English is not a transplanted form of London Cockney). New dialects typically adopt features from two or more donors. These interact as speakers accommodate to each other, and the varieties spoken by the colonial populations undergo a stage of mixing. Contact dialectologists want to find out why some features are adopted and what the criteria are that enhance their selection chances at the expense of others, for instance:

1. The surviving competitor is usually found in the majority of inputs.
2. The variants with the widest social and geographical distribution have the highest chances of being selected.
3. Regionally or socially stigmatized features are usually not maintained.

One crucial process is leveling, where factors such as status (stigma or prestige of regional/social variants), social networks, population demographics, and the frequency of competing variants all play a role. As a result, new dialects may occasionally show no regional variation, even if spoken in huge areas; in Australia, for instance, "the overall picture must remain one of a continent across whose vast reaches there is comparatively little variation" (Collins & Blair 2001: 9) and "New Zealand, like Australia, is more remarkable for the absence of regional differences" (Gordon & Deverson 1998: 126). Initial differences between dialects disappeared and leveled off when new forms were selected.

Simplification occurs when there is a reduction of irregular or redundant patterns in contact-derived varieties. A good example here is past *be, we were* vs. *we was*, in Tristan da Cunha English (TdCE), a dialect which developed in the South Atlantic from the 1820s onward and which, with only about 220 speakers, is one of the smallest varieties of English as a world language that is spoken natively (Figure 4.1). The English past *be* paradigm takes two forms for number and person (*was* and *were*), but in TdCE, Tristanians born before the Second World War extended *was* to all environments and used it with all grammatical persons (*you was, we was, they was, the dogs was*, etc.).

> VIGNETTE 4.2 Tristan da Cunha English
>
> TdCE is a small variety of South Atlantic English, spoken by some 220 native islanders in one of the world's most isolated places. The dialect has a special history. It is fairly young, as Tristan was settled in 1816, and all the settlers are known by name. There is a complete genealogical tree of the island, listing the origins of the community's founders: Kelso (Scotland), York, London, Hastings, St. Helena, Massachusetts (US), and various settings on the Continent (Netherlands, Denmark, Italy). The variety spoken on the island is a unique blend of varieties present in the feature pool, originating via dialect contact and influence from creolized (St. Helenian) English and ESL varieties.
>
> In recent years, the dialect has changed substantially as the Tristanians have become more mobile and spend more time in the UK and South Africa. Still, it is a symbol of identity, and the islanders are proud of their way of speaking.

Figure 4.1 A traditional cottage on Tristan da Cunha, where the world's most isolated dialect is spoken. Photo: Daniel Schreier.

There may also be "new" features unattested in any of the founder dialects: so-called interdialect variants. Sometimes they are intermediate between original dialect forms, or they originate in overgeneralization. In **hypercorrection**, for instance, speakers misinterpret and incorrectly generalize rules by applying them to inappropriate contexts. It occurs "when some speakers try and correct a regular feature of their dialect because they perceive it to be unprestigious, but in so doing do not necessarily attain the prestige form aimed at" (Mesthrie & Bhatt 2008: 46). To give an example: In British English, words like *grass*, *path*, *dance*, and so on have a short TRAP vowel in northern dialects and a long BATH in the South. When there is contact between speakers of northern and southern dialects, speakers may overgeneralize or hypercorrect by using the BATH vowel inappropriately in words that always take TRAP (e.g. *grand* or *cancer*).

New-dialect formation is sociolinguistically complex and may take several generations to reach completion. Dialect differences disappear when accommodation patterns between speakers in face-to-face interaction increase, and social networks are formed. Strong network ties (Chapter 3) come to function as norm-enforcing mechanisms and, based on his work on NZE, Trudgill (2004) suggested a three-step model:

1. Rudimentary leveling in the founder generation: contact, mixing, and levelling of all the dialects brought to New Zealand.
2. Feature election: The first native-born children pick and mix features from their parents' speech. Children select variants from different dialects and show extreme variability, both on interindividual and intraindividual levels. They engage in **nativization**, when the indigenous forms are developed.
3. Emergence of a new dialect: A stable, crystalized variety emerges when differences are reduced further, even to the extent that there is a remarkably small amount of regional variation in varieties such as Canadian or Australian English. There is a strong awareness of form and function of the dialect.

A particularly interesting example of new-dialect formation is multiethnolectalization. This refers to the speech of youngsters and adolescents with migrant backgrounds, who grow up in multicultural and multilingual districts of large cities in Northwest Europe. Their social conditions and everyday language experience are characterized by extensive language and dialect contact and involve a heterogeneous group of ESL speakers. Mixed varieties with multiple origins are common as there is a high degree of social contact among children and adolescents, particularly in informal contexts such as the street or in public places. The emergence of multiethnolects has been documented all across Europe, for instance in the case of **Multicultural London English (MLE)** (Kerswill et al. (2013)).

The origins of MLE can be traced to the 1950s, which saw immigration from countries in the Caribbean, Africa, and Asia regions that had been part of the British Empire and become politically independent. Some areas of London have high immigration rates (in 2006, 40 percent of all Inner London residents were born outside the UK, compared to 10 percent for the entire country). Migrant communities typically have strong ties within family and neighborhood, and there is often little interaction with the wider, mainstream community. Boroughs such as Hackney, investigated by Cheshire et al. (2011), have strong ethnic heterogeneity, high population density (with little residential segregation), and intense contacts across ethnic groups among young people. The varieties that give rise to MLE are creole-like varieties (mostly from the Caribbean), **Post-Colonial Englishes (PCE)** from Pakistan, Nigeria, and so on, EFL varieties and local London English. Some of the key questions are about what features characterize MLE, at what age(s) these are acquired and used, and how permanent they are. Its features can be traced to Caribbean or African/Asian varieties, for example:

- Narrow diphthongs and monophthongs replace broad diphthongs in FACE and GOAT: [æɪ] → [eɪ] → [eː] and [ʌʊ] → [oʊ] → [oː]
- Backing of /k/ before low back vowels to [q]
- Pronunciation of /h/ (no h-dropping, as in Cockney)
- Syllable-timed (staccato) rhythm
- Widespread use of slang terms (many of which are of Jamaican origin), including *blood* (friend), *ends* (place of residence), *mandem* (Creole plural of men "the men dem'), *rude, safe, tief* (steal), *man* (as address term), *man* (as indefinite pronoun) (Cheshire et al. 2011).

High-contact multicultural settings favor innovative patterns: Discourse markers such as still (*"I got the right moves innit but I ain't telling you though still. I ain't telling you"*). Or *this is* + Speaker as a quotative expression (*"This is me 'I'm from east London,'"*, *"this is my mum* 'what are you doing? I was in the queue before you'").

MLE is a new, mixed variety, distinct from traditional London English. It serves as a strong carrier of a local identity and is referred to as "our language," "cool," with non-ethnic associations and in strong opposition to both Cockney and Received Pronunciation. There is some variation, though most features are shared by the majority of speakers. Its characteristic features are mostly found in adolescent speakers (indexing identity) and the question is whether some features will survive and become the community's distinctive vernacular in the future.

To sum up: New dialects of English formed historically as a result of migration and colonization. The processes involved are sociolinguistically complex and influenced by the social characteristics and migration history of the speech community and contact with other groups. They form via leveling and simplification, and sometimes all the early differences can disappear and there is a striking lack of regional differentiation (as in Australia). Via continuing remigration, multiethnolects have emerged in European cities, forming out of the various dialects spoken by mixed and multilingual immigrant communities.

4.4 English in Contact with Other Languages: Jargons, Pidgins, and Creoles

English is spoken by possibly as many as 2 billion people around the world today and has been in contact with hundreds of languages; more than 100,000 loanwords have been borrowed; there has been grammatical change (restructuring) and phonological adaptation (transfer of features). Of course, the line between languages and dialects is difficult to draw sociolinguistically (mutual intelligibility is not of much help: Languages are used for intercommunication (e.g. Danish and Norwegian), whereas some dialects (e.g. Glaswegian and broad South African English) may be virtually incomprehensible to Standard speakers and each other, but we are speaking of language contact when historically and typologically different varieties interact on a regular basis (Matras 2020). Speakers in multilingual communities develop strategies so as to communicate in their everyday lives. We have already discussed code-switching and bilingualism. Alternatively, one of the languages, typically the one spoken by the colonizing power, serves as a lingua franca, a language of wider communication: for example, English used by speakers of Yoruba, Hausa, and Igbo in Nigeria. It is also possible, and this is what we look at now, that new varieties such as jargons, pidgins, and **creoles** emerge. Communities create a "makeshift" language by selecting and mixing elements, adopting loanwords and restructuring English grammar.

Extralinguistic criteria such as prestige and social status of speakers and groups are very important here, and three key terms are **superstrate**,

substrate, and **adstrate**. One of the languages, often the colonizing one, is the socially dominant superstrate, contributing most of the lexicon and serving as a **lexifier**, whereas substrates are spoken by communities that hold a socially subordinate position. Substratal influence is when a language with lower status, often an indigenous one, influences a more prestigious superstrate, mostly in the domains of morphology and grammar. In relationships of unequal power and prestige, the superstrate is adopted as a vehicle of communication at the expense of substratal languages, which in most extreme and dramatic cases can lead to language obsolescence and death (e.g. Aboriginal languages in Australia, First Nation languages in North America, etc.). The relationship is adstratal when the social hierarchy is not clear-cut, and when the languages in contact are roughly of equal status. The coexistence of Old Norse and Old English from the eighth century onwards is a good example here.

In colonial scenarios, the type of political engagement often determines the outcome of language contact: One distinguishes between settlement, trade, and exploitation colonies. The British (initially the English) spread from the early seventeenth century onward (first into the Caribbean and to North America), so the first endeavors were **settlement colonies**. In the eighteenth century, it has been estimated that more than 1 million people left the British Isles, but settler colonization boomed after 1815: About 25 million British settlers emigrated into the "New World" during the "long nineteenth century" (ca. 1789–1924), and as many as 200 million settlers of British ancestry may have lived outside the British Isles in 1930 (Britain 2020).

> VIGNETTE 4.3 The Scramble for Africa
> At the end of the nineteenth century, Africa was one of the least colonized continents, most of which was unexplored by Europeans. To avoid direct clashes and conflicts of interest, the European colonial powers (including Belgium, Britain, France, and Germany) met at the so-called Berlin Conference (1884–85) to coordinate their colonial activities. A political map of Africa shows unusually straight lines, particularly in the north, reflecting the compromise solutions agreed on by the representatives at the conference. The leading European powers split up Africa among themselves, simply drawing boundaries on maps and thus establishing new "nation states," disregarding ethnic matters, with consequences which persist to the present day. In so-called **exploitation colonies**, English was spoken by

a very small (often transient) minority with financial interests. There was no interest in setting up a permanent infrastructure, and education in the colonizer's language was left as the responsibility of clerks in the colonial administration, missionaries, and a local elite. Most (if not all) African nations are highly multiethnic, multilingual, and multicultural, with occasionally strong internal tensions between several ethnic groups. This strengthened the influence of the colonial languages as a lingua franca, as these were not originally spoken by any of the majority groups.

Figure 4.2 The 1884–85 Berlin Conference. (DigitalVision Vectors/traveler1116/Getty Images.)

So-called **trade colonies**, established along the African coast for instance, saw intense dialect interaction and occasional contact of coexisting languages. Mixed varieties of English emerged for rudimentary bartering and negotiation. There was frequent borrowing of words for flora and fauna, but the impact on the colonizers' language was limited – bilingualism was infrequent. In the absence of a lingua franca, so-called **jargons** developed. They were ad hoc interaction strategies, largely improvised with few norms or rules, makeshift vehicles of communication with small (typically specialized) vocabularies, short utterances of one or two words, and little complexity. These are the most rudimentary contact-derived languages, "a pre-pidgin, which has an unstable structure and limited vocabulary on account of sporadic use and restriction to a few domains like trade or labour" (Swann et al. 2004: 157).

Bislama, spoken on South Sea plantations from the 1850s onwards, is a good example of an English-based jargon. In the following sentence, *mi* serves as subject and object, there is a reduction of prepositions, and articles are postposed:

Buk	ia	mi	pem	Ø	long	wan	stoa	long	Niusilan
book	def	1sg	pay	Ø	in	indf	store	inf	New Zealand

"I bought *this* book in a store in New Zealand." (https://apics-online.info/surveys/23)

Developed on the spot by adults, jargons are not transmitted from one generation to the next as languages or dialects are; they modify and change quickly when acquired natively by children. They disappear from use when there is no longer a need to use them.

Pidgins emerge when stable multilingual communities have a continuing demand for a non-native language. Pidgins may develop from preceding jargons, but the dividing line is not clear-cut. Superstrates are incompletely acquired, so they are essentially formed by second-language learners who have insufficient access to the superstrate. Pidgin speakers already have native-like competence in another variety and use the pidgin as a second language or communitywide lingua franca. Many pidgins have no native speakers.

As for development, pidginization is characterized by extensive simplification. There is a strong trend toward reducing clusters of consonants and making them conform to universal syllable structures: Consonant-Vowel (CV) or Consonant-Vowel-Consonant (CVC). Consonants are deleted, syllable-initially (English *stand* > Sranan *tan*) or in clusters (English *sister* > Sranan *sisa*), or vowels are added word-finally (English *dog* > Saramaccan *dágu*). Tok Pisin, spoken in Papua New Guinea, has only seventeen consonants (Smith 2008) and five vowels: /i – e – a – o – u/ (phoneme inventories are typically small). Phonological contrasts (such as length) disappear and there are lots of phonological mergers. In Tok Pisin, /f/ and /p/ are merged to [p], and /s/, /ʃ/ and /tʃ/ are all realized as /s/ (*beach, beads, fish, peach, piss, feast, peace* all sound identical: [pis]).

Reduction is extensive, and pidgins lack morphological markers to indicate plurality, possession, or case. Nouns change little in form: Pluralization is expressed by context or the use of an added quantifier (such as *ol* "all" or postponed *dem, the boy dem* "the boys") or by reduplicating the noun (the plural of *tree* in Tok Pisin is *tree tree*). In morphosyntax, there are few word forms in pidgins; in West African Pidgin English (WAPE), for instance, tense and aspect are indicated by markers such as *don*, *bin*, or *de/di*:

Tense and aspect ... are noninflectional: *bin* denotes simple past or past perfect (*Meri bin lef* Mary left, Mary had left), *de/di* the progressive (*Meri de it* Mary is eating, Mary was eating), and *don* the perfective (*Meri don it* Mary has eaten, Mary had eaten). Depending on context, *Meri it* means 'Mary ate' or 'Mary has eaten' and *Meri laik Ed* means 'Mary likes Ed' or 'Mary liked Ed.'" (McArthur 2005)

Tok Pisin reanalyzed tense markers such as the future marker *baimbai* (shortened to *bai*) from the English superstrate *by-and-by*, for example in *em bai go long maket* "she will go to market" (Mühlhäusler 1986: 186). The pronoun for third person singular forms (he, she, it) marks the following item as a verb (or predicate), as in:

em	I	tok	se	papa	i	gat sick
he	PRED. MARKER	say	that	the father	PRED. MARKER	got sik

"he said that the father was sick". (Mühlhäusler 1986: 189)

In Tok Pisin, a sentence such as "six people are coming" is *sikspela man i kom* (translated as: "six-fellow man SUBJECT MARKER come") and *wanpela man i kom* ("one-fellow man SUBJECT MARKER come"). Possession is indicated by *bilong*, as *haus bilong John* instead of "John's house" and there are few prepositions. In WAPE, *for* is used for all kinds of prepositions: *in, at, on, to*, and so on (McArthur 2005), and we find the same process in the Pacific with *long*.

Sociolinguistically, pidgins can remain stable for generations, but their usage may be expanded to more and more domains so that the functional range and social role are expanded. Interindividual and intraindividual variability, characteristic of jargons and early pidgins, are reduced. New norms emerge, the lexicon increases in size, and grammar becomes more regular. Very often, children growing up in such an environment may adopt the pidgin as their major vehicle of communication. Conventionally, so-called creoles have been viewed as nativized pidgins. They undergo far-reaching changes in phonology, morphology, syntax, and lexicon so as to fulfil a range of functional and communicative purposes in the speech community, and they are typically unintelligible to speakers of the lexifier language, raising the interesting question of whether they are languages in their own right.

Nativization may occur when there is widespread societal bilingualism or multilingualism, a need for a lingua franca and restricted access to the lexifier language. The chain of natural transmission is broken and creoles develop "by some historical process other than normal transmission" (Thomason 2001: 74). A prototypical development jargon   >   pidgin   >   creole

might involve a jargon (spoken by adults) that is stabilized and expanded (by adults and perhaps by children also) at a pidgin stage before it undergoes nativization. As a result, there is a wide spectrum of sociolinguistic repertoires. While children acquire an expanded pidgin and set off nativization (and creolization) processes, older generations may continue using their native (substrate) languages or the pidgin. In other words, a variety may function as *both* a pidgin and a creole for different groups in the very same community, which is fascinating sociolinguistically.

During creolization, word order stabilizes further (with a strong preference for SVO (subject-verb-object) order), the grammatical system becomes more elaborate, and syntactically complex patterns emerge. Creole speakers may create new structures via **reanalysis**, the usage of an existing marker in a new category. In Sierra Leone Krio, for instance, and in Atlantic creoles generally, *se* "say" is reanalyzed into a complementizer "that," as in:

A   no   se   yu   bisi
I   know   that   you're   busy

Likewise, invariant preverbal particles express negation, tense, mood, and aspect. In Sranan, *ben* indicates past tense, *sa* future, and *e* continuous aspect, and most English-based creoles have *done* as a completive marker (*I done see that*). Often there is continuing substratal influence as temporal or aspectual categories are adopted. In Tok Pisin, for instance, verbs take a suffix *-im* to express whether or not they are transitive or intransitive:

Intransitive: *mi rid* "I'm reading; I (will) read," *mi pait* "I fight, I'm fighting"
Transitive: *mi ridim buk* "I'm reading a book," *mi paitim im* "I hit him"

Similarly, Tok Pisin has information on exclusive vs. inclusive first person plural and in addition makes a dual and plural distinction that is not found in Standard English (a sentence such as "we are going for lunch now" provides no information on whether the addressee is included in the activity or how many are going out). Tok Pisin indicates this information by using different pronouns: *yumitupela* is inclusive (addressee included), *mitupela* exclusive, *yumi* is a dual (only speaker and addressee), *mitupela* an inclusive dual, and so on (Table 4.1) – thus making Tok Pisin more complex than any English variety.

There is a lively debate on theories of origin. Creoles around the world with European lexifiers are surprisingly similar (sharing features such as negator *no*, anterior markers, progressives via reanalysis, etc.), so how can we explain this? There are several explanations:

Table 4.1 *Plural marking in Tok Pisin. Adapted from Smith (2020).*

		Singular	Dual	Plural
1st person	exclusive	mi	*mitupela*	*mipela*
	inclusive		*yumi*	*yumitupela*
2nd person		*yu*	*yupela*	*yutupela*
3rd person		*em*	*tupela*	*ol*

1. Monogenesis
   - Theory: Creoles around the world developed out of a Portuguese-based proto-pidgin spoken at sea by multilingual shipcrews. Other European colonizing powers came into contact with this pidgin and originally Portuguese words were replaced with Dutch, English, and French ones (in a process called **relexification**).
   - Criticism: Relexification would have occurred at a pidgin stage, thus prior to creolization, so monogenesis failed to account for similar yet independent developments of complexification later on.
2. Polygenesis
   - Theory: Similarities developed in parallel via substratal influence of African languages and the plantation situation under slavery conditions (plantation colonies). As language shift progressed within a few generations, the structural impact of the African languages shaped the emerging creole.
   - Criticism: The local scenarios are way too diverse to account for the simple idea that lexical items were picked up from the acrolectal lexifier and restructured via simplification. It is difficult to account for transfer and second-language learning processes.
3. Superstratum Influence
   - Theory: Creole features are remnants of archaic British dialect features or alternatively of foreigner talk or maritime jargons (nonstandardized British features included *does* and *did* as markers of habituality in the Caribbean, or *done* to express completive aspect in creoles around the world). Simplified language forms of colonists served as the role model for slaves on the plantations and elsewhere.
   - Criticism: There is haphazard matching of British dialect and creole features, at times without historical evidence. As access is limited, it is difficult to model how a fully complex system should emerge and how creoles evolve across heterogeneous environments.

4. Bioprogram Hypothesis
   - Theory: In order to create complex structures required for fully developed languages, children use innate language acquisition strategies. The "bioprogram" is an innate universal grammatical blueprint that enabled children to develop rudimentary variable pidgin forms available to them into the fully fledged grammar of a creole (Bickerton 1984).
   - Criticism: There is no clear definition of what "typical" creole features are and whether the categories investigated by Bickerton were adequate and consistent enough to allow for the generalization of findings.

In sum, the traditional view that creoles develop out of pidgins, often with a prior jargon stage:

jargon   >   pidgin   >   creole

has been much contested. Thomason (2001: 175) states that "some, perhaps many or even most, of the controversies surrounding the topic of pidgin and creole genesis will vanish if we recognize that the common assumption of a single developmental route to creole genesis – which is the main locus of the controversies – is unmotivated." This is important for all theories of origin.

Some creolists argue that the outcome of creolization depends on the social conditions of language contact (in the words of Mufwene 2001, "the ecology rolls the dice"). This is highly relevant sociolinguistically, as the contact environments of pidgins and creoles differ so much. Pidgins can only stabilize and expand if a colony, perhaps after prior jargonization, has long-term stability. Creoles, however, develop primarily in colonies where there is regular and frequent contact between colonizing and colonized populations, slaves and/or indentured laborers. Mufwene and others have argued that the difference between pidginization and creolization is predominantly a sociohistorical one, depending on contact histories and local sociolinguistic ecologies. He argues that external history is used to classify four types of creoles (plantation creoles, fort creoles, maroon creoles, and creolized pidgins), each of which is influenced by the degree of access to the superstrate. A more or less equal proportion of superstrate to substrate speakers (e.g. in slave colonies, where settler families have few slaves) would favor access to the target language, whereas large slave colonies would prohibit it.

In short, we have discussed possible outcomes of English in contact with other languages: jargons, pidgins, and creoles. In all these cases, English is simplified and restructured in multilingual communities, where several languages (with different kinds of prestige) are spoken.

4.5 The Global Englishes

English is a world language, with an estimated 2 billion speakers, and so far in this book we have seen how complex the development of local varieties is, socially and sociolinguistically. To complete the contact history of English, we now discuss the emergence of the so-called **Global Englishes** (or World Englishes), which are spoken in Africa and Asia mostly.

The plural form Englishes reflects the fact that these varieties have become different and diverse, challenging traditional classifications of English. Today, speaker numbers of Englishes in places such as Nigeria or India grow quickly. These countries have a historical, often postcolonial, relationship with Great Britain (i.e. classical "inner-circle" varieties). Their roots are in political expansionism and commerce which began with institutionalized trade contacts from the early 1600s onwards. The Global Englishes have developed in different periods of time, sociodemographic conditions, sociolinguistic scenarios, and so forth. What they have in common is that English as a superstrate gained a foothold via administration of developing colonies, first among the expatriate community and later as a lingua franca when a local infrastructure was built up. Often, English was first spoken in bridgeheads along the coast (ports such as Surat, Chennai (earlier called Madras), and Mumbai (Bombay) in India), from where it diffused into the neighboring areas and subsequently into the local communities.

Let's first look at the characteristic features in order to find out to what extent they are shared with other contact-derived varieties and whether there are resemblances between varieties (in terms of direct contact, substratum effects, independent innovation, etc.). Table 4.2 lists some features of Global Englishes around the world (taken from Mesthrie & Bhatt 2008, Schneider 2020).

These features illustrate the sociolinguistic creativity and flexibility of Global Englishes (they are often publicly visible, Figures 4.3 and 4.4). They typically originate via feature transfer and second language learning, but it is debatable as to whether (and to what extent) they are exclusive to the Global Englishes. Nearly all features make an appearance elsewhere, too, for example in pidgins and creoles, where we also find copula absence or reduced tense systems, or in British English, where FACE and GOAT monophthongs are common. The frequency of these features varies from place to

Table 4.2 Global Englishes' features around the world. Adapted from Mesthrie & Bhatt (2008), Schneider (2020).

	Feature	Example	Example in …
Morphosyntax	Variably absent definite articles or substitution by *one*	"I want to buy Ø bag"; "Here got *one* stall selling soup noodles"	Singapore English
	Singular forms used with plural reference	"This worms, they get into your body"	Native American English
	It with plural reference	"Those books are very informative. *It* can be obtained at Dillons"	Malaysian English
	Extension of plural *-s*	*staffs, furnitures, equipments*	Kenyan English, Indian English
	Zero personal pronouns	"Ø must buy for him; otherwise he not happy"	Singapore English
	Zero existential	"Is very nice food," "Here is not allowed to stop the car"	Ugandan English, Hong Kong English
	Zero past tense *-ed* marking	"We stay Ø there whole afternoon and we catch one small fish"	Singapore English
	Zero present-tense *-s* marking	"She sing Ø very well"	Indian English
	Zero copula	"The house Ø very nice"	Singapore English
	No past marking or irregular verbs	"Last time she *come* on Thursday," "He already go home"	Singapore English, Malaysian English
	Extension of progressives	"She is owning two luxury apartments,", "I am smelling bread"	Malaysian English, Nigerian English
	Prepositions used as verbs	"I told her to on the stove but she offed it"	Indian South African English
	Morphological conversion	"She was by-hearting her work," "He's always back-answering me," "He look-aftered his children very well"	Indian English, Indian South African English
Phonetics and phonology	Monophthongization	FACE and GOAT vowels	Nigerian English, Singapore English
	Reduction and loss of length quality	*ship-sheep, full-fool*	
	Consonant cluster reduction	*post* "pos," *left* "lef"	Malaysian English
	Stress change	*dedicáted, fináne*	Kenyan English
Pragmatics	Register clashes	"I am sorry to disturb you on this fine morning"	Indian English
	Invariant tags	*no?, isn't it?, is it?, true?, true or not?*	Colored South African English
	Discourse markers	*mah, leh,* or *lor* ("Hi, just come lah? – "So o.k. lah")	Singapore English

Figure 4.3 Hypercorrect article usage in a Cyprus shop. Photo: Daniel Schreier.

Figure 4.4 Consonant cluster reduction in a Cape Town parking lot. Photo: Daniel Schreier.

place; some are widespread or perhaps even near-universal, for example consonant cluster reduction, whereas others are restricted to very few or only one variety, such as discourse markers *mah* and *lor* in Singapore. As in pidgins and creoles, there is probably no single feature that characterizes the Global Englishes exclusively.

As for evolution, the functional and social adoption of English comes in several overlapping phases, as illustrated by the case of South Asian English (Kachru 2008): exploration, implementation, diffusion, and institutionalization. During exploration, missionaries and their organizations propagated the Gospel and spread of Western education and values, giving English high status. The missionaries considered this to be a "civilizing" mission and regarded it as their moral and imperial duty to bring European knowledge and Christian faith to the local population. A second phase, implementation, started in the nineteenth century and involved discussions as to what language should be used in education and how English should be made available to the local population (Kachru 2008: 9).

A British-type education system was introduced and developed in India under the British Rule from 1765 to 1947. In that period, educated English-speaking Indians assisted British officials in the administration of the colony (Figure 4.5).

Figure 4.5 The Welcome to India Arch in the British Raj, ca. 1850. (DigitalVision Vectors/duncan1890/Getty Images.)

English, the colonizing language, became extraordinarily powerful in countries such as India and over time emerged in other Asian settings, such as Sri Lanka and Bhutan, where governments embraced it as an official language. After an intense and often emotional struggle between traditional, indigenous local values and a new, Western system under British rule, English gained great influence throughout South Asia in language, literature, and society. The debate continued well into the twentieth century. As late as 1921, Mahatma Gandhi wrote that "I refuse to put the unnecessary strain of learning English upon my sisters for the sake of false pride or questionable social advantage."

Crucially, however, native speakers of English represented a small sector of the community only (clergy, clerks, teachers, missionaries, etc.). English was no more than one language among many, spoken by a newcomer community with economic interests. This changed due to social and political developments in the colonies. Political independence gave rise to a fresh round of controversies over whether the former colonies (in Africa, Asia, and the Caribbean) should keep the language of the former colonizing power for official purposes or choose a local one instead. The St. Lucian Derek Walcott, winner of the Nobel Prize in Literature, expressed it very clearly: "It's good that everything's gone, except their language, which is everything."

These conflicts laid bare the ideological issues behind language choice in postcolonial settings. They go hand in hand with identity construction: Does the community orient itself toward the "mother country" and its values and standards, or toward itself, striving to develop independent norms? English was often enshrined in the educational tier, with obvious advantages: access to a world language, availability of teaching materials, international audience and readership. The disadvantages are that large sections of the population have no or little access to education and competence in English (even in India, one of the most influential ESL countries, English is still spoken by only a minority of the population, Hindi being more widespread). These issues are difficult to resolve.

One of the cornerstones of the Global Englishes' development is that societal bilingualism and the use of (indigenous) home languages and varieties for official purposes and administration are sociolinguistically conditioned. In some cases, English has the advantage that it is not traditionally spoken by any of the regional ethnic groups. Though far from politically neutral (the injustice of colonial times is still associated with language), the status of English as a non-regional world language has helped to secure its position.

Exporting a colonial language very often changes the societal equilibrium of a speech community, so there is functional specialization. English and local languages (such as Hindi in India) are not interchangeable but used in specific contexts and settings, with different addressees and about various topics (Table 4.3).

Global Englishes emerge as second-language varieties of English in multilingual contexts. They are added to the sociolinguistic repertoire of local speech communities and spoken in official domains (administration, education, media, etc.). They thus share the following characteristics:

Table 4.3 *Functional specialization of English and Hindi in India.*

Domain	Addressee	Setting	Topic	Language
Family	Parent	Home	Planning a party	Hindi
Friendship	Friend	Cafe	Humorous anecdote	Hindi
Religion	Priest	Church	Prayer	Hindi
Education	Teacher	Primary school	Telling a story	English
Education	Lecturer	University	Solving a math problem	English
Administration	Official	Office	Getting an official document	English

1. They are primarily propagated via a local education system, typically not as a home language.
2. They are adopted in an environment where English is spoken natively by only a minority of the population.
3. They are used for a range of functions and skills (letter writing, administration, literature, advertisement, etc.).
4. They have indigenized, that is they have developed a set of distinctive local features.

Kachru (1985) suggested that English(es) be grouped into three largely concentric circles. The Inner Circle comprises countries of great historical continuity, the traditional bases of English in a sense (e.g. the UK, US, Australia), where the language is spoken natively (**English as a Native Language, (ENL)**). The Outer Circle includes countries where English is important for historical (often colonial) reasons (e.g. India, Nigeria, Pakistan, Kenya, Singapore), where it is spoken mostly as ESL and has a major role institutionally (as the language of politics, higher education, media, business, etc.). Finally, there is the Expanding Circle: Countries where English plays no historical or governmental role (e.g. China, Russia, Japan, much of Continental Europe), where it is widely used as a foreign language (EFL). Crystal (2008) estimates that the total number of English speakers in all three circles is almost 2 billion speakers worldwide (Figure 4.6).

This approach is very popular but it has sociolinguistic drawbacks. The model is static rather than dynamic (not leaving room for transition from one circle to the other) and based on geography, history, and ancestry rather than on perceptions of identity or shared linguistic features. It cannot really reconcile everyday realities of linguistic diversity within varieties and communities; should Hispanic (Latino/Latinx) English be classified as a variety of American English (thus, in the Inner Circle) or would its origins and contact conditions suggest a different classification? If so, in which circle?

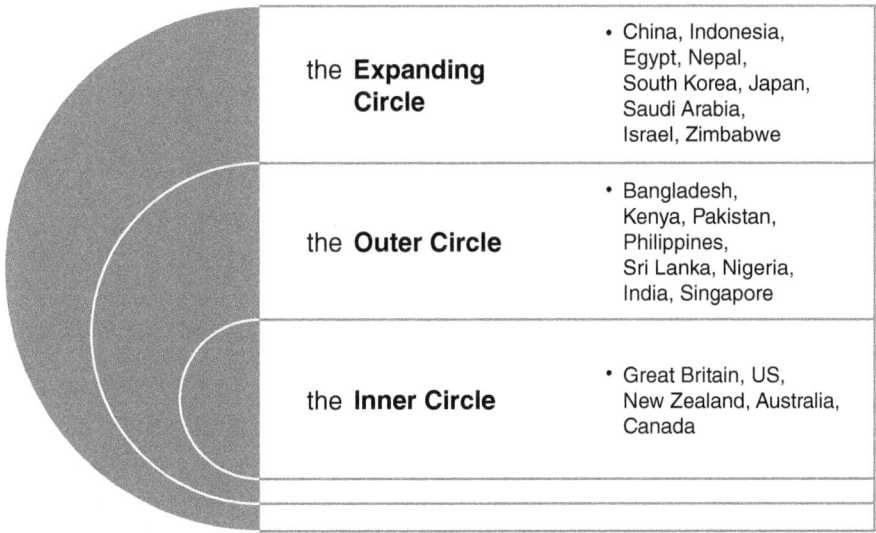

Figure 4.6 The three-circle model of English as a World Language. Adapted from Kachru (1988: 213).

It is also unclear whether (and to what extent) the inner circle (UK, US, New Zealand) should provide norms for the other circles. The question was whether the outer circle was norm-developing and the expanding one norm-dependent, relying on the standards set by native speakers. There was a lively debate on the role and function of ENL, ESL, and EFL countries: the Quirk–Kachru controversy in the early 1990s. It all started with Quirk's claim that there were parallels between non-native and nonstandardized varieties of English and that both needed access to a (native) standard variety:

> no one should underestimate the problem of teaching English in such countries as India or Nigeria, where the English of the teachers themselves inevitably bears the stamp of locally acquired deviation from the standard language ('You are knowing my father, isn't it?') ... It is neither liberal nor liberating to permit learners to settle for lower standards than the best. (Quirk 1990: 8–9)

Quirk considered ESL varieties (such as Indian or Nigerian English) as norm-dependent (on British English). Natively spoken varieties were assumed to hold an advantage over non-native ones, which were deficit deviations of the norm. Kachru's view was as follows:

> [T]he global diffusion of English has taken an interesting turn: the native speakers of this language seem to have lost the exclusive

111

> prerogative to control its standardization; in fact, if current statistics are any indication, they have become a minority. This sociolinguistic fact must be accepted and its implication recognized. What we need now are new paradigms and perspectives for linguistics and pedagogical research and for understanding the linguistic creativity in multilingual situations across cultures. (Kachru 1985: 30)

More recently, Schneider developed a life-cycle model of the evolution of what he called Post-Colonial Englishes (**PCEs**), a cover term which includes the Global Englishes as well as new dialects. Schneider suggested that:

> despite all obvious dissimilarities, a fundamentally uniform developmental process, shaped by consistent socio-linguistic and language-contact conditions, has operated in the individual instances of relocating and re-rooting the English language in another territory, and therefore it is possible to present the individual histories of PCEs as instantiations of the same underlying process. (Schneider 2007: 5)

The model involves five phases, shaped by external history, identity-building, sociolinguistic and contact-induced processes, which may overlap or occur simultaneously.

1. Phase 1, foundation, sees the transplantation of an English variety to be used alongside other indigenous varieties, with early dialect contact and initial contact phenomena, such as accommodation, leveling, simplification, and so on.
2. Phase 2, exonormative stabilization, is shaped by continuing ties with the British Isles. Identity is toward the "homeland" and the settlers often consider themselves as an outpost of the Empire (a mixed type of identity in other words). There is increasing (individual) bilingualism and a strong awareness of social differentiation.
3. Phase 3, structural nativization, is shaped by emerging local structures different to the ancestral language. Economic, sociocultural, and personal ties with the homeland weaken, the social hiatus between immigrant and indigenous population groups decreases, and there are conflicting loyalties and calls for political independence. The linguistic consequences are large-scale lexical borrowing, focusing, and continuing transfer of structures from indigenous languages. There may also be complaints about deteriorating and corrupted usage of English in the colony, compared with the allegedly "correct" ancestral variety.
4. Phase 4, endonormative stabilization, is one of political independence and goes hand in hand with cultural self-reliance and a distinctive local identity. The former colonists now see themselves as members of a young

nation and different from their country of origin, considering local forms of English as an emblem of local identity, independence, and pride.
5. Phase 5, differentiation, takes place in a context of political and sociocultural self-dependence, when the strong sense of national identity fragments into smaller, sociolinguistically characteristic communities. Social and regional differences emerge, social networks are strengthened, and communities of practice emerge.

Schneider illustrates the model in detail, drawing on examples of English in North America, Asia, and throughout the Southern Hemisphere, from Inner, Outer, and Expanding Circles, and incorporates dialect and language contact. His model reconciles many of the conflicting issues, goes a long way toward bridging the gap between koinéization and pidginization and/or creolization, and is the most influential model today.

4.6 Conclusion

Some 450 years ago, English was a minority language with only about 4 million speakers, but when the British Empire was at its height in the early 1900s, it covered over 20 percent of the world's land surface and was spoken by more than 400 million people. Today, it is estimated that some 2 billion people speak English to some extent: As Salman Rushdie famously said in 1991, "The English language ceased to be the sole possession of the English some time ago." Starting with the arrival of Germanic tribes in the fifth century, English has always been a contact language. It was shaped by the various Germanic dialects which merged into what became Old English, was enriched by contact with Old Norse, Latin, and Norman French, and the colonial era meant that speakers of English came to interact with speakers of other languages around the world. New contact-derived dialects emerged alongside pidgins and creoles, and there is sociolinguistic diversity on a global scale.

Modeling Englishes is challenging as several factors need to be considered.

- Extralinguistic ones: social history, population demographics, and educational politics.
- Social ones: identity construction and access to power and education.
- Psychological ones: language learning and identity formation.
- Sociolinguistic ones: language variation and societal bilingualism.

Various models have been developed to account for forms and functions of English as a world language, concentrating on the status of varieties, their history, and also identity-formation. Global Englishes spoken in countries with rapid population growth (e.g. India and Nigeria) are becoming more influential and there are hundreds of millions of speakers of other languages keen to learn English. The speakers in Kachru's outer and expanding circles, whatever their competence may be, increasingly outnumber those of English as a native language. In the words of Braj B. Kachru:

> the pluricentricity of English is overwhelming, and unprecedented in linguistic history. It raises a variety of issues of diversification, codification, identity, creativity, cross-cultural intelligibility, and power and ideology. The universalization of English and the power of this language have exacted a price; for some, the implications are agonizing, while for others they are a matter of ecstasy. (Kachru 1996: 135)

No doubt, sociolinguistic criteria will be paramount in shaping the future development of the English language, and we will return to these issues in Chapters 9 and 10.

Take-Home Messages

- English has had an extensive contact history, starting with the migration of Germanic tribes in the fifth century.
- Bilingualism and multilingualism are the norm in most of the English-speaking world.
- There is a distinction between English as a Second Language (ESL) and English as a Foreign Language (EFL).
- Code-switching involves the alternation of languages in speech, both in individual speech and community-wide communication.
- In diglossia, languages are functionally specialized to particular domains.
- New-dialect formation involves the processes of mixing, leveling, and simplification.
- Language contact may, under certain sociolinguistic conditions, lead to jargons, pidgins, and creoles.
- The Global Englishes have developed in different periods of time, sociodemographic conditions, and sociolinguistic scenarios. They are spoken mostly in Asia and Africa and involve second-language learning and transfer.

Activities

4.1 Look at an online map of northern England and search for placenames ending in *-by*, *-thorpe*, or *-thwaite*. Where would you say was the highest concentration of Scandinavian settlers?

4.2 Historical code-switching: The following is a personal letter written by Richard Kingston to Henry IV, where both languages are used in the same document:

> Mon tressouveraigne et tresredoute Seignour. [...] *please* a vostre tresgraciouse Seignourie entendre que a jourduy, apres *noo[ne]* [...] q'ils furent venuz deinz nostre *countie* pluis de CCCC des les *rebelz* de Owyne, Glyn, Talgard, et pluseours autres *rebelz* [...]

> ('My most sovereign and most dread Lord, may it *please* your most gracious Lordship to consider that to day, after *noon* [...] there were come into our *county* more than four hundred of the *rebels* of Owen, Glynn, Talgard, and many other *rebels* besides; English terms underlined; Schendl 2002: 254–256)

What are possible motivations for switching in this short document?

4.3 Here is a short Bislama text (from the Bislama Workbook at https://moet.gov.vu/docs/textbooks/Peace%20Corps%20Bislama%20Handbook_2014.pdf; p. 27):

> Long moning ol bank oli open long haf pas eit. Pita hemi kam long taon blong go long Vila maket. Taem market i finis, klosap long leven oklok, hem i resis kwik taem i go long bank blong tekemaot mane blong pem bensin blong enjin blong hem. Insaed long bank, hemi luk wan fren, nem blong hem Tom.

See how much you can translate, before checking the solution on p. 27 of the link. (Suggestion: Reading the text aloud helps one to understand it.)

4.4 Here is the Lord's Prayer in Tok Pisin, Jamaican Patwa, and Standard English:

Tok Pisin
Papa bilong mipela, yu stap long heven. Mekim nem bilong yu i kamap bikpela. Mekim kingdom bilong yu i kam. Strongim mipela long bihainim laik bilong yu long graun, olsem ol i bihainim long heven. Givem mipela kaikai inap long tude. Pogivim rong bilong mipela olsem mipela i pogivim ol arapela i mekim rong long mipela. Sambai long mipela long taim bilong traim. Na rausim olgeta samting nogut long mipela.

Jamaican Patwa
Wi Faada we iina evn, mek piipl av nof rispek fi yu an yu niem. Mek di taim kom wen yu ruul iina evri wie. Mek we yu waahn apm pan

ort apm, jos laik ou a wa yu waahn fi apm iina evn apm. Tide gi wi di fuud we wi niid. Paadn wi fi aal a di rang we wi du, siem laik ou wi paadn dem we du wi rang. An no mek wi fies notn we wi kaaz wi fi sin, bot protek wi fram di wikid wan.

Standard English
Our Father in heaven, hallowed be your name, your kingdom come, your will be done, on earth as in heaven. Give us today our daily bread. Forgive us our sins as we forgive those who sin against us. Lead us not into temptation but deliver us from evil.

Focus on prepositions, word order, and pronouns. What general observations can you make on English Creoles in the Atlantic and the Pacific?

4.5 The liberal discourses of *Anglicism*, whose supporters insisted on English as the language of education in order to promote Western knowledge and culture, clashed with the moral traditional discourses of *Orientalism*, the supporters of which believed that classical Indian languages (Persian, Arabic, and Sanksrit) were the most efficient way to spread European knowledge in India. Here are some excerpts from the *Minutes of Education*, written by Thomas Babington Macaulay in February 1835 (accessible at www.columbia.edu/itc/mealac/pritchett/00generallinks/macaulay/txt_minute_education_1835.html).

  [8] All parties seem to be agreed on one point, that the dialects commonly spoken among the natives of this part of India contain neither literary nor scientific information, and are moreover so poor and rude that, until they are enriched from some other quarter, it will not be easy to translate any valuable work into them. It seems to be admitted on all sides, that the intellectual improvement of those classes of the people who have the means of pursuing higher studies can at present be affected only by means of some language not vernacular amongst them.

  [9] What then shall that language be? One-half of the committee maintain that it should be the English. The other half strongly recommend the Arabic and Sanscrit. The whole question seems to me to be– which language is the best worth knowing?
    ...

  [34] In one point I fully agree with the gentlemen to whose general views I am opposed. I feel with them that it is impossible for us, with our limited means, to attempt to educate the body of the people. We must at present do our best to form a class who may be interpreters between us and the millions whom we govern, –a

class of persons Indian in blood and colour, but English in tastes, in opinions, in morals and in intellect. To that class we may leave it to refine the vernacular dialects of the country, to enrich those dialects with terms of science borrowed from the Western nomenclature, and to render them by degrees fit vehicles for conveying knowledge to the great mass of the population.

Discuss what this means for education, language politics, and also for Indian society at large.

4.6 "It is neither liberal nor liberating to permit learners to settle for lower standards than the best" (Quirk) vs. "What we need now are new paradigms and perspectives for linguistics and pedagogical research and for understanding the linguistic creativity in multilingual situations across cultures" (Kachru).

Discuss the relevance of these views in groups. What does it mean for the work of politicians, teachers, and students? Who benefits, who loses out, and what are the practical consequences for speakers of English if (1) they have to learn "the best standards" (i.e. British or American English), or (2) they learn newly merging ESL varieties?

Key Terms

adstrate
bilingualism
code-switching
creoles
diglossia
English as a Foreign Language (EFL)
English as a Native Language (ENL)
English as a Second Language (ESL)
exploitation colonies
feature pool
Global Englishes
hypercorrection
jargons
language contact
language hybridization
lexifier
lingua franca
Multicultural London English
multilingualism
nativization
new-dialect formation
pidgins
Post-Colonial Englishes
reanalysis
relexification
settlement colonies
situational and metaphorical switching
substrate
superstrate
trade colonies

Further Reading

For an excellent introduction to the consequences of language contact, check out: Matras, Y. (2020). *Language Contact* (2nd ed.). Cambridge: Cambridge University Press.

The development of World Englishes is discussed in:
Mesthrie, R. & Bhatt, R. M. (2008). *World Englishes: The Study of New Linguistic Varieties*. Cambridge: Cambridge University Press.

The development of English as a world language is:
Schneider, E. W. (2020). *English around the World: An Introduction*. Cambridge: Cambridge University Press.

A basic yet useful introduction to World Englishes is:
Melchers, G., Shaw, P. & Sundkvist, P. (2019). *World Englishes*. Abingdon/New York: Routledge.

And the theoretical implications of new-dialect formation are laid out in:
Trudgill, P. (1986). *Dialects in Contact*. Oxford: Blackwell.

CHAPTER **5**

English Historical Sociolinguistics

In This Chapter ...

... we will go back in history and discuss the historical dimension of sociolinguistics. The principle of uniformitarianism is important here, as it holds that present-day mechanisms of language change can be extrapolated to the past. We will focus on life in the British Isles in the Early Modern period and discover that the vast majority of the British population spoke regional and social varieties that contributed substantially to what the English language is today. As a result of profound changes in society, the history of English is manifold and more diverse than is insinuated by a focus on the Standard variety only. We look into language standardization in Late Modern England (1600–1900) and discuss the validity of data, particularly authenticity and authorship, as special care needs to be taken when assessing written data from times when education and schooling were a rare privilege. There is a discussion of the so-called "alternative histories of English" (Watts & Trudgill 2002) and English language ideologies in general, particularly relating to standardization and the persistence of dialect variation. We will end with a presentation of some groundbreaking studies in English historical sociolinguistics to show how one can gain insights into variation and change despite methodological challenges.

5.1	Historical Sociolinguistics: Projecting Back in Time	*page* 120
5.2	Life in England Before 1800	123
5.3	Language Standardization in Late Modern England (1600–1900)	127
	Vignette 5.1: Inkhorn Terms	130
	Vignette 5.2: Received Pronunciation (RP)	133
5.4	Literacy and Data	135
5.5	Tracking Variation and Change in Time	141
	Vignette 5.3: /h/ Insertion in the Language of Laboring Poor	144
5.6	Conclusion	149
	Take-Home Messages	150
	Activities	151

Key Terms	152
Further Reading	153

Preliminaries

The terms England/English, Britain/Great Britain, British Isles are used differently, particularly outside the region, so it might be helpful to clarify what they refer to in this book so as to avoid confusion.

- First of all, England and English are problematic. Until the 1970s, the terms were often used (particularly but not exclusively by English people) to mean Britain and British. A generic usage is still heard, for instance in the US, but is now considered at best irritating and at worst offensive in Scotland and Wales.
- Great Britain was so named after the Kingdom of England and the Kingdom of Scotland were united into one kingdom with one parliament in 1707 (though Scotland preserved a separate legal system after that date). Until that point, they were politically separate even though they had shared the same monarchs since 1603. Great Britain is the island containing England, Scotland, and Wales and has never included any part of Ireland.
- In 1800 Great Britain became the United Kingdom of Great Britain and Ireland. Following Irish independence, in 1927 it became the United Kingdom of Great Britain and Northern Ireland.
- The British Isles is a geographical and supposedly neutral term referring to all the islands, including the island of Ireland.

Using these terms, one has to tread carefully for historical, political, geographical, and social considerations. In this chapter and throughout the book, "England" refers to the country of England; Scotland, Wales, Northern Ireland, and Ireland are specifically named when discussed. Great Britain is synonymous with Britain, so the latter is used throughout. Every effort has been made to use neutral terms.

5.1 Historical Sociolinguistics: Projecting Back in Time

So far, we have seen that social organization is an important factor for language variation and change. The social fabric of a speech community, the organization of individuals into larger groups, and the formation and maintenance of social networks in combination provide the foundation of language change. We need to (1) study the sociolinguistics of both language and society and (2) compare the speech of individual speakers and different classes or ethnic groups to uncover the mechanisms involved. Such a comparison of speech from different individuals and groups rests on the **real vs. apparent time principle:**

- So-called real-time studies of language change (Labov 1994) focus on comparisons of language at different moments in time, and trace innovations diachronically (e.g. when speakers are recorded in 1990 and 2020).
- In the apparent time principle, the focus is on comparing different age-groups of the same community at one moment in time. Here, the assumption is that language stabilizes over time within speakers so that it becomes possible to compare age-groups at one period, reconstructing ongoing language change (Trudgill's Norwich sample, recorded in the 1970s, tracked ongoing change in East Anglian English on the assumption that several generations, recorded more or less at the same time, represented different stages of the local dialect).

The important question concerns how much and at what rate speakers change in their lifetimes, and **age grading** is a potential problem for apparent-time approaches: We need to recognize that "people do change the way they speak over their adult lifetimes, so that generational differences represent the effect of aging rather than change in the language" (Boberg 2004: 250–269). As a result, there are individual differences in the light of community stability, and these have to be taken into consideration carefully.

We have to address somewhat different issues when we project data back in time. As we saw in Chapter 2, one important innovation for sociolinguistics to develop out of traditional (regional) dialectology was the introduction of permanent speech records. Audio files made it possible to transcribe and cross-check speech data, providing the basis for the empirical analysis of variation and change. The downside is that synchronic studies cannot go back far in terms of time depth (applying the apparent-time construct, one can reconstruct changes roughly over the last 150 years or so). This is where the **uniformitarian principle** is paramount. When researchers want to delve back further into the history of English, they need to work with data which cannot be listened to but must be read instead. This presupposes a different methodological approach (as we will see below) and means that the availability and authenticity of data may vary significantly. Very often, it is impossible to collect more data (e.g. in the form of letters or official documents). However, if there "are relatively constant, day-to-day effects of social interaction upon grammar and phonology, the Uniformitarian principle asserts that these influences continue to operate today the same way that they have in the past" (Labov 1972a: 275). In the words of Susanne Romaine (1988: 1454), one of the pioneers of historical sociolinguistics:

> The linguistic forces which operate today and are observable around us are not unlike those which have operated in the past. This principle is of course basic to purely linguistic reconstruction as well, but sociolinguistically speaking, it means that there is no reason for believing that language did not vary in the same patterned ways in the past as it has been observed to do today.

This is encouraging, as the processes themselves may remain identical, but of course the social grounding, the values, and current attitudes of societies need to be assessed carefully as times and zeitgeists are changing. To give an example: The last forty years have fundamentally changed the way we define sex and gender as socially given criteria. The concept of a gender binary with only two groups, men and women, has been challenged and is now being actively dismantled (Kiesling 2019), so researchers need to critically rethink their approaches (Chapters 3 and 8). We need to understand how perceptions and categorizations worked in the past so as to allow for a projection back in time. Taking social-class effects as another case in point, Labov's early work showed how social stratification correlated with the usage of standard variants, so that members of social classes displayed similar frequencies of variables and participated in ongoing change in patterned ways. It is understanding the social layering of speech communities that allows us to track variation: "Not all variability and heterogeneity in language structure involves change; but all change involves variability and heterogeneity" (Weinreich, Labov & Herzog 1968: 188). In other words, once we know how society was structured in earlier times, we can apply the uniformitarian principle to uncover class-based differences as they operated in the past. But of course, social-class membership might have been stronger or different in former times.

This is particularly relevant as, in the words of Milroy, it is "*speakers*, not *languages*, that innovate" (Milroy 1992: 169). We distinguish between speaker innovation and linguistic change, and there have at all times been individual speakers who formed, picked up, and passed on new language features. We also saw that the process of language change depends on the social evaluation by speakers (Weinreich, Labov & Herzog 1968) and involves the actuation of a change in a language at a given time, the transition from one state/form to another, and the embedding in the linguistic and social structures where it emerges. There is an important difference, however: While present-day sociolinguists may explore their own speech community and collect (spoken or written) data *ad libitum*, historical sociolinguists cannot always go back to collect data. Instead, they need to work with the language materials available and develop different methodological tool kits. For instance, they may find that the evidence available is not representative; that it does not cover all social strata alike, as written materials depend on the level of literacy which, until the nineteenth century, was a privilege of the upper classes. Language histories from above (which refers to the social elite, often speaking the Standard variety) therefore contrast with the **language histories from below**, as Mattheier (2010: 353–354) maintained:

> [t]he concept of a "national language history" has dominated the view of what historical linguistics should be concerned with in relation to virtually all European languages, and continues to do so today. The theoretical starting point of this view – which at the very least needs to be seriously questioned – is that the "standard" language is the genuine teleological goal of any historical language development. And the path trodden by a speech community in developing a standard language, a unifying language, a literary language, at the same time represents the central content of language history.

Historical sociolinguistic research should therefore also focus on the varieties spoken by the underprivileged sections of society, which for centuries represented the majority of the European population. The problem is that the data available represent the mere tip of the iceberg, since we do not have spoken data and only a fraction of society was literate. Any investigation of social-class factors in sociolinguistic variation and change is dependent on the availability of written data across the social spectrum, so as to tackle the principles of (English) historical sociolinguistics. This means we need to address three points: earlier forms of society (giving us the social context), the process of standardization (providing us with information on the development of the English language in general), and methodological practices (as these were rather different to those introduced and discussed in Chapters 2 and 3), so let's discuss these issues in turn.

5.2 **Life in England Before 1800**

It is important to understand the organization of communities and social strata to understand how language is used in society at large, and a first step here is to portray society in earlier times. Needless to say, social upheaval, industrialization, and mass mobility (including changes in infrastructure and communication) had a massive impact on all aspects of language and society between 1600 and 1900. Some of these differences were slight whereas others were drastic; as Britain (2020: 210) notes, we have "to simply remind ourselves that the British Isles of two, three hundred years ago was, in some respects, rather different from now, and in others, actually, and perhaps surprisingly, rather similar."

As an illustration, pause a moment and ask yourselves when the total percentage of non-English-speaking residents in the British Isles was highest in your view:

1. 1750
2. 1850
3. 1950
4. Today.

Most students will go for Answer 4. When asked why, they point to the sociolinguistic impact of in-migration after the Second World War (see Chapter 4) and the arrival of large numbers of Hindi, Yoruba, Punjabi, Russian, and Polish speakers, from South Asia, Africa, the Caribbean, and the European mainland.

When asked to estimate how high the nonanglophone part of the population could be, estimates typically vary between 10 percent and 25 percent. It is only on second thought that some mention the earlier existence of Celtic languages; these were more frequently spoken until the early twentieth century, Gaelic being widespread in the north and west of Scotland (in fact, it was still reported as the majority language in the 1881 census). Similarly, Irish was the majority language of Ireland until nearly the end of the eighteenth century, and most areas of Wales had a Welsh-speaking majority. Communities of Welsh speakers survived in parts of England (such as Shropshire) well into the late twentieth century. In the British Isles, "it is probable that there were well over two million Irish speakers in the 1840s, 250,000 Scottish Gaelic speakers by the 1860s, and perhaps 20,000 Manx speakers. Welsh continued to a peak of 1 million in 1911" (Jupp 2001: 800). This was a criterion in traditional dialectology, as fieldworkers were instructed to focus on the use of English among:

> uneducated people, speaking an inherited language, in all parts of Great Britain where English is the ordinary medium of communication between peasant and peasant. *This limitation excludes those parts of Wales and Scotland where Celtic is habitually spoken by the natives. Ireland has*

also been excluded, except in the south-east of Co. Wexford – an old English colony – because it has otherwise a comparatively recently imported speech. (Ellis 1889: 92; emphasis added)

In other words, just over 130 years ago, most of Ireland was not surveyed in dialect surveys simply because the majority of the population spoke a language other than English. This has changed considerably: In 2011, data from the Office for National Statistics suggest that, while 7.7 percent of the population (4.2 million) of England and Wales had a main language other than English, only 1.3 percent (726,000) of the population reported that they could not speak English well and 0.3 percent (138,000) reported that they could not speak English at all. In just over a century, the pattern reversed: in the 1850s around 10 percent of the population of the British Isles spoke a Celtic language and not English. In other words, languages other than English were spoken more frequently in the UK some 200 years ago than now. The correct response to the earlier question would probably be Answer 1.

The impact of Celtic languages on extraterritorial varieties was significant as well. Speakers of Irish and Gaelic settled in Newfoundland, Nova Scotia, the Falkland Islands (Britain & Sudbury 2013), and also in the Southern Hemisphere; in Australia, "there were undoubtedly considerable numbers of Celtic speakers for over a century" (Jupp 2001: 800). These languages, along with the indigenously spoken ones, shaped the feature pools out of which English developed. They had an immense potential to influence the development of the New Englishes via language contact (Chapter 4). Consequently, the sociolinguistic ecology of language (and dialect) contact in the British Isles was considerably different in the past.

As for mobility, the eighteenth century witnessed rapid population growth. For instance, the English population almost doubled within a century, from around 5 million people in 1700 to nearly 9 million by the early 1800s (cf. the concept of **superdiversity** (Vertovec 2006) which we will discuss in Chapter 9). Work opportunities in factories and textile mills attracted the rural population from across the British Isles and there was an ever-increasing demand for cheap labor when industrialization began. Urbanization was rapid and mostly unplanned, leading to migration to the rapidly growing industrial cities of northern England, such as Manchester, Sheffield, and Leeds. In the early sixteenth century, just 3.1 percent of the population of England and Wales lived in towns with populations of over 10,000, a figure that grew to nearly 20 percent in 1800. Despite a high death rate due to poor living conditions (eighteenth-century towns were polluted, overcrowded, and insanitary, with open sewers, plagues, and epidemic diseases), by 1800 London had grown to have nearly 1 million inhabitants (almost 10 percent of the entire British population; Figure 5.1).

Figure 5.1 Scenes from a London Street in the mid nineteenth century. (DigitalVision Vectors/duncan1890/Getty Images.)

There were major changes in society, for instance increasing internal migration and high levels of mobility in the eighteenth and nineteenth centuries, particularly during the Industrial Revolution. Between 1800 and 1850 alone, an estimated one-third of the population left and moved out of their county of birth. Compared with today, most eighteenth-century towns had young populations, and young men were the most mobile members of society (those with the weakest social networks, Chapter 3). This meant that (1) British society was highly mobile from the 1700s to the late 1800s, and (2) the movement from rural to urban settings was particularly strong, accompanied by considerable mobility within rural areas as agricultural helpers were still in demand (Britain 2021).

What about education and literacy at the time (which, as we shall see, have an influence on the data available for historical sociolinguistic research)? Most of the population had no or little school education; college fees were affordable for a social elite only, but some children from non-privileged households attended Sunday and day schools run by the Church, so-called "ragged schools" for destitute children. Education only became compulsory as late as 1880, a development to which there was considerable opposition from: politicians, who felt that educating the working classes was dangerous; the Church, which wanted to maintain control of the education system and ensure that religion continued to play a major role in the curriculum; and also from parents, who needed their children at work as additional breadwinners for the family. As a result, literacy levels were low and notoriously difficult to assess (Auer, Schreier & Watts 2015), and it is well known that before the twentieth century, literacy was extremely basic (often barely functional). Historical Marriage Act records provide important evidence here. Weddings were only valid when both bride and groom and two witnesses signed the document or at least provided a mark in the parish register. In 1839, about a third of grooms and about a half of brides signed the register with a mark rather than a signature (Vincent 1989: 3). Moreover, only about a quarter of unskilled manual workers were able to sign their name on contracts (Vincent 1989: 97).

English historical sociolinguists focus on parts of society which had little access to power, authority, education, and learning and which, due to rapid urbanization and industrialization, became more mobile. This was a time of "large-scale disruption of close-knit, localized networks which have historically maintained highly systematic and complex sets of socially structured linguistic norms" (Milroy 2002: 565) but also a period of advancing literacy: In 1800, around 40 percent of males and 60 percent of females in England and Wales were illiterate, but by 1900 illiteracy for both sexes had dropped to around 3 percent (Stevens 1998). Moreover, British society at the time was multilingual and multidialectal: Society was less anglophone than it is today, the Celtic languages were more dominant, and there was extensive dialect contact, so koinéization and new-dialect formation (Chapter 4) were at work in many of the larger cities. The period from 1600 to 1900 was marked by massive changes, accompanied by shifting attitudes and ideologies concerning varieties of English, mostly the Standard vis-à-vis nonstandardized varieties.

5.3 Language Standardization in Late Modern England (1600–1900)

It may come as a surprise for some students to learn that **Standard English** (**StdE**) did not really exist before the fifteenth century. In fact, the Standard variety as we know it developed much later than some of the well-known and well-established local dialects, under special social conditions. There was a continuum from informal to formal and local to nonlocal varieties at the time (see Chapter 1), and the official language of learning and knowledge was Latin, less often French (though this was the language of the social elite between 1066 and the early 1400s). Sir Thomas More (who, by the way, latinized his surname to Thomas Morus) wrote *Utopia* in Latin, as for a long time it was thought that the language of the common people was not fit for the purpose of a literary language.

William Caxton, who had learned the printing trade on the Continent and introduced the printing press to England in the fifteenth century, reflected from a commercial standpoint as to what language to use for printing. His motivations can be followed in the personal prefaces to his books. Many of them were translations from French or Latin into English, so the language had to be acceptable and understandable for potential readers and buyers. In the preface to *Eneydos*, printed in 1490, Caxton wrote:

> Therfor in a meane bytwene bothe I haue reduced and translated this sayd booke in to our englysshe not ouer rude ne curyous but in such termes as shall be vnderstanden by goddys grace. [Translation: Therefore, as a compromise, I have translated this book into an English which is neither too coarse nor too refined, but using phrases which are understandable, God willing.]

The increase of literacy in Late Middle English society meant that publication in English was a lucrative business, and there were economic, religious, and also political considerations for a shift to English. There was a transformation from a self-sufficient feudal economy to a more competitive one, commerce and industry triggered social mobility and saw the emergence of a stronger middle class, and the belief in a divinely ordained social order dwindled. Moreover, the Protestant Reformation challenged the strong notion of Christendom (namely that the language of the Bible was Latin) and allegiance to the Pope. As the Bible was the word of God, which should reach the common people, it was subsequently translated into vernacular languages throughout Europe, a trend further strengthened by the emergence of nation states and feelings of strong nationalism generally.

Consequently, the fourteenth century saw an increase in literature written in English (Figure 5.2), yet the varieties used were local and far removed from the standard forms that developed later. Philologists and historical sociolinguists were able to trace the origins of some of the most important works: *Sir Gawaine and the Grene Knight* was most probably produced in a dialect from North Staffordshire, *Piers Plowman* in a Northwest Midlands dialect, and Chaucer wrote *the Canterbury Tales* in an East Midlands variety, though he was a great master of portraying and using different Middle English dialects. Late Middle English literature was a treasure chest

5.3 Language Standardization in Late Modern England (1600–1900)

Figure 5.2 Book printing in sixteenth-century England. (DigitalVision Vectors/clu/Getty Images.)

for language variation in writing and very different from the fixed norms of a standard that was to develop soon after.

The question, then, is why and precisely how standards developed (not only in English, as other languages formed them too). What are the typical processes of standardization, how long does such a process last and how does it diffuse through society at large? Haugen (2003: 421) argued that there were four different stages of standardization: **selection, codification, elaboration,** and **acceptance**:

- *Selection* refers to which of the competing dialects or sociolects should be adopted and elevated to the status of the standard. This is socially motivated and it is nearly always the variety spoken by the powerful and influential stratum that is selected. The model for correct English was "the usuall speach of the Court, and that of London and the shires lying about London within lx. myles, and not much above" (Puttenham 1589). Importantly, Oxford University, the oldest English-speaking university in the world, was established in the eleventh century and Cambridge University in the thirteenth century, and London was the seat of the Court.

- *Acceptance* refers to how a variety, once it is selected, gains support throughout the wider community. How are forms of an incipient standard promoted, passed on, established, and if needs be enforced? What are the roles of institutions, agencies, authorities such as schools, ministries, the media, cultural establishments, and so on? Crucially, the standard is regarded not just as the best form of a language but sometimes even as the language itself. All other social and regional varieties are dialects, which may become downgraded and stigmatized, often with some linguistic reasoning (Chapter 1).
- *Elaboration* is the necessity of a selected variety to represent desired norms and fulfil a whole range of functions (extension of the vocabulary, stylistic range, and so on). Academic and scientific writing became increasingly important due to scientific, rationalist, and empiricist motivations. New domains and situations of use, previously associated with Latin and French law, government, literature, religion, scholarship, and education were now conducted in English, which required new vocabulary items and an increase in stylistic function.
- *Codification* means that the norms and rules of grammar, use and so on are set and fixed. Normative forms are formulated (and often linguistically justified, see Chapter 1) and set down in grammars, dictionaries, spelling guides, manuals of style, texts, and so on.

VIGNETTE 5.1 Inkhorn Terms

Do you know the words *anacephalize, eximious,* or *illecebrous*?* What could they possible mean? During the Renaissance, the revival of classical scholarship brought many Latin and Greek words into Early Modern English as the classics were translated into English. The question was how this new word stock, until then reserved for the classical languages and French, was to be transformed in the new texts. Some translators had the practice of adopting words directly, at times creating them at their own will to impress readers with their education and learning, others coined new words with Germanic word elements. Writers were experimenting with the language, importing and inventing terms to meet their needs, based mostly on Latin and Greek. Neo-classical borrowings were very much a deliberate effort and the objection to so-called "inkhorn terms" was an emotive reaction against the sudden increase in English vocabulary derived from classical sources. Shakespeare's character Holofernes in *Love's Labour's Lost* is a satire of an overenthusiastic schoolmaster too fond of Latinisms. In Act 5, Scene 1, he addresses Sire Nathaniel as follows:

> Novi hominem tanquam te: his humour is lofty, his
> discourse peremptory, his tongue filed, his eye
> ambitious, his gait majestical, and his general
> behavior vain, ridiculous, and thrasonical. He is
> too picked, too spruce, too affected, too odd, as it
> were, too peregrinate, as I may call it.

The sixteenth century saw heated debates. Sir John Cheke (1514–57), a classical scholar himself, wrote to Roger Ascham (quoted from Baugh & Cable 2002: § 158):

> I am of this opinion that our own tung should be written cleane and pure, unmixt and unmangeled with borowing of other tunges; wherein if we take not heed by tiim, ever borowing and never paying, she shall be fain to keep her house as bankrupt.
>
> For then doth our tung naturallie and praisablie utter her meaning when she boroweth no counterfeitness of other tunges to attire herself withall, but useth plainlie her own, with such shift as nature, craft, experiens and following of other excellent [writers] doth lead her unto ... This I say not for reproof of you ... but for miin own defense, who might be counted overstraight a deemer of things

Interestingly, Cheke adheres to the popular myth of "pure languages" yet uses quite a few borrowings in this text himself.

There was a long and bitter ideological debate, but many objected to the introduction of a large body of new words from the classical languages. Though this was a remarkably creative period in the history of the English language, many words fell out of usage quickly.

* *anacephalize* "to recapitulate"; *eximious* "excellent, distinguished"; *illecebrous* "alluring, attractive."

There is a distinction between form-related and function-related standardization. Haugen (2003) suggested that codification and selection address the form of language whereas elaboration and acceptance address its function. He also argued that this is of central relevance for English sociolinguistics as codification and elaboration were by and large linguistically motivated, whereas selection and acceptance were mostly social processes (Table 5.1).

A large body of research on the development of StdE has concentrated on the stabilization of spelling and, less prominently, on morphology, syntax, and lexicon. As for origins, Samuels (1963) presented four types of Late

Table 5.1 *Standardization processes. Adapted from Haugen (2003: 421).*

	Form	Function
Language	Codification	Elaboration
Society	Selection	Acceptance

Middle English writing as likely sources of StdE, identified later as stemming predominantly from the Central Midlands dialect. He suggested that the spellings found in **Chancery Standard**, the spellings in documents issued from the King's secretariat, also known as the Office of Chancery, were the precursor of StdE spellings: "differences from the language of Chaucer are well known, and it is this type, not its predecessors in London English, that is the basis of modern written English" (Samuels 1963: 71). This story of the development of StdE is usually presented in textbooks. English historical linguists have tried to reconstruct the process of Chancery spellings and their influence on early StdE spellings, but the question of origins and early development is still open to academic debate.

The early stage of standardization gave rise to the reduction of grammatical and orthographical variants and saw the loss of geographically marked variants in the writing of individual writers. The eighteenth century was a period of correctness and clarity, and the fixing of rules of "good Englishe" was a prime concern. Hundreds of dictionaries, grammar books, and usage guides were published, and there was a profitable market for prescriptive language materials. The primary customers were the rising middle classes who (1) did not have yet the benefit of a liberal (Classical) education, (2) were obliged to send their children to grammar schools and charity schools, and (3) were highly motivated to move up the social scale into "polite" society. As Bishop Robert Lowth pointed out in his preface to a *Short Introduction to English Grammar* in 1762:

> The principal design of a Grammar of any Language is to teach us to express ourselves with propriety in that Language; and to enable us to judge of every phrase and form of construction, whether it be right or not. The plain way of doing this is, to lay down rules, and to illustrate them by examples. But, beside shewing what is right, the matter may be further explained by pointing out what is wrong. (Lowth 1762: 10)

The demand for grammar books was a lucrative business in the second half of the eighteenth century. Some of the books were commissioned by influential publishers and went into a large number of reprints and/or new editions. The vast majority were written by masters and mistresses at schools, for a market which involved teachers of English grammar, advocates of polite conversation, elocution, and linguistically appropriate behavior.

It was only later, in the nineteenth century, that a standardized accent emerged: **Received Pronunciation** (RP). Interestingly, when Dr Johnson wrote *A Dictionary of the English Language* in 1757, he did not comment on pronunciation. There must have been extensive phonological variation in educated society at the time, so Johnson may have felt that there was little agreement regarding "recommended" sounds. The term RP was first used by Alexander Ellis in 1869 (we discussed Ellis' work on regional dialects in Chapter 2). It gained popular usage when Daniel Jones, a famous phonetician, adopted it for the second edition of his *English Pronouncing Dictionary* (1924) to describe the accent of the social elite.

> ### VIGNETTE 5.2 Received Pronunciation (RP)
>
> RP is a unique type of accent of English around the world. We saw above that most accents carry information on the regional origins of speakers. While it is notoriously difficult to define the term dialect sociolinguistically, it is important to bear in mind that StdE is not an accent and has nothing to do with pronunciation. It refers mostly to grammar, which can be spoken with regional accents – "accent" is not "dialect". Trudgill (1983) points out that there is an inverse relationship: Whereas every RP speaker speaks StdE, not every StdE speaker has an RP accent (most British sociolinguists would probably agree that the majority of StdE speakers have regional accents). Trudgill (1983) famously estimated that 10–15 percent of the English population spoke StdE, yet only 3–5 percent had an RP accent, making it a standardized accent of StdE and not StdE itself. In his *A Glossary of Sociolinguistics*, Trudgill classifies RP as follows:
>
>> The regionless upper-class and upper-middle-class accent of British – mainly English – English which is associated with the BBC and is usually taught to foreigners learning 'British' English. The label 'received' is here used in an old-fashioned sense of 'being accepted in the best social circles'. The unusual regionless nature ... is probably the result of the unusual upper-class British educational system of non-regional residential private schools ... Only a very small minority of the population of Britain – probably three to five per cent – speak in this totally regionless way. (Trudgill 2003: 121)
>
> Recent research has shown that RP is changing indeed, though subtly (younger speakers have higher frequencies of T glottaling, fronting

> of /uː/ or /l/ vocalization). A research team led by Jonathan Harrington compared the pronunciation of vowels in Christmas speeches of Queen Elizabeth II delivered in the 1950s and 1980s and found that Her Majesty had changed to Mainstream RP over the years (probably as she accommodated to her grandchildren), which received great publicity in England.

The total number of RP speakers is sociodemographically small and probably dwindling. This contrasts with the fact that it is one of the most widely studied and frequently described varieties of spoken English, serving as a benchmark for learners of English around the world. RP is very prominent and widely used (in competition with General American) in teaching English as a foreign language.

All in all, the standardization of English spanned a process of about three centuries and involved several (overlapping) stages:

- Orthography (end of eighteenth century)
- Grammar (end of eighteenth century)
- Lexicon (dictionary) (mid nineteenth century)
- Phonology (end of nineteenth century).

"Good English" gradually came to be associated with important and careful contexts of use (literary writing, learned writing, legal writing, and the Bible) and it soon enjoyed high overt prestige. In due course, it was the "correct" usage taught to foreigners, and larger sections of society accepted its norms as a yardstick. This is precisely how standard language ideology works. Standardization follows a reevaluation of language attitudes when a normative variety is selected, accepted, and elaborated, and most of the local (rural) varieties are marginalized. At the same time, while universities, administration, and government are all involved in some way, standardization is not a coherently planned activity:

> [W]e shall see standardisation as a project, which took different forms at different times. It is only with hindsight, after all, that we can interpret the process at all: things may have felt very different in the past. One thing we can be clear about is that the process of standardisation cannot be seen as merely a matter of communal choice, an innocent attempt on the part of society as a whole to choose a variety that can be used for official purposes and, in addition, as a lingua franca among speakers of divergent dialects. It involves from the first the cultivation, by an elite, of a variety that can be regarded as exclusive. The embryonic standard is

not seen as the most useful, or the most widely-used variety, but as the 'best'. (Leith 1997: 33)

To sum up, the development of StdE was characterized by codification and correctness. A southeastern variety was selected because government and higher education were based in or around London. It was accepted as the usage of educated people, at least in formal situations, elaborated while spreading through all written discourse. As the variety of the social elite, it was not merely the language of government but of most learned and educated people. As there was increasing awareness of a societal need for StdE, it was codified through printing, for printers required norms and guidelines, and education, as the new middle classes demanded an education in English rather than French or Latin. At the end of the standardization period, it was no longer necessary for printers to ask themselves what variety they should use as a model, as William Caxton felt he had to in the late fifteenth century.

5.4 Literacy and Data

The three centuries between 1550 and 1850 were a period of transformation, both for language and society. As processes of urbanization, industrialization, and colonization unfolded, the English language changed, and a socially accepted standard variety emerged. Crucially, the selection of a prestige variety as the standard meant that the written materials available became more uniform and fixed (particularly when codification advanced in the eighteenth century). Educating the elite was of high concern and the universities catered for this purpose, exerting considerable influence on general attitudes toward language usage. There was an abundance of grammars, letter-writing manuals, pronunciation guides, rhetorical treatises, and so forth. In terms of language material, a growing body of data (or corpora) became available, and these were predominantly produced by members of the upper and well-educated strata of society. The gap between the educated people and the laboring poor widened, and there was increasing poverty as the latter represented the majority of the population. There certainly were "literate" people by 1800, that is they could write their own names and some more basic information, but not much more. Vincent (1989) estimated that around 1840, ca. 67 percent of men and 50 percent of women were literate, but he reported sharp stratification in terms of literacy rates. Only 27 percent of unskilled laborers and 21 percent of miners had some basic writing skills.

Schools opened up for the laboring poor, occasionally as private enterprises. Two Education Acts (provision of elementary schooling by government in 1870; compulsory schooling, ages 5–10, in 1880) meant the establishment of a great variety of school types in England and Wales, both day and part-time schools. The subjects taught were the so-called three Rs (reading, writing, arithmetic), needlework for girls, and of course religion in church-run schools (Figure 5.3).

Figure 5.3 An English classroom in Victorian times. (DigitalVision Vectors/duncan1890/Getty Images.)

Ironically, more and more people started to read and write yet the materials they produced were less suitable for sociohistorical analysis. This has been referred to as the **bad-data problem**: "historical documents survive by chance, not by design … [they] are riddled with the effects of hypercorrection, dialect mixture, and scribal error" (Labov 1994: 11). Data have to be handled with great care, particularly when there is uncertainty about authorship and the social dimensions of life and times in general. The challenge is to accept that, though there is ample evidence of how different life in England was three centuries ago, it is impossible to reconstruct how different it was for the people themselves (Labov 1994, Nevalainen 2010). What was the validity of modern categories such as "social class" and how were gender roles perceived and enacted in the everyday lives of speakers?

Historical sociolinguists can only make reliable assumptions about the social validity of language change when the "bad data" they are working with fulfil three requirements:

- *Empirical validity*: There have to be sufficient bodies of materials available as a baseline for comparison, particularly when studying variation. Data are needed from other contemporary writers of the same age and social status so as to allow for the comparison of data from distinct regions throughout the country and different periods of time: "In order to be able to study language change and the social dynamics of language varieties in their communities empirically in relation to external factors, the historical sociolinguist needs access to language documentation of a variety of sources" (Nevalainen 2015: 246).
- *Social validity*: One needs information on the writer's age, social status and mobility, their gender, occupation, education, and place of residence. Metadata need to be as concise and reliable as possible. While these can be collected for some writers (e.g. women of noble rank or men of the upper gentry), they elude scrutiny when letters were dictated or written professionally, which makes them difficult for a sociohistorical interpretation.
- *Historical validity*: One needs to meet and incorporate challenges of reconstruction in order to find out how language change diffuses socially and regionally. In a society rather different to what it is today (cf. the changing social conditions in preindustrialized and postindustrialized societies, discussed above), the challenge is to uncover social networks and communication channels, personal contacts, and social characteristics. Historical sociolinguists typically work hand in hand with social historians here, making every effort to reconstruct the social, economic, and cultural history of the speakers and communities they study.

Consequently, historical sociolinguists face some major methodological problems in their work: the need to ensure a sufficient body of data, reconstruct the historical context, and establish the authenticity (or representativeness) of materials available. Given the effects of social stratification with regard to literacy prior to the First Education Act (1870), for instance, there were few written sources representative of lower social strata and rural regions. It is equally difficult to obtain reliable texts untouched by editors and proofreaders or dictated to literate writers who made this a professional enterprise, all of which is necessary to produce language histories from below.

Data come from plays, trial proceedings, verbatim witness depositions and/or accounts, letters, diaries, or autobiographies, and by means of an illustration we focus on two electronic corpora: the **Corpus of Early English Correspondence (CEEC)** and the **Old Bailey Corpus (OBC)**. Letters are a particularly promising text type as authorship can often be identified (Auer, Schreier & Watts 2015; note, however, that compilations of letters cannot always be used due to copyright issues – an additional complication). Terttu Nevalainen and Helen Raumolin-Brunberg compiled the CEEC, an extensive database of historical letters containing metadata for writers (Nevalainen & Raumolin-Brunberg 2003). The CEEC contains ca. 2.7 million words and covers the period 1417–1681; there are ninety-six collections, ca. 6,000 letters, 777 writers (20 percent of them female), and the extended version (CEECE) extends the timeframe to 1800. The CEECE has a broader coverage and aims at social representativeness, but working with "bad data" means that some crucial challenges (such as sampling) remain. According to Kaislaniemi (2018: 47):

> it is worth remembering that 18th-century England was in some ways remote from what in essence was a post-medieval world. In other words, some of the inherited categories are not necessarily relevant for making sense of 18th-century England and Late Modern English. For instance, East Anglia was highly important in the Tudor period, but by the Georgian era its cultural and political relevance had waned. Similarly, the clergy were not nearly as important in 18th-century England as they had been in the 16th century, thanks to advances in literacy and the availability of the Bible in English. So, the fact that a high proportion of CEECE data comes from the professional classes and from Londoners is rather a reflection of changes in English society than of skewed data.

The CEECE represents both men and women from various social ranks and regions, and Table 5.2 (adapted from Kaislaniemi 2018: 51) illustrates some of the challenges involved. Some categories are overrepresented (women of nobility, who outnumber men of the same rank by 6:1), for others there are no data (women from the Upper Clergy), and some regions are overrepresented (London and the Home Counties). While there is a substantial body of written data for sociohistorical analysis, these caveats make it difficult to generalize the findings and extrapolate to society at large.

Another source of data comes from court cases, where trials were reported as accurately as possible. The Old Bailey Proceedings, published from 1674 to 1913 by London's central criminal court, contain almost 200,000 trials: This yields a corpus of approximately 134 million words. The full texts of the *Proceedings* are available online (www.oldbaileyonline.org) and have proven to be a valuable historical source for historians and linguists.

The OBC includes a sample of the spoken data from the *Proceedings* from 1720 to 1913, thus roughly spanning two centuries (the trials were

Table 5.2 *Social status of informants in the Extended Corpus of Early English Correspondence (CEECE) (% of running words per gender). Adapted from Kaislaniemi (2018: 51).*

		Men (%)	Women (%)	Total (%)
Social rank	Royalty	7	6	6
	Nobility	6	34	14
	Gentry (Upper)	9	3	7
	Gentry (Lower)	21	23	21
	Clergy (Upper)	6	0	5
	Clergy (Lower)	14	10	13
	Professional	30	21	27
	Merchant	3	1	3
	Other	4	4	4
	Total	100	100	100
Region	The Court	5	3	5
	London	38	58	43
	East Anglia	1	0	1
	Home Counties	17	12	16
	North	10	1	8
	Other areas	25	20	23
	Abroad	4	5	4
	Total	100	100	100

only written in direct speech from 1720 onwards). It was designed as a subset of the *Proceedings* with about 14 million spoken words from 407 proceedings altogether. It has the advantage that it includes detailed sociobiographical speaker information (gender, age, occupation, social class), pragmatic information (speaker role in the courtroom), and textual information (scribe, printer, publisher). Of course, there is no way of ascertaining the degree of accuracy of the transcripts, and the texts were written by scribes from shorthand notes of the trials and further edited before publication. There must have been some adjustments; nevertheless, the proceedings are arguably the closest one can get to how language was used in the eighteenth and nineteenth centuries.

In the following example is the court record of an eighteenth-century rape trial (from Burri 2017). A woman named Susan Marshall stood in court as an accuser of a shopkeeper (the "Prisoner"), who was on trial for rape.

PRISONER.   Vat'our it vas ven you come to mine Shop?
SUSAN MARSHALL.   What Hour? It was between Nine and Ten at Night.

Q.	Was that the first, or second Time of your being there?
SUSAN MARSHALL.	The first, for it was about Ten when I went the second Time, and I saw no body else was then in the Shop. He shut the Hatch and bolted it, and when he came to me in the Back Room he latched the Door.
PRISONER.	You vas in mine Shop but von Time dat Night.
Q.	Why did you not complain before Monday?
SUSAN MARSHALL.	Because I was afraid my Mother would beat me.
Q.	On your Oath did not you consent?
SUSAN MARSHALL.	No. I cry'd out aloud.
PRISONER.	Ven you come again to my Shop?
SUSAN MARSHALL.	Not till Monday Morning.
PRISONER.	You come on de Saturday.

(Burri 2017: 43)

The short passage contains quite a few nonstandardized features:

- Morphosyntax: no word order inversion ("Vat'our it vas ven you come"), mine for my as a possessive with a following noun ("you come to mine Shop"), was as preterit of past be with second person singular ("You vas in mine Shop"), come as a preterit form ("You come on de Saturday").
- Phonology: devoicing of labiodental fricatives ("You vas in mine Shop but von Time"), TH stopping ("but von Time dat Night").

Note too that some pragmatic conventions have changed. Asking questions was not a privilege of those in socially superordinate positions. In the Early Modern English courtroom, the role of questioners was not restricted to the most powerful speakers but was also to some extent used by less powerful defendants. The defendant himself asked some of the questions and continuously comments on the victim's evidence so as to weaken her accusations. We will see in Chapter 7 how this practice has changed today, with far-reaching consequences.

To conclude, historical sociolinguists face quite a few challenges in their work. Labov (1994: 11) famously observed that "[h]istorical linguistics can then be thought of as the art of making the best use of bad data," and he had a point for several reasons. First, it is not at all easy to obtain samples of language varieties and nonstandardized varieties, in fact any form of language that deviates from the Standard. Before the 1870s, restricted access to education and widespread illiteracy meant that members of the working and lower-middle classes wrote very little. As a result, our understanding of language as used by the lower social strata is sketchy (cf. Auer, Schreier & Watts 2015,

Elspaß 2007) and many language histories from below remain hidden. As a result, the majority of the population is underrepresented in historical sociolinguistic research (Nevalainen & Raumolin-Brunberg 2003). Second, it is not easy to obtain accurate metadata (about who the authors were, what their social and regional origins were), and sampling is often skewed. Third, context information may be missing: Historical sociolinguists rely on in-depth knowledge of the social context in which language was used, particularly when uncovering the underlying conditions of variation and change.

5.5 Tracking Variation and Change in Time

So far, the focus on challenges for historical analysis may have given the impression that historical sociolinguistics is mostly problem-ridden. This would be overly pessimistic, and I would like to end the chapter by looking at some advances and findings, showing how a critical and careful approach can help us gain a better understanding of sociolinguistic issues in the past.

Let's start with work on earlier forms of English and how they were used in dialect-contact scenarios (Chapter 4). Various corpora of emigrant letters, sent home from the colonies, offer invaluable information for sociolinguists and social historians alike (Auer, Schreier & Watts 2015, Fitzmaurice 2004). These letters mostly had a social motivation (to stay in touch with family and relatives at home, or to ask for favors). This meant they were typically intimate and personal, written by members of the lower social strata and by colonists who found themselves in unfamiliar and demanding conditions: "emigrant letters offer a window on varieties of English at key periods in their development, a window which shows usage far removed from any regulating influence of education or an emerging standard" (Hickey 2019: 5).

Emigrant letters may contain features for varieties of English which do not necessarily appear in later sources or which are not attested with the same frequency or in the same set of grammatical contexts, thus being of importance for diachronic processes. Hickey (2019: 8) suggests that emigrant letters are an important genre because they:

- reveal previously unrecorded features or confirm uncertain features
- contain features that are not attested or continued in present-day varieties
- help determining the period in which known features of a later variety probably arose
- confirm general patterns assumed for the development of varieties.

Figure 5.4 A German farmer stopping work to hear his wife read a letter from the US (nineteenth century). (DigitalVision Vectors/Keith Lance/Getty Images.)

There is a body of research on US Appalachian English and its origins in Ulster/Northern Ireland (Montgomery 1989), Southern Africa (Siebers 2015), and New Zealand (Gordon et al. 2004), to give but a few examples. Let's consider the case of Annie Carroll as a case in point (Hickey 2019). Originally from Dundalk, she emigrated to Wisconsin (US) in 1883. She then worked as a domestic servant and/or cook in Chicago, and after falling ill in 1896 could only take on minor jobs. Annie Carroll remained single all her life and wrote to her family in Ireland frequently during the 1880s and 1890s. We know that she was hospitalized in 1902; there are no more records after that.

An analysis of a small corpus of eleven letters provides evidence of (1) previously unrecorded features, (2) combinations of features not attested or not continued in a present-day variety, and (3) features known from later sources and observations of present-day speakers (Table 5.3).

The consideration of emigrant letters (Figure 5.4) shows that they provide a valuable data source for sociolinguists. While it is true that some caveats must be borne in mind, the richness of the data makes them an

Table 5.3 *Feature analysis in letters written by Annie Carroll in the 1880s and 1890s. Adapted from Hickey (2019: 18–19).*

Previously unrecorded features or confirm uncertain features	Lack of indefinite article	<before I had Ø letter from him> she got to be Ø very stout girle>
	Absence of personal pronoun	<I did not see John sence Ø got your letter> <if I had any money to send Ø would sent it>
	Unmarked third person singular	<why dont you write to minnie she think it is strange of you> <she be only glad at any down fall we or John would get>
	Unmarked genitive	<I did not get Mary last letter> <I think it for me to write you few lines I got mother letter monday 14>
	Infinitive for finite verb form	<I am sorey to here Johny Johnson wife to die (i.e. died)>
(Combinations of) features not attested or not continued in a present-day variety	Maintenance of question word order in sentential complements	<we care about what dose she say about us>
	Short /e/ raising	<I had litter from aunt Bridget>
Features known from later sources and observations of present-day speakers	Habitual with 'do' + V	<she do all ways ask when I here from you>
	Nonstandard verbal concord	<me and John is well his sisters and brothers is well>
	Second person plural pronouns	<i send you these few lines hopen to find yous all in good helth>

important source when tracking the developing of varieties of English over the past two centuries or so. In this respect, emigrant letters can join other corpora of primary data in extending the database for varieties and in providing "insights into the nature of vernacular speech before this became available in audio form during the twentieth century." (Hickey 2019: 20)

Similarly, Laitinen and Auer (2014) work with the Letters of Artisans and the Labouring Poor corpus (LALP), which contains more than 2,000 letters of application for poor relief written between 1750 and 1835. Their goal is to provide a more coherent and representative overview of language use by focusing on the lower social ranks.

> **VIGNETTE 5.3** /h/ Insertion in the Language of Laboring Poor
> Variation with regard to /h/ is perhaps one of the most fascinating variables in the history of English. /h/ can either be deleted or inserted, and there is historical evidence for both processes: "Many Early ME sources exhibit variable use of the letter *h* in syllable-initial positions before vowels (that is, in such words as *hate, hopper*). Sometimes it is omitted where it is historically expected to be present, and sometimes it is added where it is not expected" (Milroy 1992: 140). Variation has been shown for the fourteenth-century *Norfolk Gilds* and the *Paston Letters* in the late fifteenth century. Charles Dickens used it frequently in his direct wording of Working-Class London speech: "'This is the **hend**, is it?' continued Miss Squeers, who being excited aspirated her *h*'s strongly!" (*Nicholas Nickleby*, chapter 42). It features in regional dialects of English and was also exported around the globe (Schreier 2020). While the feature was under the sociolinguistic radar for a long time, prescriptive attitudes developed in the second half of the eighteenth century: "First and foremost let me notice that worst of all faults, the leaving out of the aspirate where it ought to be, and putting it in where it ought not to be. This is a vulgarism not confined to this or that province of England, nor especially prevalent in one county or another, but common throughout England to persons of low breeding and inferior education, particularly those among the inhabitants of towns" (Alford 1864: 5).
>
> Corpora such as the LALP can help us get a much better understanding of this variable. In a first study, Auer (2021) showed that both dropping and insertion were found, at times in the hand of one and the same speaker (one speaker, Frances Soundry, wrote both "so sone after" and "go hafter it"). The feature was thus flourishing in the nineteenth century.

Historical sociolinguists have contributed to our understanding of ongoing language change, and this can be illustrated with a variable we know already: multiple negation. We saw in Chapters 1 and 4 that the usage of several negators was common in earlier periods of the English language and that it featured prominently in the English complaint tradition, being commented on negatively in the eighteenth century. What we don't know is how frequently the feature occurred in written sources in the past, who used it when and how often, and how it declined over the centuries.

Nevalainen (2006: 258) aimed to "shed light on, the use of negative concord by lower social ranks in the late eighteenth century, when normative grammar was already exerting an influence on the written language."

She found that multiple negation occurs frequently in CEEC, and that its diachronic development was complex. The earliest and most frequent pattern is a sentential negator *not* followed by a negative indefinite, as in:

1. the which wollwynders be aponted to goy there wayes, sayng that thaye well *not* worke *no* more for ij s a sacke, for thaye doy not get iiij d a day. (CEEC, Sabine Johnson 1545, 417)

Only later, in the sixteenth and seventeenth centuries, was *never* used as a universal temporal negator in the past tense, as is still the case in present-day varieties of English:

2. I thinke ye weare never yet in no grownd of mine, and I never say no man naye. (CEEC, Henry Savile 1544)

Still later nonassertive forms developed: enny/enye ("I never at no sesun repordid enny shyche Wordys") and mixed constructions with both negative and nonassertive elements are still found in many present-day varieties of English (Nevalainen 2006: 258 ff.), including African American Vernacular English (Chapter 1).

Nevalainen (2006: 260) found that "the decline of negative concord and concomitant rise of nonassertive indefinites appears to have been a selective process from above in terms of the writer's education and social status." Between 1500 and 1800, there was a steady decrease in multiple negation, and the process was spearheaded by male writers with formal education and members of the upper social ranks (Figure 5.5).

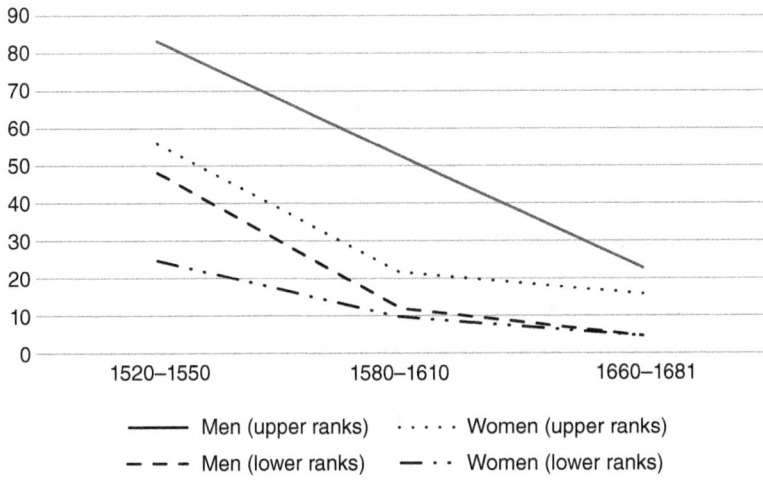

Figure 5.5 Multiple negation by social rank and gender. Adapted from Nevalainen (2006: 262).

As discussed above, this has to be handled with care as the data are sketchy and the overall sample is skewed. Data for female writers comes from the upper ranks exclusively, that is the nobility and gentry; there are hardly any documents for women from the lower social strata (due to a lack of schooling and low literacy levels overall). Though the figures for lower-rank men are less representative, the sociolinguistic trend is clear: Multiple negation occurs most often in writings produced by men and women from the upper classes.

A more fine-grained analysis (Nevalainen & Raumolin-Brunberg 2003) differentiates between (1) nonprofessional upper ranks (nobility and gentry), (2) upper-rank professionals (members of the gentry who held administrative offices or worked as lawyers or secretaries for the nobility and gentry), and (3) social aspirers (born to social ranks who showed social mobility, particularly to the rank of gentry). Table 5.4 (adapted from Nevalainen & Raumolin-Brunberg 2003: 151) indicates that, by the late sixteenth century, multiple negation disappeared quickly in the writings of men in the upper ranks, with social aspirers acting as early adopters: "negative concord had largely disappeared among the higher ranks, male and female, before the era of prescriptive grammar. In the course of the eighteenth and nineteenth centuries, the prescriptive movement stigmatized multiple negation" (Nevalainen 2006: 264).

Table 5.4 *Decline of multiple negation between 1460 and 1599, by social rank. Adapted from Nevalainen and Raumolin-Brunberg (2003: 151).*

Period	Nonprofessionals (upper ranks)	Upper-rank professionals	Social aspirers
1460–79	91% (111/120)	85% (57/67)	-
1480–1519	75% (18/24)	66% (29/44)	-
1520–59	46% (42/78)	59% (98/166)	20% (27/136)
1560–99	10% (298/330)	18% (30/163)	2% (1/55)

This intensified in the second half of the eighteenth century and negative concord continued to decline steadily (at least in writing). Sociohistorical corpora such as the CEEC provide an empirical basis to look into sociolinguistic variation and change in the period between Late Middle and Late Modern English (roughly 1400–1800). The effects of social stratification and class-based differentiation of sociolinguistic variables echo what has been found by William Labov and others in present-day English (Chapters 2 and 3), thus attesting to the strength of the uniformitarian principle.

Historical sociolinguistics has also provided valuable information on language variation in single speakers. Bergs (2015) provides a pertinent study of individual variation in writers, depending on whether they write themselves or for another person. The study is based on the Paston Letters, a collection of 421 documents with about 245,000 words, authored by fifteen family members, eleven male and four female. The Pastons were a well-known gentry family from Norfolk. Their letters come from three generations of family members, written between 1421 and 1503: Generation I represented by William I and Agnes Paston; Generation II represented by John I, his wife Margaret, Edmond I, Elizabeth, William II, and Clement II; and Generation III represented by the two brothers John II and III, Margery, Edmond II, Walter, and William III.

The number of autographed and dictated letters varies considerably. Interestingly, most letters written by males were autographed (Clement, John II, John III, Walter), whereas many of the letters by female family members were dictated – evidence of high illiteracy rates among women in the fifteenth century. Authorship is usually clear in the case of autographed letters, so they can be used for studying processes of ongoing change. Moreover, the Paston Letters are particularly relevant as some of the family members acted as both authors and scribes; family members wrote for relatives who could not read or write. The question, then, is: How do individuals vary in their writing conventions according to whether they write the letters themselves or for someone else? And how would they use traditional and innovative forms under these different circumstances?

Edmond II, John II, and John III, all representatives of Generation III, wrote both for themselves and as scribes for their mother Margaret. Bergs analyzed variation in third person plural pronouns, which were in the process of change in the fifteenth century. The Old English pronoun forms *heo* "they", *hem* "them," and *here* "their" were gradually replaced in the Middle English period by the new, innovative *th*-pronouns *they, their, them* (Watts 2012):

- Nominative: Old English *Hi(e)* → Middle English *Thei* → (Early) Modern English *They*
- Genitive: Old English *Hire/heora* → Middle English *Here/their* → (Early) Modern English *Their*
- Dative: Old English *Him/heom* → Middle English *Hem/them* → (Early) Modern English *Them*
- Accusative: Old English *Hi(e)* → Middle English *Hem/them* → (Early) Modern English *Them*

Though the origins and early diffusion of these forms remain unclear (Cable & Baugh 2002), Middle English documents showed a lot of variation. Whereas the the-pronouns were frequent in the North (which points to

Scandinavian influence), the proclamation of Henry III in 1258, produced at the Court, only had *heo* and *heom*. Chaucer mostly wrote *they* in his works, though *here* and *hem* were found as well (particularly in *The Canterbury Tales*). *Hem* survived well into the fifteenth century and was still found in the works of Thomas Malory and Caxton's *Recuyell of the Historyes of Troye* (both produced around 1470).

The question, then, is whether Generation III Pastons (Edmond II, John II, and John III) would use traditional or innovative forms in their letters, and whether they would vary depending on if they wrote letters for themselves or for their mother. Table 5.5 lists the use of pronoun forms in letters, distinguished by autographed letters and dictations.

Table 5.5 *The use of third person pronoun forms in Generation III Paston family members, acting as authors and scribes. Adapted from Bergs (2015: 124).*

	Edmond II		John II		John III	
	Author	Scribe	Author	Scribe	Author	Scribe
Hem	-	5	3	4	60	21
Them	8	9	98	4	77	11
Here	-	1	-	-	2	4
Their	1	-	15	3	57	4
% innovative forms	100.0 (total N = 9)	60.0 (total N = 15)	97.4 (total N = 116)	63.6 (total N = 11)	68.4 (total N = 196)	37.5 (total N = 40)

Of course, token counts are low and one cannot conduct statistical tests. But it is interesting that all three writers show the same pattern when it comes to variation between innovative and traditional features. For instance, Edmond II only uses traditional pronoun forms when transcribing for his mother, never for himself; John II uses both *hem* and *them* when writing for his mother, but the conservative form is found only in 2.6 percent of all possible cases in his own letters; writing for himself, John III uses *hem* in 45 percent of all cases, but when his mother dictates, the percentage increases to 65.6 percent. All three Generation III speakers vary yet they all have systematic preferences, depending on their role as writers.

How are we to interpret this? All three speakers had an identical tendency to use more conservative language in letters written for their mother. In contrast, progressive forms are used more frequently in their own writing. It is tempting to claim that this is evidence of language change in progress (the older generation using *hem/here*, the younger one *them/their*), but of course we do not know how accurately the three sons rendered the speech dictated to them. As Bergs (2015: 114) writes:

What we could and should think about though is whether the choice of pronoun forms on part of the scribe was guided by the actual language of the author, or by the way the scribe thought the author should sound like. Perhaps women generally were supposed to sound more conservative and the scribes were inclined to represent that, despite the fact that Margaret actually showed different forms in her oral performance?

It is a great pity that the historical context is missing. It simply is not possible to travel back in time and apply the principle of accountability (Chapter 2), but one notes variation and change in Margaret's language as well. Bergs found that letters written between the 1430s and the 1460s had both traditional (conservative) and innovative forms, but in letters written after 1466 (the year her husband passed away), the innovative *th*-forms were used more often. Bergs suggests three possible explanations: (1) her language may simply have changed over time; (2) being the head of the family, her social role and also her language changed after her husband's death; or (3) Margaret was accommodating to the speech of younger generations (II and III).

To summarize, historical sociolinguists have contributed significantly to complete the picture of historical variation and change in English. Their analysis of different text types (letters in particular) has shown that individuals varied with regard to whom they wrote for and what they were writing about, that different social classes had distinct preferences for the usage of sociolinguistic variables, and that emigrant documents in particular are invaluable sources for reconstructing earlier forms of the language and for pinpointing archaic forms and innovations alike.

5.6 Conclusion

This chapter has shown that the language history of English is very much based on what we know about the upper ranks of society. Sociolinguistic histories "from below" have only recently been attempted, yet these pose special challenges. These include the availability of data, as members of the lower social classes did not enjoy the privilege of schooling and education, and also changes in the production of text types. The eighteenth century saw an increase in education and literacy in general, which meant that more people could produce data needed for diachronic research. The later Education Acts were crucial in this regard, and children of all social backgrounds were able to go to school as the social conditions changed rapidly. The study of historical sources produced before 1800 showed strong effects of social stratification, gender-related differences, and individual variation.

These findings are similar to advances in sociolinguistic theory in the twentieth century and attest to the strength of the uniformitarian principle.

Processes of standardization had a profound effect on how language was written. Before 1700, writings were typically localized and individualistic, a treasure chest for regional and social analysis, but once the norms of language became fixed (via selection, acceptance, elaboration, and codification), the rich amount of variation decreased quickly. Ironically, though in the eighteenth century more language was written and preserved than ever before, the value for historical sociolinguistics reduced as materials became more uniform. Nevertheless, letters in particular provide a promising resource: Emigrants from lower ranks wrote home from English-speaking colonies all over the world and their language has further strengthened the importance of historical sociolinguistics as a subdiscipline in its own right.

> **Take-Home Messages**
>
> - In data collected for an analysis of sociolinguistic variation across individuals and groups, there are distinctions between real and apparent time approaches..
> - The uniformitarian principle assumes that the linguistic mechanisms observable today resemble those that operated in the past.
> - The social conditions of British society changed considerably between 1600 and 1900.
> - The sociolinguistic history of a language should include representative information from all social classes at all times. Many traditional histories of English have not focused on "from below."
> - The transformation of Late Middle English society favored publication in English (and not Latin or French).
> - Standardization of English spanned several centuries and included processes of selection, codification, elaboration, and acceptance.
> - Standardization involved the fixing of orthography, grammar, and lexicon in the eighteenth century and the first half of the nineteenth century. Phonology standardized only toward the end of the nineteenth century.
> - A southeastern variety of English was selected because the seats of government and higher education were based there.
> - The methods of historical sociolinguistics require data with empirical, social, and historical validity.
>
> Plays, trial proceedings, verbatim witness depositions and/or accounts, letters, diaries, and autobiographies provide primary data, letters perhaps being the most important genre.

Activities

5.1 Visit www.ons.gov.uk/peoplepopulationandcommunity/culturalidentity/language/articles/languageinenglandandwales/2013-03-04#proficiency-in-english. Track the origins and regional diffusion of three languages of choice.

5.2 This is the beginning of *Troilus and Criseyde* (late fourteenth century, written by Geoffrey Chaucer in a variety of East Midlands English). Compare the original passage with the present-day English translation and identify changes in verbal morphology (word endings), lexicon, and syntax (word order):

> 1 The double sorwe of Troilus to tellen,
> 2 That was the king Priamus sone of Troye,
> 3 In lovinge, how his aventures fellen
>
> 4 Fro wo to wele, and after out of Ioye,
> 5 My purpos is, er that I parte fro ye
> 6 Thesiphone, thou help me for tendyte
> 7 Thise woful vers, that wepen as I wryte!
>
> 8 To thee clepe I, thou goddesse of torment,
> 9 Thou cruel Furie, sorwing ever in peyne;
> 10 Help me, that am the sorwful instrument
> 11 That helpeth lovers, as I can, to pleyne!
> 12 For wel sit it, the sothe for to seyne,
> 13 A woful wight to han a drery fere,
> 14 And, to a sorwful tale, a sory chere.

And here is the translation into modern English:

> 1 Troilus's double sorrow for to tell,
> 2 he that was son of Priamus King of Troy,
> 3 and how, in loving, his adventures fell
>
> 4 from grief to good, and after out of joy,
> 5 my purpose is, before I make envoy.
> 6 Thesiphone, do you help me, so I might
> 7 pen these sad lines, that weep now as I write.
>
> 8 I call on you, goddess who does torment,
> 9 you cruel Fury, sorrowing ever in pain:

10 help me, who am the sorrowful instrument
11 who (as I can) help lovers to complain.

12 Since it is fitting to tell the truth,
13 for a dreary mate a woeful soul to grace,
14 and for a sorrowful tale a sorry face.

What strikes you most when comparing the two samples?

5.3 In his *Proposal for Correcting, Improving, and Ascertaining the English Tongue* (published in 1712). Jonathan Swift wrote:

> if it [English] were once refined to a certain standard, perhaps there might be ways found out to fix it for ever, or at least till we are invaded and made a conquest by some other state ... I see no absolute necessity why any language should be perpetually changing; for we find many examples to the contrary ... Besides the grammar-part, wherein we are allowed to be very defective, th[ose persons] will observe many gross improprieties, which however authorized, and grown familiar, ought to be discarded.

Given that Jonathan Swift was a satirist, one does not know how serious this suggestion was, but discuss whether such views can be implemented. Who benefits when "gross improprieties" in language are (or rather: can or perhaps should be) "discarded"?

5.4 Look at Table 5.3 again, bearing in mind that Margaret, as she became older, used more progressive forms in her own letters. Which of the three explanations is most appealing in your view?

Key Terms

acceptance
age grading
bad-data problem
Chancery Standard
codification
Corpus of Early English Correspondence (CEEC)
elaboration
emigrant letters
empirical validity

historical validity
language histories from below
Old Bailey Corpus (OBC)
real vs. apparent time principle
Received Pronunciation (RP)
selection
social validity
Standard English (StE)
superdiversity
uniformitarian principle

Further Reading

For an excellent collection of handbook articles on selected issues in English historical sociolinguistics, I would suggest:
Hernández-Campoy, J. C. & Conde-Silvestre, J. C., eds. (2012). *The Handbook of Historical Sociolinguistics* (Blackwell Handbooks in Linguistics). Malden, MA and Oxford: Wiley-Blackwell.

A good survey of methods and theories is:
McColl Millar, R. (2012). *English Historical Sociolinguistics*. Edinburgh: Edinburgh University Press.

The relationship between sociolinguistics and language change is clearly elucidated in:
Nevalainen, T. (2006). Historical Sociolinguistics and Language Change. In: A. Kemenade & B. Los, eds., *The Handbook of the History of English*. Malden, MA and Oxford: Blackwell, 558–588.

And one of the classic readings, with a strong focus on data handling, is:
Nevalainen, T. & Raumolin-Brunberg, H. (2003). *Historical Sociolinguistics. Language Change in Tudor and Stuart England*. London: Longman.

CHAPTER **6**

Interactional Sociolinguistics

In This Chapter ...

... we will explore language usage and interaction in general and discuss the overlap of sociolinguistics with the fields of pragmatics and discourse analysis. We will investigate the conventional patterns used by speakers when they construct, participate in, and evaluate discourse at large. The concept of face is an important one here, namely the self-image of speakers that they wish to maintain and protect via the sociolinguistic resources available to them: speech events in the form of narratives, telephone conversations, weblogs, university lectures, and so forth. Context effects on sociolinguistic interaction are discussed with examples of turn-taking, power, solidarity, and cross-cultural communication, and also with a focus on social hierarchies and language practices in the workplace. We conclude with a discussion of crossing and translanguaging in multilingual contexts.

6.1	Sociolinguistic Aspects of Interaction	*page* 155
6.2	The Sociolinguistics of Discourse Markers: The Case of *Uhm*	159
6.3	Inferencing, Contextualizing, Indexicality	163
	Vignette 6.1: John J. Gumperz (1922–2013)	165
	Vignette 6.2: Gang Graffiti as a Sociolinguistic Genre	166
6.4	Losing and Keeping Face	168
6.5	Language in the Workplace	173
6.6	Crossing and Translanguaging	178
6.7	Conclusion	182
	Take-Home Messages	184
	Activities	184
	Key Terms	185
	Further Reading	186

6.1 Sociolinguistic Aspects of Interaction

A good way of introducing this chapter is to reflect on the options speakers have when they perform everyday language tasks, no matter how frequent they may be. For instance, let's consider possible ways of asking someone for a favor, what time it is, or when a homework assignment is due. Actually, there are quite a few options for how to ask when you have to hand in your homework:

1. Homework assignment due when?
2. I am really sorry to bother you, but could you tell me when the homework assignment is due?
3. Hmmm, I can't seem to find the date for the homework assignment …

These requests vary in form and elaboration, so much in fact that sometimes it may not even be obvious that they are a request. There are thus different strategies available for us to achieve goals. As we saw in the previous chapters, speakers constantly make choices about how to use language, and these options depend on the sociolinguistic characteristics of the individuals in interaction, on context, setting, and topic (Chapter 3). We showed that sociolinguists study how language works in society on a macrolevel while also being interested in microaspects that relate to language use on a speaker level. **Interactional sociolinguistics** deals with how listeners interpret speech and how they create meaning by choosing their words or making sense of them. It is interdisciplinary and dynamic as it is placed at the intersection of discourse analysis, the ethnography of speaking, anthropology, and the sociology of language.

Discourse analysis seen through a sociolinguistic lens is a vast field and we can give only the shortest of introductions here. Generally, there is a distinction between top-down and bottom-up perspectives:

- Top-down: What is the global structure of discourse? How is a narrative structured? What major thematic blocks are used when one tells a story? How does doctor–patient interaction work, when one of the participants has more knowledge and authority?
- Bottom-up: What are the minor units that combine to make larger discursive structures? How do these utterances fit together to form larger units? What is the function of discourse markers and what cues are there so that speakers can alternate and take **turns**?

Structural approaches focus on the elements of discourse and study how they are patterned, whereas functional approaches analyze language use in a range of functions (referential, stylistic, social) to provide a broader picture of, for instance, how speakers cooperate and when they take turns in interaction. The basic assumption in both approaches is that language is adapted to different situations, functions, and uses so that it has different social values for its speakers. This is sociolinguistically relevant in that language represents a repertoire of speech styles, making discursive variation central in all kinds of speakers, hearers, actions, and events (see Chapter 1).

Research on **Conversation Analysis** has demonstrated that the way we engage in discourse is neatly ordered at every level of interaction and that the way we organize speech depends on intuitive knowledge that is shared by all participants. As a result, conversation is a special speech event with coherent structure, and we all must have some routine which helps us to produce and interpret meaning. If we did not, conversation would break down.

To give a hands-on example, discourse is structured in ritual responses to initiative utterances, the so-called **adjacency pairs**. Take the following everyday exchange as a case in point:

Pat:	Hey there.	(Greeting)
Liz:	Hi.	(Greeting)
Pat:	How's it going?	(Question)
Liz:	Not too bad I guess.	(Answer)
Pat:	Great to hear that.	(Response)
Liz:	And how are you doing?	(Question)
Pat:	Super-busy, but everything fine.	(Answer)
Liz:	Oh yeah, work work work …	(Response)

The basic organization of such exchanges is that greetings are returned, that questions are answered, requests are responded to, and so on. Speakers share these beliefs and any failure to do so is quickly noticed and occasionally commented on. At the same time, speakers do not interact simultaneously. One of them typically holds the **floor** and then there are opportunities to switch, in so-called turns, which is when others may take over and speak in their own right.

Participants in a conversation typically switch between taking on the role of speakers and hearers. We all are both, following internalized systems to indicate when our turn is no longer held and when it is handed over to another participant. This can be an active process on the part of the speaker ("What do you think?") or the result of an interruption ("sorry to interrupt …", "this reminds me of …"). A changing floor is signaled by ritual inserts ("Well …") and also by intonation and pausing.

There are major differences between speakers and communities when it comes to gaining the floor and these are of great importance for research in cross-cultural contexts. Sometimes there is a convenient pause before the floor is handed over or taken, sometimes there is struggle as speakers take the floor in a way which may come across as aggressive or rude ("Stop interrupting me!", "I'm speaking now." etc.). Speakers from different communities have various assumptions about how turns are signaled and enacted, and this is a frequent source of misunderstandings (see the concept of face below).

There are also different expectations concerning the role of listeners in an exchange. Sometimes active feedback and interaction are in order, in the forms of back-channeling and feedback ("mhm", "right"), sometimes speakers remain more silent and engage less regularly. This may also be a source of misunderstandings: Providing little reaction may be (mis)interpreted as a lack of interest, whereas a lot of feedback may come across as overzealous. This is evident in cross-cultural communication: There are different societal and cultural values in terms of floor-gaining, back-channeling, and also extralinguistic criteria such as making eye contact. When working in the US, for instance, I found it rather irritating how often I was interrupted, as in Switzerland it is customary to give someone the floor for longer periods. In sum, speech communities have different practices of gap and overlap, that is pauses in discourse and switching the floor. Some communities value silence, others avoid it at all costs – whereas the former come across as uninterested or passive, the latter are seen as highly active and overly competitive.

While turn-taking conventions help speakers to avoid gaps and overlap in conversation, to ensure an exchange is smooth and effective, there are also preference structures. These refer to differences in form and frequency of all possible sequences; for example, the first sequence is typically an invitation, the second one an acceptance, and the third one a confirmation or rejection:

Pat: Would you like to come over for dinner on Saturday?
Liz: Sure!
Pat: That's great.

Some requests are not really direct but more elaborate, containing presequences and double confirmations:

Pat:	Sorry, are you busy right now?	response, question (presequence)
Liz:	No, it's OK.	Answer
Pat:	Could you do me a favor?	question (prerequest)
Liz:	Sure.	answer (commitment)
Pat:	Could you look at my paper for me?	Request
Liz:	Sure. No problem.	agree, comment
Pat:	Great. Thanks.	comment, thanks
Liz:	No problem.	comment

Last but not least, there is also conversational **repair-work** when there is confusion or misinformation. Discursive practices of clarification and correction may contain self-, other-, and other-initiated repair:

- Self-repair:
  - I saw Judy last Tuesday – sorry, Monday.
- Other-initiated repair:
  - A: I saw Judy last Tuesday.
  - B: *Uh* Tuesday? Are you sure?
  - A: No sorry, I saw her at the gym on Monday.
- Other-repair:
  - A. I saw Judy last Monday.
  - B: No it was Tuesday.
  - A: Of course, I saw her on Tuesday.

To sum up, the way we speak is structured and patterned, with essential elements such as the floor, the turn, and repair-work. These are crucial in discourse analysis and of great relevance to interactional sociolinguistics. Sociolinguists working in this field are interested in all facets of how people use language in everyday face-to-face interaction at the crossroads of sociolinguistics, the ethnography of speaking, and discourse analysis (Figure 6.1).

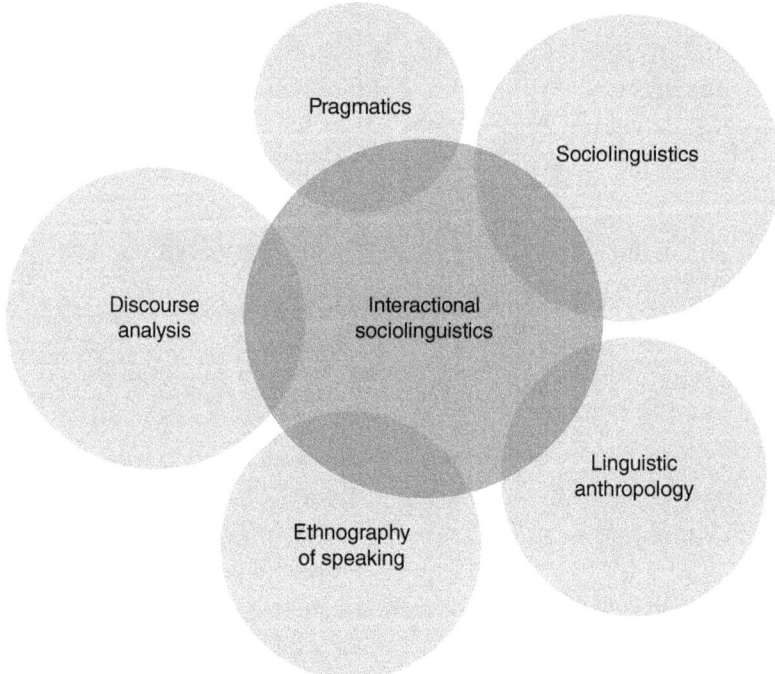

Figure 6.1 The interdisciplinary character of interactional sociolinguistics

Interactional sociolinguists assume that the knowledge of grammar and lexicon alone are not sufficient for successful interaction, and that it is the discursive context, both at microlevels and macrolevels, that helps us create meaning out of interaction. All speakers make inferences based on their intuitive knowledge, linguistic and encyclopedic, and share a set of beliefs and values that are embedded in the community's sociolinguistic repertoires. There is a common core of values and understandings of communicative goals and practices, including when and how to take the floor and take turns. Without such knowledge, conversation would be impossible.

An interesting question is how communicative practices relate to the social, cultural, and sociolinguistic world. While variable, discursive structures are patterned and sequential. Exchanges consist of recurrent pairs, preferences, repair, cues, and signals, all of which work together to create coherence in conversation. Interactional sociolinguists study how speakers signal and interpret meaning in social interaction and how they create and negotiate social identities and values as they interact. Let's illustrate this with a case study: the so-called hesitation phenomena *uhm, erm, uh* and so on.

6.2 The Sociolinguistics of Discourse Markers: The Case of *Uhm*

It should be clear by now that we have a system of sociolinguistic and discursive checks and balances, providing feedback, making sure that everything is understood properly, signaling that we are interested and following someone, and also indicating that we would like to take the floor and say something ourselves. We distinguish between understanding checks, such as *y'know, right?* or *isn't it?*, and attention signals: *m'hm, uh-huh, wow, really?* and so on. These discourse markers play an important role in the interactive relationship between speaker, hearer, and message and are crucial elements in the way discourse is structured. They are inserted regularly, very often when there is a potential turn, for instance to express a willingness to take the floor:

> Inserts ... are defined ... as a class of words: They are stand-alone words which are characterized in general by their inability to enter into syntactic relations with other structures. ... They comprise a class of words that is peripheral, both in the grammar and in the lexicon of the language. In fact, it may be questioned whether some inserts are words at all. (Biber et al. 1999: 1082)

Interesting questions in this context concern how many discourse markers there are (in different varieties of English), what their core pragmatic functions are, and how they vary and change (who uses which markers in what situation), the latter being of particular relevance here. There is no question that discourse markers are frequent. Probably all speakers of English around the world will say *well*, *okay*, and *errm* occasionally, even though they are usually not aware of this. (In my own teaching, I have become acutely aware of this when lecturing about hesitation phenomena – and it is striking to find that my students take note of this. On one memorable occasion, two students counted how often I said *okay* in a 90-minute lecture ... they obviously loved it.)

Take the following example from a rather formal setting: a live TV interview on the American National Broadcast Corporation (NBC) in 2012. The then senator Rick Santorum, who ran for the Republican nomination as presidential candidate in 2012, was interviewed by David Gregory and said the following on job opportunities in the US:

SANTORUM: Well, I, I don't – again, David, you know. I mean, I have seven kids. I can tell you, there's some who, you know, would, would do very well and excel, and others, you know what, they have, they have different skills, they have different things that they want to do with their lives. And, and the idea of sort of saying, "Well, unless you do this, then, you know, well, you're not just sort of, you know" ...
GREGORY: So ...
SANTORUM: ... "you're not sort of living up to our goals." I just disagree with that.

Isn't it striking that this short passage, taken from a highly formal setting, live on a TV show and with an audience of several millions, with maximum attention to speech (Chapter 3) and far removed from vernacular usage, contains more than a dozen discourse markers? We find eleven markers in Santorum's opening statement alone: *you know* (five times), *well* (three times), *and* (twice), *I mean* (once). Their function is to anchor the discourse, that is they are typically used at the beginning and end of utterances and provide important utterance on a pragmatic level. Discourse markers are common in all styles and kinds of speech, even at sermons and lectures.

Let's turn to the sociolinguistic importance of these markers and look at hesitation phenomena more closely: *er*, *um*, *erm*. Very often, they are considered to be characteristic of language planning, pauses in the cognitive processing of speech production (when we are searching for words in our mental lexicon), to avoid silence, or simply as hold-on markers while we are planning a next utterance (to avoid someone else taking the floor). Hesitation phenomena are frequent and carry potential for linguists who research "not only their precise function in the speech production process but also their socio-demographic distribution, their distribution in different genres, their use by non-native speakers and so on" (Staley & Jucker 2020: 21).

Historical pragmaticians (Jucker 2015) have argued that these markers have become more frequent in British and American English over the last 200 years (though one needs to take great care in interpreting written sources, particularly when it comes to typically spoken forms; cf. Chapter 5). A search of the *Corpus of Contemporary American English* (COCA) and the *British National Corpus* (BNC) retrieves many cases:

- Since having said that *erm*, I'm not immediately looking *erm*, for high expenditure, but I would hope that [BNC]
- Well Gordon and here we are with the *erm* the finished arrangement – are you pleased with it? (BNC; quoted in Tottie 2011: 182)

Tottie (2011) conducted a corpus-based study to show how sociodemographic groups vary in their frequency of hesitation phenomena. Normalizing the number of hesitators per 100,000 words, she found that *erm* and *er* occurred most frequently in male, older, and educated speakers (Figure 6.2).

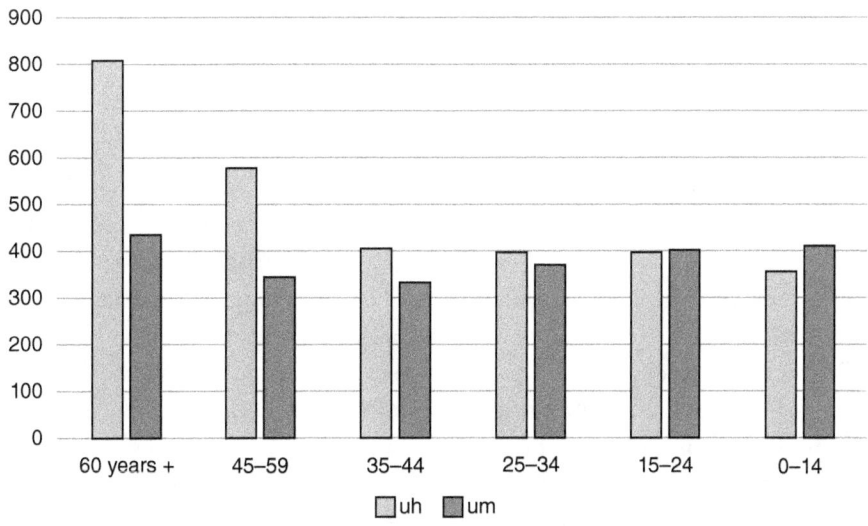

Figure 6.2 Hesitation phenomena by age-group in the BNC (normalized per 100,000 words). Adapted from Tottie (2011: 184–185).

She concluded that "the so-called filled pauses *er/uh* and *erm/um* are sociolinguistic markers that differentiate between registers of English and along gender, age and socio-economic class. Men, older people and educated speakers use more fillers than women, younger speakers and less educated speakers" (Tottie 2011: 173).

Hesitation phenomena are also important for studies of regional variation and ongoing change. Based on the analysis of Twitter data, Grieve (2014) showed that there were clear dividing lines in the US according to whether Twitter users had written *uh* or *um* in their tweets. Strikingly, the boundaries coincide with the major dialect areas: *um* is predominant in the South, New England, and the Great Lakes Area, *uh* in the Midlands and the Central states. Likewise, a comparative quantitative analysis of written and spoken corpora in several Germanic languages (English, Dutch, German, Norwegian, Danish, Faroese) and American and British English (Wieling et al. 2016) showed clear and consistent change patterns, with the use of *uhm* increasing over time relative to the use of *uh*.

Moreover, hesitation phenomena are subject to ongoing change and accommodation in migrant communities. Speakers of American English typically have filled pauses with more centralized vowels ([a ~ ə]), whereas in Spanish a lateral front vowel [e] is predominant. Erker and Bruso (2017) investigated *uh* and *em* in 24 Spanish-speaking residents of Boston, Massachusetts and reported that the usage of typically American vs. typically Spanish hesitators varied along sociolinguistic variables:

> participants who have lived in the United States for a larger fraction of their lives, who use English more frequently, and who do so more proficiently fill pauses differently when speaking Spanish than do those who have spent less time in the contact setting and whose English skills and usage are more restricted. (Erker & Bruso 2017: 205)

The longer originally Hispanic (Latino/Latinx) residents resided in the US and the more contact they had with speakers of American English, the more often they used an American English type *uh*. Individual differences correlated with contact intensity, making accommodation effects plausible (Chapter 3), which showed how sensitive these processes were. To sum up, though generally not noticed, hesitation phenomena carry a lot of sociolinguistic information on speakers and contexts. They serve as pragmatic markers, helping speakers to structure and plan discourse, hold the floor and gain attention, while at the same time they are subject to regional, social, and individual variation. Though short and barely noticeable, they fulfil a range of functions and are not stable diachronically. Remarkably, there are consistent patterns of variation and change, regardless of corpus and data used (spoken transcripts of TV shows, phonetic analysis of sociolinguistic interviews, Twitter messages, and so forth).

6.3 Inferencing, Contextualizing, Indexicality

We have seen throughout the book how important the context of utterances is for the kind of language used, in the form of different styles, dialects, address forms, or code-switching. Context is an important factor in variation as the frequency of sociolinguistic variables varies with the place and setting of an interaction (Chapter 3). Interactional sociolinguists are interested in these effects as well, yet from a different perspective. One of the major concerns is how interactants infer what others intend to communicate, particularly when the intention of an utterance is not explicit. The challenge is how speakers and hearers negotiate meaning and construct communicative meaning via the language they produce and perceive. Clearly, they must build on knowledge that is linguistic (i.e. phonological/prosodic, morphosyntactic, semantic, pragmatic), yet interpreting meaning through discourse is more than just knowing how to produce sounds and sentences. This is where issues related to **inferencing**, contextualizing, and indexicality are paramount.

Sociologists of language, such as **John Gumperz**, emphasize a relationship between language use and sociocultural embedding. Meaning is not given but jointly constructed: Social processes are interactively enacted via everyday interaction and there is a complex interplay of language and social/cultural knowledge (including communicative knowledge). While linguistic competence is necessary to produce language in everyday situations, it is our knowledge of social aspects that allows us to create, confirm, and modify meaning in interaction. There is thus a discrepancy between what is said and what is meant, and identifying intentions is in fact complex guesswork which draws on various levels of knowledge. As meaning is context-sensitive and dependent on speaker and situation, we necessarily need to know the specifics of context to create meaning.

There may be multiple ways of finding out what speakers mean when they say something. This can be illustrated with the simple word "Yes." "Yes" occurs frequently, in all styles and settings, as an expression of affirmation and acceptance, as in:

- "Is this your seat?" "Yes."
- "Did you go to the hairdresser?" "Yes."

There is a clear request for information here, so "yes" is an accurate response. But is this always the case? Consider the following exchanges:

- "Do you have a watch on you?" "Yes."
- "Do you know where Prof. Singh's office is?" "Yes."
- "Do you think it is a bit cold in here?" "Yes."

Again, there is some sort of a question-type utterance here, marked by prosody and other suprasegmental cues, which evokes a short affirmative response. However, the second set of questions differs from the first examples in that it is not an affirmation that is expected but some sort of responsive action. In other words, these are not really questions but demands disguised as questions. Whoever asks the question expects to gain information as to what time it is, to receive instructions about how to get to Prof. Singh's office, for instance, or they would like someone to get up and shut the window. Accordingly, the very same answer "yes" may be appropriate when information is requested but odd when the speaker indirectly asks for directions or active response. In other words: It is the speaker's task to interpret the meaning of questions. Phonetic and syntactic knowledge alone cannot account for how such interpretations work, so it must be the sociolinguistic competence and analysis of context (what is known about speakers and the utterance in general) that must be drawn upon here. Pragmatic knowledge allows hearers to bridge the gap between what is said and what is meant or intended.

Gumperz and Cook-Gumperz (2007) suggested that both speakers and hearers use background knowledge to coconstruct contextual presuppositions. By doing so, they use all available contextualization cues available to interpret the particular context. Cues may include prosody (tempo, volume, intonation, hesitation), repetition, formulaicity, shifts in style, and code-switching as well as all means that signal attitudes to what is said. The interpretation of contextualization cues allows participants to draw inferences about other participants and their interactional goals and to interpret special cases of meaning that are intended and not directly expressed. The relationship between context and discourse is codependent; language usage (and, for that matter, variation) is in part determined by context while it is essential in the construction of context at the same time.

Contextualization cues influence the interpretation of interactive purposes via **presuppositions**: the knowledge speakers bring into a conversation. This allows them to distinguish between what is serious and what is an ironic or flippant remark, what is essential as opposed to what is small talk, and so forth. This is of high relevance sociolinguistically, as language variation underlies the construction, maintenance, and renegotiation of identity (Chapter 3) and allows interactants to clear up potential misunderstandings in intercultural and interethnic communication.

> **VIGNETTE 6.1** John J. Gumperz (1922–2013)
>
> John Gumperz was born in Germany and emigrated to the US in 1939, where he served in the US military. He first received a BA in chemistry (as did William Labov, coincidentally) at the University of Cincinnati and then studied linguistics at the University of Michigan. His 1954 PhD was a fieldwork-based ethnographic study of the Svabian dialects spoken by German immigrants in the State of Michigan. After a two-year research stay in India (1954–56), Gumperz worked at the University of California (Berkeley), where he became Professor of Anthropology and Director of the Language Behaviour Research Laboratory.
>
> John Gumperz is one of the founding fathers of interactional sociolinguistics, and his major focus was on linking language usage with sociological theories. Among others, he worked on code-switching and multilingualism and (with Dell Hymes) on the ethnography of speaking, which argued that social norms and conventions are created via everyday language. His major theoretical contribution is the introduction of contextualization cues. According to this approach, it is not possible to separate language and social context, which is essential in the construction of meaning. Speakers share knowledge of contextual and communicative effects, which they exploit in successful interaction.

Contextualization cues play a major role in constructing social action in their function as indexical signs. Crucially, and this is where pragmatics plays a major role, it is difficult to assign referential meaning. The communicative function of these signs is mostly relational; that is, there can be no context-free interpretations as they necessarily depend on shared rules and expectations. The manner in which we contextualize meaning and interpret contextualization depends on sociocultural conventions, and all communicative cooperation rests on a shared repertoire of values and expectations (cf. also Goffman's 1983 concept of the interaction order).

Now there is a catch in here: Shared sociocultural knowledge entails familiarity with the predominant structure of communicative genres in various settings; there must be some tacit consensus on kinds of **genres** that allows speakers not only to tell a joke but also to develop an awareness of situations when jokes are appropriate in the first place. This varies from community to community: For instance, while some cultures find it appropriate to have lighthearted sermons at a funeral, sharing funny anecdotes, the same practice would be a severe breach of sociocultural conventions elsewhere. Accordingly, genres are identified as:

> frames, embodying presuppositions associated with ideological values and principles of communicative conduct that in a way bracket the talk and thereby affect the way in which we assess or interpret what transpires in the course of the encounter. (Gumperz 1999: 456)

Knowledge about the function of genres is specific historically and culturally, it overlaps with politeness theory and allows speakers to identify and solve recurrent communicative problems (such as misinterpretations of demands and questions).

VIGNETTE 6.2 Gang Graffiti as a Sociolinguistic Genre

Instances of gang graffiti are usually interpreted as markers of territory or threats to other gangs in the urban area. As Adams and Winter (1997: 338) argue, there are "few studies offering in-depth discussion of the form and frequency of the various acts that constitute it or examining its relationship to other discourse genres in the community." Based on research in Phoenix, Arizona, Adams and Winter aim to get a better understanding of the motivation and function of gang graffiti in public places. Their conclusion is that there exists a variety of utterance types and that "their interactive nature and their location reveals a more complex discourse system reflecting the social structure of the gang subculture" (1997: 338). They fulfil several functions: They are public displays to advertise gangs, give a voice to individual members in collective communities with strict values and codes, indicate social networks within and between gangs (naming friends and enemies), represent members' views of gang life and, last but not least, honor the dead. The range of functions is much broader than commonly assumed. While gang graffiti is essentially an antilanguage, created and used by a marginal group with high solidarity, it reinforces group solidarity far from the mainstream. Crossing out gang graffiti is an act of aggression and a direct threat. Consequently, graffiti excludes those outside the group and is to some extent antagonistic, territorial, and aggressive, yet functions as cooperative discourse following explicit norms and conventions. So next time you spot graffiti, try to decipher whether or not it carries meaning for individuals or entire groups.

6.3 Inferencing, Contextualizing, Indexicality

Figure 6.3 Graffiti in the inner city.

Gumperz and Cook-Gumperz (2007) provide a nice example of how meaning is negotiated on the basis of the communicative intent, inferences, and sociocultural knowledge of the participants. The context is as follows: After a graduate seminar at an American university, an African American student approached the instructor, who was talking to a mixed group of European American and African American students, and requested a letter of reference:

STUDENT: "Could I talk to you for a minute? I'm gonna apply for a fellowship and I was wondering if I could get a recommendation?"

INSTRUCTOR: "O.K. Come along to the office and tell me what you want to do."

As the instructor and the rest of the group left the room, the African American student turned his head and said to the other students: "Ahma git me a gig!"

This short dialogue demonstrates how the student distinguishes between two different **frames**, using separate indexical signs when speaking with his fellow students and the instructor. At first, the student uses appropriate contextualization cues (prosody, lexis) with the (European American) instructor but then, after being asked to follow him to the office, switches to African American English when addressing the other students, perhaps to ease the feeling of embarrassment. There are different presuppositions about interaction with the instructor and students, which is expressed with a code-switch from Standard American to African American English. Another example for frames is the use and function of insults. In some genres, they are utterly abusive, in others they serve as markers of solidarity. Ritual insults, politically incorrect and parent advisory, are used by adolescents to create identity and form in-group connections. As part of their sociocultural style, ritual insults are efficient and strong communicative practices in the construction of common identities, particularly in male-dominated subcultures off the mainstream.

To sum up, context is an important factor in variation, and interpreting meaning depends on a range of cues, genres, and inferences. Communication involves much more than linguistic information alone and depends on pragmatic and context-related knowledge as well. As a result, meaning is coproduced by interactants and allows them to construct particular cultural and social identities through communicative practices.

6.4 Losing and Keeping Face

Face is a well-known concept, often used metaphorically in everyday speech: We lose or keep face, respect someone else's face, a face can be threatened, and so forth. All this is essentially "a social phenomenon; [face] comes into being when one person comes into presence of another; it is created through the communicative moves of interactants" (Tracy 1990: 210). Successful communication is a balancing act as the faces of all participants have to be respected. Of course, language plays an important role here, in that the sociolinguistic repertoires of speakers are used as a resource to meet one's own needs while not disregarding someone else's.

The American sociologist Erving Goffman originally defined face as "the positive social value a person effectively claims for himself by the line others assume he has taken during a particular contact. Face is an image of self delineated in terms of approved social attributes" (Goffman 1955: 340). Goffman's approach to conceptualize *face* rested on several premises:

- Face is an emotive representation of a speaker's self and others.
- The general goal of social encounters is to maintain face.
- Human nature involves self-regulating participants (who follow certain standards of behavior).
- Human nature is not natural but a "ritually organized system of social activity" (discussion in Goffman 1967: 132).

All speakers have *face* wants and needs but their everyday interactive practices may threaten it in various ways. Let's take directness as a case in point: In some speech communities, requests need to be decorated and ornamented with elaborate hedges ("Excuse me, I am awfully sorry to barge in like this, but if it's no trouble I really wouldn't mind having a cup of tea.") whereas elsewhere it is accepted to be maximally direct ("Get me a tea," or even "TEA!"). This can lead to severe disruptions and misunderstandings as short direct responses are often considered rude and impolite. This is particularly pertinent in intercultural communication as some acts (e.g. requests, commands, but also invitations) are inherently face-threatening acts (see below). In such cases, social interaction involves a lot of **face-work**: "the communicative strategies that are the enactment, support, or challenge of [socially] situated identities" (Tracy 1990: 210). Goffman (1967: 34) defines face-work as follows:

> By face-work I mean to designate the actions taken by a person to make whatever he is doing consistent with face. Face-work serves to counteract "incidents" – that is, events whose effective symbolic implications threaten face. Thus poise is one important type of face-work, for through poise the person controls his embarrassment and hence the embarrassment that he and others might have over his embarrassment. Whether or not the full consequences of face-saving actions are known to the person who employs them, they often become habitual and standardized practices; they are like traditional plays in a game or traditional steps in a dance.

Goffman (2005) approaches face within a framework of the **interaction order**, which consists of spatial units (*situations*, in Goffman's terminology), verbal and nonverbal communication (*moves*), participation units (*participants*), and system and ritual constraints *(agreement or repairs)*. Constraints include, among others, contact signals that announce the beginning and end of communication, turnover signals, repair signals and norms inducing honesty (Goffman 1981: 14–15). The interaction order manifests itself in every interaction, leading to various situation-dependent utterances related to face, and is thus highly relevant for the sociology of language and sociolinguistics alike.

Brown and Levinson (1987) developed the concept further by embedding it into politeness theory, defining it as "the public self-image that every member wants to claim for himself" (61). Very much like Goffman, they stated that face "can be lost, maintained, or enhanced, and it must be constantly attended to in interaction" (62). They made an important theoretical distinction between a speaker's **negative face** ("the want of every 'competent adult member' that his actions be unimpeded by others") and their **positive face** ("the want of every member that his wants be desirable to at least some members"; 61–62). Negative face refers to the basic claim to territories, personal preserves, rights to non-distraction: all kinds of freedom of action and rejection of imposition from other parties. Positive face expresses itself in a positive self-image or amiable personality, the desire to be appreciated and approved. These two dimensions are paramount in all kinds of face threat, as they may be difficult to reconcile. When we engage in interaction, there is a permanent clash between appealing to positive face (being liked, being popular) and negative face (ensuring our own interests and stakes).

Discrepancies between the two faces occur on a regular basis: "[It] is intuitively the case that certain kinds of acts intrinsically threaten face, namely those acts that by their nature run contrary to the face wants of the addressee and/or speaker" (Brown & Levinson 1987: 62). Though we are not really aware of it, most of our interactions potentially contain **face-threatening acts** (**FTAs**), both on speaker and addressee levels, which in turn are expressed by the kind of language we use (Table 6.1).

Table 6.1 *Threats to positive and negative face in speakers and addressees. Adapted from Brown & Levinson (1987: 62).*

	Speaker	Addressee
Negative face	– Expressing thanks (Speaker admits debt) – Promises and offers (Speaker commits him/herself to future action)	– Orders, requests – Suggestions, advice – Threats, warnings
Positive face	– Apologies – Self-humiliation, self-contradiction – Confessions, admissions of guilt or responsibility	– Disapproval, criticism, contempt – Contradictions, disagreements

Brown and Levinson (1987) argue that negotiating negative and positive face is the joint responsibility of all participants and thus not exclusively under the speaker's control. FTAs can occur at any time and impede the negative or positive faces of all participants. Brown and Levinson categorize face threats according to whether they threaten a negative or a positive face and whether they jeopardize the speaker's or the addressee's face. An apology or an excuse potentially threatens the negative face of a speaker since it could be interpreted as a way of acknowledging debt or responsibility. Often, FTAs are ritualized and encoded in specific terms, resembling Goffman's (1967: 12) "habitual and standardized practices."

The problem is that we all need to carry out FTAs when imposing ourselves on the needs of an addressee or encroaching into someone else's territory somehow. FTAs are related to polite vs. impolite behavior and can take various forms. They are found both at positive and negative face levels and may occur ...

- on record without redressive action, baldly and directly:
  - "Listen, I have got an idea."
  - "Add three cups of flour and stir vigorously."
  - "Get me a cup of coffee!"
- on record with redressive action, with positive politeness:
  - "Goodness, aren't your roses beautiful! Actually, I was just coming by to borrow a cup of flour."
  - "What a beautiful vase this is! Where did it come from?"
  - "I am very sorry but I was reserving that seat for a friend."
- on record with redressive action, with negative politeness:
  - "You couldn't by any chance pass the salt, please, could you?"
  - "I'm awfully sorry to bother you, and I wouldn't but I'm in an awful fix, so I wondered if by any chance ..."
- off record:
  - "Don't you think it's a bit cold in here?" (meaning: "Please close the window.")
  - "This soup's a bit bland." (meaning: "Please pass the salt.")

This is closely related to politeness theory, which is produced interactionally between different speakers. Drawing on the two kinds of faces, positive politeness is defined on the one hand as:

> redress directed to the addressee's positive face, his perennial desire that his wants (or the actions/acquisitions/values resulting from them) should be thought of as desirable. Redress consists in partially satisfying that desire by communicating that one's own wants (or some of them) are in some respects similar to the addressee's wants. (Brown & Levinson 1987: 101)

Negative politeness, on the other hand, is:

> redressive action addressed to the addressee's negative face: his want to have his freedom of action unhindered and his attention unimpeded. It is the heart of respect behaviour, just as positive politeness is the kernel of 'familiar' and 'joking' behaviour. (Brown & Levinson 1987: 129; please note that the authors used generic *he*, which is no longer practiced today)

The connection between FTAs and politeness lies at the root of the dilemmas we encounter in our everyday lives. For instance, it is impossible to give someone an order without intruding into their self-control (thus risking loss of negative face) or to admit a serious blunder or oversight without admitting guilt or carelessness (affecting one's own positive face). Language offers a repertoire of techniques to minimize the risk of face loss, such as making compliments before asking for a favor or admitting a mistake, to use high-solidarity kinship terms or identity markers ("sorry mate, my mistake"), to avoid disagreement or insults by using diminutives ("you are not stupid but … well, just not super-intelligent"). Similar techniques are applied to avoid negative politeness, for instance by …

> … being indirect when asking for a favor:
> - "You couldn't possibly tell me the time, please?"
> - "I don't suppose I could possibly ask you for a cup of flour, could I?"
>
> … minimizing an imposition:
> - "I just came over to ask you if I can borrow a tiny bit of flour."
> - "Just a second of your precious time …"
>
> … showing deference, using honorific terms:
> - "I don't think you ought to do that, Mr. President."
>
> … using ritual apologies:
> - "I really don't like to do this, but I need to ask you to be quiet."
> - "I am very sorry, but I have been waiting for half an hour now."
>
> … impersonalizing contexts and participants:
> - "This letter has to be delivered immediately."
> - "Student papers are due today at midnight."

The question is how the weight of an FTA can be measured. Brown and Levinson (1987) suggest that three factors need to be taken into account:

1. the social distance between speaker and hearer
2. the power and authority of speaker and hearer
3. the absolute ranking of the imposition in a given culture.

These are of high relevance for Gumperz's contextualization cues, as knowledge about power, status, and cultural embedding need to be shared so as to be understood. Differences in power or social distance typically give rise to formal vs. informal styles ("Excuse me, would you by any chance have the time?" vs. "Got the time, mate?", "Excuse me sir, would it be alright if I smoke?" vs. "Mind if I smoke?"). There are also cultural differences between varieties of English, which are a reflection of distinct contextualization or (on a larger scale) politeness patterns. Whereas speakers of upper-middle-class British English would ask, "Look, I'm terribly sorry to bother you but would there be any chance of your lending me just enough money to get a railway ticket to get home?", speakers of other varieties would consider this too ornate or posh, opting for shorter and more direct requests ("Got some spare?"). The interpretation of such utterances can lead to serious conflict: Incorporating "wrong" politeness strategy (e.g. being too direct) may come across as a severe and unacceptable threat to negative face and may cause ultimately harmful conflict situations. There may be an:

> experience of emotional frustration in conjunction with perceived incompatibility of values, norms, face orientations, goals, scarce resources, processes, and/or outcomes between a minimum of two parties from two different cultural communities in an interactive situation. (Ting-Toomey & Oetzel 2001: 17)

The field of **variationist pragmatics** studies situated responses in distinct varieties, for instance the various ritualized responses to thanks across different varieties of English (Schneider 2005) or different practices to open or close a conversation.

To sum up, the concept of face is central in interactional sociolinguistics. Speakers (and hearers) are engaged in acts of keeping their own interests while at the same time risking loss of face. There is a clash between positive and negative face, the interests of being amiable and friendly impinge on one's own freedom to make decisions. This operates even in the most trivial everyday interactions such as when we are asking what time it is or when we are inviting someone for a dinner party. Language offers an array of resources to minimize face loss, though the practices may vary between communities and sociocultural groups. The concept of face has taken center stage in an influential politeness theory (Brown & Levinson 1987), where negative and positive politeness are distinguished in speakers and addressees. This has consequences for the use of language in asynchronous power relationships, as we will discover in the next section.

6.5 Language in the Workplace

The workplace is a particularly important setting for various reasons:

1. Typically, there is a strict hierarchy between employees, with various levels of administration, production and so on, allowing for sociolinguistic stratification and power relationships.
2. Workplaces have transformed radically as a result of new developments in IT and communication technology, so there are alternative communication channels and modes of speaking (Jaworski & Thurlow 2010).

3. Globalization has led to there being a larger and more mobile workforce around the world, which means that more and more people with diverse backgrounds interact on a professional basis (see Chapter 9).
4. It has become cheaper to travel, so the rise in global tourism leads to unprecedented contacts between speakers of English in holiday destinations and the emergence of grassroots Englishes around the world (see Chapter 4).

As a result, the workplace as such has become immensely diverse, from large multinational corporations to corner shops, from diving schools to coffee plantations, and there has been an increase in multicultural communication in various settings. In the words of Ladegard and Jenks (2015: 2):

> It is not only a site of employment where money is made and institutional roles are enacted through various forms of discourse; but it is also a location where people engage in social actions and cultural practices, from befriending or bullying a colleague to complimenting or gossiping about the boss. In other words, the workplace is a host of cultural and linguistic norms and there are various sociolinguistic conventions for engaging in work- and non-work-related activities.

This is of particular relevance for interactional sociolinguistics, as solidarity, hierarchy, and intercultural communication all play a role (Holmes 2006, Holmes & Stubbe 2003). It is impossible to do justice here to the full breadth of language in the workplace, so let's illustrate its implications with two studies from language brokering in a small multilingual cleaning business in the US and the usage of grassroots English in the Tanzanian tourist industry.

As for multilingual workplaces, Gonçalves and Schluter (2017: 241) look at "the covert language policy and micro-language planning practices" of a Portuguese/American business owner in the US. They argue that the current practices of a local, blue-collar workplace reflect macrosocial structures, class differences, and asymmetrical power relations. Embedded in a framework of critical ethnography, they emphasize the importance of **language brokering**, as not all employees have access to (or speak) English, which is the language of the customers: "Language brokers facilitate communication between two linguistically and/or culturally different parties. Unlike formal interpreters and translators, brokers mediate, rather than merely transmit, information" (Tse 1996: 485). The company studied is a small cleaning business run by a Luso–Brazilian American woman, whose employees are monolingual speakers of Spanish, European Portuguese, and Luso-Brazilian Portuguese (Figure 6.4).

6.5 Language in the Workplace

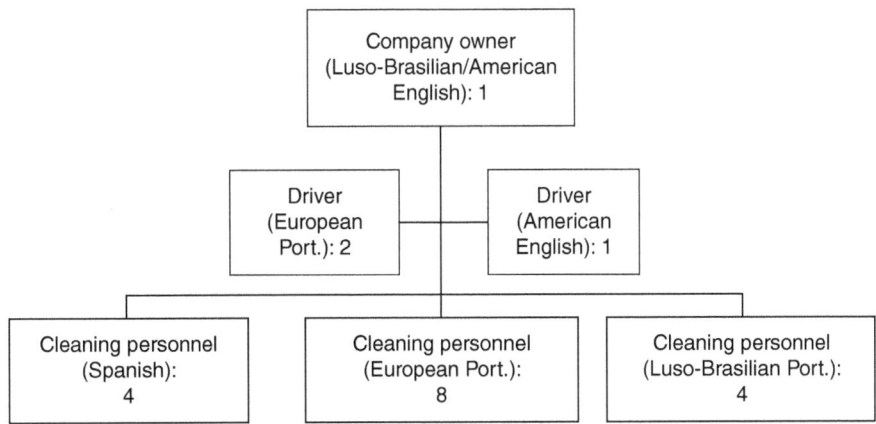

Figure 6.4 The hierarchy of a small cleaning business in the US. Adapted from Gonçalves & Schluter (2017: 247).

Gonçalves and Schluter (2016: 247) aim to uncover the language practices of the company and are interested in how the owner (herself a Portuguese–English bilingual) legitimates the domination of her employees through the quasi-exclusive use of a "superordinate" language. How do her language-brokering practices and language choices (both in oral and written channels) affect "inter-employee" and employee–client communication, and what discourse strategies does she employ to assert authority as the manager of the company?

They found that communication is divided between company-internal and company-external staff. Internally, the company language is Portuguese, spoken by the staff majority (who are preferably hired and have no fixed contracts). There is little need for English language proficiency among the cleaning personnel, and the manager speaks Luso–Brasilian Portuguese with most of the employees. As for interaction with the clients and customers, English is the language of choice, making it the language of economic gain and symbolic capital (Chapter 9). The knowledge of two languages allows the manager to exert legitimate domination over her employees, who in fact depend on her language skills. The manager acts as a broker in this multilingual and culturally diverse workplace, translating but at the same time mediating information between her employees and customers. In fact, she is highly aware of the advantage bilingualism provides her with and exerts the sociolinguistic power relationship via strict top-down communication structures. She gives the clients explicit instructions not to communicate with the cleaning personnel, justifying this as follows:

> "No, I don't tell them 'don't communicate', there, there is erm, erm, a paragraph [in the 7-page company booklet handed out to all clients] that says 'Do not leave a note because most of the cleaning ladies do not speak English' so they may not understand and we really want to do a good job ... if you leave a note, you leave it to me so then I can you know, tell the cleaning lady this, this and that and erm you know, there's no miscommunication in there ... I tell some customers, 'If you leave a note for her, she's gonna take that note for me, so if you're asking her to do something, it may not get done.'"

In other words, Portuguese/English bilingualism is exploited for professional purposes in this particular work setting, putting the manager at the top of the company hierarchy, not only in terms of company structure but also in terms of her sociolinguistic repertoire and skills. The knowledge of English gives her symbolic power and puts her in a superior position, manifesting asymmetrical power relations in the company. However, the manager stands up for her personnel in case there is conflict with clients, mediating culturally but also using on-record directness when necessary. Though this is a Portuguese-run company, the manager is a "language policy agent" (Gonçalves & Schluter 2017: 253) who takes advantage of English proficiency to maintain and legitimate her dominant position and authority, thus making English a gatekeeper and a means of social control (Chapter 8).

The second case in point that serves as illustration here is taken from Schneider (2016), who reports on idiolectal acquisition of English and the development of grassroots English in tourist destinations as diverse as India, Indonesia, and Tanzania. English as the lingua franca of tourism is spoken by a majority of the visitors in these locations. Information has to be made available in the language of the tourists, so the burden to acquire English is on the local population, who financially rely on interaction with travelers paying for various services. As a consequence, the distribution of the roles of English and local languages is uneven. English is used as an additional language (Chapter 4), in a heterogeneous set of intercultural and multi-ethnic settings, often acquired ad hoc, without formal instruction or schooling. The motivation (or, depending on the viewpoint, pressure) to obtain some proficiency in English is immense:

> Rather than having been disseminated, as has been the case traditionally, from above, a process of growth of English from the ground, as it were, can be observed these days – and while this is not a wholly new process in itself, its breadth, regularity and intensity have reached a novel quality in the 21st century. The English language is undergoing a new kind of

expansion and transformation, with 'grassroots Englishes' emerging in many countries and contexts. (Schneider 2016: 3)

Among others, Schneider discusses English proficiency in northern Tanzania, where tourism (such as climbing Kilimanjaro) is a lucrative business. As many of the tourists come from English-speaking countries or are at least to some extent anglophone, English is the language of economic prosperity and social progress. Schneider finds that most of the porters on the tour speak Swahili (or other local languages) but very little English (if any). Such competence is a prerequisite to move up the social ladder and receive better-paid jobs in transport or administration, and these entail increasing contacts with (English-speaking) visitors. The workplace in the local tourist industry typically entails a couple of years as a porter, during which some rudimentary English is acquired (occasionally via direct contact with the visitors, and there is no official instruction). There are no standards to be met and no tests, the only goal is basic intelligibility. Schneider (2016: 8–9) reports the speech of one of the guides as follows:

> After we reaching Saddle we may finding the cooker is already there, we gonna maybe you have a lunch dere, or we can, we're going to ask him the cooker if you will gonna have a lunch, pocket lunch, on the way, or we're gonna have hot lunch, right? It just depending, with the cooker, how, and we gonna see how you, how you, how, how you fitness you are, right? If you walking very slowly we can decide for all of us, we can make me pocket lunch for you, but if you have a go with the hard time, is better for us to go to have a lunch in, in the Saddle Hut, hot lunch, right? Because sometime we will gonna walking slowly, sometime, just depending how our body [ac]climatization [xx] is, all right?

Proficiency is somewhat higher (because English is taught as a foreign language at Tanzanian high schools), but still there are some typical examples of grassroots Englishes (that interestingly resemble a jargon, Chapter 4): copula absence, missing number concord, *-ing* forms rather than infinitives with modal verbs, progressive forms with stative verbs, double prepositions and lexical creativity ("the cooker"). English is the key to economic advancement and progress, correlating with the type of work opportunities available for the workforce. It is thus a symbol of inequality and power, an issue to which we will return in Chapter 9.

To sum up, language in the workplace is an important object of study for those interested in interactional sociolinguistics. It involves multiple interactants, often with differential status and authority, and various levels of contextualized discursive practices. The picture has become more complex via processes of globalization and ongoing diversification of workplaces, both on a global scale and also via technological developments. The workplace, whether virtual or real, lends itself ideally to the study of language as a means of solidarity and authority, the analysis of face in uneven hierarchic relationships, but also of accommodation, language brokering, and the exploitation of multilingualism as language practice.

6.6 Crossing and Translanguaging

Language and identity are closely interwoven. Identity-related language choices manifest themselves in all facets of everyday lives and are shaped by sociolinguistic characteristics of speakers and contexts (Chapter 2). The question of relevance here is how national, social, or ethnic identities are expressed via speaker resources, and how bilingual and multilingual individuals use their repertoire to create their own identity in a range of settings (Joseph 2004). Rampton (1995) coined the term **crossing** for this purpose: It "involves code alternation by people who are not accepted members of the group associated with the second language that they are using ... switching into varieties that are not generally thought to belong to them" (Rampton 1995: 485). In other words, speakers adopt dialect features they would not normally use as they are motivated to create some sense of identity within the group or community.

We saw above that a traditional approach to sociolinguistic variables (e.g. class, ethnicity, gender, etc.) would hold that they are fixed concepts formed in childhood and adolescence through local community networks and socialization (Chapter 2). In opposition, a more semiotic approach would postulate that they represent a "socio-cognitive category that is activated in different ways in different contexts" (Rampton 1995: 485). Ethnicity, for instance, would be a flexible, negotiable concept that is renegotiated in an interaction as perceptions and expressions of identity increase or decrease. Rather than being set and given, a sense of identity is created actively, which is very much in line with third-wave variationist sociolinguistics (Chapter 3). These practices can follow different trajectories, such as to embrace and cultivate one's own identity or to distance oneself from those of others in the community or peer group.

Rampton investigated language crossing in a multiethnic and diverse school in Southeast England. In a sense, this is pioneering work on multi-ethnolectalization (Chapter 4), as interactions between adolescents from different ethnolinguistic backgrounds saw the creation of "a local multi-racial vernacular" (Rampton 1995: 492). The main agents were adolescent groups speaking local varieties of Anglo British English, Asian Englishes, Caribbean Creoles, and other languages (e.g. Panjabi). These varieties had different levels of indexicality: Asian English carried negative associations whereas Creole was highly prestigious among the adolescent peers, stereotypically representing toughness and opposition to authority. Rampton argued that adopting someone else's ethnicity or creating a new, group-based identity was common in multiracial and multiethnic interactions. He used qualitative methods for data collection: radio-microphone recording, interviews, retrospective participant commentaries on extracts of recorded conversation (Rampton 1995: 489). Participants went to the same school and lived in the surrounding neighborhood; though they belonged to different networks and communities of practice, they were mutually familiar to some extent. Membership of peer groups was primarily determined by the individuals' gender and ethnic backgrounds (though some groups were mixed).

Crossing is not a matter of proficiency in one or several varieties alone. Rampton (1995) showed that using other dialect features was an instrumental part of youth culture, and that a tacit understanding was collectively shared as to when such a practice was out of bounds. Outgroup languages were used as "auxiliary adjuncts in a range of activities that formed a basic part of the daily round of peer group recreation" (Rampton 1995: 492), such as listening to music, football, and ritual abuse. Though attitudes varied between groups, language crossing was a sign of peer-group membership, indicating familiarity and solidarity, particularly when values and beliefs were shared. By adopting and using features of other varieties, speakers transgressed ethnic and peer-group boundaries, associating themselves with the ethnicity of different groups. However, adolescents practicing crossing neither attempted to actually claim ethnic identity as such nor were they entitled to "move unproblematically in and out of their friends' heritage language in any new kind of open bicultural code-switching" (Rampton 1995: 502).

Thinking about this further, there is a close connection with Gumperz's contextualization cues as the interpretation of interactive purposes depends on the contextual principles shared by the adolescents. There is a shared code about when and when not to cross, and in some circumstances or situations it is strictly prohibited, at the risk of severe conflict. It is simply not the case that anything goes. For instance, Anglo British adolescents using Creole features are in real trouble as this was considered "(a) as a derisive parody, and hence as an assertion of white superiority, and (b) as a further white appropriation of one of the sources of power" (Hewitt 1986: 162). As a result, crossing was not tolerated when it came from middle-class Anglo adolescents. Knowing how to "cross" requires a good understanding of its (implicit) rules and codes. In moments of distress or conflict, crossing had to be avoided at all costs. As a result, "ethnic descent was credited with a lot of authority in routine social reality, but it was regularly transgressed in liminal moments and events when adolescents invoked, explored and momentarily inhabited ethnicities other than their own" (Rampton 1995: 508). This resembles the code of honor of ritual insults in African American youth culture, which has had so much influence around the world.

Identity is also at issue in **translanguaging**, when speakers engage in processes of creative mixing in communities where there is a high degree of multilingualism. While one can arguably cross with little knowledge of other varieties, contextual knowledge being paramount, translanguaging involves the integration of bilingual and multilingual resources by speakers who have proficiency in at least two varieties. It has been defined as the "ability of multilingual speakers to shuttle between languages, treating the diverse languages that form their repertoire as an integrated system" (Canagarajah 2011: 401). The ensemble of languages is seen as an active resource for the creation of a speaker's identity: "Meaning-making is not confined to the use of 'languages' as discrete, enumerable, bounded sets of linguistic resources" (Blackledge & Creese 2013: 127, quoted in Joseph 2004). Instead, the focus is on the speaker's choices, on a personal and not on a structural level, and mixing languages represents an act of identity. Translanguaging

> shifts the lens from cross-linguistic influence to how multilinguals intermingle linguistic features that have hereto been administratively or linguistically assigned to a particular language or language variety. (García 2009: 51)

There has been much work on Hispanic (Latino/Latinx) English-speaking communities in the US (García 2009), but the concept has also been investigated in South Africa. As is well known, the sociolinguistic situation of South Africa changed profoundly after the end of the Apartheid system in 1994, and the "Rainbow Nation" has brought together languages such as Zulu, Xhosa, Tswana, English, and Afrikaans in various interethnic and multilingual settings. There have been claims (Banda 2018, Makalela 2015) that increasing contact between historically divided groups and social mobility within society at large have given rise to extensive translanguaging, particularly in multilingual speakers who strive to create a sense of order in a quickly transforming society. These practices are greeted almost euphorically in some places, including in higher education, as it is seen as a new innovative practice to overcome old racial barriers and language-based discrimination.

For instance, a multilingual pedagogical approach is considered a "socially just response to calls for decolonial education in South Africa" (Hurst & Mona 2017: 131), and social justice can be "interpreted as social and civic responsibilities, commitment to promoting the common good, and participation in democratic processes and cultural diversity" (Cumming-Potvin 2009: 84). Education must help the development of students in the form of an appropriate multilingual pedagogy (see also Chapter 9).

Translanguaging may give rise to lexical innovation, as Wei (2018: 11) notes in an Asian context. Here, English utterances are reappropriated with entirely different meanings for communication between Chinese speakers of English. These new words are very often used on social media. They are in accordance with English morphology (via blending mostly), yet there are Chinese twists and some meanings are difficult to understand for outsiders (Wei 2018: 12), for example:

- *Chinsumer*: a mesh of "Chinese consumer," usually referring to Chinese tourists buying large quantities of luxury goods.
- *Democrazy:* "democracy + crazy"; mocking the so-called democratic systems of the West and in some parts of Asia where certain legislation (such as the ownership of firearms) can be protected due to political lobbying and, in the case of Taiwan, parliamentarians get into physical fights over disagreements (widely used after Trump's victory in the 2016 US presidential election).
- *Harmany*: the Chinese Communist Party's discourse on "harmony" is turned by the bilingual netizens into harm + many, as many people feel that the social policies imposed on them brought harm rather than cohesion.
- *Smilence:* "smile" + "silence," referring to the stereotypical Chinese reaction of smiling without saying anything.

While the concept of translanguaging has some appeal, particularly in language and identity and applied sociolinguistics (Chapter 7), a couple of theoretical issues remain unclear. For instance, it is not certain how a speaker-based perspective should integrate principles of contact linguistics (Chapter 4), that is whether there is a potential overlap with jargons and code-switching, which of course may serve identity purposes as well. There is a lack of conceptual transparency, and Wei (2018: 9) certainly has a point when stating that there "is considerable confusion as to whether Translanguaging could be an all-encompassing term for diverse multilingual and multimodal practices, replacing terms such as code-switching, code-mixing, code-meshing, and crossing." Moreover, translanguaging, reflecting attitudes to language diversity and multilingualism, has far-reaching pedagogical consequences for applied sociolinguistics in the multilingual classroom.

To sum up, crossing and translanguaging represent proactive practices to create identity and transcend social boundaries by making use of a speaker's language resources. They are much more microoriented, by focusing on speakers and small groups, and involve the transformation of ethnic belonging or creation of a new self-definition. Formerly static sociolinguistic variables such as race or ethnicity represent flexible and dynamic concepts which, depending on the situation, enable or disable the practice(s) of multilingual identity-formation. There is no complete adoption of another identity (i.e. claiming to be Afro-Caribbean or Asian, etc.). Both crossing and translanguaging rely on an intimate knowledge of the speakers' situation and contextualization cues/indexical signs, and it is perhaps no surprise that they are predominantly found and studied in vibrant and dynamic youth cultures and applied contexts. Their use, whether involving bilingual or multilingual mixing or not, is subject to constraints and may be sanctioned when felt to be sociolinguistically inappropriate (as an expression of superiority or appropriation). There is a clear understanding of who can engage in such practices and who cannot.

6.7 Conclusion

Situated at the crossroads of sociolinguistics, the ethnography of speaking, pragmatics, and discourse analysis, interactional sociolinguists study how people use language in everyday face-to-face interaction and how they create meaning via discursive practices. The overlap with pragmatics is particularly fruitful, as "people who study pragmatics are interested in when language is used, where it is used, who it is used by, how it is used, what it is used for, and, perhaps most importantly, how it gets interpreted as doing the things it is used for by the people who use it when they do so" (Merrison et al. 2014: 43). Knowledge of grammar and lexicon alone are not sufficient for successful interaction as it is interpreting discourse, both at microlevels and macrolevels, that is essential when meaning is identified in interaction. This depends on speakers sharing a set of beliefs and values, taking advantage of their sociolinguistic repertoires and making various kinds of inferences.

One of the principal research questions concerns how communicative practices relate to social, cultural, and communicative backgrounds, and how they are shaped by universal and locality-specific characteristics. While varying between speech communities and cultural groups, discourse structures have clear and orderly patterns that are socially constructed. Exchanges consist of recurrent pairs, preferences, repair, cues and signals, all of which create coherence in conversation. Speakers signal and interpret meaning in social interaction, they manage social identities and activities as they interact. As a case in point, hesitation phenomena (or filled pauses) are subject to regional, social, and individual variation; often overlooked, they carry a lot of sociolinguistic information on speakers and contexts in that they function as pragmatic markers, helping speakers to structure and plan discourse, hold the floor and gain attention, and so forth.

We further saw how important context is in structured variation, and that it would not be possible to create and interpret meaning without the intimate knowledge of a range of cues and genres. Communication involves much more than linguistic information alone and depends on pragmatic and context-related knowledge also. As a result, meaning is coproduced by interactants (often via inferences), which allows them to construct cultural and social identities through communicative practices. The concept of face is central here: Speakers (and hearers) are keeping their own interests while at the same time risking the loss of face. There is a clash between positive and negative face, interests of being amiable and friendly on the one hand and being in charge of one's own decisions on the other. Language offers an array of resources to minimize the danger of face loss, though practices typically vary between communities. The concept of face has taken central stage in politeness theory, where negative and positive politeness are distinguished, both in speakers and addressees. This has consequences for the use of language in unbalanced power relationships. Language in the workplace is a showcase scenario as it involves several interactants, often with differential status and authority, a place that has been transformed via globalization and the digital revolution. It lends itself to focal areas of interactional sociolinguistics, such as the study of language as a means of solidarity and authority, the analysis of face in uneven hierarchic relationships; but it also lends itself to the study of accommodation, language brokering, and the exploitation of multilingualism as language practice.

Last but not least, crossing and translanguaging are proactive means to create identity and transcend social boundaries, making use of a speaker's multilingual resources. These involve transforming and adjusting ethnic membership by appropriating features from other varieties. Sociolinguistic variables such as race or ethnicity are interpreted as flexible, dynamic, and interpretable concepts. Both crossing and translanguaging rely on an intimate knowledge of the speakers' situation and the contextualization cues/indexical signs used, and are particularly frequent in youth language, where search for a personal identity is paramount. Notwithstanding, the process of mixing codes, whether bilingual or multilingual, is subject to constraints and may be sanctioned when felt to be sociolinguistically inappropriate (as an expression of superiority or appropriation). All speakers have access to interpretative processes by establishing links between speaking activities in an ongoing interaction, decoding the social context while being aware of cultural beliefs and taboos (including communicative norms, expectations, etc.).

Take-Home Messages

- Interactional sociolinguistics studies how people use language in everyday face-to-face interaction, and how they create meaning via discursive practices.
- The knowledge of grammar and lexicon alone is not sufficient to successfully interpret meaning in interaction. Inferences and contextualization cues are of particular importance here.
- Meaning is coproduced by interactants (often via inferences) who construct particular cultural and social identities through communicative practices.
- Discursive structures provide all kinds of linguistic, extralinguistic, and metalinguistic information. They are inherently variable and structured.
- Positive and negative face are central concepts, referring to a speaker's needs and interests and their aspiration to be friendly and amiable. Linguistic resources offer a variety of possibilities to minimize face loss.
- Crossing and translanguaging are proactive means to create identity and transcend social boundaries, by making use of a speaker's intimate contextual knowledge and their multilingual language resources.

Activities

6.1 It is rare that one person speaks to an audience without being interrupted (exceptions are speeches, lectures, sermons, etc.). As most participants have the possibility to speak, they must know how to take the floor – even if this means they have to interrupt someone. Discuss what possibilities there are to announce that you would like to say something and how you would interrupt someone speaking. You may collect samples from your surroundings and make a list with your observations, distinguishing between intralinguistic and extralinguistic cues when the change is signaled. Which of the two is more important in your view? And in case there are misunderstandings: What are the consequences and how are they addressed?

6.2 Jokes provide a particularly interesting, culturally sensitive genre. Select ten jokes in English and/or a language of your choice. What are the cultural implications of understanding meaning and how do these depend on the hearers' contextual (social and cultural) knowledge? Who would tell a joke in what context(s), and what attributes are associated in different cultures with those people who do?

6.3 Schneider (2016: 6) reports another example of grassroots English from Indonesia:

> If de people going to de cem-, if now die, looking for good -, looking, eh, Balinese calendar, when I can bring to cemetery, but if we do cemetery, around four o'clock, five o'clock, before de, uh, sun down, maybe around five o'clock, and den, you give in[?], with many people. If here, if, uh, if I always come when the neighbor co-[?] dead, the neighbor have, uh, something, and then I hel(e)p him, evry[?],evry[?], uh, neighbor dead, yeah, neighbor, I have, dead, I come. When I die also come. When me lazy, only my family. There is dis[?] difficul' here in, uh, in Bali. Also, I am not from Lovina, when in Lovina I live with, rent a house, yeah, but I'm from de mountain here. If my neighbor in de mountain dead I come with motorbike go home. Sometime alone. If I have ceremony, one bike, four people: my daughter, my son, my wife, and suitcase behind. My daughter fourteen years, my son ten years, and small motorbike. But I have only one motorbike. But now I must try another motorbike.

Go through this passage and note all the "grassroots" features of interest. To what extent is this different to the process of jargonization discussed in Chapter 4?

Key Terms
adjacency pairs
contextualizing
contextualization cues
Conversation Analysis
crossing
interactional sociolinguistics
face

face-threatening acts
face-work
floor, turns
genres, frames
Gumperz, John
Inferencing
indexical signs

interaction order
language brokering
negative face
positive face
presuppositons

repair-work
translanguaging
turn-taking
variationist pragmatics

Further Reading
For an introduction to the work of John Gumperz on interactional sociolinguistics, read:
Gumperz, J. J. (1982). *Discourse Strategies* (Studies in Interactional Sociolinguistics 1). Cambridge: Cambridge University Press.

Two suitable handbook surveys are:
Jaspers, J. (2011). Interactional Sociolinguistics and Discourse Analysis. In: J. P. Gee & M. Handford, *The Routledge Handbook of Discourse Analysis*. Abingdon: Routledge, 135–146.
Schiffrin, D. (1995). Interactional Sociolinguistics. In: S. McKay & N. Hornberger, eds., *Sociolinguistics and Language Teaching* (Cambridge Applied Linguistics). Cambridge: Cambridge University Press, 307–328. doi:10.1017/CBO9780511551185.014.

CHAPTER **7**

Applied Sociolinguistics

In This Chapter ...

... we investigate how sociolinguistic theory overlaps selected areas of applied linguistics. We revisit the question of how discrimination operates in the language ideology of Standard English and find out how this may entail serious impediments in domains such as education and health advice. We look at how anthropological and ethnographic issues have an impact on cultural misunderstandings, how insights from variation and change can be used to help improve children's reading and writing skills, and discuss the involvement of sociolinguists in dialect maintenance and revival issues. There are special sections on forensic sociolinguistics and legal aspects of language usage, and we present hands-on cases of real-life issues where sociolinguistics has been relevant, particularly the court case following the shooting of Trayvon Martin in 2013.

7.1	Applying Sociolinguistic Knowledge	page 188
7.2	Linguistic Discrimination	192
	Vignette 7.1: The 1996 Oakland Controversy	195
7.3	Forensic Linguistics	198
	Vignette 7.2: Identifying the Unabomber	201
7.4	Educational Failure	203
7.5	Language and Social Justice	211
7.6	Conclusion	215
	Take-Home Messages	217
	Activities	217
	Key Terms	219
	Further Reading	219

7 Applied Sociolinguistics

7.1 Applying Sociolinguistic Knowledge

We have already found that sociolinguistics is a highly interactive discipline, overlapping and drawing from research traditions in ethnography, sociology, anthropology, pragmatics, and so on, which gives it such a vibrant and energetic character. No matter whether the object of interest is social stratification, historical sound change, the creation of meaning in social interaction, or the emergence of new contact-based varieties, sociolinguists by necessity focus on the social embedding and environment of speakers. Some would go as far as to claim that language-related research is irrelevant if language is detached from social context (William Labov hesitated to use the term sociolinguistics for many years as he felt it was redundant, linguistic theory itself being socially based). As language is deeply rooted in society, affecting all our lives in profound ways, the question we ask here is how insights from sociolinguistics generally can be returned to society so as to benefit speakers and communities.

One point of concern is the public's strongly perceived sense of dialects' inequality, which was discussed in Chapter 1. While there are no formal and functional *linguistic* criteria to argue in favor of some dialects' superiority over others, there is a strong and persistent *social* belief that this should be so, with attempts at linguistic justification, often from a prescriptive standpoint. While such views developed historically and are a corollary of language standardization (Chapter 5), they are extremely powerful in public perception today. In the words of Lippi-Green (1997: 41):

> Standard language and its corollary, nonaccent, ... need not be understood as any specific language, but ... a collectively held ideal, which brings with it a series of social and regional associations ... it is useful to consider standard language and nonaccent both as abstractions and as myths. ... Myths are magical and powerful constructs; they can motivate social behavior and actions which would be otherwise contrary to logic or reason.

Accordingly, one area we need to look at is how social inequality is created via language evaluation, particularly when prescriptive views lead to discrimination against all those who do not speak a standard variety (who in all societies represent the large majority). It is a sad fact that speakers of stigmatized dialects (social, regional, or ethnic) generally have fewer opportunities in life, whether it be for job applications, apartment searches, or educational opportunities. So it is no surprise at all to find that equal rights for speakers of all dialects is an urgent concern for the application of sociolinguistic theory. Let's illustrate these points in a short introduction, with examples from the classroom, the court, and patient–doctor interaction.

A first setting is the classroom, and the question of how dialect (and, of course, language) diversity should be incorporated in the teaching syllabus. Most classrooms in the world are characterized by heterogeneity and increasing diversity, as students from various regional and social backgrounds and different family histories come together in one of the most important formative phases of their lives. The challenge for educationalists and teachers is twofold:

1. to raise awareness of dialect diversity, so that variation is seen as an asset and not as a burden, and
2. to implement programs that assist students who did not grow up in a standard-speaking environment, to help them advance their skills and open up opportunities for further learning and education.

First, let's look at efforts to redress reading failure and ask how dialect curricula are used in teaching. Linguists have been instrumental in applying their expertise for local schools engaged in language planning. In the US, language experts such as Geneva Smitherman have acted as chief advisors to the National Council of Teachers of English (NCTE) and made sure that information about language variation was implemented in policy-making decisions. Similarly, the Center for Applied Linguistics produced materials such as the Sheltered Instruction Observation Protocol (SIOP) for English language learners (Center for Applied Linguistics, 2011: www.cal.org/siop/), which is made available online and used in classrooms throughout the country.

Similarly, sociolinguists have developed programs for dialect awareness. Walt Wolfram and his associates from North Carolina State University developed a curriculum for eighth-grade students on Ocracoke Island, which has been expanded to reflect language variation across North Carolina and is part of the social-studies curriculum statewide (Reaser & Wolfram 2007). They keep emphasizing that social-studies curricula benefit from the inclusion of knowledge about local culture, as they allow educationalists to draw from the students' familiar worlds and enhance their learning success.

A second focus is on the usage of language data as evidence in the courtroom. This is particularly important in cases when audio recordings or written samples are used as evidence in court, for instance regarding blackmail, threat, or abduction. Here, language (whether spoken or written) is instrumental for the jury's verdict on whether a plaintiff is guilty or not. The area of **forensic linguistics** is becoming increasingly important as "[o]ver the past 30 years there has been a rapid growth in the frequency with which courts in a number of countries have called upon the expertise of linguists" (Coulthard & Johnson 2012: 105). By way of an illustration, let's consider an anonymous kidnapper who leaves a message demanding a ransom; their voice is the only piece of evidence. If that person is later caught and facing trial in court, the recording may be the only means to decide whether or not they committed the crime – and a professional linguist may be the only expert who can decide whether two voice samples come from the same person or not.

The classic case here is as follows: In the early 1980s, an anonymous caller made bomb threats to a Pan American counter at Los Angeles airport. Paul Prinzivalli, a cargo handler born in New York, who was thought by Pan American to be a disgruntled employee, was accused of the crime, arrested, and jailed. The judge believed that Prinzivalli's voice sounded like the tape recordings of the threat caller, who, he thought, was from New York as well. The defense team sent William Labov tapes in the hope that he might be able to distinguish different kinds of New York City accents and help them provide evidence that Prinzivalli was innocent. However, Labov quickly realized that the man who made the bomb threats did not come from New York at all but from Boston, and used phonetic data science to prove to a West Coast judge (who could hear no difference between Boston and New York City speech) that the two samples were not identical. Prinzivalli was set free, which Labov considered one of the biggest achievements of his career.

Adding to what was said in Chapter 6, anthropological knowledge of speech communities helps clear up or avoid misunderstandings. Anthropological linguists can adopt a brokering role and help transmit information, not only in immigrant communities, where there may be little competence in the local language(s), but also when it comes to clearing up different cultural conceptions, which may be harmful. A good example comes from the Health Care system, where adequate instructions are potentially lifesaving. In Australia, communication between White Australian healthcare workers and Indigenous Australian patients has long been notoriously difficult. As many of the latter group are bilingual in English and their native Aboriginal language, it is not really language competence but the cultural evaluation of context and participant roles that affect interpretation. This can cause major harm; in the words of Amery (2017: 13):

> The communication gap between health professionals and Indigenous Australians has a significant impact on health outcomes. Limited health literacy is not confined to Indigenous people, but it is greatly magnified for speakers of Indigenous languages in comparison, for example, to non-English speaking migrants.

Health care may pose serious challenges for effective cross-cultural communication between professionals and patients. While doctor–patient interaction is of special concern for sociolinguists, given that it occurs in settings characterized by sharp stratification and predefined authority roles, the Australian context is particularly upsetting. According to Australian census data, the life expectancy of Indigenous residents in rural Australia (who often do not speak Australian English as a first language) is significantly lower than that of those resident in urban areas (Amery 2017: 13), which mirrors findings from other places.

However, and this is reason for concern, speakers of indigenous Australian languages are shown to have more difficulties understanding health-care instructions than non-English speaking migrants in Australia. Why should that be so? One problem is that the specialized vocabulary and medical jargon which seems normal for health-care workers is in fact a barrier for communication, as Indigenous Australians, especially in rural areas, have comprehension issues (Amery 2017: 14). Likewise, simple phrases used by health professionals can be grossly misunderstood, for instance when the phrase "keeping an eye on it" (14) might be taken literally (an eye should be placed on an injury).

Moreover, indigenous patients may also struggle with quantitative concepts. Some Aboriginal languages have radically different numbering systems: Languages such as Anindilyakwa, Kokata, and Yolngu have few numerals beyond 5. Instructions about how many pills to take may therefore not be understood. In their study of cross-cultural communication between members of the Yolngu tribe and White Australian health professionals, Cass et al. (2002: 469) reached the depressing conclusion that, at the dialysis unit where they researched, the "percentage of renal function, number of drinks consumed, amount and frequency of medication …, length of time without dialysis, high and low blood pressure" meant nothing to the Indigenous patients, whereas "Yolngu ways of expressing quantity and spatial and temporal concepts were completely unknown to staff." There is no need to stress how dramatic, indeed life-threatening, cross-cultural communication differences are when patients and medical staff, although both are fluent in English, have fundamentally different cultural understandings and concepts. The insights of sociolinguists and anthropological linguists are of paramount importance in order to raise some awareness and develop efficient and culturally sensitive instructions for the benefit of health-care workers and patients alike.

These and many other issues are important for society at large. There is a growing understanding that sociolinguists need to bring in their expertise and advice, first, because they have firsthand knowledge of the social and language-related factors involved, and second, because it is their responsibility to return their expertise for the benefit of the communities they work(ed) with. Labov (1982) called this duty the principle of "error correction" and "debt incurred," according to which popular misconceptions have to be addressed and repaired, and Wolfram (1993) postulated a principle of "linguistic gratuity," which means that researchers have to make every effort to return the favor to the speech community. In what follows, we look at four of these areas in more detail: linguistic discrimination in general, forensic linguistics, reading failure, and social justice.

7.2 Linguistic Discrimination

Languages and dialects are used in different contexts and for different purposes, carrying different connotations. We have already learned that standardization processes and the emergence of a high-prestige variety are primarily the result of social, political, and economic factors – not of linguistic ones. In other words, all statements about dialects are social evaluations in disguise: Few varieties of English enjoy prestige whereas most of them are stigmatized somehow. At the risk of some simplification, standards are spoken by the social elite and members of upper classes, non-standardized ones are typically spoken by residents of rural areas and members of lower social classes. In the words of Fasold (2006):

> When linguists use the term "standard language" they mean an arbitrary standard. ... In English, there is a general tacit agreement on what these standards are. ... It is general social acceptance that gives us a workable arbitrary standard, not any inherent superiority of the characteristics it specifies. The upshot is that "correct English" is "correct" only in the sense that people have agreed that it is correct.

This view is uncontroversial and one of the few general statements all sociolinguists would subscribe to wholeheartedly. Still, the question remains of how we should cope with and address the occasionally strong views about regional and social dialects, attitudes held by the vast majority of our population. In my courses, I am continually amazed to find time and time again that students may be highly sensitive to various forms of prejudice yet give little thought to the consequences of their own attitudes toward language. The **Standard Language ideology** (Watts 2011)) means that there is a pervasive belief in the superiority of an abstracted and idealized form of language, along with some linguistic justification. Since rural or working-class dialects and Standard English share much vocabulary, they are considered the same language and any differences in phonetics and morphosyntax are often perceived as inaccuracies or "bad English." Other reasons for negative attitudes are that Standard English is used in published texts and, as the educational language in Britain, it has a long historical tradition and a body of literature. Other dialects are either not standardized or they have only recently been used in literature or media discourse. As a result, there is a persistent belief that local dialects are fine for informal communication but should have no place in the school, where the standard is tacitly accepted as the norm (see Section 7.4).

It is perfectly normal for speech communities to have language attitudes, and different views about dialects have been recorded throughout the history of English. In the *Polychronicon*, written in the first half of the fourteenth century, Ranulph Hidgen commented on the northern dialects as follows (ironically, in Latin):

> Tota lingua Northimbrorum, maxime in Eboraco, ita stridet incondita, quod nos australes eam vix intelligere possumus. ('All the language of the Northumbrians, above all in York, shrieks in such an undisciplined way that we southerners can hardly understand it.')

When John Trevisa translated the *Polychronicon* into English in 1387, he rendered *ita stridet* (literally "it so screeches") as <ys so scharp slytyng & froting & unschape> ("is so sharp, cutting, frothing and unshapely"), thus making the description even more unfavorable. Is it not striking how this view from the fourteenth century mirrors present-day views? The belief that varieties are not equal is strong and persistent, as are judgments and evaluations based on characteristics such as the ethnicity of the speaker, their gender, social class, education, or region (Niedzielski & Preston 2000: 41).

The problem increases when negative views have an effect on the lives of speakers. **Linguistic prejudice** has real and direct negative effects, particularly when it comes to discrimination and those on the receiving end. This has been demonstrated in: employment, where a negative evaluation of accents reduces job opportunities (Pedulla & Pager 2019); education, where children with local accents consistently have a lower success rate in tests (Baugh 2018); and the judicial system, where non-standardized dialect speakers are less credible as witnesses (Rickford and King 2016; see Section 7.6). Lippi-Green (1997) provides a thorough and harrowing account of studies conducted in North America and provides firm evidence of how widespread discriminatory attitudes toward accented speakers are. In the words of Rickford and King (2016):

> [c]onsiderable research … demonstrates that speech perception and evaluation are significantly influenced by listeners' attitudes, often by biases from factors like race, ethnicity, geography, and social status.

To give but one example, Munro (2003: 43) discusses the case of a human-rights ruling from British Columbia (Mirek Gajecki v. Board of School Trustees, School District No.36 (Surrey), 1990). Gajecki emigrated to Canada from Poland in 1970. He obtained a Quebec teaching certificate and taught at a technical institute in Montreal. After moving to Vancouver in 1979, he worked as a substitute teacher at a high school, teaching mathematics, computer science, and physics. Though Gajecki's didactic and professional skills had been evaluated positively, he was informed that he would no longer be hired as the school board had concerns about his accent. Even when facing court, a representative of the board justified the decision stating that "kids might seize on mispronounced words and fool around with it and whether or not the children would understand the teacher [sic]" (quoted in Munro 2003: 44). The tribunal upheld the complaint and ordered the school board to pay compensation of $630 for lost wages and $2,000 for hurt, indignity, and embarrassment.

Sociolinguists can do more than they have been doing in the past and many feel there is a moral responsibility to address social injustice and discrimination (Baugh 2018). They should provide their expertise to demonstrate that negative perceptions are linguistically unfounded and should make every effort to stand up for those who are disadvantaged due to the way they speak. This is most urgent in cases of **linguistic discrimination/linguicism**. The challenge is twofold: First of all, it is crucial to educate the general public that dialect differences are systematic and regular not corrupt versions of the standard with a deficient grammar; second, sociolinguists need to develop a methodological tool kit to measure and show dialect perceptions.

Let's start with attitudes in the general public. Very often, there is profound ignorance in these matters and people have no idea at all how dialects function and how they are structured. We saw in Chapter 1 that African American English (AAE) is one of the most thoroughly researched varieties of English around the world, and that it is structurally different from other dialects it has been in contact with. Take the case of habitual *be*, which is "a major characteristic of AAE and helps distinguish it from other varieties of English" (Green 2004: 81). Sentences (from Green 2002: 35) such as

1. "Breakfast be ready at 8."
2. "The children be at school when I get home."

are considered ungrammatical by speakers of Anglo American English, who fail to understand the meaning of *be* here. They just do not know that AAE has a more complex aspectual system in that it distinguishes between actions that are sporadic and those that occur more than once. Habitual *be* "marks the recurrence of an eventuality" (Green 2002: 52) and means that something occurs more than once and at regular intervals, so the two sentences

3. "Breakfast is ready at 8." (or "Breakfast ready at 8.", with copula absence)
4. "Breakfast be ready at 8."

do not mean the same at all for an AAE speaker. Here, (3) means that on a specific day (today or tomorrow), breakfast is ready at 8 o'clock – but this is something that happens on that occasion only. On the other hand, (4) is recurrent – breakfast is often or always served at 8 o'clock. In other words, whereas in Anglo American English varieties, habitual aspect is expressed through adverbs, such as *usually* or *always*, AAE uses verbal morphology to emphasize that an event or state is repeated or that it happens on a regular basis (Green 2002: 47).

Now, what will happen if someone is not familiar with this distinction (probably the majority of the American population, in fact). Sentences such as "Breakfast be ready at 8" will be interpreted as bad grammar, corrupt versions of (mainstream) American English, as lazy and uneducated, and speakers will be stigmatized as they apparently do not know the rules. AAE speakers are judged as less credible, accurate, trustworthy, more deceptive, and as having less prestige (Frumkin 2007, Rickford and King 2016) and it is only a short step for them to be disadvantaged. Sociolinguistic research has shown that African Americans are systematically discriminated against when applying for apartments (Baugh 2018, Rickford and King 2016) or are attacked as witnesses in court (see Section 7.5). Sociolinguists often focus on applied issues to show how AAE features produce dominant stereotypes. In their attempts to raise awareness for dialect differentiation, they use public relations, attendance in the media, lectures to the interested public, lobby and give advice to political decision-makers, and so on. It is a struggle that has kept sociolinguists busy for six decades now and will go on for quite some time.

VIGNETTE 7.1 The 1996 Oakland Controversy
On December 18, 1996, the Oakland School Board resolved to recognize Ebonics (a then popular name for African American English, a blend of the words Ebony and Phonics) as the "primary language of African American children," which should be implemented in Language

> Arts lessons. The School Board aimed at "maintaining the legitimacy and richness of such language … and to facilitate their [pupils'] acquisition and mastery of English language skills." Soon afterward, a major controversy erupted. Political leaders, from both left and right, criticized the decision, arguing that it would harm educational standards in schools. Civil rights leaders such as Jesse Jackson expressed concern that African American students were more likely to fail as they were barred from learning Standard American English. There was confusion and potentially deliberate fake information, for example that all instruction would have to be offered in African American English or that African American children would be forced to attend ESL courses. Richard Riley, then Secretary of Education, publicly declared that:
>
>> Elevating 'Black English' to the status of a language is not the way to raise standards of achievement in our schools and for our students … the administration's policy is that 'Ebonics' is a nonstandard form of English and not a foreign language.
>
> Linguists and educators (among them William Labov) joined educators from Oakland in providing pro-Ebonics testimonies at a US Senate Hearing on Ebonics on January 23, 1997. Senator Arlen Specter, the Chairman of the Committee that supported the Standard English Proficiency program, did not withdraw funding, but later directed $1 million toward research on the relation between the home language of African American students and their success in learning to read and write in Standard English. In January 2007, the Linguistic Society of America passed a resolution in which hundreds of linguists confirmed that the Oakland School Board's intention and decision were correct.

Second, sociolinguists have been instrumental in developing methods to study and quantify language attitudes empirically. Perceptual dialectology is concerned with answering the following questions:

> What do non-specialists have to say about variation? Where do they believe it comes from? Where do they believe it exists? What do they believe is its function? (Preston 1999: xxv).

Put simply, perceptual dialectologists are interested in how "people react to spoken language" in a certain geographical area (Montgomery & Beal 2011: 121). Language attitudes need to be inferred. For this purpose, sociolinguists develop direct (via questionnaires), indirect (such as **matched/verbal guise techniques**), or societal treatment methods (content analysis). The use of questionnaires involves asking about language attitudes directly whereas indirect approaches infer attitudes by speaker evaluations (e.g. via matched-guise and verbal-guise tests). So-called direct approaches typically use elicitation tasks and direct questioning via surveys, questionnaires, or interviews. Questionnaires and surveys can either be compiled on paper (in person or by sending them postally) or online. Interviews are led in person, with individuals or a group of participants. Some researchers leave the room and let the participants discuss issues by themselves, but this does not always work. Alternatively, participants are invited to note key words of associations they may have with a particular language variety.

In a matched-guise technique, participants listen to different dialects and rate them along various dimensions (friendliness, politeness, education, etc.). Though they are rating different sound samples, listeners are probably less aware that their ratings implicitly display underlying language attitudes. To avoid preference of voice qualities, the same (bidialectal) speaker records passages using different dialects. This technique was applied in the US and Britain (see the discussion of perceptual dialectology in Chapter 1; Preston 1993) but also in studies on World Englishes, as in Guyana, where the same speaker recorded passages in Guyanese Creole and Guyanese English (Rickford 1985), and Singapore, where a speaker recorded an excerpt of her Sunday morning routine in Singapore Standard English and Singapore Colloquial English (reported in Cavallaro & Chin 2009).

Finally, societal treatment studies are interested in finding out the value of varieties in different societies "by examining material such as the language use in the education system, in cartoons, in novels or advertisements ... [they] highlight how different languages convey cultural resonances in a particular culture" (Garrett 2010: 142). Direct approaches allow sociolinguists to elicit conscious attitudes, whereas indirect methods as used in societal treatment aim to look at implicit attitudes "behind individuals' social façades" (McKenzie 2010: 45). Implicit attitudes are elicited through indirect measures such as the traditional approach of listening to recordings. While some methods focus more strongly on implicit beliefs, others elicit explicit associations; in combination, they allow a rigorous data-based analysis of attitudes and evaluations of language variation.

No matter what method is used, the ultimate goal is to provide an empirical baseline to study emotional and ideological language issues and to allow researchers and authorities to explore attitudes and thus redress a "bias toward an abstract, idealized homogenous language, which is imposed and maintained by dominant institutions and which has as its model the written language, but which is drawn primarily from the spoken language of the upper middle class" (Lippi Green 1997: 64). This is particularly pressing in cases when minorities are discriminated against because their dialects are socially stigmatized.

7.3 Forensic Linguistics

Sociolinguists are regularly required as experts when it comes to analyzing speech samples in court cases. The field of forensic linguistics:

> is a sub-field of linguistics that is particularly engaged with professional and institutional interaction in legal contexts. It is also an applied discipline, in that it has real-world applications and its findings can be applied in professional practice. (Coulthard & Johnson 2007: 14)

Take, for instance, cases when the only piece of evidence is linguistic, such as letters or voice messages (threats, blackmail, etc.). To verify authorship, some sort of linguistic knowledge has to be applied so as to substantiate legal advice. The founder of the field was Jan Svartvik, a Swedish linguist, who became well-known for his stylistic analysis of confession statements in British murder cases in the 1960s (Olsson 2009: 2). Forensic linguistic analysis took some time but then developed quickly in the 1990s, with the International Association of Forensic Linguistics and the first Forensic Linguistics Institutes being founded (Coulthard & Johnson 2010: 1) and becoming internationally renowned via high-profile cases (such as the identification of Ted Kaczynski, the Unabomber, in 1996; see Vignette 7.2).

Forensic sociolinguists assist in legal matters when language-related evidence is needed (e.g. to determine a person's origins, which is particularly pressing in asylum interviews (Singler 2004) or when there is potential language discrimination in court against minorities or members of different cultural backgrounds; Bucholtz 2009; see also Section 7.5). Research involves all linguistic branches, in the analysis of both written and spoken domains: phonetic/phonological, morphological, syntactic, lexical, discursive, pragmatic, and textual. For instance, sociophoneticians typically analyze prerecorded audio recordings made available to them by prosecutors or defense attorneys; distress calls, threat calls (Labov 1988), wiretap surveillance recordings and official recordings of police interrogations (Bucholtz 2009); and of course they may provide expertise when evidence is based on written documents alone (threats, ransom notes, etc.; Butters 2007).

The two main branches involved are the language of the legal process itself (written language of the law, interaction in the legal process) and language as evidence (Coulthard, Johnson & Wright 2017 7). Whereas the first field falls under (critical) discourse analysis and pragmatics and will not be discussed here, the second one concerns the analysis and identification of authorship, that is the determination of an author or caller, which is a sociolinguistic concern. Authorship analysis "describes the process of examining the characteristics of a piece of work in order to draw conclusions on its authorship" (Bouanani & Kassou 2014: 22) and involves three categories:

- *Authorship attribution or identification:* The goal is to provide probabilistic evidence about whether or not a person may be the author of a text, based on the comparative analysis of other works produced by that person.
- *Authorship profiling or characterization:* The goal is to give a better understanding of the profile or characteristics of the person who produced a particular text: their gender, educational background, cultural background, language familiarity, and so forth.
- *Similarity detection:* The goal is to compare several pieces of work and to determine how likely it is that they were produced by the same person.

For written data, the method used to analyze authorship analysis draws on so-called stylometry, which refers to statistical analysis of literally style and studies patterns of sociolinguistic variation (Chapter 3) such as style markers, but also textual features such as mean sentence length and punctuation:

> Stylistic approaches to authorship analysis operate within a paradigm of linguistic variation and involve the analyst identifying 'style markers', that is the author's 'choice from optional forms', which are the observable results of the habitual and usually unconscious choices an author makes in the process of writing. (Coulthard, Johnson & Wright 2017:155).

This is a challenging task (in some ways resembling the work of historical sociolinguists, Chapter 5). Data are sparse and they often come from various genres (social media, essays, letters), which makes comparison difficult. Unique, idiosyncratic features are rare, so authorship analysis is based on a comparison of features whose combination is particularly likely to occur in the writing of a particular person (Coulthard 2005).

Even small amounts of data can be important here. This is illustrated by the Jenny Nicholl murder case in Britain (full discussion in Coulthard, Johnson & Wright 2007: 159 ff.). In June 2005, Jenny Nicholl, a teenager in the North of England, vanished under mysterious circumstances. After her disappearance, four text messages were sent from her mobile phone, first to some of her friends and then to her father. There was some unease about these, and her family was doubtful about whether they had been written by Jenny or by someone else using her phone. One of the messages read as follows:

> <Y do u h8 me i know mum does.told her i was goin.i aint cumin back and the pigs wont find me.i am happy living up here.every1 h8s me in rich only m8 i got is jak.txt u couple wks tell pigs i am nearly 20 aint cumin back they can shite off>

Comparing the language used here and contrasting it with other messages written by Jenny before her disappearance, using similarity detection, forensic linguists uncovered a number of inconsistencies (Table 7.1). Though the dataset was small (four messages containing a mere 180 words), the analysis strongly suggested that this was not Jenny's texting style. There was some suspicion that her estranged partner had abducted and killed her, trying to cover his tracks by sending texts to Jenny's family and friends, so his texts were studied as well. Evidence relied on **consistency** and **distinctiveness** of features used; it is not sufficient for a particular feature to occur just once, as it might be a typo, and it needs to be consistent:

> A person's style is the combination of choices across variables ... when writing texts of the same type or genre (e.g. email, text message, tweet), one can assume that there will be an observable 'consistency' in their choices across these texts ... no absolute consistency required but variants have to be evaluated in terms of degrees of consistency ... the 'weight of evidence' which may be placed on any style marker. (Coulthard, Johnson & Wright, 2007: 157–158)

Table 7.1 *Differences in the text messages written by Jenny Nicholl and her alleged murderer. Adapted from Coulthard, Johnson & Wright (2007: 158).*

Feature	Jenny Nicholl	Suspicious text
Habitual spacing	<word9word>	<word9 word>, <word 9word>
Signoffs	<cu>, <x>	<cya>
Taboo language/accent	<shit>	<shite>
Possessive/accent	<my>, <myself>	<me>, <meself>
Spelling	<fone>	<phone>
Contractions/accent	<ive>, <have2>	<ave (2)>
Negative markers/accent	<im not>, <havnt>	<aint>

Distinctiveness, however, refers to the extent to which styles of several persons are similar or different. If distinctiveness in a sample is limited, then it has to be reinforced by the presence of other consistently distinct features. The corpus in the Jenny Nicholl murder case was small and most of the features were found only a few times, but this had the advantage that they were both consistent and distinctive; the four messages were most likely written by someone else. The evidence brought forward was so compelling that her former partner was found guilty of Jenny's murder and sentenced to life imprisonment. The judge declared that:

> After he killed her, the defendant retained her mobile phone and on two separate days sent bogus text messages from the phone – as if from her – first to her friends and then to her father, cruelly pretending that she was still alive and that she had run away. He was of course intending, thereby, to prevent the missing person inquiry turning into a murder investigation. (quoted on https://www.thenorthernecho.co.uk/news/2061825.devious-liar-continues-prolong-familys-anguish/)

The accused appealed against the verdict in vain. Ironically, he also put forward forensic analyses in his defense, but this was not successful.

VIGNETTE 7.2 Identifying the Unabomber

Between 1978 and 1995, the US public was increasingly alarmed by a series of bomb attacks; parcels with explosives were sent to various institutions through the regular postal service, killing three and injuring almost two dozen people. The main targets were universities (the first attack occurred at the University of Chicago) and airlines. It was clear immediately that there was a terrorist who built bombs with materials bought in regular hardware stores throughout the country; the person was extremely skillful in not giving away any clues, left false trails, and even threatened to blow up airplanes. At some stage, more than 150 FBI agents worked on what became known as the Unabomber (Una: universities and airlines) case; based on the forensic analysis of bomb materials, addresses were targeted, places where the parcels were posted from were screened, and the backgrounds of victims were checked out. Soon there was some speculation that the attacker had been born in the Chicago area and later lived in Salt Lake City and the San Francisco Bay area. However, their gender and profession remained unclear, and the FBI profiled a range of potential attackers from disgruntled scientists to aircraft mechanics. For a long time, there was no real breakthrough, even though this was one of the most expensive investigations in FBI history. The terrorist simply left no trace.

It was only in 1995, seventeen years after the first attacks, that some evidence became available. The Unabomber sent a long essay explaining their motives and views on modernized technological society, demanding it be published in the *Washington Post*. After a lengthy discussion about whether the manifesto was authentic or not, whether publishing it would be an act of surrender to terrorists or whether it could even serve as an inspiration for copycats, the FBI director Louis Freeh and Attorney General Janet Reno authorized publication, in the hope that some information about the author's identity might come in from the public. Indeed, thousands of comments were sent in when the manifesto was reproduced, and one of them became top priority: A man by the name of David Kaczynski informed the FBI about his brother Ted, who had grown up in Chicago, taught at the University of California at Berkeley, then lived for some time in Salt Lake City before giving up his academic career and moving to a cabin in the forests near Lincoln, Montana. David's wife had noticed some special phrases, idioms, and oddly familiar ideas in the text, and these reminded her of Ted Kaczynski. She made letters and other correspondence available for analysis, and a linguistic comparison of these documents strongly suggested identical authorship. This very loosely matched the profile the FBI had constructed of the suspect, and on April 3, 1996, investigators arrested Kaczynski in his home. They located incriminating evidence there, such as bomb components, the original manifesto and some 40,000 handwritten journal pages, and a detonating device ready for posting.

Ted Kaczynski was jailed for life and died in prison on June 10, 2023. The search for the Unabomber is remembered vividly today and was the subject of mainstream movies and television series.

Language-based evidence is also important in the case of asylum seekers. It is a sad fact that millions of people are forced to flee their home countries for fear of prosecution or punishment; they often arrive in unfamiliar countries and surroundings, without documentation of their origins and nationality as they cannot present passports. Host countries face the problem of deciding whether fugitives qualify for political asylum or are economically motivated, that is driven by a desire for better living conditions. Governments around the world rely on linguists' opinions, based on the assumption that speech provides vital information about origins (Chapter 3).

A so-called **language analysis for the determination of origin** (**LADO**) is carried out to identify national, social and/or ethnic identity, and a language profile is set up for individual asylum seekers. Interviews are recorded and analyzed, idiosyncratic, distinctive, and diagnostic features are noted (accent, morphosyntax but also lexicon and loanwords). Cultural and geographic knowledge is tested to provide further evidence. Linguists have argued that it would be simplistic to assume a straightforward connection between region of origin and dialect/language spoken, particularly in the case of traumatized fugitives who have suffered prosecution and torture at home and spent years escaping these conditions, but sometimes language is the only piece of evidence available. This is important lifesaving work, and professional linguists have the necessary know-how to make such decisions:

> As a profession we are working towards a utopian future where anyone who is arrested both understands and is able to claim their rights; where anyone who needs the help of an interpreter is able to have one and where the prejudicial effect of interpreting on the legal process is reduced to an absolute minimum; where all legally significant interactions are audio- or video-recorded; and where all expert opinions, whether on the origin of an asylum seeker, the authorship of a disputed text, the comprehensibility of a text or the confusability or two trademarks are reliable and reproducible. (Coulthard & Johnson 2010: 614)

No matter whether assessing written or spoken language, establishing authorship, or verifying national, regional, or ethnic origins, language-based evidence is crucial in legal and political contexts. These decisions can be made with a direct comparison of text messages (as in the (2008) Jenny Nicholl murder case), involve a quantitative evaluation of stylistic variation, or be based on the phonetic analysis of recordings (as we saw in Labov's Prinzivalli case), or be crucial in determining speaker origins. In the case of immigration, such analyses are key factors in decisions on whether asylum seekers are granted right of residence or are sent back to their insecure home countries.

7.4 Educational Failure

Addressing educational consequences of reading failure has been a particularly pressing concern for sociolinguists since the 1960s. This was the time when the relationship between social dialects and language learning appeared on the radar and when some first awareness of the consequences of using nonstandardized dialects in the classroom developed. There was a lively discussion about whether the use of American Standard English would favor the socially dominant groups (thus ensuring they maintained their status, getting access to better education and job opportunities), whereas minority groups would be disadvantaged in the educational progress. Some argued that the discrepancy between socially valued varieties and stigmatized ones was a social problem, and the question arose of how insights from dialectology and variationist sociolinguistics (Chapter 2) could be applied to language teaching.

In the controversial work of Basil Bernstein, a British sociologist, he claimed that "language was a set of rules to which all speech codes must comply, but which speech codes are realized is a function of the culture acting through social relationships in specific contexts" (Bernstein 1970: 161). Language usage was a consequence of socialization, "a complex process of control, whereby a particular moral, cognitive and affective awareness is evoked in the child and given a specific form and content" (1970: 162). Bernstein argued that there were essentially two codes (he named them **restricted code and elaborated code**), which were a function of socialization and social-class membership. He argued that the two codes were linguistically different because:

- Syntax was "more formally correct" (Bernstein 1970: 164) in the elaborated code and less complex in the restricted code: for instance, the elaborated code had more subordinate clauses and fewer unfinished sentences.
- There were more logical connectives like *if* and *unless* in the elaborated code, whereas the restricted code used simple coordination like *and* and *but*.
- Elaborated code had higher originality whereas restricted code used more clichés.
- Reference was more explicit in the elaborated code and rather implicit in the restricted code: The restricted code had more pronouns.
- The elaborated code was used to convey facts and abstract ideas, the restricted code attitudes and feelings.

Bernstein illustrated the existence of codes in the case of 5-year-old children, working-class and middle-class, who were given a series of three pictures showing boys playing football and breaking a window. Here are two samples of how a representative of each group described the events:

- *Elaborated code:* "Three boys are playing football and one boy kicks the ball and it goes through the window and the ball breaks the window and the boys are looking at it and a man comes out and shouts at them

because they've broken the window so they run away and then that lady looks out of her window and she tells the boys off."
- *Restricted code:* "They're playing football and he kicks it and it goes through there it breaks the window and they're looking at it and he comes out and shouts at them because they've broken it so they run away and then she looks out and she tells them off."

Sociolinguists such as William Labov pointed out that Bernstein made inaccurate and negative statements about African American English (Labov 1970). There was debate as to how to interpret these samples and a dispute between proponents of language difference and language deficit. The **deficit hypothesis** proponents held that children from economically poor homes or ethnically different families were linguistically deficient (Chapter 1), that is their dialects were linguistically inferior when compared to the standard. In other words, in order to help students from these backgrounds, teachers should give them some knowledge of the standard so as to progress and be successful. Accordingly, minority and ethnic dialects or English-based creoles (such as those spoken in Hawai'i and the Caribbean) had to be kept out of the classroom as much as possible, so that Standard English could become the sole target of formal education. We have already discussed the Standard English ideology (Chapter 4) and the view that Standard English is the key to academic and economic success.

However, sociolinguists such as Bill Labov, Walt Wolfram, John Baugh, and others strongly argued that non-mainstream dialects were not "restricted code," that their tense and aspect systems were in fact more complex and, in the case of AAE in particular, that they came from cultures in which rhetorical and expressive styles skills were highly valued. As dialects had different social functions, the selection of Standard English as the sole medium of instruction was an important reason for educational failure. Moreover, it was not realistic to aim at making a diverse classroom entirely Standard English-speaking. Language testing was seen as problematic as standardized tests were developed on the basis of the distribution of scores over a sample of the general population. Such a practice was biased against children whose speech was systematically different when compared to the mainstream population's. This had dramatic consequences: Students scoring below a normal range were diagnosed as having language disorders and grammatical deficits.

To give an example: The island of Tristan da Cunha hosts one of the most isolated English-speaking communities in the world. Located in the middle of the South Atlantic Ocean, it has just over 200 inhabitants (Schreier 2003). From the Second World War onward, a local infrastructure, including a local school, was built up; before that, children were educated in Sunday school. The local dialect is unique in the world for a number of reasons (see Chapter 4), and outsiders find it difficult to understand, particularly when the Tristanians speak among themselves. Dialect differentiation posed considerable problems for education. Evans (1994) collected the prevailing views of teachers in the 1950s and 1960s and assessed the situation as follows:

> Throughout the story of schooling on Tristan teachers noted the particular language style of the islanders, seeking on one hand to preserve its special characteristics, and on the other to teach standard English. For example, many years later, Miss E. Harvey, a teacher from Norfolk, reported: For the first two days I found the Island speech difficult to understand. Often Islanders ask a question in the form of a statement, only the lifting of the voice showing that a question is intended. 'Sidney, what time it is?' or 'Good morning Teacher. How you is?' She found that many words were pronounced differently — 'rop' for rope, 'sop' for soap, 'larning' for learning, 'coating' for courting. She was addressed as 'Missarvey'. Jim Flint, a later head teacher, commented: 'In the islanders' Dickensian speech Vs become Ws and extra Hs abound — one islander told him — 'Hi didn't was want to went hout hin the dark.' The children simply spoke two languages — School English and Island English. An attempt to change something which I believed worth preserving played no part in our English course.' (Evans 1994: 275)

Though most teachers appreciated the local dialect, they reported that it posed considerable problems for their teaching as all materials were based on Standard English. In the words of one of the teachers, "Sometimes I have to make them [the schoolchildren] repeat sentences slowly, before I can be sure of the meaning. They have two distinct languages, and they have forgotten school speech during the holiday" (quoted in Evans 1994: 288). Educationalists later claimed that the isolation of the island, alleged inbreeding, and the lack of mental stimulation combined to explain educational failure, and the 1977 *Education Report* concluded that:

> By the time children reach the Senior Class, environmental factors are a great problem. Very few Tristan homes have any books. The Tristan vocabulary in general use is very limited and then in a dialect based on the spoken word and not the written. Such deficiencies are very difficult to overcome. This is coupled with an innate lack of drive for a goal. (quoted in Evans 1994:304)

The question then is what kind of education was best fitted to the everyday practices and sociolinguistic experience of the local schoolchildren.

A number of practical educational issues need to be considered here. First, the requirement to teach in spoken Standard English posed problems for teachers who spoke nonstandardized varieties. Second, as the vast majority of students speak a local, highly distinctive dialect, overt correction of nonstandardized speech was likely to have negative effects on learning and motivation. Third, a forced switch to Standard English, even if possible, might change the students' perceptions of identity and of their own family histories and ways of life, and might have harmful effects. Sociolinguistically speaking, the enforcement of RP or General American English accents in the classroom is simply not practicable here, and the best practice adopted on Tristan was that islanders were hired for teaching after having received some training in Britain.

The situation is somewhat different when it comes to teaching reading and writing. Some suggest carrying out early education and reading in the native vernacular, followed by a gradual move to standard spelling – an approach which does not have unanimous support from educational scientists and is criticized within the community also. This is different in the domain of writing and dialect readers, as it is generally questionable whether differences in linguistic structure are responsible here.

Let's take the Caribbean as a case in point. This is an extremely heterogeneous setting in terms of contact-induced language change and the formation of pidgin and creoles (Chapter 4). Six languages have official status: Spanish, French, English, Dutch, Haitian Creole, and Papiamento, plus some languages that are symbolic nationally but do not have official status (such as Arawak languages or Jamaican Creole). The clash between official language and mother tongue is evident:

> What is known as the English-speaking or anglophone Caribbean might be more usefully described as the English-official Caribbean, that is areas of the Caribbean in which English functions as an official language but not necessarily as a mother tongue or a vernacular variety used in unofficial and informal contexts. (Alleyne 1985)

In Jamaica, the local creole (Patwa) is used for everyday, informal situations, at home, with family and friends, whereas Jamaican Standard English is the language of education, high culture, government, the media, and official/formal communication (this resembles the classic case of diglossia, as discussed in Chapter 4). Only a small minority of Jamaicans (mostly upper-class and upper-middle-class) speak Jamaican StdE natively. As on Tristan da Cunha, the question is how Patwa should be incorporated into the teaching curriculum for the benefit of children, most of whom have little access to the Standard and struggle at school. They are effectively forced to get some education in a variety they have to learn first, a situation similar to that of migrant children elsewhere. Accordingly, linguists such as **Hubert Devonish** claimed that Patwa should be used as the medium of instruction. Creoles should be used in education so as to enhance the official status of Creole in the public and administrative domain. He argued that the stigma in education led to negative attitudes in society, which further marginalized its usage in the classroom as part of a vicious circle.

This idea has some appeal. First, it gives credit to the fact that the community's majority language is Patwa. Second, endorsing Creole as a medium of instruction would enlarge the pool of potential teachers (as many of them are Patwa speakers themselves), and make it more accessible for the children, who have firsthand knowledge of it. Devonish, a former professor of linguistics and coordinator of The Jamaican Language Unit (JLU) at the University of the West Indies, lobbied for protection from language discrimination to be included in the Charter of Rights. He developed and tested alternative curricula and a bilingual program to enhance literacy with positive learning effects, thus giving Patwa higher societal status.

Fred Cassidy from JLU took this a step further by developing a new writing system, which is closer to spoken Patwa:

> The more the creole differs phonemically from the lexicalizing language (English, French, Dutch – whatever), the more it must differ in its orthography. It should be taught and learned in a system of its own ... Paramount should be a phonemically accurate, consistent, autonomous system. (Cassidy 1993).

The system includes double letters to indicate vowel length and new combinations of consonants to indicate local pronunciation (Figure 7.1).

Spelling reform remains an emotional issue. *Alfabet ina Jamiekan* is certainly radical and has been criticized by educationalists, parents, and lawmakers alike. There were objections on several counts. First of all, a radical reform would shift the goalposts, as one important aim of formal education has been to develop proficiency in Standard English reading and writing. Accordingly, students should spend as much time as possible learning the standard – any time dedicated to dialects in the classroom would have no benefit and could in fact disadvantage the children's development by confusing the varieties (Siegel 2006: 46). There was a "ghettoization" concern that students in special programs, receiving education in their home dialects, would be further isolated by not having the opportunity to interact with students who speak varieties closer to the standard (Siegel 2006: 51), thus cutting them off from all opportunities. The latter concern is

ALFABET INA JAMIEKAN

a aki ackee	**aa** baal ball	**ai** laim lime	**b** baibl bible	**ch** choch church	
d daag dog	**e** eg egg	**f** feda feather	**g** guot goat	**hn** kyaahn cannot	
i igwaana iguana	**ie** kiek cake	**ii** tii tea	**j** joj judge	**k** kait kite	
l lamp lamp	**m** manggo mango	**n** nuoz nose	**ng** king king	**o** okro okra	
ou kou cow	**p** pila pillow	**r** ron run	**s** sing sing	**sh** shaak shark	
t tiebl table	**u** uman woman	**uo** buot boat	**uu** shuuz shoes	**v** venda vendor	
w waal wall	**y** yam yam	**z** zuu zoo	**zh** chrezha treasure	a aa ai b ch d e f g hn i ie ii j k l m n ng o ou p r s sh t u uo uu v w y z zh	

Figure 7.1 *Alfabet ina Jamiekan*. Courtesy of The Jamaican Language Unit.

held mostly by parents, who remain skeptical about the value and practicality of dialects in the classroom. This has consequences: Even though the Bidialectal Communication Program was implemented to improve reading in the US, it failed because of the many negative reactions from parents and teachers (Labov 1995).

Consequently, language choice remains a thorny issue for education. It is a great challenge to ensure consistent access to and competence in the medium of instruction, particularly in heterogeneous and diverse classrooms where children have different sociolinguistic repertoires. At the same time, there is persistent unease with the idea of implementing dialects in the curriculum. One way out of this dilemma would be to implement local dialects considering instrumental, accommodation, and awareness concerns:

1. *Instrumental:* A local dialect may be used as a medium of instruction to teach initial literacy, for example via immersion in content subjects such as mathematics, science, and health (in Australia or in the case of Haitian Creole-speaking immigrants in the US). Alternatively, students may learn to read with materials in their home varieties first (which is practiced in Scandinavia) and then "bridge" to Standard English varieties. A transitional bilingual education approach is where the vernacular is gradually replaced by English as the main language for teaching school subjects. The use of a child's vernacular may, however, still be used.
2. *Accommodation:* Students' vernacular varieties are not actively taught and used but are accepted in the classroom. The standard remains the only medium of instruction, spoken by all teachers, but students can respond in their local dialects. This is practiced in Hawai'i and in higher-level education in Caribbean settings, such as Trinidad and Tobago; note this means teachers have to be speakers of these varieties themselves.
3. *Awareness:* The standard language remains the medium of instruction, but students' varieties are seen as a resource for learning the standard – and for learning in general, rather than as a deficit impeding their progress. Australia, for instance, has a "Two-way English" program for students in Western Australia who speak Aboriginal English.

To sum up, educational failure has been a great concern for applied sociolinguists. The challenge is to draw on the students' sociolinguistic resources, which typically do not (or only sporadically) include standard varieties, so as to enable them to progress in their education, maintain their identity, and not cut them off from economic and professional advancement. There has been resistance to using dialects in the classroom due to persistent misconceptions about the nature of educational programs using local varieties. On the one hand, there have been strong expressions of allegedly detrimental effects, entailing even stronger social stigmatization. On the other hand, it is recognized that there are benefits to using vernacular varieties in the classroom: the same classroom activities can be used for speakers of all varieties, both stigmatized and standardized, to fight against dialect prejudice. Speakers of nonmainstream varieties can discuss their own language in the classroom, which increases linguistic self-respect. Programs designed to increase awareness make students notice linguistic differences, which might help them develop bilingualism and increase their competence in reading and writing in standard.

No matter what policy is adopted and what sociolinguists have to say on educational matters, this is a most pressing concern in the light of the continuing diversification of classrooms around the world: Whatever approach is endorsed, we should not forget that "the minority differential in U.S. literacy is parallel to the literacy problems of many countries where the home language of children differs markedly from the first language of reading instruction" (Labov 2003: 131).

7.5 Language and Social Justice

The last domain considered here is the courtroom, where language also plays a major role. Sociolinguists have long been interested in power relationships as reflected by different discursive strategies, in methods to provide evidence (see Section 5.3) and, more recently, in addressing issues of social injustice. Let's remember that perhaps as much as 90 percent of the British population speak a regional, social, or ethnic form of English, while only very few of the remaining 10 percent who speak Standard English have an RP accent (this is Trudgill's 1998 estimate). Consequently, "speakers have virtually the same recognition of authorized usage, but very unequal knowledge of this usage" (Bourdieu 1991: 62). Language functions as a gatekeeper in a sociolinguistically imbalanced system, and Piller (2020) argues that this mismatch is increasing for two reasons. First, even though legislation has made considerable progress in addressing discrimination based on ethnicity, religion, and origins, the attitudes toward language-based prejudice have not disappeared. The problem is that, despite all efforts, it is still not recognized that stigmatizing people because of their language is on a par with other forms of discrimination. Second, due to large-scale migration and population movement, our social environment is diversifying quickly:

> migration has resulted in a significant increase in linguistic diversity and institutions are not always well-equipped to adapt to the changing linguistic needs of their clientele. Given that all social life is inevitably conducted through the medium of a particular language, a lack of proficiency in the medium of an institution constitutes a significant disadvantage. (Piller 2020: 4)

Such attitudes have dramatic consequences, not only in the classroom but also at court. They become most evident when the defense is built on damaging witness credibility based on the way they speak:

> in the United States and around the world in which witnesses or defendants use a vernacular rather than the mainstream variety, they tend to be misunderstood or discredited, and encounter dialect unfamiliarity. (Rickford & King 2016: 950–951)

Prejudice against African American English in the US judicial system has been documented thoroughly. Court recorders are not aware of the intricacies of AAE tense and aspect systems, which really matter in eyewitness accounts. Green (2002) describes cases of erroneously transcribed accounts in courtrooms that involve "come," a marker of indignation, not being recognized: *He come tell (me) bout I'm gonna take the TV* (was transcribed as <??? I'm gonna take the TV>). The witness expresses irritation that another person wants to remove a TV set, not that they are physically taking it, an important difference obviously.

Similarly, completive or resultant state *don* means that an action has been completed (as "I don eat the pie"). It is potentially harmful when a statement such as "They done tore that room up" was mistranscribed as <They just tore that room up>; for one, this is not the meaning intended, and second, the rendering as "just" adds another type of meaning, as if they had destroyed the room without a purpose or warning. A third example involves immediate future *finna/fitna* (lexicalized from *fitting to*), a preverbal marker which indicates immediate future (*I am finna leave*, "I am just about to leave"). A statement such as *I'm fitna be admitted* was mistranscribed as <I'm fit to be admitted>, which is simply not what the witness intended to say. There is no need to stress the consequences of a lack of understanding of social and ethnic dialects.

Brown-Blake & Chambers (2007: 277) report a striking case of intelligibility error in Britain, involving both syntax and phonology, in the account of a Jamaican Creole (JC) speaker testifying in a police interview. Here is what the witness said:

> "wen mi ier di bap bap, mi drap a groun an den mi staat ron." ('when I heard the bap bap [the shots], I fell to the ground and then I started to run')

This was transcribed as:

> <When I heard the shot (bap, bap), <u>I drop the gun</u>, and then I run>. (emphasis added, DS)

The error involves the misidentification of *drop* as a transitive rather than an intransitive verb, *a* as a Standard indefinite article and not as a Creole preposition meaning "to," and the misinterpretation of JC *groun* (/groŋ/) "ground" as /gon/ "gun." *Drap a groun* does not mean "drop the gun" at all, and it is easy to imagine what consequences such a mistake has; it is only when native interpreters are hired to countercheck that such errors can be cleared up (as happened in this case). This may be expensive, but it is essential to keeping innocent speakers from being punished for crimes they did not commit.

The adequate translation provided and checked by native speakers is important, but anthropological and ethnographic issues also play a role. Australia provides a case in point here:

> The likelihood Aboriginal people have of coming into contact with the criminal justice system is twenty times that of non-Aboriginal Australians ... and the ways in which they use language have a significant bearing on the outcomes of their involvement with the law. (Malcolm 2018: 540).

Different expectations of behavior can have negative consequences when speakers of Australian Aboriginal English have to testify in court. Analyses of testimonies of Aboriginals (Eades 2000: 163) demonstrate that Native Australians are not culturally used to direct question–answer patterns, which is the principal method of inquiry in witness cross-examinations. Direct questions are considered as face-threatening (Chapter 6), even taboo in some Aboriginal communities, and hence are avoided. Similarly, there are different perceptions of silence as an appropriate reaction (cultural practices of "no-gap-no-overlap," Chapter 6). While remaining silent is a most respectful and appropriate response in some Aboriginal communities, in court this may be interpreted as an attempt to withhold information and refusing cooperation, which damages the perceived trustworthiness of an indigenous witness. This is also reported as a barrier to communication in US American Navajo school settings.

Eades (2000: 190) reports a problematic tendency in courtroom discourse for judges and attorneys. Some of them commonly silence indigenous witnesses in situations where they do not follow their explanations related to culture and lifestyle, or deem them to be irrelevant to a case. One good example is explanations of kinship terms, which may seem straightforward to speakers of mainstream Australian English but are ambiguous for indigenous speakers and need explanation. Similarly, an indigenous person's lawyer may lack sufficient cross-cultural communication skills to fully understand a client's explanations and fail to represent them adequately. There is a need for more sociolinguistic knowledge and increased awareness of discourse conventions among legal practitioners, so as to avoid bias against Indigenous Australians. In the words of Rickford & King (2016: 951), "lawyers, judges, and foundations committed to social equity and justice seem almost completely uninformed about how 'language can stand as a barrier to justice or equal opportunity'." With this aim, handbooks such as the *Aboriginal English in the Courts* (Queensland 2001) have been made available to help fill this need. However, Eades (2004) reports that in some cases awareness of intercultural communication has been used to manipulate cross-examination, for example by "scaffolding" answers through the choice of questions. Of course, native-speaker knowledge of Indigenous Australians would be of great benefit here, but this population is virtually absent in the Australian legal profession.

Perhaps the most perfidious strategy in court is to directly harm witness credibility because of the dialect they speak. A recent example of such practices is the "State of Florida vs. George Zimmerman" case. Trayvon Martin, a 17-year-old African American from Florida, was on his way home from a convenience store on February 26, 2012 when he met George Zimmerman, a member of the community watch. Shortly after Zimmerman reported the allegedly suspicious behavior by Martin to the police, there was an encounter between the two and Zimmerman shot Martin in the chest. Zimmerman himself had minor injuries and he said he had acted in self-defense, so was not charged at the time.

It was only after the case was picked up by national and international media that Zimmerman had to stand trial. The key witness was a 19-year-old high-school student, Rachel Jeantel, with whom Martin had been on the phone just seconds before he was shot. Jeantel, a speaker of African American English with some influence from Caribbean Creole English, "was not properly heard (understood, responded to) in the courtroom, and ... this fundamentally and negatively affected the believability of her testimony in the Zimmerman trial" (Rickford & King 2016: 957). She testified for nearly six hours longer than any of the other witnesses, in fact, but in the end her account was not considered by the jury at all (Figure 7.2). The fact that Jeantel's socially stigmatized way of speaking was sometimes not understood led the jurors to question her credibility and disregard her statement (Rickford &

Figure 7.2 Rachel Jeantel testifying in court. (Pool/Getty Images News.)

King 2016: 957), so the jury ended up acquitting Zimmerman of second-degree murder and manslaughter in July 2013. This lays bare some deep-rooted societal problems, as Rickford & King (2016) emphasize:

> It is important to note that such discrimination, which Baugh has called 'linguistic profiling', should not necessarily be attributed to racial prejudice on the individual level, but to institutional racism at the societal level, a distinction that news media commentaries failed to make in the Trayvon Martin case. (Hodges 2015: 978)

Of course, this goes far beyond the realm of English sociolinguistics, as societal, historical, cultural, and linguistic aspects all play a role in discrimination and institutional racism. But language does play a major role in linguistic profiling and the consequences of linguistic discrimination need to be assessed and discussed by the wider public. This is a major societal concern. The acquittal of Zimmerman sparked protests against the injustice African Americans face in seeking restitution in the courts, and these saw the beginnings of the **#BlackLivesMatter** movement, one of the most influential civil rights movements in American history.

To sum up, the courtroom is a major site for applied sociolinguists. Based on the language used and evaluated in such settings, juries make decisions about whether to find someone guilty or whether to acquit them, and attorneys and judges evaluate language use in their decisions. Language contributes to and fosters inequality, as linguistic discrimination is not on the radar as other forms of discrimination are. Sociolinguists make every effort not only to bring in their expertise to cross-check and translate spoken statements but also to educate decision-makers about the social and cultural backgrounds of the parties who come together in the courtroom. Judges have to understand what it means ethnographically when Aboriginal Australians or First-Nation Americans are silent during cross-examination, that this is not a sign of admitting guilt or refusing to cooperate. They must be alerted that this behavior respects their cultural practices. Applied sociolinguists are called upon to alert the public when "vernacular speakers are ... misunderstood or unfairly assailed and misjudged in court" (Rickford & King 2016: 952). Knowledge of dialect diversity and cultural differentiation is crucial; it can help save lives.

7.6 Conclusion

Sociolinguists work with data drawn from speech communities and on occasion become part of the social lives of the speakers whose language they study. They should consider it a responsibility to share their knowledge and step in when language attitudes cause harm, particularly when the Standard English ideology is involved. No matter whether it is the principle of "error correction," "debt incurred" (Labov 1982), or proactive "linguistic gratuity" (Wolfram 1993), sociolinguists bring in their expertise and advice for a variety of societal concerns: linguistic discrimination, forensic linguistics, educational failure, language in the courtroom, and linguistic profiling. It is they who have firsthand knowledge of language-related issues, including the function and structure of nonmainstream varieties which are so often misinterpreted and misunderstood by the general public.

In forensic linguistics, sociolinguists may use written and spoken language to establish the likelihood of authorship, to verify national, regional, or ethnic group membership of asylum seekers, and give testimony in legal and political contexts. In educational issues, they promote awareness of the complexities of nonmainstream varieties and develop programs which enable children, no matter what dialect they speak, to make good progress in their education. Teachers and educationalists need to be made aware of the benefits of using vernacular varieties in the classroom. Students should draw on their sociolinguistic resources as much as possible to avoid stigmatization and enhance linguistic self-respect. The challenge is to help them develop bidialectalism and increase their competence in reading and writing the standard variety. This concern is particularly urgent in light of the continuing diversification of classrooms around the world. Last but not least, the courtroom is another major site for applied sociolinguists. Sociolinguists share their expertise when it comes to cross-checking and translating spoken statements, advising decision-makers about social and cultural diversity in the courtroom, and also discuss cases where linguistic discrimination leads to the stigmatization of witnesses. The situation is aptly summarized by Rickford & King (2016: 949):

> The central role of the Zimmerman trial in the birth of the influential #BlackLivesMatter movement and the central role of AAVE in the ignoring of Jeantel's testimony in that trial remind us of the central importance of language in the lives of individuals and societies. Working for justice can take many forms, but for linguists, we believe it should include listening to vernacular dialects more closely and hearing their speakers more clearly and more fairly, not only in courtrooms, but also in schools, job interviews, apartment searches, doctors' visits, and everywhere that speech and language matter. Dispelling fictions about and prejudices against vernacular speech is a task that linguists are best qualified to undertake.

Some progress has been made over the years, but so much still needs to be done. There remains a feeling of unease that decades of sociolinguistic research have not more successfully ensured that those members of communities, who have no privilege or opportunity to speak the standard variety, the vast majority in fact, are still treated unfairly because of the way they speak.

> **Take-Home Messages**
> - Sociolinguists use their knowledge to benefit speakers and communities, particularly those with nonstandardized varieties.
> - This has been labeled the principle of "error correction" and "debt incurred" (Labov 1982) or "linguistic gratuity" (Wolfram 1993).
> - Often, prejudice and discrimination come from ignorance about linguistic systems, which are interpreted against the Standard language ideology.
> - Forensic sociolinguists assist in legal matters where language-related evidence is of legal relevance.
> - There have been numerous programs to draw on pupils' sociolinguistic repertoire so that they can make progress in reading and writing. Enforcing standard pronunciation is not practical, however.
> - In court, sociolinguists bring in their expertise to cross-check and translate spoken statements, to educate decision-makers about the social and cultural backgrounds of all parties involved, and also to raise awareness if dialect differences are used to discredit witnesses.

Activities

7.1 The following is a real case (reported in Garcia 2016: 345):

> Manuel Fragrante immigrated to Hawaii at the age of 60. Upon arrival, he began searching for a job. He applied for a clerk position at the City of Honolulu's Division of Motor Vehicles and Licensing. The position required taking an exam that tested "among other things, word usage, grammar and spelling." Fragante scored the highest out of 721 test-takers. Shortly after, he was interviewed for the position. During the interview, the interviewers had a difficult time understanding Fragante due to his accent. The employer concluded that his accent "would interfere with his performance of certain aspects of the job." As a result, Fragante dropped from the

first to the third position on the list of applicants and subsequently filed a Title VII claim alleging accent discrimination. At the trial, two expert witnesses testified that, even though Fragante spoke with a heavy accent, his speech was comprehensible. However, they also stated that due to a history of discrimination against foreign accents like his, listeners may "turn off" and not understand him.

Discuss factors that speak in favor of and against employment. How would you measure and access the importance of "intelligibility" in such a position?

7.2 Read the following article about forensic linguistics: http://news.bbc.co.uk/2/hi/science/nature/7600769.stm.

Then go through some of your own text messages. What features would you single out that would lend themselves to analysis? How would you assess their degree of consistency and distinctiveness? Compare your notes with those of others. Are your observations similar?

7.3 According to what you have heard about restricted and elaborated speech codes, would you agree with Bernstein's claim that "the bottom line is that if you can't handle elaborated code, you are not going to succeed in the educational (and therefore higher class) system"?

7.4 McWhorter (1998, 2000) strongly argued against the use of African American English (and other nonstandardized dialects) in the classroom as a bridge to learning Standard English. His arguments were the following:
1. *Immersion:* The best technique to acquire a new variety is by immersion, not by making use of the first language or dialect.
2. *Similarity:* Linguistic differences between varieties are not that significant.
3. *No positive effects:* There is no conclusive evidence that children learn better when their native dialect is used in the educational process, so there is no reason to develop special language programs focusing on these students.
4. *Practicality:* It is impractical to bring vernaculars into formal education. Nonstandardized dialects have not been codified; even if they could be standardized, the cost of developing written materials would be prohibitive.

Discuss these arguments in turn. What do you think?

7.5 Discuss whether creole-speaking children are disadvantaged when they are not allowed to use their home language, and give reasons. Imagine you were in charge of implementing one of these programs (instrumental, accommodation, or awareness) at your local school: Which one would you choose and why?

7.6 Watch the news clip on the George Zimmerman trial at: www.youtube.com/watch?v=GnXZY4rogo8.

Discuss how the cross-examination is portrayed and what stance is taken toward the questioning of Zimmerman's defense team.

Key Terms
#BlackLivesMatter
code, restricted and elaborated
consistency
deficit hypothesis
Hubert Devonish
distinctiveness
forensic linguistics
language analysis for the determination of origin (LADO)
linguistic discrimination/linguicism
linguistic prejudice
matched/verbal guise techniques
Standard Language ideology

Further Reading

The following is a good introduction to forensic linguistics:
Coulthard, M. (2010). Forensic Linguistics: The Application of Language Description in Legal Contexts. *Langage et société*, 15–33. doi:10.3917/ls.132.0015. URL: www.cairn.info/revue-langage-et-societe-2010-2-page-15.htm.

An excellent overview of language in the courtroom, from an Australian perspective, is found in:
Eades, D. (2011). Sociolinguistics and the Law. In: R. Mesthrie, ed., *The Cambridge Handbook of Sociolinguistics* (Cambridge Handbooks in Language and Linguistics). Cambridge: Cambridge University Press, 377–395. doi:10.1017/CBO9780511997068.028.

The shocking analysis of "State of Florida vs. George Zimmerman" is found in:
Rickford, J., & King, S. (2019). Language and Linguistics on trial: Hearing Rachel Jeantel (and Other Vernacular Speakers) in the Courtroom and Beyond. In: J. Rickford & G. Sankoff, *Variation, Versatility and Change in Sociolinguistics and Creole Studies*. Cambridge: Cambridge University Press, 245–300. doi:10.1017/9781316091142.014.

And an excellent introduction to language attitudes is:
Garrett, P. (2010). *Attitudes to Language*. Cambridge: Cambridge University Press.

CHAPTER 8

Language Planning and the Law

In This Chapter ...

... we look into a range of sociolinguistic aspects involved in politics and nation building. Some language issues may have a political dimension, and English has played a major role in this around the world. One important issue here is whether English should be adopted to serve in all official functions as a national or official language, which is particularly important in postcolonial contexts, or whether a local language, accessible to larger sections of a community, should be adopted instead. We will discuss how and to what extent governments should plan and orchestrate language-related activities in education and public discourse, and we look at language policies implemented in the US and Ireland (concerning history, socioethnic varieties, bilingualism, and multilingualism) as cases in point. We also discuss the impact of governmental bodies on language planning when focusing on the Speak Good English movement in Singapore, and present efforts to achieve language revitalization, which are preeminent given the increasing rate of language obsolescence and death around the world. The chapter ends with a look at language rights in the case of migrant communities.

8.1	Language Planning: Basic Issues	*page* 221
8.2	Language Policies in the US: A Case in Point	226
	Vignette 8.1: Gutierrez v. Municipal Court	229
8.3	Language Obsolescence and Revitalization	232
	Vignette 8.2: Reviving Cornish	236
8.4	Speak Good English in Singapore	240
	Vignette 8.3: Esperanto	240
8.5	Language Rights vs. Language Survival	244
8.6	Conclusion	247
	Take-Home Messages	248
	Activities	249
	Key Terms	250
	Further Reading	251

8.1 Language Planning: Basic Issues

Language planning involves a deliberate effort on the part of governments, nongovernmental organizations, or individuals to shape and influence the function, structure, or acquisition of a particular language. The goals of language planning may differ depending on agent and purpose but generally involve decisions that affect speech communities in regions or nations. Among others, sociolinguists are interested in three related questions:

1. What do we understand by the term language planning, what are the processes involved and how are these enforced?
2. What are the motivations behind regulating language at a state or national level, and who benefits from such practices?
3. How effective are language-planning policies, and why are they successful or counterproductive?

Let's start with a hands-on example. We discussed the emergence of the New Englishes in Chapter 4 and found that Indian English was one of the key players among Global Englishes, both in terms of speaker numbers and supraregional, perhaps even global, influence. The history of English in India is long and complex. The roots of English there can be dated to the seventeenth century, when merchants associated with the East India Company set up local trade centers, and the first missionaries arrived. English was the language of the British expatriate population and a small local elite, who cooperated with the British and served their commercial and political interests while themselves profiting financially. English served as the language of education and learning for this group, and after the Crown took over administration from the East India Company, English progressively turned into a second language. Bilingualism, involving indigenous languages and English as a Second or Foreign Language, in due course became more widespread in Indian society.

The function and status of local languages were reevaluated toward the end of British colonial rule. The early twentieth century saw some attempts to instate local languages in elementary schools, and an ideological debate occurred when India sought political independence after the Second World War. The function of English was still strong as it was the language of the Indian National Congress and a new political leadership. Mahatma Gandhi was fluent in English, as he had been exiled earlier in his life to South Africa. The question was whether a newly independent India should adopt English as the national or official language or whether one or several of the local languages should be chosen instead. Gandhi, who had protested and demanded an end to British rule, in a parliamentary speech (which ironically was given in English) argued in favor of abandoning the former colonial language from all public life. In 1933, he wrote:

> I know this tussle between English and Hindi is almost an eternal tussle. Whenever I have addressed student audiences, I have been surprised by the demand for English. You know, or ought to know, that I am a lover of the English language. But I do believe that the students of India, who are expected to throw in their lot with the teeming millions and to serve them, will be better qualified if they pay more attention to Hindi than to English. I do not say that you should not learn English; learn it by all means. But, so far as I can see, it cannot be the language of the millions of Indian homes. It will be confined to thousands or tens of thousands, but it will not reach the millions.

The dilemma was that English represented a global language, an international lingua franca, but it was not available to hundreds of millions of Indians. Gandhi argued that a local language such as Hindi would have wider currency in the country, so it should be adopted instead. The struggle about the future of English intensified after the Second World War, when India cut ties with Britain. After intense debate, article 343 of the 1949 Indian constitution stipulated Hindi as the official language, with English as a second official language for a period of fifteen years. After that, Hindi should have become the single national language and served as a symbol of national unity, spoken in government and administration. However, this was met with fierce protests throughout India, as it was objected that the adoption of Hindi would be advantageous to the (Hindi-speaking) north and discriminatory elsewhere. Indians from the mostly Dravidian South strongly opposed this policy. There were violent upheavals and civil unrest against the phasing-out of English, and in 1967, a new "Three-Language Formula" was implemented in the Language Act. Hindi was to become the new official and national language, regional languages were to be strengthened until English would eventually disappear and become dispensable. In the *Year Book of the Commonwealth* (Great Britain: Foreign and Commonwealth Office 1985: 212), it said that:

> The Constitution [of 1947] laid down that after 1965 Hindi should be used for all official purposes. The official Languages Act, 1963, however, provided for the continued use after 1965 of English, in addition to Hindi, for all official purposes of the Union and for the transaction of business in Parliament. Under this Act a Parliamentary Committee was set up in 1975 to review the progress made in the use of Hindi.

Article 345 of the Constitution provided for the adoption by States Legislatures, for official purposes of the State, of any of the fourteen regional languages, listed in the Eighth Schedule to the Constitution.

These were Assamese, Bengali, Gujarati, Hindi, Kannada, Kashmiri, Malayalam, Marathi, Oriya, Punjabi, Sanskrit, Tamil, Telugu, and Urdu. A fifteenth, Sindi, was subsequently added. Sanskrit, which is a scholarly language used primarily in religious or poetic contexts, has not been adopted for official use by any State.

With hindsight, it is remarkable how sociolinguistically wrong Gandhi was, as he obviously underestimated the antagonistic views that existed toward Hindi in much of the country. English could not be kept out at all, simply because the alternative was bitterly opposed. Only half a century later, the anglophone Indian population outnumbered the total population of the British Isles, and Indian English is one of the most widely spoken varieties of English around the world today. Still, Gandhi's concerns continue to have some relevance as the large sections of the Indian population who are not fluent in English face significant barriers to education and employment. Looking back now, it is clear that India's postindependence policy did not work in this regard. English is still in place today, in fact is more important than before (Chapter 4), and it has a strong position as an official language in public life and all formal domains. All efforts to do away with the former colonial language were unsuccessful and it is now the second official language in the Indian Constitution. English is used in the domains of education, administration, law, mass media, science and technology, trade, and commerce. Any attempts to remove it from official functions now would surely meet with vehement protests.

There are similar cases of language selection throughout the English-speaking world. After the Second World War, many of the former colonies cut their ties with Britain. Between the 1940s and the 1970s, most overseas territories gained independence, yet maintained political, economic, and also symbolic ties with the British Crown and the Commonwealth. As a result, the importance of English remained paramount: Education was in English, and so was all official communication. In many of these countries, the question concerned what language status should be given to English vis-à-vis local languages and whether or not it should be recognized as an official language. At the risk of some overgeneralization, these debates boiled down to the two opposing views of **vernacularization** and **internationalization.**

- Vernacularization refers to the selection and restoration of an indigenous language that is adopted as an official language (e.g. Hebrew in Israel or Quechua in Peru).

- Internationalization is pursued when a non-indigenous language is given official status in particular domains, as happened in Singapore, India, the Philippines, Guyana, Papua New Guinea, Namibia, and many other places.

The question was whether there should be one single official language or several, which languages should have national or regional status, and so on. Very often, multilingualism and linguistic pluralism were important because language policies had to ensure social peace in societies where multiple languages were spoken (e.g. Hindi, Telugu, regional languages, and English in India). Accordingly, in the early twenty-first century, English has several language statuses around the world in no less than 84 countries (Crystal 2009: 62–65; see Table 8.1).

Table 8.1 *The language statuses of English around the world. Adapted from Crystal (2009: 62–65).*

Status	National/regional	Example
Sole official language	National	Former territories of the British Empire, but also Namibia and Burundi
Joint official language	National	English, Afrikaans, Zulu, Xhosa and other languages in South Africa
Promoted language	No official status but used for specific functions	West African Pidgin English in Cameroon

Today, English is the sole official language of the Commonwealth of Nations and the Association of Southeast Asian Nations (ASEAN), and is one of the official languages of the United Nations, the European Union, the African Union, the North American Free Trade Agreement (NAFTA), and the Organization of Islamic Cooperation, to name but a few international bodies.

As Crystal (2009) points out, there is a distinction between de facto and de jure statuses. For instance, English may be adopted as a **de jure official language** in a country, effectively functioning as a primary language, so that it has been legally established as the national language of the country (examples in this category include Namibia, where it is the sole official language). English can also be adopted as a de jure co-official language, as in South Africa, where several languages such as Zulu, Xhosa, and others have the same status; or in Canada, which pursues a bilingual policy and endorses more than one language to avoid promoting one group of speakers over another. Multilingual communities typically opt for a co-official approach to avoid clashes between different speaker groups.

In other countries, English serves as a **de facto official language**, which means that it does not have explicit legal status. In countries such as the US, Australia, and New Zealand, it is a primary language not legally recognized but spoken by the majority of the people (note that English is not the de jure official language of the US, at least not on a national level). As such, it enjoys a demographic and very often a historical advantage. As a result, the UK and the US grant English no legal status in their constitutions, an issue which repeatedly sets off political debates and tensions. Most countries have one or two official national languages and give them judicial status, while the US and the UK do not have such legal protection.

Very often, criteria such as language history, cultural orientation, and colonial and postcolonial experiences go hand in hand with national identity. To promote the latter, closely related varieties may be selected as separate languages, perhaps ultimately due to political reasons: Danish and Norwegian are mutually intelligible yet have legal status as separate languages. Serbia and Croatia have adopted different writing systems: Cyrillic for Serbian and Roman script for Croatian. Similarly, countries such as Papua New Guinea have adopted local pidgins like Tok Pisin as official languages (Chapter 4), which reflects the controversial relationship between English, the varieties it gave rise to under contact conditions, and the preexisting local languages.

It is clear that languages have different types of "weight" in communities (see Chapter 9), with English giving its speakers an advantage. Tensions of this kind have been discussed with reference to **linguistic imperialism**, a hotly debated issue:

> A working definition of English linguistic imperialism is that the dominance of English is asserted and maintained by the establishment and continuous reconstitution of structural and cultural inequalities between English and other languages. (Philipson 1992: 47)

This is most controversial in terms of language obsolescence and death, as it implies that English is responsible for the disappearance of thousands of languages around the world. We will return to this in Chapter 9.

To summarize, English language planning involves three major domains, relating to status, form, and function, which can be outlined as follows:

- **Status planning:** The allocation or reallocation of a language or variety to certain functional domains within a society. These planning decisions affect the status, or standing, of a language vis-à-vis other languages.

For instance, policymakers decide what official language(s) postapartheid South Africa should endorse, or whether West African Pidgin English, spoken by millions in a large geographic area in West Africa and the global diaspora as well, should be given special legislative status.
- Corpus planning: This refers to language-authoritative actions that concern the *form* of English. Corpus-planning decisions affect the structure of a language, for instance when it comes to spelling reform or grammar testing. The selection and codification of Standard English is a good example here (Chapter 5).
- Acquisition planning: This is when a national, state, or local government makes decisions which affect schooling and education and also the usage of language in childhood and adolescence. These planning decisions involve various levels of language usage, such as status, context, and literacy through education and ensure language rights. Language revival (e.g. via language nests in New Zealand) is a good example, but languages can also be prohibited from use in public. Minority languages may be banned from kindergartens and schools, very often to weaken the cultural identity of their speakers or to promote a national identity at the expense of a minority one. So-called **language proscription** (i.e. varieties discouraged by official sanction or restriction) has been implemented to weaken Basque and Catalan in Spain (during Franco's regime), Breton in France (marginalized during the nineteenth century and later the Third Republic), and German in the US (after the First World War).

We saw in Chapter 5 that the processes underlying Standard English involved various levels of language planning. It has been codified in grammar mostly, a new standard reference accent marginalized regional ones, and there were far-reaching ideological consequences on a global stage as well: "The creation of a standard, national, variety of language is undoubtedly a means by which a nation imagines itself; in intangible ways it can give the nation, so constituted and associated, considerable power, both internally, and on the international stage" (McColl Millar 2005: 200). Language planning is a complex process, politically, socially and sociolinguistically speaking, as it involves the status and function of a local reference variety and its relationship with other languages. Let's illustrate this by looking at language policies in the US.

8.2 Language Policies in the US: A Case in Point

North America has a long history of language contact, involving European (English, French, and Spanish) and Native American languages (Iroquois,

Algonquian, etc.). There are certain parallels with other parts of the world with British colonial influence. In the 1840s, federal government and missionary bodies started the first schools for Native Americans, teaching them English and basic skills such as reading and writing. The quality of schools and reservation life were controlled through agencies such as the Bureau of Indian Affairs (BIA, established in 1824) and, at the beginning of the nineteenth century, tribes such as Cherokee, Creek, and Seminole all had their own school systems. In 1852, the schooling system implemented for the Cherokee tribe used both English and Cherokee in an early immersion program, but during the 1861–65 Civil War, both the Union and the Confederacy became more aggressive in enforcing English culture on native Americans. Many of the established schools were closed by federal order so only a few were still in place at the end of the nineteenth century.

A policy of coercive assimilation with the aim of deculturation and domestication was enforced, and in the 1880s the IBA set up an education system of English-only boarding schools. Native American children were separated from their families at a young age, which was also common practice in Canada and Australia, and access to their ancestral cultures was cut off. Speaking native languages was prohibited and punished in most schools, and every effort was made so that children would no longer speak the languages of their parents. There was harsh punishment when children did not follow school rules or when they were caught speaking languages other than English (humiliation in class, corporal punishment, or having their mouths washed with soap). This had a disastrous effect on the usage of native languages and permanently weakened the heritage tradition and transmission of customs.

The case of Hispanic/Latinx Americans is both different and similar. English and Spanish have a long contact history in what is now the US Southwest, as several states there historically belonged to Mexico. American expansion into the Southwest was gradual and, after the 1835–36 revolution in Texas and particularly after the 1846–48 US–Mexican war, large portions of Mexican territory at the time (Texas, New Mexico, California) were annexed by the US. A sharp increase of Anglo-American settlement led to gradual naturalization of the inhabitants, including historically indigenous peoples in the present-day US. Tensions were intense, not surprising given the sociodemographic conditions, and today a sizeable minority of the total population (in some parts even the majority, as in San Antonio, Texas) refer to themselves as Hispanic/Latinx in official US censuses. Indeed, the Pew Research Center estimated that the US Hispanic/Latinx population reached ca. 63.6 million in 2022 and that they are in the demographic majority in some parts of the country and major cities. In four states (California, Arizona, New Mexico, and Texas), they represent more than 25 percent of the entire state population (Table 8.2, adapted from the Pew Research Center's 2022 analysis of the US Hispanic/Latinx population).

Table 8.2 *The Hispanic/Latinx population in the US (% of total population by state). Calculated and adapted from Pew Research Center tabulations of the American Community Survey provided through Integrated Public Use Microdata Series from the University of Minnesota.*

Total Hispanic/Latinx population in the US	Selected states
More than 10 million	Texas, California
1 million–10 million	Washington, Arizona, New Mexico, Colorado, Florida, Georgia, North Carolina, Illinois, Pennsylvania, New York, New Jersey
500,000–1 million	Oregon, Nevada, Utah, Indiana, Ohio, Michigan, Virginia, Maryland, Delaware, Massachusetts, Rhode Island
100,000–500,000	Idaho, Nebraska, Kansas, Oklahoma, Arkansas, Louisiana, Minnesota, Wisconsin, South Carolina, Tennessee, Kentucky, Alabama, Washington DC
0–100,000	Montana, North Dakota, South Dakota, Wyoming, Missouri, West Virginia

Today, first-language and heritage speakers of Spanish represent the largest language minority in the US. This can be explained by the steadily increasing immigration of Mexican workers to the US throughout the twentieth century. A significant percentage of immigration is also from various Central American countries and, most recently, there has also been substantial immigration from South America, Venezuela in particular. For example, between 1990 and 2002, the Mexican-born population residing in the US more than doubled from 4.3 million to 9.8 million immigrants, and speakers of Mexican Spanish now represent the largest Hispanic/Latinx group. There are differences in the language usage of the Hispanic sector of the US population. Data from the 2002 census show that 23% of Mexican Americans indicate they are English-dominant, 26% bilingual, and 51% Spanish-dominant. Puerto Ricans were 39% English-dominant, 40% bilingual, and only 21% Spanish dominant. However, Salvadorans, Dominicans, Colombians, and other Central and South American groups tended to be more Spanish-dominant.

What does this mean in the context of language policies? Until the 1970s, there were frequent attempts to devalue the Spanish language and to discourage Hispanic/Latinx children from using it at school. Like their Native American peers, children from these communities were segregated in the Southwest. They were forced to attend Spanish-speaking schools and local high schools were attended by Anglo-American children only. Their schools were underfunded and had fewer teachers and more children per class compared to regular public schools. "No Spanish" rules were implemented by school boards in the Southwest, Florida, and New York City in the 1960s. Between 1855 and 1968, teaching in any language other than English was illegal in all of California. Children speaking Spanish on school grounds, even on playgrounds, were punished with detention, fines, and expulsion. One should note that these laws were implemented despite the Treaty of Guadalupe Hidalgo (1848) between the US and Mexico, which guaranteed all Mexicans residing in US territory the right to maintain their language and culture.

Discrimination against minorities was met with a fierce struggle for linguistic rights by Spanish speakers, and the first calls for affirmative action were made by President John F. Kennedy in 1961. Any requirements that only English should be spoken at the workplace were judged illegal because such rules would have set off discriminatory employment practices toward people who did not speak English as a primary language (Chapter 6). In 1970, the Supreme Court ruled that segregation was unconstitutional and the Civil Rights movement successfully lobbied for a Bilingual Education Act, to ensure equal opportunity for all non-English speaking children by law. However, all programs were transitional in nature and the "original purpose was and continues to be the rapid anglicization of language minority children; the right to an education in one's native language simply does not exist" (Hernández-Chávez 1995: 152). There was separate and unequal treatment even in integrated schools, and in 1997, Californian voters supported Proposition 227 to end bilingual education in public schools. Though English is not granted official status at the national level, thirty US states have adopted English as the official language today.

VIGNETTE 8.1 Gutierrez v. Municipal Court

In March 1984, an African American employee of the Southeast Judicial District of the Los Angeles Municipal Court complained that Spanish speakers were making fun of her in Spanish. Consequently, the managers instated a rule that English had to be spoken at all times, with the exception of translation work. This policy was later modified so as to exclude breaks and lunchtime. However, Alva Gutierrez, a Hispanic deputy court clerk, decided to sue the Municipal Court. She argued that bilingual Hispanic American employees were forbidden to speak their native language and discriminated against. The employer justified their decision to enforce "English only" at work, claiming that:

1. The US and California were English-speaking.
2. Speaking other languages was disruptive, creating a "Tower of Babel" atmosphere.
3. An "English Only" rule created racial harmony.
4. The Court could only guarantee that its employees were working efficiently if they communicated in English.
5. The rule was required by the California Constitution.

Crucially, there had been a similar court case back in 1980, Garcia v. Gloor, where the plaintiff, Hector Garcia, a native American of Mexican descent and salesman at Gloor Lumber & Supply, had been made redundant after speaking Spanish to another employee. The company pursued a policy that employees were prohibited from speaking Spanish unless they were doing business with Spanish-speaking customers. The court ruled against the plaintiff and held that federal law did not grant an employee the right to speak a particular language at work.

In Gutierrez v. Municipal Court, however, the court agreed that the cultural and ethnic identity of speakers was tied to language use. Any rule prohibiting employees from speaking a language other than English, except when necessary to translate for the non-English-speaking public, constituted national-original discrimination in violation of Title VII. The mere fact that an employee was bilingual did not therefore eliminate the relationship between their first language and cultural ethnicity. Although Hispanics learn English and become assimilated into American society, their first language remained an important link to culture and identity.

In a note of dissent, three judges quoted Garcia v. Gloor and stated that national origin was not to be equated with language usage. Further, they claimed that the policy had widespread employee support and that ethnic tensions would increase if languages other than English were allowed: "When employees bring their private language into a public work-place, this creates a difficult and sensitive problem for those around them who do not speak the language" (discussed in Gibson 2004). Language diversity at the workplace remains a controversial issue to the present day.

Tensions remain between the imposition of English and support for linguistic diversity. In public and political discourse, there is occasionally strong resentment toward speakers of Spanish in the US vis-à-vis the continuous influx of immigrants from Central America. The Pew Research Center estimates that the total amount of the population born in Mexico rose to 25 percent in 2018 (45 million in total) and that hundreds of thousands attempt to cross the border between Mexico and the US each year. This is a heated political issue: The "big, beautiful" wall, to be paid for by the Mexican government itself, was a key promise made by Donald Trump in the 2016 presidential campaign, but these views are by no means new. In the 1990s, Republican senator Pat Buchanan argued for a temporary stop to immigration, claiming that minorities needed to be assimilated first:

> If America is to survive as 'one nation, one people' we need to call a 'time-out' on immigration, to assimilate the tens of millions who have lately arrived. We need to get to know one another, to live together, to learn together America's language, history, culture and traditions of tolerance, to become a new national family, before we add a hundred million more. And we need soon to bring down the curtain on this idea of hyphenated-Americanism. (Buchanan quoted in MacGregor-Mendoza 1998: 62)

And in 2007, Newt Gingrich famously claimed that:

> The American people believe English should be the official language of the government … We should replace bilingual education with immersion in English so people learn the common language of the country and so they learn the language of prosperity, not the language of living in a ghetto … we should establish that citizenship requires passing a test on American history in English. And if that's true, we do not have to print ballots in any language except English. (Discussed in Dennis Baron's Web of Language: https://blogs.illinois.edu/view/25/1792.)

The rapid growth of the Spanish-speaking population evokes resentment and fear of a competing culture within parts of the English-speaking majority, and these feelings of antipathy are channeled in the New Nativism or the **English Only Movement**. Supporters of this movement promote English as the language of national unity and of integration. These efforts, it is claimed, are necessary because Spanish-speaking immigrants and citizens retain their ancestral language and refuse to learn English, which is seen as disloyal to American traditions and values. Sociolinguistically speaking, the complex language situation of bilingual and multilingual communities and their relationship with identity formation is either not properly understood or else wilfully misrepresented, depending on the viewpoint. Proponents of the English Only Movement fail to understand that speaking more than one language is a symbol of family history, an essential component of an individual's sociolinguistic repertoire and by no means disloyal:

> "Integration" into the dominant society is seen as a proper objective only insofar as this means the cultural adaptation of the minority to the norms of the majority rather than the full and equal participation by all groups. (Hernández-Chávez 1995: 158)

As a result, language policies in the Southwest have changed at the expense of the Hispanic minority. After initial de jure equality of English and Spanish in several states, measures have been implemented to establish English as the official language and to play down the role of Spanish in public life. There has been some jerrymandering as well: Boundary lines of political districts were redrawn deliberately to create counties with English-speaking majorities and so exclude the Spanish language from politics and law, for example in legal documents, ballots, courts. These efforts are immensely harmful. As we saw in Chapter 7, a better understanding of the sociolinguistic realities of bilingual speakers is needed to limit the damage of misleading, often populist, claims. Bilingual education policies and a positive attitude toward societal multilingualism help bilingual children advance and get a better education, they facilitate the entry into the job markets for adults, and are essential for tolerance and mutual respect in our society.

8.3 Language Obsolescence and Revitalization

One of the most awkward questions one can ask linguists is how many languages there are in the world. Frankly, the answer is: Nobody really knows, at least not exactly. The most important reason for this is that there is no clear criterion to distinguish between languages and dialects. Mutual intelligibility is simply not a suitable yardstick. Languages such as Serbian and Croatian or Norwegian and Danish generally do not pose problems for cross-communication, whereas other languages are fragmented in regionally distinct varieties which differ substantially in grammar and sound system. Chances are that an American from Iowa will seriously struggle with understanding a Glaswegian, and I remember when I was living in New Zealand watching a TV documentary on the economic situation of working-class Australian fishermen; their strong local accents were given subtitles. As a result, language status is not a linguistic issue but attributed according to historical, cultural, and very often political criteria. Even though there is no precise number, linguists estimate that there are 6,000–7,000 languages in the world right now, most of them spoken in Africa and the Pacific.

However, there is general consensus on another issue: The total number of languages is going down rather dramatically. Some world languages, such as English, Arabic, and Mandarin, have hundreds of millions of speakers, whereas the vast majority of languages have lower numbers.

Measuring **language vitality** depends on sociodemographic, historical, cultural, and also political criteria. First of all, absolute and relative numbers of speakers are important, and we need to assess how many members a community has, by itself and also vis-à-vis the mainstream community it is in contact with. We need reliable statistics on who speaks the minority language when and on what occasions (see Chapter 4), whether it is transmitted to younger generations, and what attitudes speakers have. Last but not least, it is crucial to assess whether it is endorsed in education and whether it has special political status. There are macrocriteria such as:

- extranational issues: globalization, digitalization, and social media
- national issues: language policies, educational support, federal support
- regional issues: regional autonomy, population density, contact patterns.

These gain complexity via microlevel issues such as attitudes, human resources, correlation with cultural values, traditions and/or religion, levels of literacy, and finally financial resources (Figure 8.1).

As we saw in Chapter 4, intergenerational transmission is considered the most important criterion in general, not only in change processes but also when it comes to the maintenance or disappearance of languages. A cross-sectional analysis of the community, with focus on whether languages are handed down the generations or not, is important in this context. We need to assess whether all generations, including children, fluently use the language, whether it is spoken by parents/grandparents but not by children who are still able to understand it, or whether it is only the grandparents and older generations who have active and passive knowledge. The following is a ten-step categorization system for intergenerational transmission (Grenoble & Whaley 2006: 6):

A   a language is spoken by all generations, including all, or nearly all, of the children
A- a language is learned by all or most children
B   a language is spoken by all adults, parental age and up, but learned by few or no children

8 Language Planning and the Law

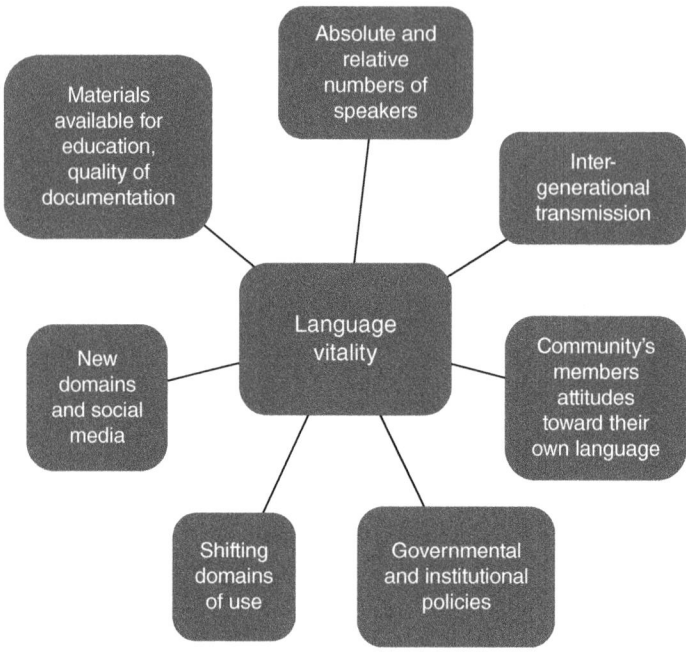

Figure 8.1 Language vitality

B- a language is spoken by adults in their thirties and older but not by younger parents
C a language is spoken only by middle-aged adults and older, in their forties and up
C- all speakers are in their fifties and older
-D all speakers are in their sixties and older
D all speakers are in their seventies and older
D- all speakers are in their seventies and older, and fewer than 10 speakers
E a language has no more speakers.

This system can be translated into a general category of language endangerment and loss based on all these criteria (Table 8.3).

What is alarming is that the vast majority of the world's languages fall into the last four categories: They are disappearing, near extinction or practically dead. According to Ocal Oguz from the Turkish National Commission for UNESCO:

> Nearly 2,500 languages face extinction because the number of their speakers is very low. Unfortunately, according to statistics and compiled data, one of these languages disappears every 15 days. (interview on BBC, February 2021: www.aa.com.tr/en/culture/2-500-languages-face-extinction-unesco-official/2152541).

Table 8.3 *Levels of language endangerment and loss.*

Level of endangerment	Characteristics	Examples
Safe	• All generations use the language in all or nearly all domains • Language of government, education, and commerce • Official or recognized status	English, German, Yoruba, Mandarin
At risk	• Vital, but lacks some of the properties of a safe language (status, speaker numbers, etc.) • Mostly bilingual speakers	Basque, Welsh
Disappearing	• Observable shift toward another language	Scottish Gaelic, North Sami (Finland and Sweden)
Moribund	• Not transmitted to children	Western Aleut (Alaska), South Sámi (Finland)
Nearly extinct	• Only a handful of speakers of the older generation remains	Hundreds of Native American and Aboriginal languages
Extinct	• No remaining speakers	Kiksht/Upper Chinook (USA, 2012), Dyirringani (Australia; early 20th century), Dalmatian (Europe, late 19th century)

This is a sociolinguistic and anthropological tragedy. Cultural and traditional knowledge is lost forever, particularly when the communities whose language is obsolescent have no tradition of writing down what they know and pass it on only orally. The disruption of intergenerational transmission has disastrous effects, particularly in the Americas and in Australia. Languages are cultural treasures and their disappearance is irreparable.

In the light of these worrying trends, some attempts have been made to revitalize obsolescent languages. For instance, countries such as New Zealand have implemented total immersion programs, whereby all New Zealand children attend so-called language nests, speaking Māori exclusively. Other countries have partial immersion or bilingual programs, where the minority language is a second or foreign language in the curriculum. There are also community-based programs, where native speakers teach their language to members of mainstream society, for instance in master–apprentice programs created to pass on Native American languages in California. Less frequently, there are **language reclamation** models, for example where dead languages are reconstructed, codified, and learned by individuals.

> **VIGNETTE 8.2** Reviving Cornish
>
> Cornish is a Celtic language which survived in southwest England until the eighteenth century; its last speaker, Dolly Pentreath, reportedly died in 1777. Throughout the nineteenth century, there were attempts, by the Celtic scholar Edward Lhuyd among others, to save as much of the linguistic heritage as possible and document the language. Lhuyd invented his own orthographic system to record sounds specific to Cornish. The revival movement of Cornish is said to have begun with Henry Jenner's now famous *Handbook of the Cornish Language*, published in 1904. With the help of Late Cornish sources, Jenner tried to develop a modern orthography. Jenner selected Middle Cornish as a starting point, possibly because there was a sizeable number of texts available for this period.
>
> Likewise, between 1920 and 1940, Robert Morton Nance based his attempt at reconstructing Cornish on Middle Cornish. His version of Revived Cornish, which included a new spelling system, became known as Unified Cornish. In the 1970s, focus began to shift away from the written to the spoken language, but there was no agreement on what period of traditional Cornish should be targeted for the spoken variety. Three recommendations for a reconstructed form were suggested: (1) It should follow the grammar of Middle Cornish; (2) It should have a regular phonological system; and (3) The orthographic system was to be phonemic. These were taken up by the Cornish Language Board in 1987, which implemented what it called Common Cornish, and soon there were heated discussions and debates. An eminent scholar and supporter of the revival of Cornish, Richard Gendall, "angrily left [the language movement]" (Bock 2005: 20), and developed Revived Late Cornish, a variety rooted in seventeenth-century and eighteenth-century Cornish. A further attempt to recreate Cornish, Unified Cornish Revised, was suggested by Nicholas Williams in the 1990s. This means that there are now several competing forms of the language, all of which could potentially be used for the revival process. Though it has only a few thousand speakers at most, the British government recognized Cornish under the European Charter for Regional or Minority Languages in 2002 and funded bilingual language programs. Ironically, despite the stormy debates, Cornish was taken off UNESCO's "extinct" languages list in 2010 and is now taught in some nurseries and primary schools.

Let's check out efforts in two major English-speaking countries, New Zealand and Ireland, and see what political decisions have to be made to safeguard indigenous languages. We begin with New Zealand, where Māori is mostly spoken in the North Island. As for population demographics, according to the National Census (2018), 775,836 New Zealand residents claimed Māori ethnicity (ca. 16.5%). Some 95.4% of the total population indicated they were speaking English and only 4% claimed to be able to speak Māori. Moreover, 78% claimed to speak one language only and 17% reported themselves to be bilingual, using two languages regularly. Only ca. 20% of (self-identified) Māori stated they had conversational knowledge of their ancestral language, and again only around 6.5% (i.e. 1.4% of the Māori population overall) claimed to be able to speak Māori with full competence. In other words, while speaker numbers are still considerable, Māori is endangered.

How did this happen? In 1800, Māori was the predominant language in all of New Zealand, spoken along with some Polynesian languages. Then, after colonization by English speakers, it became a minority language vis-à-vis the socially dominant English language, with rules soon implemented to discourage the usage of Māori, such as forbidding it in school. In the late nineteenth century, a UK-style school system was introduced for all New Zealanders. Still, Māori functioned as the first and home language for hundreds of thousands until the Second World War, with newspapers and literature written in the language as well. By the 1980s, however, fewer than 20% of the Māori community self-indicated to be native speakers, and there were increasing concerns that the language was dying out.

As a result, there were some rather symbolic actions first, such as a Māori Language Day and a Māori Language Week. The first officially bilingual school was set up in 1978, and kindergartens and day-care centers known as the Kōhanga Reo, or language nests, adopted Māori. The first Māori-language radio station, Te Reo-o-Poneke, was set up in 1983, and the 1980s saw the revival of te reo and Māori language recovery programs. Then, the **Māori Language Act** was passed in 1987, which gave the language official status and ensured that it could be used in legal and formal settings such as the courts and Parliament. The Māori Language Commission was instated with several prominent New Zealand linguists serving as members. It promotes the use of the language and gives advice as to when and how to use it.

Ireland has a history of language contact and shift as well. The indigenous language was Irish, and English arrived toward the end of the twelfth century. The Statutes of Kilkenny (1366) set in place discriminatory laws to prevent English settlers from speaking any other language. Education was forbidden under Penal Laws in 1703–04, and when it was allowed again, then only under the condition that all classes were conducted in English, which meant that pupils speaking Irish in or outside the classroom were punished severely. Attitudes toward English were supportive; as the influential Irish politician Daniel O'Connell (1775–1847) put it, "I am sufficiently utilitarian not to regret its gradual abandonment ... The superior utility of the English tongue, as the medium of all modern communication, is so great that I can witness without a sigh the gradual disuse of Irish." Still, a majority of the population, particularly in the rural areas, spoke Irish.

The Great Famine (1845–49) dealt a horrible blow to the Irish language. An estimated 1.5 million Irish people died or emigrated to English-speaking countries elsewhere. The forced social mobility saw a rapid move toward societal bilingualism and – a few generations later – English monolingualism. In fact, the proportions of language usage in Ireland were turned upside down in the nineteenth century. Whereas in 1800, some 40% of the population were monolingual Irish speakers, only 1% were monolingual in Irish in 1891, with 86% stating they were English monolinguals. There was little bilingualism, and rapid language shift took place within a few generations of speakers.

The Gaelic League (*Conradh na Gaeilge*) was established in 1893 to promote the usage of the Irish language and create a link between language and national identity. Language revival efforts were boosted when the Irish Free State was founded in 1922. As a political act to express independence, Irish was made the official first language and the government adopted a remarkably protectionist policy. Article 8 of the Constitution states:

8.1 The Irish language as the national language is the first official language.
8.2 The English language is recognized as a second official language.

Irish became compulsory in several domains and by law:

- had to be used on all official documents and signs
- was required as a prerequisite for civil-service jobs
- was a compulsory subject at school
- was promoted in all state-funded media.

Moreover, the Gaeltacht areas were established. These regions in the western parts of the country were where Irish remained the community language. According to the 2016 census, the regions had 96,090 inhabitants, with 66.3% claiming to speak Irish yet only 21.4% saying they spoke the language daily outside the education system.

This raises an important question. Irish was obsolescent and heavily endangered, yet the twentieth century saw far-reaching political efforts to promote its usage in the general population. Ireland thus provides a showcase scenario to investigate whether language shift can be reversed. In terms of sociodemographics, the total number of speakers aged 3 and over has more than tripled over the last 100 years (from ca. 540,000 in 1926 to ca. 1,760,000 in 2016), and there seems to be reason for optimism. However, and this is cause for concern, language proficiency in Irish has not increased. We saw that usage in sociolinguistic domains is an equally decisive factor. Irish is compulsory in schools and all Irish schoolchildren must learn the language, which means most come into contact at a young age and learn it as a second language. But still: of the more than 1,700,000 speakers of Irish in the 2016 census, only about 3% indicated speaking it on a daily basis.

However, some 70% of those who reported being able to speak Irish also indicated they would never use the language in their everyday lives. The Irish linguist Ray Hickey interprets this as follows: "The only answer is that they once learned the language (in school), have not used it since, but view the remnants of their knowledge of Irish as an ability to speak the language." In an interview with *The Irish Times* on March 16, 2011, language commissioner Seán Ó Cuirreáin somewhat soberingly stated that "Children [are] leaving school after 1,500 hours (14 years) of Irish without a 'basic ability' to speak the language." In other words, the majority of those who claim to be competent in Irish do not really speak it and have passive competence at best. They are claiming to speak Irish because the attitudes toward the ancestral variety are so positive that even people with little competence in the language claim that they are Irish speakers: "Most of the people who, in the census, claim to be Irish speakers are expressing an attitude rather than ability" (Watson 2007: 355–356). In other words, despite all efforts and a sense of national pride, the status of Irish is by no means safe.

Comparing the Irish and New Zealand scenarios, we find there is a positive and favorable stance towards ancestral languages in both countries. Both countries have implemented policies and taken active steps to ensure the maintenance of indigenous languages after long periods of discrimination and stigmatization. However, despite all efforts, Irish and Māori are not safe, notwithstanding high speaker numbers and supportive attitudes. Still, it is remarkable that governments should invest so much to the benefit of speech communities and view language survival as an asset for the nation as a whole. Multilingualism is seen as a positive symbol for political unity. Sadly, speakers of thousands of languages around the world are not that privileged.

8.4 Speak Good English in Singapore

We now turn to the various agents involved in language planning. Whereas individuals are instrumental in codification (Chapter 5), producing grammar books and dictionaries, occasionally inventing languages, governmental bodies are central in implementing policies that favor or disfavor language choice and usage. On occasion, they may even turn against a part of the population by invalidating their dialects, spinning it positively as an effort to help speakers "improve" to get better access to the job market.

> ### VIGNETTE 8.3 Esperanto
>
> Esperanto is one of the most widely used artificial languages in the world. It was invented by the Russian ophthalmologist Ludwik Zamenhof, whose goal it was to create a neutral language to foster a sense of collectivism and world peace. He was convinced that such a language had to be learnt easily, that is it had to have a simple morphology and basic syntax so that an international community would resort to it as a lingua franca. He called this new language Esperanto; it had no grammatical gender, no cases, no syntactic redundancy, and morphemes did not change in form. All the rules were outlined in the book *Unua Libro*, "First book", published in 1887. The language spread quickly and within twenty-five years it had its own journal, there were Esperanto Societies on all continents as well as a World Congress. Though speakers of Esperanto were discriminated against in the world wars (the German Esperanto Society was prohibited by the Nazis), the language gained popularity in the second half of the twentieth century; there are Esperanto speech communities in Brazil, Japan, and China. It is an official school subject at some Hungarian schools, Radio Vatikan has weekly contributions in Esperanto, and Duolingo, the web-based service that offers language courses, has lessons in Esperanto as well.
>
> It is unclear how many speakers there are, and estimates range from several hundred thousand to 10 million. Ethnologue.com estimates a number of around 2 million, but it remains unclear what language proficiency they have and when and how often Esperanto is used. There has been some repeated criticism of the structure. Its word stock is European-based, mostly on Romance languages, yet its orthography is Slavic, words are bisyllabic with stress on the ultimate syllable, and there is no regional variation as Esperanto was highly codified. Furthermore, although it competes with several world languages, it is

> artificial and lacks a native-speaker tradition and sizeable body of literature. For these reasons, it is seen as less useful than well-established languages such as English. Nevertheless, it is unusual that a language invented as an individual effort spread around the world and is now used by hundreds of thousands of speakers.
>
> While it is remarkable that it gained users and is still used, Esperanto also pales quite dramatically when compared to speaker numbers in organic speech communities and the regional spread of former colonial languages (English, French, Spanish, etc.). Perhaps it is most accurately characterized as a fairly unique development, with a relatively small number of passionate, motivated users.

Singapore is a good case in point for direct government interference: The country has about 3.5 million inhabitants, who mostly speak English, Malay, Mandarin Chinese, and Tamil. Mandarin Chinese is a relatively new phenomenon, only growing in importance with the recent economic power of mainland China. It is sometimes forgotten that the established Chinese speech communities in Singapore mostly spoke other languages, Hokkien in particular. Accordingly, though Mandarin has been promoted successfully by the government in top-down fashion, it is not the heritage language of most Singaporeans nor is it representative of the population historically. Originally, there was competition between the British and the Dutch Crowns in Asia. In 1819, Thomas Stamford Raffles arrived on the island and signed a contract with the Malay Sultan which guaranteed the British a free harbor here. Singapore became a British colony in 1824 and a crown colony in 1867, attracting numerous traders and growing quickly. Like many former colonies, Singapore declared its independence from the UK in 1963, then after a brief period as part of the Federation of Malaysia, became a self-governing state in 1965. Its economy, at first based mostly on local trading and fishing, shifted to industrialization after independence, and the country became one of the Asian tiger states, gaining wealth through export and financial services.

Singapore has a long history of language contact. Malay, Indonesian, Southern Chinese, and Indian traders were present when the British arrived, and a local "capitán" system divided the community into Malays, Chinese, and Indians. English thus came to be used in an environment characterized by language diversity and multilingualism, and contact-derived varieties (Chapter 4) such as Bazaar Malay and **Singlish** developed early on. In the nineteenth century, English was mostly the language of the local elite while the majority of the population continued to be taught chiefly Malay, Tamil, and a dialect of Chinese. As in India, language usage was class-based and subject to strong attitudes; there were some early comments that the local Singaporean's English was imperfect and corrupt, but by 1900 the upper classes enjoyed a "much greater degree of English language proficiency" in a "much wider occupational range" (Lim and Foley 2004: 2–3). English gradually took over in the twentieth century: In the 1920s, a program was launched to make English teaching compulsory for all students, and, while bilingual education continued, an English-medium education only came into place in 1987 (Lim & Foley 2004: 4–7).

Today's population of ca. 5.3 million (2010 census) is divided into four major groups:

- Chinese (from different Chinese regions): 74%
- Malays (Malaysia and Indonesia): 13%
- Indians (India, Pakistan, Bangladesh, Sri Lanka): 9.2%
- Others (Eurasians, Europeans, Japanese, Arabs, etc.): 3.8%.

Singapore has four official languages today: English, Malay, Mandarin, and Tamil. English has no specific ethnic affiliation, serving as a neutral language for the Singapore population (Wee 2004: 1019). It is the standardized and high-prestige language used in administration, education, commerce, science, and technology. In terms of educational policy, two languages are institutionalized in the school system:

- English, officially labeled the "First Language" due to its association with modernization, international banking, and tourism (Bao 2001: 69–70)
- an Asian "mother tongue Second Language" (i.e. Chinese, Tamil, or Malay, depending on a child's ethnicity) due to their association with traditional Asian values and cultural orientations.

The former "capitán system" between the different ethnic groups of Malaysians, Indians, and Chinese has been maintained so that the policy of multilingualism pays tribute to ethnically based diversity.

While ethnically based bilingualism seems a good compromise, there are some critical issues to consider. So-called **English-knowing bilingualism** means that children should learn both English and their mother tongue, yet the official language policy does not always adhere to sociolinguistic realities. Official mother tongues are not always spoken at home, making it difficult to reconcile language usage in diverse classrooms with the competence of children from several ethnic backgrounds (Wee 2004). Also, such a policy fails to include multilingualism in local languages other than English. As a result, English is used as a first language for an increasing number of

Singaporeans (Deterding 2007: 85), and reports of English as a home language (children growing up in such families count as native speakers of English) rose from about 32% in 2010 to about 48% in 2020. This weakens the status of the second languages and might give rise to ethnic struggles:

> there has always been a tension between the pragmatic view of English as a neutral language and the discourse of multiracialism, which assumes a close connection among race, "mother tongue", culture and identity. In this context, English is no longer the neutral medium of international communication and modern knowledge, but is viewed as a carrier of Western decadent values and undesirable influences to which Singaporeans, especially the "heartlanders", are particularly vulnerable. (Rubdy 2001: 351)

Moreover, the focus on English saw another debate: the status of the local variety of Singlish. There exists a language continuum and, as in most places around the world, the majority of Singaporeans do not speak the acrolectal variety but a local form which differs strongly from the standard. Singlish has seen extensive contact with the Chinese varieties of Hokkien and Cantonese, Malay varieties and Tamil, as well as clashes with Standard Singapore English. It is not clear exactly when and how Singlish originated but most evidence suggests that it developed at some stage in the nineteenth century, as a contact-based lingua franca in a multilingual community where English functioned as the acrolect (Chapter 4). Today, Singlish carries a strong sense of being local and is the home language for hundreds of thousands of Singaporeans. They speak English at home, but their language is neither socially valued nor promoted by schools and educational authorities. The clash is rather complex: On the one hand, Standard Singapore English is the language of economic progress and is claimed as providing a new national identity. Singlish, on the other hand, stands for the community's history and is a symbol of local pride and identity for a large part of the population.

The government has a clear position and has decided to stigmatize Singlish as much as possible. The Speak Good English Movement was initiated in 2000, originally as a year-long campaign to educate the population about good language usage (Chapter 5) and to raise awareness of the dangers of using Singlish. This was a top priority and followed former Prime Minister Lee Kuan Yew's remark in 1999 when he referred to Singlish as a "handicap we must not wish on Singaporeans" (see Chapter 1).

The government made various efforts to stigmatize the usage of Singlish in schools, among the general public, and in families. It lists mistakes, gives advice for parents on how to help their children get rid of errors, and actively attempts to eradicate the language spoken by a vast number of Singaporeans. What they speak is some sort of English, but it is not perceived to be the form that allows economic and social progress, so the government has decided to take an active role in trying to change how the general population speaks. It is deeply ironic that while the usage of English is actively endorsed and supported, the local English variety is stigmatized and discouraged. It will be interesting to see how these efforts continue.

8.5 Language Rights vs. Language Survival

The last point we need to address here concerns the various types of language rights, which is most important in terms of minority speakers and immigrants. We have already seen that many languages are disappearing quickly around the world. The question is whether governments or nongovernmental organizations should make efforts to preserve them: Is it a human right to speak one's own language or not? We will now look at the previous discussions through the lens of language rights.

First, there are countries with one main language where immigrants seeking full citizenship are expected to have a degree of fluency in that language. Australia, for instance, pursues a policy of **linguistic assimilation**. There is a strong belief that every citizen, irrespective of their native language, should learn and use the dominant language of society at large, which is also propagated by opponents of the English Only Movement in the US. Of course, this may favor language obsolescence, as the most vulnerable languages are the ones that need protection the most – standard varieties have sufficient speaker numbers, enjoy legal status, and are safe on all counts. According to Freeland & Patrick (2004), language rights protect minority language speakers from disadvantage or discrimination, whereas **language survival** efforts foster the vitality of a threatened language, which means it should be spoken as much as possible. Language protection and human language rights pose challenges for acquisition planning in education. An awareness of these complications:

> comes in part from an increased understanding of the academic disadvantages that children face when they are educated in an imposed language … an awareness that has arguably been the major force behind the drives to make education in vernacular languages a universal right. (Freeland & Patrick 2004:1)

Of course, the dilemma is that strengthening some languages may lead to the loss of others, so supporting the use of an immigrant language typically means fostering bilingualism in their native and the local language. For instance, Hungarians immigrating to Australia should be allowed to continue speaking their ancestral language while at the same time becoming competent in Australian English, which is a challenge for educational institutions and job markets. It has become widely recognized that:

> bilingual education is a central part of national or regional language planning that, on some occasions, seeks to assimilate indigenous and immigrant minorities, or integrate newcomers or minority groups. On other occasions, bilingual education is a major plank in language revitalization and language reversal (e.g. among Native American Indians, the Sámi in Scandinavia, and the Māori in New Zealand). (Baker 2003: 95–96)

There should be support for multilingualism, with the fostering of proficiency in the national/official language as an Additional Language. Different policies have been implemented, ranging from assimilation to societal bilingualism and multilingualism to efforts at language revitalization. Generally, one distinguishes between several types of planning processes (adapted from Baker 2003).

Type 1: Majority-Language Integration for Speakers of Minority Languages

- Integration of a minority language and gentle transition of minority-language speakers to the majority language. The main goal is proficiency in the majority language and social integration in mainstream society.
- Example: Spanish–English bilingual education in the US, AAVE "dialect readers" (Rickford 1999a), which start in AAVE and gradually move toward Standard American English.

Type 2: Minority-Language Maintenance

- Stronger support for the minority language, typically in isolated ancestral communities with little access to the majority language.
- Example: Miskitu in Honduras, whose speakers do not use Spanish, the national majority language.

Type 3: Minority-Language Maintenance for Minority/Majority-Language Bilinguals

- Stronger commitment to the minority language, implemented when all or most of the minority-group members speak both minority and majority languages. Both languages are officially endorsed, but the majority one is not allowed to dominate.

- Example: Basque is supported in the Basque Country, often in preference to Spanish (Haddican 2005).

Type 4: Minority-Language Integration for Minority-Language Semi-Speakers

- Stronger commitment to the minority language. A significant part of the minority group only know the majority language, and bilingualism is widespread. The motivation is perceived aestheticism and ancestry, and generic claims about the benefits of knowing additional languages.
- Example: The "Twf" ("growth") movement in Wales, originally designed to inspire confidence in reluctant Welsh-speaking parents to use more Welsh with their children (Edwards & Newcombe 2005).

Type 5: Minority-Language Integration for Nonspeakers of the Minority Language

- Typically employed when very few or no native speakers remain. The policy is targeting majority-language speakers with no prior exposure to the minority language, including those with no ancestral links. The focus is on creating new speakers via education with the aim of increasing speaker numbers and social awareness of the minority language.
- Example: Cornish in Cornwall, Irish in Ireland, Scottish Gaelic in Scotland.

No matter what policy is adopted, it is important to bear in mind that these decisions have far-reaching consequences for speech communities. Language-planning activities are extraordinarily complex, involving social, political, and cultural issues, and one should always bear in mind that they depend on a country's financial situation. Bilingual education is expensive as teaching materials have to be created and teachers have to be given extra training. The ancestral tradition of indigenous languages has to be taken into consideration, particularly in postcolonial settings, and the costs and benefits of language maintenance vs. language hegemony deeply affect all forms of social interaction in a society. Perhaps the most essential question is whether there is a basic right to speak *all* languages, whether usage should be promoted or limited, or whether mainstream, often colonial, languages should be offered to everyone, making them mandatory in education and formal discourse. Official languages are the key to professional success and economic prosperity, so the support for minority languages is sometimes seen as cutting speakers off from financial benefits.

There are national considerations as well; pressure is exerted on immigrants to learn the (main) language of the country they reside in, and linguistic assimilation goes hand in hand with cultural assimilation. Often, the maintenance of these languages, be they ancestral (such as Gaelic in Scotland, Hopi in the US Southwest, or Djamindjungan in Australia) or immigrant ones (such as Polish in London or German in Wisconsin), is eyed with some suspicion. The lack of sociolinguistic accommodation, no matter whether it is an act of choice or because the target is not available, makes these speakers an easy target for xenophobia, discrimination, and linguistic racism (Chapter 7). Marginalization by the mainstream community may speed up language loss as speech communities undergo language shift.

A good example is the German-speaking community in the US. Germans migrated in several waves to North America, and it is estimated that up to 50 million Americans have German ancestry. This was a most influential group: In 1900, the US had more than 600 newspapers in German, hundreds of German schools and church services; and in some places, German was more widely used than English. The First World War and its aftermath changed this, and speaking German in public was considered unpatriotic and rebellious. It was forbidden to use the language in public places, schools were closed, and nearly all the newspapers disappeared. Americans of German descent anglicized their last names to show assimilation (Schmidt became *Smith*, Schneider *Taylor*, and Müller was changed to *Miller*). Even though a federal court rule (Meyer v. Nebraska) reversed the decision to outlaw the usage of German in private schools and most bans of language use were lifted, speaker numbers dropped quickly within a generation or two. Surely, the outcome would have been different if bilingualism had been considered an asset, even more so if there had been official support for bilingualism and language maintenance.

8.6 Conclusion

In this chapter, we have looked at basic issues of language planning. We found that there are different activities in terms of corpus, status, and acquisition, and sociolinguistic issues come into play in all decisions about how languages are codified and elaborated, how their status is enhanced in society at large, and how transmission is ensured via processes of language adoption in schools and educational facilities. There is a close link with standardization at large, as these decisions directly involve language-related policies. The selection of one variety sets its place in education and official discourse; codification and elaboration relate to how it is used grammatically and orthographically; whereas acceptance changes language attitudes in general, often leading to stigmatization and negative views toward minority languages. Selection and codification involve form-related policy planning, acceptance, and elaboration function-related policy-planning. This is summarized in Table 8.4 (adapted from Hornberger 2006: 29).

Table 8.4 *Language policy and planning goals.*

Type of planning	Form-related policy planning	Function-related policy planning
Acquisition	Education, literacy, mass media, work	Maintenance, shift, curricular planning, literacy
	Selection	**Acceptance**
Corpus	Standardization, orthography	Modernization, renovation of functions
	Codification	**Elaboration**
Status	Officialization, nationalization	Revival, maintenance, international and intranational communication

Different viewpoints clash in political discussions about whether to give immigrant or indigenous communities the right to maintain their native languages in education and other sectors. Some propound that these speakers should start using the mainstream language whereas others strongly support their right to use ancestral languages. A discussion of the language situation in the US, with focus on Native and Hispanic Americans, showed the complexity of decisions and political issues at play.

When addressing language obsolescence, we saw that absolute and relative numbers of speakers are important and that we need reliable sociolinguistic information on who speaks the minority language when and on what occasion, whether it is transmitted to younger generations, and what attitudes speakers have. The vitality of languages depends crucially on whether they are endorsed in education or not and if they are granted special political status. Extranational issues (e.g. globalization, digitalization, and social media), national issues (e.g. language policies, educational support, federal support) and regional issues (e.g. regional autonomy, population density, contact patterns) all have to be considered.

Take-Home Messages

- English language planning involves governments, nongovernmental organizations, and individuals in shaping and influencing the function, structure, and acquisition of a particular language. It involves status, corpus, and acquisition-planning processes.

- Vernacularization refers to the selection and restoration of an indigenous language as an official language.
- English has a special officialized language status in 84 countries around the world.
- Languages differ dramatically in terms of speaker numbers. Whereas world languages have more than 100 million speakers, more than a dozen languages only have one speaker left. It is estimated that more than 1,000 languages will die out in the twenty-first century.
- Language vitality depends on sociodemographic, historical, cultural, and political criteria.
- Some governments (e.g. in Singapore) take a proactive role in promoting international standards at the expense of local vernaculars.

Activities

8.1 Do some research on the language policies of the following countries: Ghana, Namibia, Hong Kong, and Australia. What is the status of English there and on what grounds have these planning decisions been supported politically?

8.2 Gingrich's comments gave rise to a heated debate. He was criticized by leaders of the Hispanic community and challenged by Democrat politicians. Gingrich reacted with a public statement in Spanish, where he apologized and explained what he had really meant. His statement, in Spanish with English subtitles, can be watched at: www.youtube.com/watch?v=sg-0aB7jf_c.

What are the main arguments in favor of immersion and what does Gingrich have to say about the maintenance of Spanish in the US?

8.3 There is an increasing demand in European countries for immigrants to have to learn and adapt to the predominant language and culture.

Where do you see similarities and/or differences with the situation in the US (e.g. education)? How compatible do you think the right to retain one's language and culture is with political realities such as integration?

8.4 Which of these two claims is true?
1. "It is more likely for languages in the world to have more than 1 million speakers than to have fewer than 1,000."

2, "It is more likely for languages in the world to have fewer than 1,000 speakers than to have more than 1 million speakers."

Now visit www.ethnologue.com and check out which claim is accurate (and of course you might ask yourself whether all these are really languages and not dialects ...).

8.5 How do you interpret the scale in Grenoble & Whaley (2006: 6)? What is the cut-off point when we should start worrying whether a language is disappearing?

8.6 Do some research on how the revival of Welsh in Wales resembles and differs from the Irish scenario outlined in this chapter. Discuss.

8.7 Visit the website: www.languagecouncils.sg/goodenglish/resources/grammar-rules/grammar-gaffes. It asserts that there are typical "mistakes" in English and claims that "This compilation of corrections to common grammar gaffes may save you from unintended awkward moments." Go through the list and discuss how often these occur in other varieties of English you may know. Are some of them constrained to formal contexts or indicative of social class?

On a more general level, discuss in groups where a government should influence the economic survival or the cultural identity of a country through language planning. Is English rather a "neutral" language or the bearer of "Western values"?

8.8 Compare the language-policy decisions in Australia and New Zealand. How do these countries differ from each other in their approaches to ancestral and immigrant languages?

Key Terms

de facto official language
de jure official language
English-knowing bilingualism
English Only Movement
function planning
internationalization
language planning
language proscription
language reclamation

language survival
language vitality
linguistic assimilation
linguistic imperialism
Māori Language Act
Singlish
Speak Good English Movement
vernacularization

Further Reading

For a good introduction to language planning, I would recommend:

Ferguson, G. (2006). *Language Planning and Education*. Edinburgh: Edinburgh University Press.

Kaplan, R. B. & Baldauf, R. B. (2007). *Language Planning from Practice to Theory*. Clevedon: Multilingual Matters.

The sociolinguistic complexity of policymaking is introduced here:

Spolsky, B. (2009). *Language Management*. Cambridge: Cambridge University Press.

Wiley, T. G. (2003). Language Planning and Policy. In S. McKay & N. H. Horberger, eds., *Sociolinguistics and Language Teaching*. Cambridge: Cambridge University Press, 103–147.

CHAPTER 9

The Sociolinguistics of Globalization

In This Chapter ...

… we will look at a field that has received much theoretical attention lately: sociolinguistic aspects of globalization. The sociolinguistic turn meant that language-external variables moved to the center of research, which in subsequent waves were modified and reinterpreted as society became more flexible and social barriers were permeated. The changes brought about by the emergence of the "global village" have intensified such trends, and today language variation is no longer seen as static, in a socially stratified and rather rigid system. Rather, language is approached as a negotiated system and a fluid form of identity construction that is characterized by ever-widening social networks in both the real and the increasingly digital world. We will first critically look at superdiversity, presented as a chief characteristic in the postmodern world, and effects of mobility on sociolinguistic repertoires. Building upon this, we will present some theoretical and methodological issues, both geopolitically and geoculturally, and introduce the World Language System, which orders the world's languages into different layers according to criteria such as usage, function, and speaker numbers. Finally, we look at winners and losers of language and globalization (countries, companies, and individuals) so as to assess general sociolinguistic trends in a postmodern world.

9.1	Language in a Globalizing World	*page* 253
9.2	Mobility and Superdiversity	253
9.3	Sociolinguistics Goes Global	256
	Vignette 9.1: Jan Blommaert (1961–2021)	257
9.4	The World Language System	259
9.5	Winners and Losers	264
9.6	Conclusion	268
	Take-Home Messages	269
	Activities	269
	Key Terms	271
	Further Reading	271

9.1 Language in a Globalizing World

The world as we know it has changed fundamentally over the last two decades, and so have our views on global affairs, our attitudes toward diversity, and our perception of interconnectedness involving all aspects of social life. For instance, many of us have become more mobile in recent years, traveling more often and covering wider distances. Air travel, once a luxury, became a commodity, and manufacturing and goods production have been shifted from the global North to the global South. We are more frequently in contact with people from different places and different backgrounds, communication channels have been modified, and social media provide us with new platforms for global interaction. Commuting to work or university has become a regular part of every day for many of us.

This chapter looks into some sociolinguistic consequences of globalization and asks how well-established approaches need to be complemented and revised in the light of such complexity. There is a diachronic perspective inherent in this; as Blommaert (2010) put it, "understanding globalization is understanding a historical process" (137) as it represents a succession of activities, carried out by actors with distinct social relationships. This intensification means there is a continuously stronger flow of speakers, products, entertainment artefacts, or memes around the globe, and advances in communication science and IT are groundbreaking, "resulting in new patterns of global activity, communication organization and culture" (Blommaert 2010: 12). Given that language is a social phenomenon, our social fabric (Chapter 1), we need to ask how the transformation changes and challenges traditional beliefs about linguistic diversity, our language attitudes, and also how it affects the sociolinguistic choices we make on a daily basis. Let's begin with a concept that has received a lot of attention in the literature: the idea of superdiversity.

9.2 Mobility and Superdiversity

We saw in Chapter 2 that space, in all its manifestations, holds a central place in sociolinguistic theory. Traditional dialect geography was interested in horizontal space, and language variation was primarily considered a function of regional distance. Later, the sociolinguistic turn led to a strong focus on vertical space and social stratification in particular. These rather static categories have been challenged by what has become an increasingly important aspect of our ordinary lives: **mobility**. Blommaert (2010) argued that movement, in terms of sociolinguistics at least, is a "trajectory through different stratified, controlled and monitored spaces in which language 'gives you away'" (Blommaert 2010: 6). Accordingly, the sociolinguistics of mobility is involved when the "movement of language resources is seen as a movement in a horizontal and stable space and in chronological time" (2010: 4).

Britain (2010) has theorized the concept of space and argued that it is to a considerable extent negotiated and defined by its speakers. Our use and conception of space varies as it fulfils various functions. Space can mean and represent different experiences for us. A park, for instance, can be a place where joggers work out in the morning, a picnic and playground for families in the afternoon, and a meeting point for members of societal subcultures at night. Space can thus have different objectives for society at different points in time and involve different communities of practice, who engage in their own interaction patterns with different routines. In other words, place has become dynamic; it is negotiated and shaped by its users.

Cities are the most obvious site here. For one, neighborhoods change quickly in terms of population set-up, infrastructure, and lifestyle. The Lower East Side, where Labov conducted his landmark New York City study in the 1960s and 1970s, used to be a heterogeneous community with various ethnic groups living next door to each other (Chapter 2). When Labov and his associates carried out their fieldwork, it was a traditional immigrant, working-class part of town, with well-known neighborhoods such as the East Village, Chinatown, Little Italy, and the Bowery, where descendants of Irish, German, Jewish, Ukrainian, Italian, Chinese, and Puerto Rican immigrants lived in close proximity. Though they were separate communities, perhaps speaking separate ethnolects, their networks overlapped in everyday interaction. This has changed drastically, and the Lower East Side today has little if anything in common with how it used to be fifty years ago. It is no longer a district for lower-middle and working classes as there has been rapid gentrification over the last twenty years. Apartments have become unaffordable for most residents. In 2008, the National Trust for Historic Preservation listed the Lower East Side as one of America's Most Endangered Places.

Or take the case of London: A few generations ago, the East End was renowned for **Cockney**, the well-known London working-class accent. Starting in the 1950s, there was large-scale in-migration from countries other than the UK, when former colonies became politically independent (Chapter 4). There was extensive contact between (white) Anglo British residents and immigrants from Africa, the Caribbean, and Asia (India, Pakistan, etc.). In districts such as Hackney, more than 60 percent of today's population claim ancestry from outside the UK. There are few opportunities for interaction with the wider, mainstream, mobile sectors of London society, and the local community is characterized by dense family and neighborhood networks, ethnic heterogeneity, and intense contacts across ancestral and immigrant society sectors, particularly among the younger population. This is a relatively new phenomenon.

The increase in immigration means that London has become a much more multilingual place than it was a hundred years ago. Recent census data indicate that at least 250 languages are spoken by sizeable speech communities. In the 2011 census:

- Some 1.7 million Londoners indicated speaking a main language other than English at home (that's the total population of cities such as Barcelona or Philadelphia, Pennsylvania)
- Around 700,000 local residents indicated speaking a main language that was European but not of British origin. There were almost 150,000 speakers of Polish alone: One should note that the expatriate Polish population in the UK in June 2020 was 816,000 – higher than that of Kraków, Poland's second-biggest city.
- More than 500,000 people spoke a South Asian language as their main language.
- Some 100,000 spoke an East Asian language as their main language.
- More than 130,000 people spoke an African language as their main language (London has more than 115,000 Nigerian-born residents alone, which is almost as much as the population of Norwich).

This is the setting that gives rise to multiethnolectalization (Chapter 4), which, in combination with the construction of new towns in the former countryside, fundamentally changes the sociolinguistic landscape of large cities. Many members of the earlier Cockney-speaking community left the East End to take up residence elsewhere. According to Paul Kerswill:

> in much of the East End of London, the cockney dialect that we hear now spoken by older people will have disappeared within another generation. People in their forties will be the last generation to speak it and it will be gone within 30 years. Since the 1950s and the New Town movement, more affluent east Londoners moved out of the capital and into Essex and Hertfordshire, especially to places like Romford, Southend and Hemel Hempstead, and they took their accent with them. (www.lancaster.ac.uk/news-archive/D47105465E6D082B8025775300374D2E.php)

These changes correspond with what is happening around the globe. Cities have grown disproportionately (the population of Istanbul almost doubled from ca. 8.7 million in 2000 to ca. 15.6 million in 2022), there is much more mobility, both nationally and internationally, and rural populations continue to decrease. The World Bank estimates that some 56 percent of the global population today – ca. 4.4 billion inhabitants – live in cities. This tendency is very likely to continue so that the urban population will grow, while rural areas will have fewer if any inhabitants. Accordingly:

> the nature of immigration to Britain has brought with it a transformative 'diversification of diversity' not just in terms of ethnicities and countries of origin, but also with respect to a variety of significant variables that affect where, how, and with whom people live ... [including] a differentiation in immigration statuses and their concomitant entitlements and restrictions of rights, labour market experiences, gender and age profiles, spatial factors, and local area responses by service providers and residents ... The interplay of these factors is what is meant here, in summary fashion, by the notion of 'super-diversity'. (Vertovec 2006: 1)

The concept of superdiversity suggests that the world today is more mobile than ever, that certain societies are superdiverse, particularly in high-contact urban settings, which is a recent societal phenomenon: "'Super-diversity' is a term intended to underline a level and kind of complexity surpassing anything previously experienced in a particular society" (Vertovec 2007: 3).

This has been criticized as a rather uninformed view of sociolinguistic, historical, and sociodemographic developments in the English-speaking world, particularly when considered from a diachronic perspective. In Chapter 6, for instance, we saw that the population of London grew from 40,000 in 1500 to 900,000 in 1801 (an approximate 22-fold increase in just three centuries!) so one should not underestimate earlier patterns of mass migration for economic and political purposes. One should also bear in mind that in the eighteenth and nineteenth centuries, industrialization gave rise to rapid urbanization, and the societal changes of that time in no way fell short of what has been labelled superdiverse today. Still, population diversity has a strong economic, social, and political undercurrent and there is no doubt that recent events will continue to challenge our sociolinguistic models.

9.3 Sociolinguistics Goes Global

Among other issues, Blommaert (2010) concentrated on "super-diverse patterns of urban multilingualism" (13) in his critical work on the sociolinguistics of globalization. He distinguished two components:

- A geopolitical one: the "slow, deep process of globalisation, affecting the deep social, political and economic fabric of societies" (2010: 13).

- A geocultural one: the "more recent developments within globalization, largely an effect of the emergence of the new communication technologies, increasing and intensified global capitalist processes of accumulation and division of labour, and increased and intensified global inequalities resulting in new migration flows" (ibid.).

For Blommaert, the character of language is necessarily fluid and mobile, resting on mobility as a central element. This includes the mobility of linguistic and sociolinguistic resources, which is taken to mean that "'sedentary' or 'territorialized' patterns of language use are complemented by 'translocal' or 'deterritorialized' forms of language use, and that the combination of both often accounts for unexpected sociolinguistic effects" (Blommaert 2010: 4). Globalization is a historical phase, characterized by the flow of speakers, products, images, and discourses around the globe.

> **VIGNETTE 9.1** Jan Blommaert (1961–2021)
>
> **Jan Blommaert** was a Belgian sociolinguist and linguistic anthropologist. Born in 1961, he was Professor of African Linguistics and Sociolinguistics at the University of Ghent, then at the University of London and later at the University of Tilburg, where he was director of the Babylon Centre for the Study of Superdiversity. He held honorary posts in China and South Africa as well. His scientific interest was focused on the theoretical and empirical study of globalization, migration and superdiversity, and the consequences for language and society. Given his strong interest in Critical Discourse Analysis, language ideology, and sociolinguistics, his special focus was on language hegemony and the consequences of globalization on power structures generally and the variable manifestation of language in political and social structures. In his late work, Blommaert turned to language in cyberspace and the connection of online and offline communication.
>
> After a short illness, Blommaert passed away on January 7, 2021, in Antwerp, Belgium.

Blommaert makes a further theoretical distinction between what he called the sociolinguistics of distribution and the sociolinguistics of mobility.

- Sociolinguistics of distribution is concerned with language. The "movement of language resources is seen as a movement in a horizontal and stable space and in chronological time" (Blommaert 2010: 4).
- Sociolinguistics of mobility refers to "actual language resources in real sociocultural, historical and political contexts … language in motion

[through] various spatiotemporal frames [called scales] interacting with one another" (5).

History is thus seen as a succession of activities, carried out by actors who stand in and perform various relationships. This means that one cannot study historical language processes without considering power, hierarchy, authority, and normativity. As a result, we have a new "kind of sociolinguistics ... in which we de-synchronize and historicize sociolinguistic phenomena" (Blommaert 2010: 145), and this involves a paradigm shift away from language structure to a renegotiated function in speech communities.

One challenge is to identify the relevance, distribution, and negotiation of linguistic resources and to concentrate on sociolinguistic motivations. As we saw in Chapter 6, language sociologists such as John Gumperz have argued in favor of an interrelation between language use and sociocultural embedding. Meaning is constructed via joint interaction so that it represents a complex relationship of linguistic and social/cultural knowledge (including communicative competence). While purely linguistic knowledge is necessary to produce language in everyday situations, it is the knowledge of social aspects that enables speakers to establish meaning while they interact. Meaning is constantly created via contexts, depending on speaker and situation, and needs to be reevaluated and assessed.

A globalized sociolinguistic theory means that concepts such as contextualization and indexicality need to be reconsidered as well. There is an "intrinsic historicity in every language fact" (Blommaert 2010: 138), and this allows us to define and use stable patterns of socially constructed meaning in language, such as genre, register, and normativity. The ordering of indexicality is important for outlining patterns of social order that rest on convention and normativity created via language use. There are various competing centers of power and authority in the world, from which such normative pressures emerge: For English, this would be the UK and the US (Kachru's inner circle), for other languages it would be China, Brazil, or India. As a result, English is still most influential in terms of language hegemony, but countries with other languages emerge as new powers. It remains to be seen how they change the global balance and hegemony of world languages.

Blommaert suggested that this happens through a process of reshuffling of stratified and ordered indexical processes. New orders of indexicality (see discussion in Chapter 6) have developed, and every horizontal space (i.e. a neighborhood, region, etc.) may intertwine with a much more mobilized vertical space (class, gender, age, etc.). Social stratification is a characteristic of Western societies that carries over from generation to generation via transmission (cf. Chapters 3 and 4), yet it has become more situationally variable due to recent events. Most societies today allow some sort of social mobility or change in people's positions, and these may typically be upward and downward but can also manifest themselves horizontally. Social stratification involves social (in)equality and also shared beliefs and common interests – perhaps even language ideologies, as well.

9.4 The World Language System

As we have seen, it is impossible to give the precise number of languages spoken around the world, but most linguists would estimate between 6,000 and 7,000. These languages differ on a number of counts, typologically and structurally, but also in terms of regional diffusion, speaker numbers, and function (Chapter 8). The WLS, to which we turn now, springs from the assumption that there is global hierarchy of languages and "a surprisingly efficient, strongly ordered, hierarchical network, which ties together – directly or indirectly – the 6.5 billion inhabitants of the earth at the global level" (de Swaan 2010: 56). This network can be subdivided into four major categories: hypercentral, supercentral, central, and peripheral (Figure 9.1).

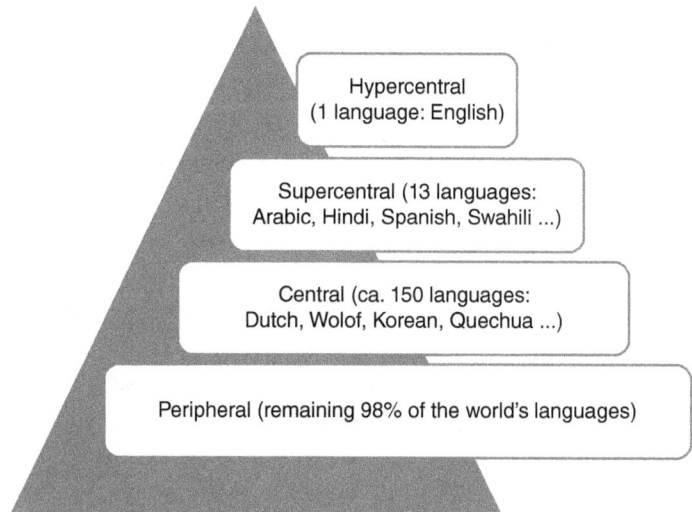

Figure 9.1 The World Language System

These four levels can be summarized as follows:

- Hypercentral: currently only one language, English (relevant to all other languages in the world as a language of international communication)

- Supercentral: transnationally important, these have demographic weight and often histories of imperialism, colonialism, and migration (there are "about a dozen" such languages according to de Swaan 2010: 57): Arabic, Chinese, French, German, Hindi, Japanese, Malay, Portuguese, Russian, Spanish, and Swahili
- Central: typically standardized official languages of small and medium-sized nation states ("there may be some 150 languages" of this kind, de Swaan 2010: 57): Dutch, Finnish, Korean, Wolof, Quechua, and so on
- Peripheral: nearly all of the world's languages are in this category; they have neither demographic weight nor institutional support. There are more than 6,000 such languages.

The hub of the WLS is therefore English, which serves as the language of global education, science, business, and the media. This is the language that carries a strong function as a second language and is widely learned and spoken as a foreign language around the world. With an estimated 2 billion speakers, it has the furthest reach of all languages (Chapter 4). One layer down, we find the supercentral languages; these are very widely spoken, they have sociodemographic weight, and their transnational appeal has historical, political, and economic causes. Though they may have large speaker numbers (in fact, the native Spanish-speaking population outnumbers the English-speaking one already and this trend is predicted to increase further in the next twenty years), they are not widely used as second languages or linguae francae (Chapter 4). There exist differences between languages in this category. While Spanish has been transplanted via colonialism and is now the most widely spoken language in South and Central America, Swahili is important in the wider Southern African and diasporic contexts but lacks demographic weight, whereas Japanese has demographic weight but limited transnational reach. These languages often have colonial traces and "were once imposed by a colonial power and after independence continued to be used in politics, administration, law, big business, technology and higher education" (de Swaan 2001: 162).

The central group includes ca.150 languages, spoken by a majority of the world's population. Many of them have midsized speaker numbers and are used in education, media, and administration. Typically, they are prominent on a national level and given legal protection as an official language – often they have been codified and standardized. In the fourth category, the bottom of the pyramid, so to say, we find the peripheral languages; there is a sharp statistical mismatch here as 98 percent of the world's languages have peripheral status, yet they are spoken by less than 10 percent of the world's population. This is particularly striking if we remember that as many as one in four speakers globally can be classified as a speaker of English. Unlike central languages, these are "languages of conversation and narration rather than reading and writing, of memory and remembrance rather than record" (de Swaan 2001: 4). Most of these languages are regionally confined, spoken by small, occasionally migrating, speech communities at the social and economic margins of society. They typically serve as first languages, mostly in marginal sectors of society at large, and it is unusual for them to be learned as second or foreign languages. A large number of these peripheral languages are threatened by extinction (Chapter 8), and it is no exaggeration to say that, by the end of the century, more than a thousand of them will have disappeared forever.

For three main reasons, de Swaan's model is highly relevant for the sociolinguistics of globalization. First, it is dynamic in that it allows for the transition from one level to the next. The gradual tendency is for speakers to move up one or two levels, via learning of or shifting to central and/or supercentral languages. The more benefit speakers see in a language as the medium of learning and economic success, the more likely they are to use and acquire it, provided that access is possible, of course, so that they can move up the hierarchy and start using a language with wider currency. To give two examples: Speakers of Sámi, a peripheral language, are learning Finnish, a central one, as this is the language used at school; and speakers of Breton are using French, a supercentral language, as this allows them to communicate regionally and to move on professionally. Of course, one should not forget that often there are also social and educational pressures to use the supercentral language. Speakers of supercentral languages, in their turn, are learning the hypercentral language as this is the medium of global interaction, of commerce, science, education, and entertainment. It is also possible for speakers of peripheral languages to skip levels and learn the hypercentral language right away, which is what happens in Australia and North America, where speakers of Aboriginal and First Nation languages shift to English. However, movement down the language hierarchy, say from supercentral to peripheral language, is less common. This accelerates the rate of language obsolescence and death dramatically, as we saw in Chapter 8.

Second, the WLS accounts for increasing multilingualism. The majority of the world's population are multilingual, and this follows a pattern: if additional languages are learned and spoken, they typically come from the higher levels of the WLS. de Swaan argues that speakers of a peripheral language acquire the central language and native speakers of the central language learn a supercentral language. In other words, two languages combine to represent the speaker's sociolinguistic repertoire, each with their own connotation and spheres of usage. The supercentral or hypercentral language is used for official purposes with high function (education, administration, etc.), the central or peripheral one is used in the home domain with the family and so on. Languages from different hierarchical levels carry different functions and are used for various purposes. The notion of "symbolic capital" has been developed in Bourdieu's work (1982, 1991) with reference to the *marché linguistique* (**linguistic marketplace**). Alongside the notions of economic, social, and cultural capital, Bourdieu defined symbolic capital as the "form that the various species of capital assume when they are perceived and recognized as legitimate" (1989: 17). Moreover:

> Owing to the fact that symbolic capital is nothing other than economic or cultural capital when it is known and recognized, when it is known through the categories of perception that it imposes, symbolic relations of power tend to reproduce and to reinforce the power relations that constitute the structure of social space. (Bourdieu 1989: 21)

The recognition and social value inherent in symbolic capital reflect other forms of capital. Bourdieu describes power in terms of "symbolic capital," which comes along with social position and prestige. However, it is immaterial; although apparently conceptually existing alongside the other "capitals," symbolic capital is not a different form of capital but rather a legitimated, recognized form with a representative function (Bourdieu 1982). The power relationships and competition between Bourdieu's different kinds of capital have been discussed extensively, and the theoretical debate has addressed institutional domination, counterbalancing effects of different aspects of capital in a state of competition as well as the identification and negotiation of symbolic capital by individual members.

All this is relevant for sociolinguistics. As we saw in Chapter 5, the social meaning of language is negotiated by the particular speech communities (in the form of social stratification in urban populations to acts of identity, indexicality, and enregisterment in communities of practice). After all, "one of the major topics in sociolinguistics is the study of language variation and change with its inevitable relationship to social forces" (Fasold 1992: 223). The WLS takes into account the language-external criteria that underlie the spread, function, and prestige of languages. Another advantage is that it allows us to critically assess one of the most diverse and controversial concepts in sociolinguistic theory: prestige. Societal multilingualism with languages from several WLS levels typically reflects the social prestige of languages. Whereas (some) peripheral languages survive because they carry strong local prestige due to their covert prestige (Chapter 2), standard languages are spoken to avoid social stigma and facilitate international communication. At the same time, standard language ideologies can be incorporated into this system as well, as "symbolic capital is a credit: it is the power of those who have obtained sufficient recognition to be in a position to impose recognition" (Bourdieu 1989: 23).

A final point to consider is that the WLS is a contemporary reflex of historical processes, with de Swaan arguing that there has been constant evolution. Languages obtained supercentral status when the first agrarian societies began to migrate and extended their residential areas. There was extended language contact, as communities speaking local or peripheral languages interacted with the language of socially superior groups, perhaps with emerging bilingualism. In other words, languages spread with socially dominant communities via imperialism and colonization, and the model can account for this well.

A good example is Latin, which diffused out of Italy along the Mediterranean coast into what is now Asia and northern Africa, and also north into territories where Germanic and Celtic languages were spoken. Latin was a widely used lingua franca in Europe for more than four centuries, and it was the language of commerce, trade, and politics in much of what is now Europe. Similar processes toward central and supercentral usages operated with the spread of Spanish, Persian, and other languages, as a direct consequence of migration, colonialism, and imperialism. Languages (e.g. English, French, Spanish) achieved their status because they were transported by their speakers to other continents. There is a flow of people, goods, and languages, which makes sociolinguistics global and, as Blommaert stated, ahistoric. The downside, of course, is that languages forcefully entered the sociolinguistic ecologies of indigenous populations and became more widespread as European colonization intensified, so that indigenous populations and their languages were relegated to the social periphery (Chapter 4).

To sum up, de Swaan suggests that the world's languages can be grouped into four hierarchical levels: peripheral, central, supercentral, and hypercentral. The WLS is essentially a sociological classification that takes sociodemographic weight and the social role of languages into account. There are thousands of peripheral languages in the world, connected to one of a hundred central languages, and one hypercentral language. There is mobility between these levels as speakers typically move up into the next category, though they can also skip levels and start using the hypercentral language right away. Consequently, the system reflects human traffic and historical population movements, taking into account the prestige of languages.

9.5 Winners and Losers

From a macrosociolinguistic perspective, the study of language in society involves a range of perceptions and value judgments (Chapter 1). Linguistically, all forms of language varieties are equal, yet socially speaking, they are not. From a personal perspective, I have taught a number of courses on sociolinguistic issues only to read in end-of-term papers that my students still claim some varieties are more "correct" or "expressive" than others. While this is not true, it attests to the strength of individual beliefs and societal ideologies: We have to accept that we just cannot leave language alone. Its role is too powerful in our lives.

Accordingly, the social transformation into a global village has led to a reconsideration of well-established categories. Not only have new stalls been added to our sociolinguistic marketplace, but existing sections have extended and undergone wholesale internal reorganization. Today's world has only a slight resemblance to how it was two generations ago. The economic and social changes of these processes are way too complex to be rendered here, but over the last half century, there has been a sharp increase in international trade, export of all kinds of goods, a greater mobility of workforces and capital, and an ever-increasing interdependence of society and economy. The list of winners includes countries, companies, and individuals:

- Some countries have benefited from this transformation, particularly those that can provide low-cost workforces and have a sufficient infrastructure to export their manufactured goods. Korea, Vietnam, and Thailand are good candidates. These are countries where export goods as a proportion of Gross Domestic Product (i.e. the total monetary or market value of goods and services produced within a country's borders) have increased significantly over the last forty years. As a consequence, such emerging economies have seen the growth of a wealthy middle class, whose real incomes have grown by taking advantage of the new economic opportunities.
- A second category of winners includes transnational firms with global reach, for example financial services, high-tech software firms, or pharmaceutical companies. Multinational companies take advantage of tax breaks and lower-cost labor abroad, producing and shipping goods over large distances to cut production costs. Some global companies such as Amazon and Google set up subsidiaries in countries like Ireland and Luxembourg for tax reasons, and financial services have established their headquarters in the Caribbean for similar reasons.

Production of goods is increasingly globalized, with products being designed in North America or Europe and manufactured in Asia. This creates new job opportunities and attracts highly qualified (anglophone) personnel from around the world.
- A third category comprises some individuals who benefit from global changes through opportunities to invest internationally and take advantage of lower tax rates. These are very often the highest earners, who can negotiate higher wages. The World Bank reports that between 1988 and 2008, the real income of the world's top 1 percent of the world's earners went up by more than 60 percent. Similarly, workers gain employment as new jobs are created in export industries, and greater movement of labor has made markets more flexible. A good example here is health care, where an increasing demand for carers is met by employing foreign-born personnel.

The list of losers can be presented equally by countries, companies, and individuals:

- First, some countries with developing economies lack the infrastructure and are not capable of developing a manufacturing sector for export of goods. The agricultural sector, for instance, has seen comparatively smaller growth in profit than IT or finance sectors, putting these countries and regions at a disadvantage.
- Second, the companies that are not able to operate and compete internationally lose a crucial part of their markets. Some manufacturing sectors of high-cost labor countries in Europe and North America are no longer competitive with newly emerging economies that have the advantage of lower labor costs.
- Third, unskilled manual workers are suffering from a decline in employment opportunities due to the structural changes of their local economies. Some countries are losing their highly skilled workforce, who take up job opportunities in countries offering higher incomes. The World Bank estimates that top earners and the middle class have seen rising incomes, whereas the real incomes of the poorest 5 percent of the world's population continue to be alarmingly low. Almost 700 million people (8.5 percent of the global population) live on less than $2.15 per day, which has been set as the extreme poverty line for low-income countries (www.worldbank.org/en/topic/poverty).

Human migration, whatever its motive, is emerging as a new sociolinguistic variable in the postmodern world. Blommaert's sociolinguistics of mobility means that language is brought from home to host countries, and that the sociolinguistic ecology of both environments is fundamentally altered.

Arguably, the amount of language contact (Chapter 4) has never been more intense than it is now, and this has a strong impact on the usages, forms, and functions of English as a world language. Being at the hub of the WLS, English offers a range of advantages in a globalizing world. It is the world's lingua franca for technology, finance, education, politics, media, and entertainment, and some basic knowledge of English is required for many of the higher or better paying jobs. Some have argued that this gives an unfair advantage to those who have language competence, particularly when they have the added bonus of being able to set and prescribe language standards (Chapter 6). This is the issue of linguistic imperialism we encountered in Chapter 8, and accounts for the rapid spread of Grassroots English as well.

Dominance of English is asserted and maintained by the establishment and continuous reconstruction of structural and cultural inequalities between English and other languages. The structural and cultural inequalities ensure the continued allocation of more material resources to English than to other languages and benefit those who are proficient in English (Philipson 1992: 47).

This is a highly emotional and ideological debate, and there are several challenges to the view that English is a killer language that "preys" upon local languages. Arguably, the globally ubiquitous model of the nation state has a more significant role in centralizing national languages and pushing out local ones than a single language such as English does. Philipson may consequently approach language obsolescence from the wrong angle. At the same time, processes operating on a global scale are certainly related, but not necessarily implicated as directly as nationalization is, when it comes to marginalizing local languages. And last but not least, one must be cautious not to anthropomorphize English. As tempting as the metaphor may be, languages themselves do not act as killers; switching to languages is a consequence of economic and social decisions made by individuals, as is evidenced by the spread of grassroots English (Chapter 4). If anything, individuals switching to English could be categorized as killers of their heritage languages, but this seems far too harsh and out of touch with social realities.

The claim about structural inequalities is controversial, but the hegemonization of English, in the form of the social, cultural, ideological, or economic influence some groups have over others, is widespread. It certainly has sociolinguistic consequences. For one, it may lead to or speed up the loss of varieties that are not primarily used within the dominant political and economic systems: In theory, that refers to 98 percent of the world's languages. In the words of Blommaert (2010: 182), "where English occurs, indigenous (and especially minority) languages are threatened, first with attrition and eventually with language death." Thus, the WLS theorizes that language groups are engaged in unequal competition on different levels globally. It examines competition and language shift through a global lens and establishes that its sociolinguistic function goes hand in hand with political, economic, cultural, and ecological aspects, many of which underlie language choice and the instrumental motivation to learn foreign languages. As today's constellation of languages is the result of colonization and domination, it shapes and strengthens relations of power and exchange. While speakers of peripheral languages learn more central languages for financial, educational, and social reasons, languages considered less desirable or useful are in danger of becoming extinct as global contacts and communication increase.

In other words, the core countries, some of which are anglophone, are favored in the WLS because they are sociolinguistically privileged. After all, it is their language that increases in importance. Economic growth and language status therefore go hand in hand. The semiperipheral countries maintain economic and financial trade with both periphery and core countries, so it is these languages that are brought into both groups by human traffic in both directions.

At the end of the day, the societal and political processes that underlie globalization are complex and diffuse. As unapproachable as the decision-making processes seem, they affect the everyday lives of hundreds of millions of speakers around the world. But one thing is clear: English has become an asset for a combination of social, economic, and historical reasons, whereas other languages have been marginalized. As a consequence, hundreds of millions of people are actively learning English in some way, for example in grassroots environments (Chapter 4). These motivations are often instrumental and monetary, as proficiency in English is the key to professional success and social advance in various economic sectors: tourism, commerce, and so on. A good example here is the call-center industry, which has sprung up in various Asian settings (Bolton 2013), in which English is the prerequisite for better-paid and well-paid jobs. The world of big data and digitization has opened up new opportunities, and English is the language of information technology, the main medium of the internet and cyberspace in general. All this gives English an advantage and helps explain why those who have little or no knowledge now find themselves in the backseat. In the words of Freeland & Patrick (2004: 1), there are worries, "voiced in particular by linguists, over the rapid decrease in the number of languages throughout the world as they are pushed aside by state education policies or by the wider processes of globalization," and Blommaert (2010: 3) states that:

Most people in the world still have no access to the new communication technologies that offer shortcuts to globalization, they live, so to speak, fundamentally un-globalized lives; but the elites in their countries have such access and use it in the pursuit of power and opportunities – a pursuit which does affect the lives of the "un-globalized" citizens.

It would be simplistic to turn languages into agents; after all, it is speakers who use them, and individuals enact power relationships and social differences via the linguistic resources available to them. But then again, some languages are placed at eye level in the shelves of the linguistic marketplace, whereas others are stocked out of sight. I am fully convinced that language inequality is one of the major challenges for the twenty-first century, and the sociolinguistics of globalization may provide a key to redress these issues and to find good solutions.

9.6 Conclusion

Globalization is a complex phenomenon, at the same time concrete and abstract, and it has far-reaching effects on our everyday lives. As so often happens, unprecedented new opportunities create winners and losers. Some social groups get marginalized along with their "particular cultural features, identities, practices and resources such as language" (Blommaert 2010: 154), whereas others gain in importance. Whether or not we subscribe to the idea that society is subject to unprecedented superdiversity, mobility, and travel opportunities, along with the communicative potential offered by social media and the digital turn, these opportunities have widened social contacts and brought us into contact with an ever-widening social net around the world. It has never been easier for someone from Aberdeen to chat with a person in Kuala Lumpur or Bloemfontein. The consequences are, in the words of Blommaert (2010: 1), that "globalization forces sociolinguistics to unthink its classic distinctions and biases and to rethink itself as a sociolinguistics of mobile resources, framed in terms of trans-contextual networks, flows and movements."

Blommaert's approach invites us to reflect on the shift from a static, totalized, and immobile view of language to a dynamic, fragmented, and mobile one. There is an interesting link with the emergence and balance of the WLS, which is arguably eroding its base as thousands of peripheral languages are threatened by extinction. These trends will continue via sociodemographic developments, increasing multilingualism, and also as a consequence of active efforts to learn hypercentral and supercentral languages: "Such markets naturally include winners and losers, and many people nowadays find their linguistic resources to be of very low value in globalized environments" (Blommaert 2010: 3).

Take-Home Messages

- Our social lives have been diversified and complicated by globalization.
- Mobility and population movement have increased, which has brought many of us into contact with speakers from around the world, thus extending our social networks considerably.
- Sociolinguistics of globalization distinguishes between geopolitical and geocultural processes.
- There is an important distinction between the sociolinguistics of distribution and the sociolinguistics of mobility.
- The World Language System hypothesizes a global hierarchy of languages, organized in different layers.
- Bourdieu argued that languages are organized in linguistic marketplaces, where they vie for function and usability.
- Some have argued that the spread of global languages such as English turns them into killer languages via processes of linguistic imperialism.

Activities

9.1 Visit the London census online at https://worldpopulationreview.com/world-cities/london-population.

What can you find out about local residence patterns of various population groups? In what parts of the city is the concentration highest and what could this mean for interaction patterns and dialect contact?

9.2 **Dunbar's number** is a suggested number of the amount of people with whom we keep up stable social relationships. At the risk of some simplification, it indicates the size of an individual's social network. The number was first suggested in the 1990s by the British anthropologist Robin Dunbar, who argued in favor of a correlation between primate brain size and average social group size. By comparing our average human brain size with those of primates, he suggested that humans can maintain 150 stable relationships, "the number of people you would not feel embarrassed about joining uninvited for a drink if you happened to bump into them in a bar." On the periphery, the number also includes past colleagues, such as high-school friends or old acquaintances, with whom one would want to catch up again. Dunbar further suggested that numbers larger than this generally require more restrictive rules, laws, and enforced norms to maintain an organized social group.

What do you think of this theory? Would you support the idea that there is a fixed average of contacts we can have? And how would such a number vary and change over time, in your opinion, both across generations and in an individual's lifespan?

9.3 We discussed Kachru's model of World Englishes in Chapter 4. The idea was that there are three circles: inner, outer, and expanding. Discuss this model with what de Swaan suggests for the WLS. What are the differences and similarities? How permeable do you think are the borders between the various categories or circles? What would have to happen for these systems to change?

9.4 Christian Mair adapted de Swaan's WLS to English, calling it the World System of Standard and Nonstandard Englishes (Mair 2013). Mair defined "the English Language Complex as ... a surprisingly efficient, strongly ordered, hierarchical constellation of varieties, styles and registers which ties together – directly or indirectly – the 1-billion-plus regular users of English at the global level." He suggested these four levels:
1. The hub/hypercentral variety: Standard American English
2. Supercentral varieties:
   - standard: British English, Australian English, Indian English, Nigerian English, and so on
   - non-standard: African American Vernacular English, Jamaican Creole English, popular London English, and so on
   - further domain-specific uses in English as a Lingua Franca: science, business, international law
3. Central varieties:
   - standard: Irish English, New Zealand English, Jamaican English, and so on
   - nonstandard: US "Southern" and so on
4. Peripheral varieties: all traditional rurally based nonstandard dialects, plus a large number of ex-colonial varieties, including pidgins and creoles.

Would you support or question this classification?

9.5 Create a list of winners and losers of the WLS, then discuss in groups what sociolinguistic consequences you would diagnose for each. Can you think of global trends that will affect the balance of languages around the world? Who, in your view, benefits/suffers the most? How is language competence and individual and/or societal multilingualism related to this? Take the case of speakers of English: Are there winners and losers in this group?

9.6 At the 4th World Congress of the Finno-Ugric Peoples, held in 2004, Tove Skutnabb-Kangas, then at the University of Roskilde, Denmark, argued that "It is these killer languages that pose serious threats towards the linguistic diversity of the world. As I said, English is today the world's most important killer language, but there are many others, large and smaller."

Discuss this claim in groups and try to find sociolinguistic arguments in favor of and against the existence of "killer languages."

Key Terms

Jan Blommaert
Cockney
Dunbar's number
marché linguistique (linguistic marketplace)

mobility
superdiversity
World Language System (WLS)

Further Reading

The sociolinguistics of globalization has been explored theoretically in:
Blommaert, J. (2010). *The Sociolinguistics of Globalization*. Cambridge: Cambridge University Press.

The following is a clear and hands-on introduction to the World Standard System:
de Swaan, A. (2001). *Words of the World: The Global Language System*. Malden, MA: Polity Press.

And for an application to the English-speaking world:
Mair, C. (2013). The world system of Englishes: Accounting for the transnational importance of mobile and mediated vernaculars. *English World-Wide*, 34(3), 253–278.

CHAPTER **10**

A Tribute to Sociolinguist(ic)s

In This Chapter ...

… you will notice differences in content and structure compared to those you have read and worked with so far. You will already have noticed that the introductory "In this chapter …" looks different, longer, and there are no key terms and take-away messages. Over the generously counted four years I spent writing this book, for the longest time I had no idea what to do with Chapter 10, to be frank. It was clear that the textbook, like all books, needed to finish in style to come full circle, but I came to realize that a simple chapter summary was neither necessary nor exciting. For a while, I was toying with the idea of bringing some big themes together – variation, identity, data, attitudes – but I could not really envisage something that would satisfy my own expectations or benefit BA students learning about sociolinguistics. As we have seen how diverse the field is, how much there is to learn and discover and research, synthesizing it all and then coming up with my personal interpretation or even projection of future developments seemed a bit, well, presumptuous. I was at a loss about what to do.

And then one day, for no particular reason, I looked at the Post-it I had put on my computer screen: "Always remember to write the book you would have wanted to work with when you were a student." I walked down memory lane back into the 1990s, when I was a student of English at the Universities of Basel and Neuchâtel, and thought about the courses I had taken: "Varieties of English around the World," "Language and Society," "Language Variation and Change." When I started my studies, I had no idea that one day I would do sociolinguistics for a living; in fact, I did not even know linguistics existed as a separate field of English Studies. I was extremely privileged that as a student I had two wonderful professors, both outstanding sociolinguists with global reputations: Peter Trudgill and Jenny Cheshire. They were warm and generous people as well, and their courses inspired and engaged me like no others could. When Peter Trudgill offered me an assistantship to write a PhD, I did not hesitate for a second and never looked back.

Looking at the twenty-eight years I have been in the business now, I remember what a strange experience it was to gradually enter the world of English sociolinguistics, and how amazed I was to get to know the people whose work I had read and who had inspired me. I recall how much I was in awe to meet Lesley Milroy, Dennis Preston, and William Labov at conferences, and how impressed I was at finding how friendly, genuinely interested, and supportive they were and are. People who write books are behind a canvas somehow, and I still experience this with my students today. When they have a question about a publication and I encourage them to contact the colleague and ask them directly, they typically look at me and ask: "Can I really do that?" Of course, sociolinguists, like most academics, are happy when their work is noticed and discussed and do not mind sharing their personal insights or advice. In fact, many of them feel honored. I have made this experience this time and time again.

And so I came up with the idea of giving the last word of this introductory textbook to my colleagues. Looking back to when I was a student, I thought it would be interesting for all those working with this book to have a personal input from the sociolinguists they had read about, to learn how they became sociolinguists in the first place and how they reflect today on their work and what future opportunities and challenges they predict.

I contacted colleagues around the world (in alphabetical order: Anita Auer, David Britain, Jenny Cheshire, Ana Deumert, Lisa Lim, Dennis Preston, John R. Rickford, Sali Tagliamonte, Lionel Wee, and Walt Wolfram) and asked them to send in short answers to the following questions:

- How did you become a sociolinguist in the first place?
- What do you consider to be your most important contribution to sociolinguistics?
- What advice would you give students of sociolinguistics today?
- How do you think your field will branch out and develop in the coming years?

Moreover, for the benefit of students working with this book, I sent my colleagues one or two questions concerning the area of specialization discussed here, and all of them agreed to participate. It is only fitting that the last word goes to colleagues and friends around the world, who have been very important in driving sociolinguistics forward and have at the same time shared their enthusiasm with generations of younger scholars. Enjoy, let the journey continue – and keep it up!

Anita Auer: Historical Sociolinguistics

Anita Auer is a historical sociolinguist with a special interest in diachronic and synchronic aspects of language variation and change. Her research themes involve: the role of historical urban vernaculars in standardization processes; the language of the laboring poor in Late Modern England; alternative histories of the English language; and language maintenance and shift among Swiss-heritage speakers past and present in North America. Anita Auer worked in the Netherlands and in England and has been Professor in English Linguistics at the University of Lausanne (Switzerland) since 2014.

How Did You Discover Sociolinguistics in the First Place?

When doing a degree in English, Psychology, and Philosophy (teacher trajectory) at the University of Vienna (Austria), my favorite subjects were English historical linguistics/history of English and social psychology. While I was not aware of the field of sociolinguistics at the time (1990s), questions related to power relationships between dialects and a standard language, sociolinguistic variation, and identity construction through language have always fascinated me (given that I grew up as a dialect speaker in a small village). In fact, it was only during the early stages of my education at the University of Manchester (England; first Erasmus programme, then PhD) that I was introduced to sociolinguistics. The key moment was a talk by Emma Moore (now Sheffield) about her PhD thesis, in which she aimed at applying Penny Eckert's Community of Practice approach to a school in Bolton. I was completely fascinated by this type of research and started reading up on sociolinguistics and models of language change. As my PhD focus was on historical linguistics in English and German but sociolinguistic questions became more and more prominent in my work, one of my PhD supervisors at the time, Prof. Martin Durrell, invited me to attend a conference on *Linguistic Purism in the Germanic Languages* at the University of Bristol in 2003. This conference saw the launch of the Historical Sociolinguistics Network (HiSoN); the rest is history (as people say).

What Do You Consider to Be Your Most Important Contribution to Sociolinguistics?

Generally, aiming to apply sociolinguistic theories (that are still largely based on phonology) to historical data while trying to be philologically accurate with regard to the data and considering the contemporary sociohistorical contexts. This is well reflected in the projects *Emerging Standards: Urbanisation and the Development of Standard English, c. 1400–1700* and *The Language of the Labouring Poor in Late Modern England*, in which we retrieved the data from archives and transcribed them ourselves. We did our best to pay special attention to the writer/scribe (and the text-production circumstances) when analyzing the data and describing language variation and change.

What Advice Would You Give Students of Sociolinguistics Today?

Do not focus only on sociolinguistics but get training in different related fields as well. This allows you to take different perspectives on the data and to open up new research directions.

What Are the Biggest Challenges and Perspectives in Historical Sociolinguistics?

Data are crucial in the field of historical sociolinguistics, that is finding different types of data and then determining details about the writers. Even though retrieving new data from archives and finding information about the writers/scribes can be time-consuming, I think that the future of our field lies in working with new and different types of data that can then be analyzed with the help of digital tools. At the same time, the philological (and more detailed) perspective still seems very relevant to me as it can allow you to explain interesting linguistic patterns.

How Do You Think Your Field Will Branch Out and Develop in Coming Years?

This depends on the development of linguistic theories/fields and data available for historical sociolinguistics. For instance, one research direction that is developing quickly in the field of historical sociolinguistics is the application of heritage linguistic theories to historical data, which then includes questions related to bilingualism, language acquisition, attrition, dialect/language contact, and so forth, and how historical data can provide answers.

David Britain: Language and Space

David Britain is a dialectologist and sociolinguist interested in: variation and change in contemporary English; the dialectological consequences of geographical mobility, especially dialect contact; the dialectology/human geography interface, especially with respect to mobility, isolation, and the

Figure 10.1 David Britain

urban–rural dichotomy; language ideologies as they relate to non-standard dialects; and dialectological data collection using mobile phone apps. David Britain worked in the UK and in New Zealand and has been Professor in English Linguistics at the University of Bern (Switzerland) since 2010.

How Did You Become a Sociolinguist in the First Place?

I had originally gone to the University of East Anglia in Norwich in eastern England to study French and German, but alongside this we had also had to choose courses in literature, linguistics, and history. Literature was absolutely a no-no for me, I enjoyed my contemporary German history courses, but linguistics was, for me, a new subject and it pretty quickly lit my fire, especially courses that involved language variation. I took one course taught by Dr. Ken Lodge on the history of English phonology, much of which was about how we account for contemporary dialect variation in England by looking back at the phonological processes involved in the linguistic changes of earlier centuries. For that course, I had to record someone and do some analysis of the recording. I recorded my dad, born and bred in Wisbech in eastern England, who had spent almost all his adult life working as a farm laborer nearby. Dad was, essentially, a NORM. I found the task interesting – Dad had Canadian Raising of /ai/ – but I was still finding my ear, and Ken was able to point out things in the recording that I hadn't noticed (partly, I suspect, because I also spoke that dialect at the time and for me it was too familiar, rather than an object of enquiry that I could step back from and look at from outside). But that project energized me and Ken suggested I might want to consider taking the dialectological investigation of the area further. Prof. Peter Trudgill had just moved from the University of Reading to nearby Colchester in Essex, so I applied to study for a PhD with him there, beginning in 1987. I wasn't, to be totally honest, a sociolinguist at that point. I was still a (very rudimentary) dialectologist. But my time at Essex during the PhD changed that – I was able, thanks to Peter, to begin teaching sociolinguistics, to study and work alongside other sociolinguists, and to find my feet. After the PhD, I went for a two-year postdoc to Victoria University of Wellington in New Zealand, to work with Janet Holmes and Allan Bell. These were my two most sociolinguistically formative years, and very very happy years too.

What Do You Consider to Be Your Most Important Contribution to Sociolinguistics?

I know I have been a bit of a fox rather than a hedgehog and dipped and delved into several things over the course of my career, but I think my long-standing research interest in new dialect formation, dialect contact, and its outcomes is the one theme that has been most central for me. Keeping *rural* varieties on the sociolinguistic map in this work has been important to me too, whether they be in rural parts of England (such as my work on the Fens, or on the consequences of counter-urbanization for dialects of rural East Anglia) or isolated insular communities far away, like the work I have been carrying out with colleagues on the Englishes of Micronesia and the Falkland Islands. I was once at an Arabic sociolinguistics conference in southern France and was confronted with the, for me, bizarre view that linguistic change in urban areas was special, of a different kind to that in rural areas, since dialect contact was an urban phenomenon. Having worked almost exclusively on *rural* dialect contact all my life, and having found exactly the same types of change that they had found in Arab cities, it was clear to me that what was important was contact and not "urban-ness" in accounting for the changes found. So I've been on a bit of a mission since then to "defend" the rural, to explore its diversity, and to scrutinize the way that "the rural" and rural dialects are represented in the media.

What Advice Would You Give Students of Sociolinguistics Today?

I'm not sure I am the right person to give advice, really. I personally feel that I have meandered in several directions, rather than focused doggedly on one, and I am fortunate that, despite that, I've managed to keep myself fed. Sociolinguists, though, have to be human and humane – we have to be able to engage and talk to people, laugh with them, enjoy their company. I would encourage young sociolinguists to find their site – whether that's a city, an island, a rock band, or a crochet group – and dive in, immerse fully, and enjoy what that can bring. Be open-minded, critical, and do what you think is interesting. Don't be a clone. Work with lots of different kinds of (nice) people. If I had my time again, I would almost certainly want to be a human geographer, and diving into this literature constantly fills me with ideas that inform my sociolinguistics. Read what you want to read, not just what is in the canon.

How Do You Think Your Field Will Branch Out and Develop in the Coming Years?

We are already in one of those periods of "critical excitement," I think. This is partly fed by new technologies facilitating not only data collection but also data processing and analysis on a very large scale. Forced alignment and other such recent advances mean we can process thousands of vowels very quickly, so Big Data seems to be one disciplinary fashion. Another seems to be Small Data, an analysis of variant choice in a short comedy sketch or a TV ad or in a tweet, with the emphasis on the ideological stances performed by particular deployments of particular variables. So very first or very third wave. I just hope we don't forget *people* as we move ahead, real people in real communities who we can sit down with and whose stories we can listen to and cherish. And I hope we don't become totally engulfed in the statistical fetish, one consequence of which is that we lose sight of people and lose sight of rich socially motivated and well-researched explanations for the patterns that R has spat at us.

What Are the Biggest Challenges and Perspectives in Doing Research on Language and Space?

Theoretically, what I find fascinating is the comparison of, on the one hand, what is actually going on geographically with people's dialects and, on the other, how these geographical dialects are represented and portrayed ideologically in the media and so forth. Sometimes they appear to be completely at odds with one another – a dialect can have lost a particular salient feature, but the media represent that dialect by emphasizing the very feature that has been lost: Spaces as geographical areas versus spaces as constructed discourses can be very very different indeed.

Methodologically problematic for a long time has been how to collect systematic data from across a whole region, rather than from one neighborhood in a city. The Survey of English Dialects, after all, took twenty years to complete, and to do this again in the same way would be unimaginably expensive and time-consuming. We probably wouldn't want to do it that way again anyway. Our English Dialects App (and before it the Swiss German Dialäktäpp) were some of the first to experiment with the affordances of new technologies to collect dialect data. These techniques also have problems, of course, and for us the EDA has been a fascinating learning exercise, a methodological journey into what works and what does not. Collecting regional data remains a challenge moving forward.

Over the last decade, I've been especially interested in mobility, especially small-scale, mundane everyday mobility. I think we all realize its potential impact on dialect maintenance, but operationalizing mobility in dialect studies is notoriously difficult, something the Milroys realized when they pioneered their social network analyses of Belfast. We attempted to build it into the EDA, looking at travel-to-work distances and how often users had moved in the last ten years, but the results were not entirely easy to interpret. How we can holistically assess the key factors about mobility which appear to be especially deleterious for dialect maintenance is therefore another hurdle we face.

What is important across all of these questions is that we listen to the geographers – this is their bread and butter. We have the linguistic tools, but they have the geographical ones, and I'm rather sorry that more of us don't engage more systematically with contemporary human geography in the way we have done with sociology, anthropology, and social psychology, for example.

Jenny Cheshire: Multiethnolectalization

Jenny Cheshire has a broad range of interests, including language variation and change, language contact and dialect convergence, applied sociolinguistics, and language in education, with a focus on conversational narratives and spoken English, adolescent speech, and Multicultural London English. Jenny Cheshire studied in France and England, worked among other places at Birkbeck College, the Universities of Neuchâtel and Fribourg (Switzerland), and then at Queen Mary, University of London.

Figure 10.2 Jenny Cheshire

How Did You Become a Sociolinguist in the First Place?

I've been interested in language for as long as I can remember. As a small child growing up in what was then a very monolingual part of East London, I could hardly believe that there were children just like me, only 100 miles or so away across the English Channel, who spoke a completely different language. When I got to secondary school, I was thrilled to be able to learn that language – French – as well as another language that people used to speak hundreds of years ago: Latin. So when I got to university, I was happy to find not only linguistics but also a field within linguistics that was all about people and how they use language.

There were two topics in my sociolinguistics course that intrigued me more than the others. The first was the study of the social stratification of English, first in New York City, and then in Norwich, England. I was intrigued by Labov's and Trudgill's findings that phonetic variation turns out to be regular and systematic if you take account of differences between speakers and differences in style, and I wanted to see if grammatical variation was systematic, too. The second topic was avoidance behavior in some Australian languages where, for example, a man could not talk directly to his mother-in-law but had to address her through a third person or, if no-one else was present, via the doorpost. It seemed a fascinating way to be polite. So I became interested in language variation and use early on.

What Do You Consider to Be Your Most Important Contribution to Sociolinguistics?

I think Dani is expecting me to say it's my research on multiethnolects, because the last two questions he asked me were about these. This is certainly what I've been working on most recently, along with my colleagues Sue Fox, Paul Kerswill, and Eivind Torgesen for Multicultural London English and Penelope Gardner-Chloros and Maria Secova for Multicultural Paris French. But I'd like to think my most important contribution is on grammatical variation and change. That's what I started out trying to find out about, inspired by the work of Labov and Trudgill, and I'm still trying to understand it. I've realized just how different grammatical variation can be from phonetic variation, because we can't avoid using grammar to negotiate meaning. It stands between phonetics, semantics, and pragmatics, and often we need to take account of all these aspects of language as well as general communicative principles such as politeness. Very often we can't understand grammatical variation unless we look at how people use it in spontaneous interaction, and most of my work has focused on this.

What Advice Would You Give Students of Sociolinguistics Today?

I'm very conscious that William Labov has said "the one error that I have been trying to avoid is telling other people what to do" (quoted in Tagliamonte 2015: 169)! Nonetheless, I can't resist the invitation to offer some advice. To students interested in doing their own research I would say, follow your interest – focus on any topic that inspires you and that you would love to find out more about. Begin by reading as much as possible on that topic so you know what other researchers have done and which approaches you like, because then you'll get a better idea of how to deal with your chosen topic. If you don't want to do your own research but are simply generally interested in sociolinguistics, I would say read as widely as possible on different topics in the field, not only the ones you find the most interesting. Everything in sociolinguistics is interrelated, so reading widely helps to get a better understanding of how individuals use language and how language relates to social issues. It's interesting, too, to think about how what you're reading relates to the language use you know about from your own life history and your own language use.

I'd also advise students of sociolinguistics, whether research-oriented or not, to think about how the other linguistics disciplines you're studying relate to sociolinguistic issues. For me, the most exciting insights into language variation and change have come from working with – or even just from talking to – colleagues with expertise in formal syntax, pragmatics, semantics, historical linguistics, psycholinguistics, phonetics, and corpus linguistics. I've probably missed out some other fields from this list, but my point is that all these different perspectives contribute to a better understanding of what language is and what we do with it.

How Do You Think Your Field Will Branch Out and Develop in Coming Years?

I think we will see more interdisciplinary work involving linguistic variation and other fields of linguistics. When I started out as a sociolinguist, my field was often dismissed by colleagues working in other fields. They saw sociolinguistics as a marginal field, and in fact at that time it was usually offered to students only as an optional module in the undergraduate program. Sociolinguistics has a far more central place in the curriculum now, and the achievements of researchers in the field have (deservedly) won the interest of linguists working in other fields, so there are plenty of opportunities for interdisciplinary research. I think sociolinguists will reach out beyond linguistics, too, in their search for explanations for linguistic variation. This has always happened to some extent, but it seems to be increasing now. One fairly recent example is work on language variation and change and game theory, from applied mathematics (Mühlenbernd & Quinley 2017). All this interdisciplinary work is greatly advancing our understanding of how and why language varies and changes.

I think we'll see more work on the social meaning of grammatical variation, too, drawing on both semantics and pragmatics as researchers look for parallels between sociophonetics and what are coming to be known as sociosyntax, sociopragmatics, and sociosemantics. A survey of research of this kind was given by Beltrama (2020).

Finally, I think we'll see researchers sharing data more frequently than they do at present. This will be especially useful for the study of grammatical variation, where ideally researchers carry out both quantitative and qualitative analyses of the variable they are interested in. Quantitative analyses need large amounts of data because grammatical variables are inevitably less frequent in speech than phonetic variables. Qualitative analyses, however, are best carried out with smaller amounts of data so that we can see how speakers use the variable as they interact with one another, and so that we can take account of speakers' life histories. Sharing datasets makes it easier for researchers to combine these approaches.

I hope I'm right in these predictions – they may simply reflect my hopes for sociolinguistics, but there are signs that these things are happening already.

What Is Your Opinion of the Effect of Multiethnolects on the Dialect Landscapes of Major Societies?

This is an interesting question, and a very difficult one! So far, the effects seem to vary from one society to another. In several European cities the multiethnolect is seen as a youth vernacular, associated with adolescents living in multilingual and multiethnic areas of cities; this is the case for *Kiezdeutsch* in Berlin, for example. This suggests to me that speakers will stop using the multiethnolect as they become adults, so the effect on the dialect landscape will be limited. In other cities, some of the linguistic forms originally associated with the multiethnolect have been sociolinguistically reallocated or recontextualized: In Copenhagen, for example, some are being mapped onto social stratification and status (Madsen 2013) and are no longer associated with speakers of recent immigrant origin. In London, and perhaps beyond, Multicultural London English, or MLE, has become recontextualized for some people as a marker of a Black British identity (Ilbury & Kerswill 2023).

The situation for London is complex, however, since at the same time there are indications that MLE could be here to stay as a new London working-class dialect. The characteristic phonetic features of MLE are used by children as young as 4–5 from a range of ethnic groups. An online survey of attitudes to MLE of 800 Londoners showed that 16.4 percent, representing a wide spread of ethnic and social groups, claimed to be speakers of it (Kircher & Fox 2019: 853).

The limited research there has been in the UK on multiethnolects outside London has found MLE-type features used by young people in Birmingham in the Midlands and Manchester in northwest England, in both cases alongside local dialect features. Drummond (2018) has suggested, as a result, that this is evidence of an overarching Multicultural (Urban) British English. We do not know for sure whether the MLE features diffused from London or whether they emerged independently in multilingual areas of Birmingham and Manchester, but in any case their existence has certainly had an effect on the dialect landscape of English cities.

The short answer to the question, then, is that in my opinion there is evidence of some very interesting effects on the dialect landscape of major urban societies, but we do not yet know if the effects will be temporary or longer-lasting.

Do You Think Multiethnolects Should Be Incorporated in School Curricula in Some Form?

Yes, I do! Learning about multiethnolects means students can learn about the emergence of new dialects, the effect of immigration on language, young people's language, and many other interesting and important sociolinguistic topics. Multiethnolects are often seen negatively, probably because they are associated with low-status groups in inner-city areas, but also, quite simply, because they are new dialects; so learning about them should lead to younger generations being less linguistically prejudiced. Multiethnolects, in fact, are an excellent example of social integration, since they are spoken by young people of all ethnicities, including the dominant ethnicity in a society.

References
Beltrama, A. (2020). Social meaning in semantics and pragmatics. *Language and Linguistics Compass*, 14(9), e12398.
Drummond, R. (2018). *Researching Urban Youth Language and Identity*. Palgrave Macmillan.
Ilbury, C. and Kerswill, P. (2023). How Multiethnic is a Multiethnolect? The Recontextualisation of Multicultural London English. In: B. A. Svendsen & R. Jonsson, eds., *Routledge Handbook of Language and Youth Culture*. London: Routledge.
Kircher, R. & Fox, S. (2019). Attitudes towards Multicultural London English: Implications for attitude theory and language planning. *Journal of Multilingual and Multicultural Development*, 40(10), 847–864.
Madsen, L. M. (2013). "High" and "low" in urban Danish speech styles. *Language in Society*, 42, 115–138.

Mühlenbernd, R. & Quinley, J. (2017). Language change and network games. *Language and Linguistics Compass*, 11(2), e12235.

Tagliamonte, S. A. (2015). *Making Waves: The Story of Variationist Sociolinguistics*. Oxford: Wiley-Blackwell.

Ana Deumert: Multilingualism

Ana Deumert is Professor of Linguistics at the University of Cape Town. Her research program is located within the broad field of sociolinguistics and has a strong transdisciplinary focus. She has worked on the sociolinguistic history of Afrikaans, coauthored *Introducing Sociolinguistics* (2009, with Rajend Mesthrie, Joan Swann, and William Leap) and the *Dictionary of Sociolinguistics* (2004, with Joan Swann, Rajend Mesthrie, and Theresa Lillis). She has also worked on multilingual mobile communication practices and recently completed the edited collection *From Southern Theory to Decolonizing Sociolinguistics* (2023, with Sinfree Makoni). Her current work focuses on language and sound as well as the use of language in insurgent political movements, looking, in particular, at the anticolonial struggle.

Figure 10.3: Ana Deumert

How Did You Become a Sociolinguist in the First Place?

I became a sociolinguist by chance and good fortune. I had originally studied history and literature, and had always enjoyed questions of language, and how history and language were entangled with one another. And then in 1994, when I had just moved to South Africa, I read Joshua

Fishman's work on the sociology of language and thought immediately: *This is the kind of work I would like to do!* In the following years I combined my interest in history with sociolinguistics in my PhD work and, while completing my PhD, also began to teach a new postgraduate course on language policy at the University of Cape Town. Since then, my work has moved into many different directions; but I do maintain a strong interest in history and the poetic, an interest that is grounded in my early training.

What Do You Consider to Be Your Most Important Contribution to Sociolinguistics?

I think only others would be able to answer this question – it would be presumptuous for me to even try. In my research I have been driven by a passion for knowledge and a deep-seated commitment to social justice. As a result, my work is very varied: I have worked within the variationist paradigm as well as macrosociolinguistics, contact linguistics, and the broad tradition of linguistic anthropology. More recently I have been inspired by poststructuralist approaches and, especially, decolonial theory. I have analyzed spoken language as well as written language (online and in archives), and I have published work on art, politics, and music. Who knows what I will be writing about in five years' time?

What Advice Would You Give Students of Sociolinguistics Today?

Keep an open mind, read widely, follow your heart, and always keep history and politics in focus. Language is never neutral, it can be used to oppress and to empower, it can close our minds and open our minds. Importantly, enjoy what you do – that way you will do excellent work. Also, as you do your own work and research always remain critical – not everything that one finds in books is correct or matters. Too often, scholars overestimate academic knowledge and discount the many knowledges that people have. As William James said in the early twentieth century: 'No professor's lectures can save us.' The world is always so much bigger than the lecture hall, and our futures demand that we listen beyond the academy.

How Do You Think Your Field Will Branch Out and Develop in Coming Years?

I hope that our work will become much more transdisciplinary, breaking through the modernist confines of disciplinary knowledge. I also hope that we will open our minds to other ways of thinking and being, resist the desire for expertness and remain very humble. I often think of Archie Mafeje's reflections on anthropology. He wrote the following in his text *Anthropology and Independent Africans* (1998): "As I conceive of it, ethnography is an end product of social texts authored by the people themselves ... In my view, this [marks] a definite break with the European epistemology of subject–object ... [it is] a recognition of the other not as a partner in knowledge making, *but as a knowledge-maker in [their] own right*." And I would argue that the same applies to sociolinguistics: We can learn so much by listening carefully.

How Do You Think Increasing Multilingualism Will Affect English as a World Language?

I don't think that multilingualism is actually increasing; it was always there. Multilingualism is how people live, wanting to speak to one another, to communicate and relate to one another. Speaking other languages is thus not unusual or new, and multilingual practices have always affected the linguistic ecologies in which we live. However, what is perhaps new is that schools and policymakers now pay attention to it and have begun to value and cherish it. This has led to the emergence of empowering and politically nuanced discourses about multilingualism. Ideally, such discourses will lead to a situation where the hegemony of English is diminished and, importantly, not replaced by a new hegemony; a world in which all languages and ways of speaking can thrive.

What Is Your Professional Advice on How Endangered Languages Can Be Protected?

As I noted above, I am critical of positioning myself as someone who is an expert, as someone who gives advice to others regarding what they should do. I am, of course, interested in language, interested in meaning and in what people do with language and other signs. But I do not necessarily know more than them – I would always take my guidance from those who wish to maintain and protect their language. I would want to listen to them, not the other way around. And in the process, I will learn. Maybe sometimes I will have something to say, and maybe sometimes what I think could be helpful. At other times we might work together, finding new paths together, learning from one another. But the most important principle is that those who speak the language, who identify with the language, who long for the language, will always be the experts. Not me.

Lisa Lim: Language Contact

Lisa Lim is an Associate Professor in the Department of Linguistics at the University of Sydney. Her interests involve language contact and evolution of the New Englishes, Asian varieties in multilingual ecologies, language shift, endangerment, revitalization, and postvernacular vitality in minority and endangered language communities, such as the Peranakans in Singapore and the Malays of Sri Lanka. She's also researching the sociolinguistics of globalization, with interests in mobility, urban multilingualism, computer-mediated communication, and their impact on contact dynamics.

Figure 10.4 Lisa Lim

How Did You Become a Sociolinguist in the First Place?

I didn't start off a sociolinguist per se. I'm probably a good example of how one's interests and career develop via serendipitous moments in one's life, through professional but also personal choices and trajectories. Having graduated from the National University of Singapore (NUS) with a First Class Honours in English Language, I was offered an overseas scholarship to do my PhD. Although my Honours thesis was in pragmatics, at the interview I was asked, "Do you like phonetics?" – because they needed to nurture a future professor in that discipline. Being the quite eclectic, catholic scholar-to-be (as well as typical dutiful Singaporean student), I said, "Um, yes …." So off I went and trained in instrumental acoustic phonetics, returning to direct the phonetics lab and courses at

NUS; a few of my students were inspired to continue their training as speech and language therapists. But I've always had a passion for the close relationship between language and society. My Honours thesis had addressed cultural differences in pragmatic preferences in Singapore. My PhD was the first of that era to examine ethnic group differences in prosodic patterns in Singapore English (SgE), and, while centered on phonetics, had been informed by the sociolinguistic research of one of my supervisors, Paul Kerswill.

My career has seen a certain amount of mobility, for professional and personal reasons. I left my tenure at NUS and, together with my partner Umberto Ansaldo – typologist and contact linguist, with whom I collaborate – spent years at institutions in Europe, Asia, and now Australia. Mobility experiences are time-consuming and energy-consuming, and most unsettling, but they also have provided precious opportunities to engage with diverse fields and cultures, broaden my horizons, and reinvent myself – several times over! At the Universiteit van Amsterdam I was employed more pointedly in sociolinguistics and enriched by the sociolinguistics and multilingualism research group. Vibrant research networks in Europe, South Africa, and the UA embraced my then World Englishes (WE)/linguistics-situated focus and ushered me more profoundly into explorations of contact linguistics, creole studies, language endangerment, linguistic citizenship, and the sociolinguistics of globalization.

What Do You Consider to Be Your Most Important Contribution to Sociolinguistics?

I have done my small part in taking Asian contact varieties and positioning them beyond both the realm of WE and their market value within only Asia, where they had been for a while, and bringing them to the fore and demonstrating their significance more broadly in contact linguistics and sociolinguistic theory. My scholarly work has always aimed at restructuring through a sociolinguistics lens. An early paper on SgE particles, though initially approached from a more descriptive WE perspective, ultimately tied structure intimately to social history, encompassing migration and language policy, and to ecology and typology. My work also centers around minority communities and their languages, which are often invisible in the official statal narrative: the nonofficial Chinese "dialects" and "non-Tamil Indian languages" in Singapore's ecology; and Hong Kong's linguistic minorities. And my research on the Peranakan communities of Singapore, addressing early English adoption, identity politics, postvernacular vitality, succeeded in articulating – beyond the interest they had attracted previously solely for their endangered vernacular Baba Malay – their wider significance for sociolinguistics.

What, in Your Opinion, Is the Contribution of Newly Emerging Varieties of English to Current Models of English as a World Language?

First, ecology and typology are significant. Multilingual ecologies, especially with languages of diverse typologies, are extremely instructive for the potential and eventuality of the emergence of new varieties. Features such as (lexical) tone, and particles – not traditionally considered part of the typology of English – can emerge in contact varieties of English. This clearly demonstrates that anything is possible, as long as the ecology and typologies of languages therein allow.

Second, history is significant. We need to give face not only to more dominant language varieties in an ecology, but also consider different dominances across different eras, as well as recognize founder populations. Newly emerging varieties offer unique histories and ecologies whose study brings important considerations to our models.

Third, computer-mediated communication (CMC) and social media are significant. In communities where English is not dominant, these comprise a significant platform on which English is used more than in "normal" non-CMC contexts, and where creative translanguaging practices support intense contact and restructuring, and thus catalyze evolution.

Finally, studying newly emerging varieties of English also compels us to reflect on what a "World Language" entails. Just as the world maintains infinite diversity, in spite of connectivity and influences, so too does the English language – thus we do better to speak of "Englishes", or perhaps "Englishes as World Language varieties." Similarly, just as the world is constantly evolving, so too are our Englishes.

Is It Likely or Unlikely That New Pidgins and Creoles Will Form in the Near Future?

A most recent instance is the emergence of Manila Chinese English in the multicultural urban ecology of metropolitan Manila, due to extensive contact between Manila English and local varieties of Chinese Filipinos such as Philippine Hybrid Hokkien and Tagalog. As long as human beings continue to communicate, in ecologies involving more than one language variety, and in the diversity of cultural and linguistic practices that exist, contact dynamics and human creativity will see to it that new contact languages evolve. Multilingual urban centers have, in particular, for a while now been recognized as important sites for language contact and evolution of new varieties. And in particular, English-based contact varieties stand to continue to have much vitality, given the positioning of English as a World Language with much economic, cultural, symbolic, and social capital, globally, within local contexts and on virtual platforms.

Dennis Preston: Folk Linguistics

Dennis Preston is Regents Professor and Co-Director of the Center for Oklahoma Studies, Oklahoma State University, and University Distinguished Professor Emeritus, Michigan State University. His work focuses on sociolinguistics and dialectology, folk linguistics, language variation and change, and the form and function of American English generally. He is an Erskine Fellow of the University of Canterbury (New Zealand) and a Fellow of the Japan Society for the Promotion of Science, and of the Linguistic Society of America. Dennis Preston was awarded the Officer's Cross of the Order of Merit of the Polish Republic in 2004.

Figure 10.5 Dennis Preston

How Did You Become a Sociolinguist in the First Place?

I think I will answer in the fourth place, touching first on my inclinations to be one. First, I grew up somewhat bilingually (100 percent Hungarian on one side) and was made aware when I was very young from others outside the South that I sounded like a cowboy. Second, my father, in spite of his late-learned English, was an elaborate, decorative speaker. He indulged in and was expert at such matters from phonetic modification to elaborate metaphoric flights, bringing language to a level beyond the purely communicative. Third, after all this priming, my main linguistic training was historical and dialectological, both with my esteemed dissertation director Prof. Frederic G. Cassidy. What a setup: change and variation. So, fourth, when *The Social Stratification of English in New York City* arrived in my mailbox barely a year after publication, I had the *Aha!* moment you seek.

What Do You Consider to Be Your Most Important Contribution to Sociolinguistics?

I believe that, with *folk linguistics* (which is as much the child of my former student, coauthor, and friend Nancy Niedzielski) and the additional work on *perceptual dialectology* and *language regard*, I have played some role in influencing the field to take more seriously what Weinreich, Labov, and Herzog called the problem of evaluation. Approaches that allow the exploration of various means, from the experimental to the discursive, in discovering and making use of what nonlinguists think about and respond to in the world of language structure and use, are in stark contrast to the denigration of all such matters, as in Bloomfield's famous "tertiary responses" article. I also hope this trend has provided further grounding in the well-known sociolinguistic struggle against linguistic prejudice.

What Advice Would You Give Students of Sociolinguistics Today?

If you believe there is any value in what I say in my answer just above, the most important thing you can do is talk with people. You'll learn a lot about language and social life from such practice, and I guarantee it will only enhance your professional abilities.

How Do You Think Your Field Will Branch Out and Develop in Coming Years?

If I may be allowed to substitute "hope" for "think," I hope language variation and change will never hamper itself by insisting on a monotonic approach or by disregarding its practitioners who value a variety of approaches in seeking answers to the big and little questions of language variation and change.

What Are the Biggest Challenges and Perspectives in Perceptual Dialectology Today?

Perceptual dialectology was never meant to be simply the collection of hand-drawn maps by nonlinguists. That it has been characterized as such has allowed the seriousness of it as one of a wide array of approaches to folk knowledge to be overlooked as a sort of fun game. I fear that the perspective that it is, because of its immediate attractiveness and popularity, a linguistic party game does not allow for its rightful place as an effective tool in the study of linguistic folk knowledge.

What New Methodologies Do You Envisage in Your Field?

At the risk of being curmudgeonly, I hope for no downgrading of the effectiveness of the sociolinguistic interview, but I believe I have already advanced that concern in my advice to young sociolinguists. Of course, I look forward to advances in speech and recording technologies, and, even more specifically, the development of computer-assisted map-drawing opportunities that will allow for effective collection and rapid statistical treatment and display of data investigations, work which is already under way. And I would be worse than a curmudgeon if I did not recognize how the many advances in perceptual dialectology, folk linguistics, and language regard have been made and are being made by my brilliant and hardworking students and even some who did not suffer my tutelage, a fact which leads to another piece of advice that I might give young sociolinguists: As you progress, please remember that you are not just there to teach your students; you must learn from them or the full process of education has not carried through.

John R. Rickford: Activist Sociolinguistics

John R. Rickford, born in Guyana in 1949, is Professor Emeritus at Stanford University. His research focuses on sociolinguistics, the relation between linguistic variation and change and social structure, with a special interest in the relation between language and ethnicity, social class and style, language variation and change, pidgin and creole languages, African American Vernacular English, and the applications of linguistics to educational problems.

How Did You Become a Sociolinguist in the First Place?

In 1971 I graduated from the University of California Santa Cruz (UCSC) with a major in sociolinguistics (see Rickford 2022: 76), perhaps the first person to do so anywhere. I had switched from literature to an

Figure 10.6 John R. Rickford

independently designed major in sociolinguistics because of the novelty of the field, the opportunity to do original work on important social issues, and the fact that UCSC's innovative character facilitated this. Early work by Charles Ferguson, Joshua Fishman, Dell Hymes, and William Labov, among others, inspired me, but Le Page's (1968) paper on problems with using English in education in my native Guyana and other West Indian territories really drew me in.

What Do You Consider to Be Your Most Important Contribution to Sociolinguistics?

More than fifty years later, I would say that my most important contributions have been on descriptive, methodological, and theoretical issues in the study of American English, African American Language or Vernacular English, and Caribbean English-based creoles (see e.g. Rickford 1979, 1987, 1999a, 2019). But for the past dozen years, my focus has been on activist sociolinguistics, including the contributions we can make to the *education* of vernacular speakers (see Rickford et al. 2013), and to their treatment in *criminal justice* systems which often disregard, disbelieve, or disparage speakers of vernacular or nonstandard varieties.

As noted in my foreword to Lawson and Sayers (2016), the community studies of sociolinguists in the 1960s often *did* have an activist orientation, especially in relation to "redressing educational inequities linked to vernacular dialects." But for various reasons, "applied issues have usually taken a back seat to analytical and theoretical issues in sociolinguistics." Moreover, activism on criminal justice issues is relatively new. So I'll focus on them in reporting on my work in activist sociolinguistics.

I have been involved in several cases involving criminal justice, most often in showing that police transcripts of the speech of African American defendants were inaccurate in significant ways (as others have shown too, e.g. Jones et al. 2019). But the case which is best known is discussed in Rickford and King (2016), which won the LSA award for the best article published in *Language* that year. In it, we showed that the unfamiliarity of jurors (and the general public) with the highly systematic AAVE of Rachel Jeantel *may* have contributed to their disregard of her crucial earwitness testimony on the murder of her friend Trayvon Martin by George Zimmerman (see also King and Rickford 2023). But perhaps an even bigger factor was their prejudice against vernacular speech like hers, and their tendency, as in other cases, to view it as not credible. This extends even to cases in which Black speakers are using colloquial English expressions like "I'm good" to mean "No thanks," as I showed in a 2018 Expert Notice in a New Mexico court case involving a Drug Enforcement Agency's illegal body search of an African American woman (see Rickford 2022: 101–103).

What Advice Would You Give Students of Sociolinguistics Today?

My answer is that you need to know enough linguistics to give specific technical analyses of the features of the varieties in question to convince educators, judges, or juries of the validity of your points (e.g. Labov 1997 on the distinction between Boston and New York City accents in the Prinzivalli case; or Shuy (1998) on the distinction between simple and compound clause types in the speech of wrongly accused African American Louisiana teenager Michael T. Carter who, like Prinzivalli, spent 15 months in jail for a crime he didn't commit). And you need to understand enough of the social context you're investigating (educational, legal, and so on) and its relation to language to understand their mutual effects (e.g. Eades 2010, Gonzalez Van Cleve 2016). So, as a sociolinguist you need to know as much as any good linguist should know, and then more.

How Do You Think Your Field Will Branch Out and Develop in Coming Years?

It is my fervent hope that research in activist sociolinguistics will grow, and that this research will be used to improve the life chances of vernacular and dialect speakers around the world (see Wright (2023), which won the award for the best article published in *Language* in 2023, and the work of Baugh (2003) and others it drew upon). From the references in King and Rickford (2023) and other sources, this appears to be happening, and it gives to sociolinguistics an urgency and impact that go beyond the descriptive and theoretical issues – important as those are – with which so much of academia is absorbed.

References

Baugh, J. (2003). Linguistic Profiling. In: S. Makoni, G. Smitherman & A. K. Spears, eds., *Black Linguistics: Language, Society and Politics in Africa and the Americas*. New York: Routledge, 155–168.

Eades, D. (2010). *Sociolinguistics and the Legal Process*. Bristol: Multilingual Matters.

Gonzalez Van Cleve, N. (2016). *Crook County: Racism and Injustice in America's Largest Criminal Court*. Stanford, CA: Stanford Law Books.

Jones, T., Kalbfeld, J., Hancock, R. & Clark, R. (2019). Testifying while Black: An experimental study of court reporter accuracy in transcription of African American English. *Language*, online edition for Public Policy.

King, S. & Rickford, J. R. (2023). Language on trial. *Daedalus*, 152(3), Summer, 178–193.

Labov, W. (exact date unknown). How I got into linguistics, and what I got out of it. *University of Pennsylvania*. www.ling.upenn.edu/~wlabov/HowIgot.html.

Lawson, R. & Sayers, D. (2016). *Sociolinguistic Research: Application and Impact*. London: Routledge.

Le Page, R. B. (1968). Problems to Be Faced in the Use of English as the Medium of Education in Four West Indian Territories. In: C. A. Ferguson, J. A. Fishman & J. Das Gupta, eds., *Language Problems of Developing Nations*. New York: Wiley & Sons, 431–442.

Rickford, J. R. (1979). Variation in a Creole Continuum: Quantitative and Implicational Approaches. PhD dissertation: University of Pennsylvania.

Rickford, J. R. (1987). *Dimensions of a Creole Continuum: History, Texts and Linguistic Analysis of Guyanese Creole*. Stanford, CA: Stanford University Press.

Rickford, J. R. (1999a). *African American Vernacular English: Features, Evolution, Educational Implications*. Oxford: Blackwell.

Rickford, J. R. (2019). *Variation, Versatility and Change in Sociolinguistics and Creole Studies*. Cambridge: Cambridge University Press.

Rickford, J. R. (2022). *Speaking My Soul: Race, Life and Language*. London: Routledge.

Rickford, J. R & King, S. (2016). Language and linguistics on trial: Hearing Rachel Jeantel (and other vernacular speakers) in the courtroom and beyond. *Language*, 92(4), 948–988.

Rickford, J. R., Sweetland, J., Rickford, A. E. & Grano, T. (2013). *African American, Creole and Other Vernacular Englishes in Education: A Bibliographic Resource*. New York: Routledge; and Urbana, IL: National Council of Teachers of English.

Shuy, R. W. (1998). *The Language of Confession*, Interrogation and Deception. Thousand Oaks, CA: Sage Publications.

Wright, K. M. (2023). Housing policy and linguistic profiling: An audit study of three American dialects. *Language*, 99(2), e58–e85.

Sali A. Tagliamonte: Variationist Sociolinguistics

Sali A. Tagliamonte holds the Canada Research Chair in Language Variation and Change at the University of Toronto. Previously, she worked at the University of York in the UK. Her research interests span the fields of variation and change, new-dialect formation, internet and youth language, and the history of Canadian English. Sali Tagliamonte is the author of *Making Waves: The Story of Variationist Sociolinguistics* (Tagliamonte 2015), which tells the human story of the field (based on interviews with 43 of the most famous scholars) and served as an inspiration for this concluding chapter.

Figure 10.7 Sali A. Tagliamonte

How Did You Become a Sociolinguist in the First Place?

I grew up in the shadow of one of the largest copper mines in the world in northern Quebec, Canada. Twin smokestacks dominated the landscape, and the topography of the town reflected the social structure of the community: The mine manager had the biggest house at the top of a hill, the various heads of operations lived in grand but lesser houses, in a long line leading down the street, and the hundreds of miners had modest cookie-cutter homes near the mine. The dominant population of the community were francophones; the rest of us were a mixed group whose parents or grandparents had migrated to Canada from the UK, EU, and Asia. Together, we were called "The English." Variation was all around me — in the way people spoke and in the way people lived.

I did not know anything about linguistics then, but I was born with the "antennae" for language and with that natural penchant one is drawn to words and expressions. I think it's almost like you do not discover sociolinguistics, it emerges in you. Later in life, I went to university. I studied English literature with the intention of becoming a poet. But with the voices of so many interesting people, friends, and relations in my head, I took a course in dialectology and then linguistics. My poetry professor said linguistics would "maim me for life," but for me, it opened a whole new world of understanding and curiosity that has been my passion ever since.

What Do You Consider to Be Your Most Important Contribution to Sociolinguistics?

In reflecting on my academic accomplishments, I wish I had access to the innumerable letters of reference my academic supporters have written for me to verify what other scholars think is my most important contribution to sociolinguistics. If I had to guess, my most potent successes as an academic would be: (1) my contributions to comparative sociolinguistics; (2) my ability to make method and analysis comprehensible; and (3) my studies of linguistic variables from phonology to discourse and pragmatics.

I pride myself on noticing unstudied linguistic phenomena and bringing to the field understanding and explanations of their patterns of variation and trajectories of change. I am also very proud of the many corpora I have collected, including the York English Corpus (1997), the Roots Corpus (2003), and the Ontario Dialects Project, which to date has data from over 1,000 individuals in twenty-one communities, and is still growing at 11 million words: vernacular Ontario English from the late 1800s to the present day (at the time of writing, 2022). To me, the joy of being a sociolinguist is to sit across from a stranger and hear their stories and learn about their lives. I have gained insight and understanding of human life from the hundreds of interviews I have done in the field, and I see this experience as one of the greatest gifts of my professional life.

What Advice Would You Give Students of Sociolinguistics Today?

My best advice to students intrigued by sociolinguistics is this tried-and-true strategy: Follow your curiosity. Make a plan. Be intrepid. Go to the field! Embrace local practice by "walking a mile in another's moccasins" or at least listen with wonder and try to imagine it. Transcribe with a strategy. When you come up with an idea, go exploring in the available data immediately. Early probing into the viability of good ideas is critical for maintaining purpose and having the most fun. If it doesn't work out, keep looking. If it gets hard, keep going. If you can't figure it out, try again.

How Do You Think Your Field Will Branch Out and Develop in Coming Years?

Science is always changing. Sometimes there is a phase of consolidation; then expansion which leads to fragmentation. In the early twenty-first century, sociolinguistics is diffuse, driven in many directions, often by ideology rather than by science. However, we are living in interesting times of social change, economic upheaval, and global problems. As long as linguists are well trained in theory, method, and analysis, and the wise scholar holds fast to evidence-based inquiry, the study of language in society will continue to provide us with the potential to change the world. Even if you don't aspire to change the world, you'll have an interesting life.

In Your Opinion: Is There a Fourth Wave of Sociolinguistic Theory Coming Up?

Sometimes people think of developments in sociolinguistics as waves, counting them first, second, third. Is a fourth wave coming? Definitely. We already see this happening. Scholars are beginning to build teams of interdisciplinary talents. Syntacticians are doing experiments; semanticists are studying words; typologists are studying dialects; phonologists are building labs; and sociolinguists, as usual, are implicated everywhere. If not, they should be. As teams of scholars work toward understanding what is going on in the languages of the world and ask the question *Why?*, I think language will keep being the bellwether of human development from the ground up and into the future.

What Are the Most Important Methodological Skills Younger Sociolinguists Should Acquire Today? What Is Your Advice?

When you study language, the most important skill is to understand linguistic variation, knowing how to define the dependent variable and to model the multifaceted independent variables that influence it. The rest is about how clever you can be in finding the explanation.

References
Tagliamonte, S. A. (2015). *Making Waves: The Story of Variationist Sociolinguistics*. Oxford: Wiley-Blackwell.

Lionel Wee: English As an Asian Language

Lionel Wee received his PhD from the University of California at Berkeley and is Professor at the Department of English Language and Literature at the National University of Singapore. His research interests focus on language policy (especially in Southeast Asia), the grammar of Singapore English, metaphorical discourse, and general issues in sociolinguistics and pragmatics.

Figure 10.8 Lionel Wee

How Did You Become a Sociolinguist in the First Place?

My PhD training was in cognitive linguistics, but immediately upon returning to Singapore (I was in UC Berkeley on a scholarship) I was asked to help with a dictionary of Singapore English. And this immediately forced me to confront sociolinguistic dimensions of language, such as whose usage is to be taken as correct, the bases on which normative judgments are made, and how matters of orthography (for words that had hitherto been used only in spoken communication) are to be settled. This, combined with the fact that I majored in sociology as an undergraduate, brought home to me that it is in the social aspects of language that most of the really interesting questions lie.

What Do You Consider to Be Your Most Important Contribution to Sociolinguistics?

I think that is something for others to decide: Whether I have made any contribution at all! But I will say that a consistent preoccupation of mine has been to deconstruct assumptions about the nature of language. This was a theme in my work on language rights, it was also a focus in my work with Joseph Park on the commodification of English, and it remains a major concern in my current work on the use of automation in communication.

What Advice Would You Give to Students of Sociolinguistics Today?

Be interdisciplinary. As I work on the questions that arise from trying to deconstruct language (so as to better understand its nature), I realize the importance of integrating insights from anthropology, sociology, philosophy, politics, and so on. As sociolinguists, we have much to learn from the work that goes on in other fields, and vice versa.

How Do You Think Your Field Will Branch Out and Develop in Coming Years?

I am not sure because academia can be extremely conservative, and outdated and problematic ideas about language are difficult to dislodge. I can only hope that a more interdisciplinary approach will lead to great convergences between sociolinguists and scholars from other fields, so that we can make greater progress toward understanding what it is we actually do, what actually happens, when we communicate or think we communicate!

In Your Opinion: How Will English Continue to Diversify in Various Asian Settings?

In many Asian countries, an argument given to more conservative groups (such as governments or educational institutions) is one based on some notion of diglossia. The nativized variety will "only" be used in informal domains and a standard variety in formal ones. In some places such as Singapore, however, we see early attempts to use the nativized variety as a "High," which is very interesting. It's not clear if these attempts will succeed and whether other countries might follow suit. And it's also not clear if the use of a nativized variety as a "High" will gradually lead it to converge with a standard, thus eroding the differences between the two, in the course of which it would be the nativized variety that lost much of what makes it distinct.

What is the Potential and Possible Effect of Grassroots Forms of English?

I think that depends on what segments of the grassroots we are talking about. For simplicity's sake, let us just consider two broad groups: one where many of the individuals are competent in a standard; and one where many are not. There is some broad correlation between the two kinds of competence and socioeconomic status and educational qualifications, especially in Singapore, but we can put that aside for now.

For the first group, nonstandard usage will likely be the result of deliberate attempts at playfully departing from the standard. Grassroots forms, then, have to be understood as highly performative (in Coupland's sense of a performance continuum). They are intentional, even staged.

For the second group, nonstandard usage will likely be the result of the lack of competence in the standard. The grassroots forms, in this case, will occupy the other end of the performance continuum. They are more routinized and lacking in strategic character. And it could well be that the patterns of usage associated with this second group might be appropriated by the first group as part of the latter's highly performative uses of English (in plays, novels, advertising, or as interactional exchanges among friends to signal "local," "non-elite" identities).

Walt Wolfram: Sociolinguistic Outreach

Walt Wolfram (born in 1941 in Philadelphia) is William C. Friday Distinguished University Professor at North Carolina State University, where he directs the North Carolina Language and Life Project. His research interests include variation and change, varieties of American English, with a focus on African American English and English in North

Figure 10.9 Walt Wolfram

Carolina, promoting sociolinguistic gratuity and work within the speech communities researched.

How Did You Become a Sociolinguist in the First Place?

Although the field of sociolinguistics did not exist at the time, I was born to be a sociolinguist. I was reared by German-speaking immigrant parents in working-class, urban Philadelphia, where German was the language of the home, the church, and some of my neighborhood. I was born in 1941, during the Second World War, when most of the world was at war with Germany. As a child, I was conflicted by anti-German sentiments around me while all my relatives lived in fear of death in Germany during the war. My parents spoke heavily accented English that would obviously not be an appropriate norm for me growing up. Wanting to escape the stigma of being German in the 1940s, I turned outside of my family for English-language norms and customs. I wanted identity as an American, so I paid attention to local models of behavior and the speech of my native Philadelphia English-speaking cohorts. In the process, I became sensitive to different ways of acting and speaking from an early age, and this set the stage for my life as a sociolinguist.

Reared in a highly religious home, I committed to becoming a missionary and translating the Bible into an indigenous language in South America. Pursuing this goal as an undergraduate student, I tended to excel in language courses and linguistics courses, majoring in cultural anthropology. That led me to graduate school to get a PhD in linguistics before I left for the mission field. My mentor, Roger Shuy, one of the first sociolinguists, invited me to work on the Detroit Dialect Study in 1965. I chose to study social stratification in the Black Detroit community because it was a radically different linguistic situation typical of many large urban areas in the US. At the same time, I started a family and applied to go to the mission field, but the mission organization required applicants to raise their own finances. I was unable to do so but needed to support my family. At that point, Roger Shuy offered me an opportunity to do research at the Center for Applied Linguistics in Washington, D.C. in an area related to my dissertation. And that began my journey into the field of sociolinguistics. Because of all these circumstances, I often say that I am an "accidental sociolinguist," but in retrospect, my undergraduate major in cultural anthropology combined with my linguistic graduate training was the perfect combination for the emerging discipline, along with the personal socialization from my youth. Actually, I never had a course in sociolinguistics: There were none until we started the first sociolinguistic program at Georgetown University in 1970.

What Do You Consider to Be Your Most Important Contribution to Sociolinguistics?

I would like to say that my major contributions include both research and engagement. I have researched a number of ethnic and regional language situations: African American Language, Appalachian English, Vietnamese English, Native American Lumbee English, Hispanic English, and Southeastern Coastal English, among others. So I have become one of the sociolinguists who describe socioethnic communities. At the same time, I subscribe strongly to the notion that "If you have knowledge, it is worth sharing," not just with academic peers but with the communities who fuel your research and the general public. In this capacity, I have been executive producer of more than fifteen television documentaries on American English varieties (winning several Emmy Awards), established permanent and temporary exhibits in museums, developed a formal textbook for teaching North Carolina social studies and language variation, and have presented over a thousand workshops for practitioners and teachers. Given the misunderstanding and myths that exist in popular culture about language variation, even in our institutions of higher education, this remains the biggest challenge for sociolinguists in their public lives, and this commitment has consumed my professional passion in the latter stages of my career. There are plenty of brilliant, capable sociolinguists, the descriptive and theoretical field is advancing nicely, but the public understanding of language and social equality is still in a primitive state and needs much more intense engagement by scholars.

What Advice Would You Give Students of Sociolinguistics Today?

The field has advanced immeasurably in technology-based programs and its quantitative sophistication. Accordingly, students need to keep up with the ever-progressing state-of-the-art computational programs for analysis. But that is more of a requisite than advice at this point. Students need to find topics that they are passionate about for one reason or another and pursue the underlying issues that make them important. They need to identify what is an important issue in sociolinguistics and frame their studies in this context. It is not enough simply to describe: Students must further ask themselves why these issues are important for sociolinguistic understanding and how they relate to social justice around the world today.

How Do You Think Your Field Will Branch Out and Develop in Coming Years?

The continued technological advances of analytic procedures will continue in the coming years. It is a necessary, requisite skill for students to be flexible and to learn the most efficient methods of analysis. But I fear that the field may lapse into methodological reductionism, consumed by the programs of analysis. At the same time, there has been an acceleration of the trend to address fundamental issues of sociolinguistic justice and equality in society by a smaller group of sociolinguists. Both of these trends are admirable, but I fear that the so-called descriptive-theoretical and operational are not meshing as they should. We must be careful not to categorize these trends with elitist evaluative metrics like "theoretical" or "real" versus "applied" or "outreach" that prioritize the intellectual value of one over the other. Personally, I don't want to live in a world where my research focus has no application to the lives of those I associate with in my public life. I want everyone to be affected by the insights of sociolinguistics – it is operationally relevant and significant!

What Is Your Personal Assessment of Feedback from the General US Public about Your Recent Activities?

We have been greatly gratified by our public outreach in the state of North Carolina, where our major programs take place. We have a number of stable programs that address the public, including regular documentaries. We are currently completing a five-part series, *Talking Black in America*; the first of its kind, that ranges from the presentation of the diasporic roots of African American Language to its socioeducational implications for social justice. These documentaries are currently integrated into more than 200 university classes around the country and are shown in secondary schools, corporate institutions, even in public movie theaters. Our regular exhibit booth at the State Fair attracts thousands of people each year, and folks return to see our latest dialect buttons and discuss dialects with our staff. People also know our trade books, particularly *Talking Tar Heel* which is used regularly in teacher training. Our programs on the dialects of North Carolina have been highlighted in state and national media, including major television and radio stations, like CNN and National Public Radio. Just about everywhere we go in the state, people know our program and appreciate the fact that we are celebrating the dialect heritage of North Carolina. We also have a dialect curriculum which can be taught to Grade 8 students in social studies that is officially endorsed by the State

Department of Public Instruction. When I received the North Carolina Award, the highest honor given by the state to a citizen, the Governor of the State said, "So even a linguist can win this award," noting the exceptional impact of our program.

In What Ways Should Sociolinguists Around the World Become More Engaged – and What Are the Most Pressing Issues?

I have often stated that popular beliefs about language variation are akin to a modern geophysicist maintaining that Planet Earth is flat. Citizens think that dialects are simply "a collection of random errors" without any systematic organization or sociohistorical legacy. Every sociolinguist should be actively engaged in debunking current language myths, which are unfortunately held even by our fellow, progressive academicians in our own universities. Furthermore, these ideologies form the basis for much of the sociolinguistic inequality in the world – and these misconceptions need to be addressed by socially responsible sociolinguists.

Every language speaker should have the right to respect and celebrate their language variety as a cultural icon. Personally, I think that we need to make the sociolinguistic perspective on language and equality an integral, required part of formal education so we can dispel the myths that have persisted for so long in the public conversations about language variation. It's not an option; it's an obligation.

Appendix: Phonological Symbols and Lexical Sets

The following is a list of phonological symbols and associated lexical sets developed by Wells (1982: 120) commonly used to refer to vowels in Englishes around the world. The keyword KIT, for instance, is used with reference to /ɪ/, a short front unrounded vowel. RP refers to Received Pronunciation (standard British English), GenAm to General American English, so this chart illustrates pronunciation differences in the two major varieties (and can be extended with varieties elsewhere, of course).

	RP	GenAm	Lexical set		RP	GenAm	Lexical set
1.	ɪ	ɪ	KIT	13.	ɔː	ɔ	THOUGHT
2.	e	ɛ	DRESS	14.	əʊ	o	GOAT
3.	æ	æ	TRAP	15.	uː	u	GOOSE
4.	ɒ	ɑ	LOT	16.	aɪ	aɪ	PRICE
5.	ʌ	ʌ	STRUT	17.	ɔɪ	ɔɪ	CHOICE
6.	ʊ	ʊ	FOOT	18.	aʊ	aʊ	MOUTH
7.	ɑː	æ	BATH	19.	ɪə	ɪr	NEAR
8	ɒ	ɔ	CLOTH	20.	ɛə	ɛr	SQUARE
9.	ɜː	ɜr	NURSE	21.	ɑː	ɑr	START
10.	iː	i	FLEECE	22.	ɔː	ɔr	NORTH
11.	eɪ	eɪ	FACE	23.	ɔː	or	FORCE
12.	ɑː	ɑ	PALM	24.	ʊə	ʊr	CURE

Adapted from Wells (1982: 120)

Glossary

accent the way a language is spoken by individuals, with reference to the sound system and the production of speech sounds

acceptance a process by which a selected standard gains support throughout the wider community; how forms are promoted, passed on, established, and if needs be enforced in wider society

acquisition planning when a national, state, or local government makes decisions that affect schooling and education and determine the usage of language in childhood and adolescence

adjacency pairs pairs of utterances that go hand in hand in conversation, as in thank you/welcome, greetings, or compliments

adstrate two (or more) languages that have equal social status in a contact scenario

African American Vernacular English (AAVE) the distinctive variety (varieties) that developed over centuries in the African American community in North America

age grading age-related and age-specific differences in the use of vernacular and supralocal features, commonly used in adolescence, subject to societal pressure in adulthood, and occasionally resurfacing in later periods

audience design when speakers vary and shift the way they speak in response to their interlocutors

bad-data problem historical data that can typically not be replicated or checked alternatively, and were produced only in writing by a minority of the literate population

bilingualism individuals and communities using and/or speaking two languages on an everyday basis, with frequent switching between them

#BlackLivesMatter a transnational and decentralized political, social, and civil movement with the aim of eradicating racism, discrimination, and racial inequality in society

Blommaert, Jan a Belgian sociolinguist and linguistic anthropologist (1961–2021), famous for his work on the sociolinguistics of globalization

Chancery Standard the language used in documents issued from the English King's secretariat, also known as the Office of Chancery, in the late Middle Ages, sometimes believed to be the precursor of Standard English spelling

Cockney the working class (distinctive and widely known) variety that developed over centuries in the East End of London

code, restricted and elaborated developed by Basil Bernstein; speech codes are characteristic of different social classes and show different types of complexity and elaboration

code-switching shifting from one language to the next for various purposes

codification a process by which the norms and rules of standard grammar, use, and so on are set and fixed (and often linguistically justified) in grammars, dictionaries, or spelling guides

community of practice an aggregate of people who engage in activities with a common purpose, as a result of which practices such as ways of talking, beliefs, values, and power relations emerge in different contexts

complaint tradition the century-old custom in the British Isles (and the anglophone world) of treating variation and change in English as decay

consistency stability with which features are used in texts

contextualization cues features used to represent speakers' ways of creating meaning that are essential in constructing the common ground for interpretation of utterances

Conversation Analysis the study of the structure and function of conversation

Corpus of Early English Correspondence (CEEC) an extensive database of historical data containing metadata for writers with a size of ca. 2.7 million words produced between 1417 and 1681

corpus planning language-authoritative actions that concern the form and structure of a language (e.g. via spelling reform)

covert prestige when speakers dissociate themselves from standard varieties and prefer local (typically nonstandardized) variants for reasons of group identification and peer pressure

creoles varieties that emerge in large-scale language contact and are acquired and used by children and adolescents, often as a first language, when there is restricted access to the lexifier language

crossing switching between codes, very often by adolescents (for reasons of language identity) who are not accepted members of the group associated with the features adopted

de facto official language a language that does not have explicit legal status but is spoken by the majority of the people in wider society

deficit hypothesis theory that children from economically poor homes or ethnically different families are linguistically deficient due to socialization effects

de jure official language a primary language that has been legally established as the national variety of the country

Department Store Study the 1960s study of social stratification of language variation, researched in the three New York Department stores Macy's, Saks, and Calvin Klein

Devonish, Hubert Caribbean linguist who argued that Jamaican Patwa should be used as the medium of instruction to enhance the official status of Creole in public and administrative domains

dialect a regionally distinct variety of a particular language, with specific and recognizable morphological, grammatical, and lexical features

diglossia two languages are functionally specialized to particular domains in society, one typically of high standard in public discourse and one local and in the home domain

distinctiveness features or combinations of features that are characteristic for individual speakers

Dunbar's number a hypothetical number for the amount of people with whom speakers keep up stable social relationships and networks

early adopters central members of a community, with strong social ties and highly conforming to group norms, who provide models for other noninnovative members of the group

elaboration the development of a selected variety so that it represents all desired norms and fulfils the whole range of functions required (e.g. extension of the vocabulary, stylistic range, etc.)

emigrant letters letters written and sent home by migrants from overseas; these are most valuable as some writers had semiliterate status so features of spoken language may have surfaced in writing

empirical validity historical data have to be available in sufficient amounts to represent a baseline for comparison, particularly when studying variation (writers of the same age, region, and social status)

English-knowing bilingualism children in Singapore learning and speaking both English and their mother tongue

English Only Movement a movement in the US that promotes English as the language of national unity and of integration

enregisterment a sociolinguistic process by which speakers come to associate strictly linguistic forms with social meaning about speech communities or dialect regions (e.g. Pittsburghese)

envelope of variation a set of contexts and conditions in which sociolinguistic variation is possible, for instance rhoticity or was/were alternation

face developed by the US sociologist Erving Goffman, this concept refers to the representation of a speaker's own and others' personality through language resources

face-threatening acts utterances that directly or indirectly attack the self-perception of participants in a given conversation (threats, insults, etc.)

face-work the strategies that individual participants employ to save or threaten the perception of face (of themselves or others)

feature pool the total of all features (phonetic/phonological, morphosyntactic, lexical) found in all the cooccurring dialects from which a new dialect selects its features

floor a person who speaks at a given moment in a conversation and who actively is entitled to (and at times defends the right to) speak; important in the analysis of turn-taking, politeness, and power in conversation

forensic linguistics the study of language for legal purposes, for example the identification of speaker voice in threat calls

frames the means and ways in which linguistic resources are used to shape and create meaning in discourse

genres the type and mode of discourse written or spoken, with a basic distinction of content, language, form, and function

Global Englishes varieties of English around the world that have formed via language contact and multilingualism, typically in ESL contexts

Gumperz, John One of the founders of interactional sociolinguistics, Gumperz worked on code-switching, multilingualism, and the ethnography of speaking and argued that language is essential to create social norms and conventions

historical validity historical data need to provide the context of when they were produced: social setting, networks, patterns of contact, and so on

hypercorrection when speakers misinterpret and incorrectly generalize rules by applying them to inappropriate contexts

indexical signs a term coined by John J. Gumperz to refer to contextualization cues that signal meaning by direct association between sign and social context of an utterance

indexicality conventional/stereotypical relationships between linguistic forms and social meanings in a community that emerge in a range of communicative practices, styles, and registers

inferencing the meaning we create indirectly, by using implicit knowledge to understand indirect speech acts or humor (irony)

innovators speakers who are central in creating and bringing in linguistic innovations

interaction order speech situations, verbal and nonverbal communication (moves), that form the basis of conversation

interactional sociolinguistics a field of sociolinguistics, intersecting with discourse analysis, the ethnography of speaking, anthropology, and the sociology of language, that studies how speakers interpret language and create meaning by choosing words or making sense of them

International Phonetic Alphabet A special alphabet set up by the International Phonetic Association to provide accurate and detailed symbols for all the speech sounds in the world's languages

internationalization a nonindigenous language (such as English) is given official status and used in public domains

jargons interim makeshift, simplified varieties, created ad hoc by adults, largely improvised and not learnt, with specialized vocabularies and little grammatical complexity

Labov, William the American founder of variationist sociolinguistics (born 1927–2024), who set up both its methodological and theoretical foundations

language analysis for the determination of origin (LADO) a program put in place to identify national, social and/or ethnic identities, and language profiles of asylum seekers

language brokering strategies used to facilitate communication between linguistically and/or culturally different parties. Language brokers mediate in diverse sociolinguistic environments

language contact the (occasionally unprecedented) interaction between speakers of different languages, that may lead to simplification and the emergence of new varieties

language histories from below documentation and analysis of nonstandard (i.e. not socially prestigious) varieties of a language, typically neglected in textbooks and language histories

language hybridization languages that merge into a new linguistic system in a given contact scenario

language planning efforts by governments, political groups, or nongovernmental organizations to influence the function, structure, or acquisition of language in speech communities or societies, very often via language politics

language proscription when varieties are discouraged by official sanction or restriction, often with the aim of threatening the vitality of minority languages

language reclamation when de facto or nearly extinct languages are reconstructed, codified, and learnt by individuals (e.g. Hebrew or Cornish)

language survival efforts to foster vitality of a threatened language so that it is spoken as much as possible, for instance via acquisition planning in education

language vitality a range of political, sociological, or psychological factors that determine how widely used and positively perceived a language is

lexifier the language that contributes most of the lexicon in conditions of language contact and creolization

lingua franca a language that serves as a means of communication for speakers who have no language in common

linguistic assimilation strong belief that every citizen, irrespective of their native language, should learn and use the dominant language of society at large

Linguistic Atlas of New England the first larger project to study regional dialect variation in North America (conducted by Hans Kurath)

linguistic discrimination/linguicism bias toward individual speakers based on the way they speak, including all kinds of stigmatization

linguistic imperialism the dominance of a language (e.g. English) that is asserted and maintained by the establishment of social and cultural inequalities between languages

linguistic norm any linguistic feature that is found regularly in the speech of more than one speaker in a community (i.e. any feature that is not idiosyncratic)

linguistic prejudice bias toward individual speakers based on the way they speak

linguistic profiling identifying social characteristics of speakers (ethnicity, social class, etc.) based on their accent or dialect

linguistic variable any linguistic feature that is realized by more than one form and that takes several variants (e.g. lexical forms, pronunciation of vowels, etc.)

Māori Language Act passed in 1987, this law gave the indigenous language official status in New Zealand and ensured its use in legal and formal settings, court, and parliament

marché linguistique **(linguistic marketplace)** developed by Paul Bourdieu, (1930–2002), a French sociologist, languages carry "symbolic capital" by having different functions and usages in society at large

Martha's Vineyard an island off the coast of Massachusetts, where William Labov conducted his first sociolinguistic study on the social meaning of language variation

matched/verbal guise techniques methods used in perceptual dialectology, in which the same speaker is included in an experiment, speaking different dialects (elimination of voice effects)

mobility an increase of individual and group movement in time and space, central to contact linguistics

Multicultural London English   a mixed dialect that has multiple origins and developed via social contact among multiethnic and multilingual children and adolescents in London, UK

multiethnolectalization   the language that emerged in the speech of adolescents with migrant backgrounds in multicultural and multilingual cities in Africa and Europe

multilingualism   using several languages on a regular basis, either on individual or societal levels

nativization   when a new dialect, pidgin, or creole is spoken by younger members of the community and thus acquires native speakers

negative face   speakers have a desire that they can make their own actions and decisions, and that others do not interfere

new-dialect formation   the emergence of a new dialect via processes of contact between several social or regional dialects

NORMs   local participants in villages (Nonmobile, Older, Rural Males). Fieldworkers in the Survey of English Dialects project were instructed to record and collect data from NORMs

observer's paradox   a conundrum social scientists face when they want to observe the social behavior of speakers and by their very presence influence the behavior they study

off-the-shelf features   features that diffuse quickly through the English-speaking world; they typically are cognitively and linguistically simple, frequent, and regular

Old Bailey Corpus (OBC)   a corpus of verbatim transcripts of court cases from 1720 to 1913 by London's central criminal court, containing almost 14 million words

orderly heterogeneity   language usage is not random, but patterned and constrained, reflecting order and structure

overt prestige   when speakers of nonstandardized dialects openly endorse and adopt standard forms, (often with a social motivation) that may later become accepted by the community as a whole

perceptual dialectology   the study of "folk" views about language, general attitudes toward social attributes of language

pidgins   varieties that emerge when a multilingual community has a continuing demand for a non-native language; they typically have small lexicons and restructured grammars

positive face   speakers have a desire that they are desirable in a group or community and popular with other speakers

Post-Colonial Englishes   varieties of English spoken in former colonial possessions of the British Empire that became politically independent in the twentieth century

prescriptivism vs. descriptivism   the distinction between studying a language via description (for research) and proscriptive views and rules about varieties (typically favoring the standard)

presuppositions   propositions which speakers must assume as given in order to know that what they say is appropriate in a certain context of use (e.g. formality)

quotative "like"   a grammatical item used to introduce a direct quote in speech ("she was like 'this is so cool'"); subject to internal constraints and diffusing rapidly in the English-speaking world

real vs. apparent time principle two constructs in language change research: Apparent time studies language at a particular point in time, with two or several population samples; real-time data from two points in time are used to observe change directly in a community

reanalysis the adaptation of a grammatical structure for a different purpose in a contact variety, such as future tense or habituality

Received Pronunciation (RP) the high-prestige accent that emerged as a late consequence of standardization, adopted from the social elite in Great Britain: court, government, etc.

relexification when the grammatical system of a contact language increasingly adopts words from the high-status lexifier variety

repair-work when something goes wrong in communication (e.g. a misunderstanding), then speakers may engage in culturally and socially set strategies to establish clear meaning

S-curve linguistic change does not operate in a linear and equal speed over time, regional and social space(s); it is characterized by several stages: initiation, expansion, and termination

selection a socially motivated process by which one of the competing dialects or sociolects is adopted and elevated to the status of standard, typically the one spoken by the powerful social elite

settlement colonies a type of colonization that involves human traffic and the settlement of overseas territories for agricultural or industrial purposes

Singlish a local variety of Singapore English that developed out of contact between English and Asian languages such as Malay, Hokkien, and Tamil

situational and metaphorical switching situational code-switching is a consequence of changes in a social setting; metaphorical switching is triggered by the content and topic of a conversation

Social Connotation Hypothesis opinions about languages (and dialects) that are basically a function of positive or negative associations with extra-linguistic factors

social networks the social relationships formed by individual speakers, characterized by density (how often there is interaction) and multiplexity (in how many levels interaction occurs)

social stratification the differentiation of society into different social layers, defined by sociological, economic, and linguistic criteria

social validity historical data need to be as socially balanced and representative as possible to allow for studying historical variation and change

sociolect the variety spoken by a particular social class (e.g. the Lower Working Class in Singapore)

sociolinguistic repertoire the entire range of varieties and styles individual speakers have at their disposal

sociolinguistic variable any linguistic feature that covaries not only with linguistic factors but also with independent nonlinguistic ones, such as social class, ethnicity, gender, age, or contextual style

Speak Good English Movement originally a year-long campaign, the Singapore government aimed to educate the population about good language usage and to fight the (in politicians' views) social and educational dangers of speaking Singlish

SPEAKING model an influential model developed by Dell Hymes, a US linguist and anthropologist, to model the parameters that influence language variation in individual speakers

Standard English the socially prestigious variety of English that emerged over centuries, involving processes of selection, codification, elaboration, and acceptance

Standard Language ideology the pervasive and historically grown belief in the superiority of a high-prestige language variety, backed up by linguistic justification

status planning the allocation or reallocation of a language or variety to certain functional domains within a society (e.g. as a standard variety)

stereotypes generalizing truths about language variation, selecting individual features, and overestimating its frequency and use in communities

style alternative definitions: Traditionally, style was seen as controlled by extralinguistic factors such as attention to speech, later as an active resource to shape, and create a speaker's persona and/or identity

stylistic continuum a range from formal to informal speech in speakers using several varieties of a language or two or more dialects

substrate the language in a contact scenario, often the local one, that is not socially dominant yet is essential in shaping the emerging grammar of a contact-derived variety

superdiversity the theory that our world today is more mobile than ever as a recent societal phenomenon, particularly in high-contact urban settings via migration

superstrate the language in a contact scenario, often the colonizing one, that is socially dominant, contributing most of the lexicon and serving as a lexifier

Survey of English Dialects a large project to study regional variation in England and Wales that was carried out in the 1950s and 1960s and involved fieldwork in more than 300 towns and villages

trade colonies a type of colonization that involves industrial production and export, so that communication is mostly professional, with comparatively little human traffic from Europe

translanguaging strategies of bilingual or multilingual speakers to shift resources of different languages, merging through diverse varieties via creatively and flexibly making use of sociolinguistic repertoires

turn/turn-taking when the floor changes and another participant takes over as active speaker in a conversation

under-the-counter features features that are local and restricted to individual speech communities; they are linguistically constrained and structurally complex, typically found in close-knit communities

uniformitarian principle assumption that effects of social interaction on variation and change are constant and stable, so that they continue to operate the same way today as they did in the past

variationist pragmatics studies how social factors interact and influence each other via language usage during an interaction (e.g. greetings)

vernacular in traditional Labovian sociolinguistics, this refers to the speech context in which speakers are least aware that they are being observed and studied

vernacularization the selection and restoration (or elaboration) of an indigenous language that is adopted as an official language

Wenker, Georg A German pioneer in the questionnaire-based study of regional dialect variation

World Language System the model of a global hierarchy of languages with four different categories: hypercentral, supercentral, central, and peripheral

References

Adams, K. L. & Winter, A. (1997). Gang graffiti as a discourse genre. *Journal of Sociolinguistics*, 1, 337– 360.
Alford, H. (1864). *The Queen's English*. London: Strahan & Co.
Alleyne M. C. (1985). *A Linguistic Perspective on the Caribbean*, Washington D.C: Latin American Program Woodrow Wilson International Center for Scholars.
Amery, R. (2017). Recognising the communication gap in Indigenous health care. *Medical Journal of Australia*, 207(1), 13–15.
Auer, A., Schreier, D. & Watts, R. J., eds. (2015). *Letter Writing and Language Change*. Cambridge: Cambridge University Press.
Auer, P. (2021). Reflections on linguistic pluricentricity. *Sociolinguistica*, 35(1), 29–47.
Bailey, C. J. N. (1973). *Variation and Linguistic Theory*, Arlington, VA: Center for Applied Linguistics.
Baker, C. (2003). Education as a site of language contact. *Annual Review of Applied Linguistics*, 23, 95–112.
Banda, R. (2018). Translanguaging and English-African language mother tongues as linguistic dispensation in teaching and learning in a Black township school in Cape Town. *Current Issues in Language Planning*, 19(2), 198-217.
Bao, Z. (2001). The origins of empty categories in Singapore English. *Journal of Pidgin and Creole Languages*, 16(2), 275–319.
Baugh, A. C. & Cable, T. (2002). *A History of the English Language*. London: Routledge.
Baugh, J. (1996). Perceptions within a Variable Paradigm: Black and White Detection and Identification Based on Speech. In: E. Schneider, ed., *Varieties of English Around the World: Focus on the USA*. Philadelphia, PA: John Benjamins, 169–182.
Baugh, J. (2003). Linguistic Profiling. In: S. Makoni, G. Smitherman & A. K. Spears, eds., *Black Linguistics: Language, Society and Politics in Africa and the Americas*. New York: Routledge, 155–168.
Baugh, J. (2018). *Linguistics in Pursuit of Justice*. Cambridge: Cambridge University Press.
Bell, A. (1984). Language Style as Audience Design. In: N. Coupland & A. Jaworski, eds., *Sociolinguistics: A Reader and Coursebook*. New York: St Mattin's Press, 240–250.

Bell, A. (1999). Styling the other to define the self: A study in New Zealand identity making. *Journal of Sociolinguistics*, 3(4), 523–541.

Beltrama, A. (2020). Social meaning in semantics and pragmatics. *Language and Linguistics Compass*, 14(9), e12398.

Bergs, A. (2006). Language change and the role of the individual in historical social network analysis. *Logos and Language: Journal of General Linguistics and Language Theory*, 2, 30–54.

Bergs, A. (2015). The Linguistic Fingerprints of Authors and Scribes: A Medieval Whodunnit. In: R. Watts, D. Schreier & A. Auer, eds., *Letter Writing and Language Change*. Cambridge: Cambridge University Press, 156–181.

Bernstein, B. (1970). *Education cannot compensate for society*. London: New Society.

Bernstein, B. *(*1970*)*. Education cannot compensate for society. *London: New Society*, 38, 344–347.

Biber, D., Johansson, S., Leech, G., Conrad, S. & Finegan, E. (1999). *Longman Grammar of Spoken and Written English*. Harlow: Pearson Education Limited.

Bickerton, D. (1984). The language bioprogram hypothesis. *Behavioral and Brain Sciences*, 7(2), 173–188. doi:10.1017/S0140525X00044149.

Bishop, D.-L. (2022). Tha's a rummun ent it: Why does the East Anglian accent get overlooked? *Eastern Daily Press*, January 16. www.edp24.co.uk/news/20635145.thas-rummun-ent-east-anglian-accent-get-overlooked/.

Blackledge, A., & Creese A. (2013). Heteroglossia in English Complementary Schools. In: J. Duarte & I. Gogolin, eds., *Linguistic Superdiversity in Urban Areas*. Amsterdam/Philadelphia, PA: John Benjamins, 123–142.

Blommaert, J. (2010). *The Sociolinguistics of Globalization*, Cambridge: Cambridge University Press.

Bloomfield, L. (1933). *Language*. New York: Holt, Rinehart & Winston.

Boberg, C. (2004). Real and apparent time in language change: Late adoption of changes in Montreal English. *American Speech*, 79, 250–269.

Bock, A. (2005). History of Cornwall – Timeline. In: H. Birkhan, ed., *Bausteine zum Studium der Keltologie*. Vienna: Edition Praesens.

Bolton, K. (2013) World Englishes, Globalisation and Language Worlds. In: N.-L. Johannesson, G. Melchers & B. Björkman, eds., *Of Butterflies and Birds, of Dialects and Genres: Essays in Honour of Philip Shaw*. Stockholm: Acta Universitatis Stockholmiensis, 227–251.

Bouanani, S. & Kassou, I. (2014). Authorship analysis studies: A survey. *International Journal of Computer Applications*, 86(12), 22–29.

Bourdieu, P. (1982). Les rites d'institution. *Actes de la Recherche en Sciences Sociales*, 43, 58–63.

Bourdieu, P. (1989). Social space and symbolic power. *Sociological Theory*, 7(1), 14–25.

Bourdieu, P. (1991). *Language and Symbolic Power*. Harvard University Press.

Britain, D. (2010). Conceptualisations of Geographic Space in Linguistics. In: A. Lameli, R. Kehrein & S. Rabanus, eds., *Language and Space: An International Handbook of Linguistic Variation. Volume 2: Language Mapping*. Berlin: De Gruyter Mouton, 69–97.

References

Britain, D. & Sudbury, A. (2010). South Atlantic Ocean: Falkland Island English. In: Daniel Schreier, Peter Trudgill, Edgar Schneider and Jeffrey Williams, eds., *Lesser Known Englishes*. Cambridge: Cambridge University Press, 209–223.

Britain, D. (2020). A Sociolinguistic Ecology of Colonial Britain. In: D. Schreier, M. Hundt & E. W. Schneider, eds., *The Cambridge Handbook of World Englishes* (Cambridge Handbooks in Language and Linguistics). Cambridge: Cambridge University Press, 145–159.

Britain, D. (2021). Grammatical Variation in the Contemporary Spoken English of England. In: Andy Kirkpatrick, ed., *The Handbook of World Englishes (Fully Revised Second Edition)*. London: Routledge, 32–58.

Britain D. & Sudbury, A. (2013). Falkland Islands English. In: D. Schreier, P. Trudgill, E. W. Schneider & J. P. Williams, eds., *The Lesser-Known Varieties of English: An Introduction*. Studies in English Language. Cambridge: Cambridge University Press, 209–223.

Brown, P. & Levinson, S. C. (1987). *Politeness: Some Universals in Language Usage*. Cambridge: Cambridge University Press.

Brown-Blake, C. & Chambers, P. (2007). The Jamaican Creole Speaker in the UK Criminal Justice System. *International Journal of Speech Language and the Law*, 14, 269–294.

Bucholtz, M. (2009). Captured on tape: Professional hearing and competing entextualizations in the criminal justice system. *Text & Talk*, 29(5), 503–523.

Burri, S. (2017). Power and Gender Relations in the 18th Century Courtroom: A Corpus and Discourse Study of Power Relations Across Gender and Speaker Roles in the Rape Trials of the Old Bailey Proceedings. Unpublished MA thesis, University of Zurich.

Butters, R. R. (2007). Sociolinguistic Variation and the Law. In: R. Bayley & C. Lucas, eds., *Sociolinguistic Variation: Theories, Methods, and Applications*. Cambridge: Cambridge University Press, 318–337.

Cable, T. & Baugh, A. C. (2002). *A History of the English Language* (5th ed.). London: Routledge.

Cameron, D. (1995). *Verbal Hygiene (The Politics of Language)*. London & New York: Routledge.

Canagarajah, S. (2011). Translanguaging in the classroom: Emerging issues for research and pedagogy. *Applied Linguistics Review*, 2, 1–28.

Cass, A., Lowell, A., Christie, M., Snelling, P. L. et al. (2002). Sharing the true stories: Improving communication between Aboriginal patients and healthcare workers. *The Medical Journal of Australia*, 176(10), 466–470.

Cassidy, F. G. (1993). On Creole orthography. *Journal of Pidgin and Creole Languages*, 8(1), 135–137.

Cavallaro, F., and Chin, N. B. (2009). Between status and solidarity in Singapore. *World Englishes*, 28(2), 143–159.

Chambers, J. K. (2008). Sociolinguistic Theory (3rd ed.). Oxford: Wiley Blackwell.

Chambers, J. K. (1992). Dialect acquisition. *Language*, 68(4), 673–705.

Chambers, J. K. & Trudgill, P. (1998). *Dialectology* (2nd ed.). Cambridge: Cambridge University Press.

Cheshire, J., Kerswill, P., Fox, S. & Torgersen, E. (2011). Contact, the feature pool and the speech community: The Emergence of Multicultural London English. *Journal of Sociolinguistics*, 15(2), 151–196.

Coates, J. (2004). *Women, Men and Language: A Sociolinguistic Account of Gender Differences in Language* (3rd ed.). New York: Routledge.

Collins, P. & Blair, D., eds. (2001). *English in Australia*. Amsterdam and Philadelphia, PA: John Benjamins Publishing.

Coulthard, M. (2005). The linguist as expert witness. *Linguistics and the Human Sciences*, 1(1), 39.

Coulthard, M. (2010). Forensic linguistics: The application of language description in legal contexts. *Langage et Société*, 15–33.

Coulthard, M. & Johnson, A. (2007). *An Introduction to Forensic Linguistics: Language in Evidence*. London: Routledge.

Coulthard, M. & Johnson A. (2010). Concluding Remarks: Future Directions in Forensic Linguistics. In: M. Coulthard & A. Johnson, eds., *The Routledge Handbook of Forensic Linguistics*. New York: Routledge, 473–486.

Coulthard, M. & Johnson, A. (2012). *An Introduction to Forensic Linguistics: Language in Evidence*. London: Routledge.

Coulthard, M., Johnson, A. & Wright, D. (2017). *An Introduction to Forensic Linguistics: Language in Evidence* (2nd ed.). London: Routledge.

Coupland, N. (1980). Style-shifting in a Cardiff work-setting. *Language in Society*, 9(1), 1–12.

Crystal, D. (1981). English on the air – Has it degenerated? *The Listener* (July 9), 37–39.

Crystal, D. (2003). Final frontiers in applied linguistics? *British Studies in Applied Linguistics*, 18, 9–24.

Crystal, D. (2008). *A Dictionary of Linguistics and Phonetics*, New Jersey: John Wiley & Sons.

Crystal, D. (2009). *English as a Global Language* (2nd ed.). Cambridge: Cambridge University Press.

Cumming-Potvin, W. (2009). Social justice, pedagogy and multiliteracies: Developing communities of practice for teacher education. *Australian Journal of Teacher Education*, 34(3), 82–99.

de Swaan, A. (2001). *Words of the World: The Global Language System* Malden, MA: Polity Press.

de Swaan, A. (2010). Language Systems. In: N. Coupland, ed., *The Handbook of Language and Globalization*. New Jersey: John Wiley & Sons, 56–76.

Deterding, D. (2007). *Singapore English*, Edinburgh: Edinburgh University Press.

Drummond, R. (2018). *Researching Urban Youth Language and Identity*. London: Palgrave Macmillan.

Eades, D. (2000). I don't think it's an answer to the question: Silencing Aboriginal witnesses in court. *Language in Society*, 29(2), 161–195.

Eades, D. (2004). Understanding Aboriginal English in the legal system: A critical sociolinguistics approach. *Applied Linguistics*, 25(4), 491–512.

Eades, D. (2010). *Sociolinguistics and the Legal Process*. Bristol: Multilingual Matters.

Eades, D. (2011). Sociolinguistics and the Law. In: R. Mesthrie, ed., *The Cambridge Handbook of Sociolinguistics* (Cambridge Handbooks in Language and Linguistics). Cambridge: Cambridge University Press, 377–395. doi:10.1017/CBO9780511997068.028.

Eades, D. & Queensland Department of Justice and Attorney-General. Court Strategy and Research Branch. (2000). *Aboriginal English in the Courts: A Handbook*. Brisbane: Dept. of Justice and Attorney General.

Eckert, P. (2000). *Linguistic Variation as Social Practice*. Oxford: Blackwell.

Eckert, P. (2005). Variation, Convention, and Social Meaning. In: *Annual Meeting of the Linguistic Society of America. Oakland CA*, 7.

Eckert, P. (2012). Three waves of variation study: The emergence of meaning in the study of sociolinguistic variation. *Annual Review of Anthropology*, 41, 87–100.

Eckert, P. & McConnell-Ginet, S. (1992). Think practically and look locally: Language and gender as community-based practice. *Annual Review of Anthropology*, 21(1), 461–488.

Eckert, P, & McConnell-Ginet, S. (2003). *Language and Gender*. Cambridge: Cambridge University Press.

Edwards, V. & Newcombe, L. P. (2005). When school is not enough: New initiatives in intergenerational language transmission in Wales. *International Journal of Bilingual Education and Bilingualism*, 8(4), 298–312.

Ellis, A. J. (1889). *On Early English Pronunciation, with Especial Reference to Shakspeare and Chaucer: Existing Dialectical as Compared with West Saxon Pronounciation*, vol. 2. London: Philological Society.

Ellis, J. (1992). *The English Language in a Social Context*. Cambridge: Cambridge University Press.

Elspaß, S. (2007). 'Everyday language' in emigrant letters and its implications for language historiography – the German case. *Multilingua – Journal of Cross-Cultural and Interlanguage Communications*, 26(2–3), 151–165.

Erker, D. & Bruso, J. (2017). Uh, bueno, em …: Filled pauses as a site of contact-induced change in Boston Spanish. *Language Variation and Change*, 29(2), 205–244.

Evans, D. (1994). *Schooling in the South Atlantic Islands 1661–1992*. Oswestry: Anthony Nelson.

Fasold, R. (1984). *The Sociolinguistics of Society*. Oxford: Basil Blackwell.

Fasold, R. (1992). Linguistics and Grammatics. In: M. Pütz, ed., *Thirty Years of Linguistic Evolution*. Amsterdam: John Benjamins Publishing Company, 161–176.

Fasold, R. (2006). The Politics of Language. In: R. Fasold and J. Connor-Linton, eds., *An Introduction to Language and Linguistics*. Cambridge: Cambridge University Press, 371–400.

Ferguson, C. A. (1959). Diglossia. *WORD*, 15(2), 325–340.

Ferguson, G. (2006). *Language Planning and Education*, Edinburgh: Edinburgh University Press.

Fitzmaurice, S. M. (2004). The Meanings and Uses of the Progressive Construction in an Early Eighteenth-Century English Network. In: A. Curzan & K. Emmons, eds., *Studies in the History of the English Language II*. Berlin and New York: Mouton de Gruyter, 131–176.

Freeland, J., & Patrick, D. (2004). Language Rights and Language Survival. In: J. Freeland and D. Patrick, eds., *Language Rights and Language Survival*. Abingdon and New York: Routledge, 1–34.

Fridland, V. (June 16, 2020). The sound of racial profiling: When language leads to discrimination. *Nevada Today*. www.unr.edu/nevada-today/blogs/2020/the-sound-of-racial-profiling.

Frumkin, L. (2007). Influences of accent and ethnic background on perceptions of eyewitness testimony. *Psychology, Crime & Law*, 13(3), 317–331. https://doi.org/10.1080/10683160600822246.

García, O. (2009). *Bilingual Education in the 21st Century: A Global Perspective*. Malden, MA and Oxford: Wiley-Blackwell.

Garcia, M. (2016) Accent discrimination towards bilingual employees in the workplace. *University of San Francisco Law Review*, 51(2), 345–369.

Garrett, P. (2010). *Attitudes to Language*. Cambridge: Cambridge University Press.

Gauchat, L. (1902). L'unité phonétique dans le patois d'und commune. *Aus Romanischen Sprachen und Literaturen; Festschrift Heinrich Morf*. Halle: Max Niemeyer. 175-232.

Gibson, K. (2004). English only court cases involving the US workplace: The myths of language use and the homogenization of bilingual workers' identities. *Second Language Studies*, 22(2), 1–60.

Giles, H., Bourhis, R., Lewis, A. & Trudgill, P. (1974). The imposed norm hypothesis: A validation. *Quarterly Journal of Speech*, 60(4), 405–410.

Goffman, E. (1955). On face-work: An analysis of ritual elements in social interaction. *Psychiatry*, 18(3), 213–231.

Goffman, E. (1967). *Interaction Ritual: Essays on Face-to-Face Behavior*. New York: Pantheon Books.

Goffman, E. (1981). *Forms of Talk*. Philadelphia: University of Pennsylvania Press.

Goffman, E. (1983). The interaction order: American Sociological Association, 1982 Presidential Address. *American Sociological Review*, 48(1), 1–17.

Goffman, E. (2005). *Interaction Ritual: Essays in Face-to-Face Behaviour*. American Sociological Review, New Brunswick: Transaction Publishers.

Gonçalves, K. & Schluter, A. (2017). "Please do not leave any notes for the cleaning lady, as many do not speak English fluently": Policy, power, and language brokering in a multilingual workplace. *Language Policy*, 16(3), 241–265.

Gonzalez Van Cleve, N. (2016). *Crook County: Racism and Injustice in America's Largest Criminal Court*. Stanford, CA: Stanford Law Books.

Gordon, E. & Deverson, T. (1998). *New Zealand English and English in New Zealand*. Auckland: New House.

Gordon, E., Campbell, L., Hay, J., Maclagan, M., Sudbury, A. & Trudgill, P. (2004). *New Zealand English: Its Origins and Evolution*. New York: Cambridge University Press.

Great Britain: Foreign and Commonwealth Office (1985). *Year Book of the Commonwealth 1985*. London: HMSO.

Green, L. (2002). *African American English: A Linguistic Introduction*. Cambridge: Cambridge University Press. doi:10.1017/CBO9780511800306.

Green, L. (2004). Research on African American English since 1998: Origins, description, theory, and practice. *Journal of English Linguistics*, 32(3), 210–229.

Grenoble, L., & Whaley, L. (2006). *Saving Languages: An Introduction to Language Revitalization*. New York: Cambridge University Press.

Grieve, J. (2014). A Comparison of Statistical Methods for the Aggregation of Regional Linguistic Variation. In: B. Szmrecsanyi and B. Wälchli, eds., *Aggregating Dialectology, Typology, and Register Analysis: Linguistic Variation in Text and Speech*. Berlin/New York: Walter de Gruyter, 53–88.

Gumperz, J. J. (1982). *Discourse Strategies* (Studies in Interactional Sociolinguistics 1). Cambridge: Cambridge University Press.

Gumperz, J. J. (1999). On Interactional Sociolinguistic Method. In: S. Sarangi & C. Roberts, eds., *Talk, Work and Institutional Order: Discourse in Medical, Mediation and Management Settings*. Berlin: Mouton de Gruyter, 453–472.

Gumperz J. J. & Cook-Gumperz, J. (2007). A Postscript: Style and Identity in Interactional Sociolinguistics. In: P. Auer, ed., *Style and Social Identities: Alternative Approaches to Linguistic Heterogeneity*. Berlin: Mouton de Gruyter, 477–502.

Haddican, W. (2005). Standardization and Language Change in Basque. *University of Pennsylvania Working Papers in Linguistics*, 11(2), 105–118.

Haugen, E. (2003). Dialect, Language, Nation. In: C. B. Paulston & G. R. Tucker, eds., *Sociolinguistics: The Essential Readings*. Oxford: Wiley-Blackwell, 410–422.

Henderson, A. (2001). Is Your Money Where Your Mouth Is? Hiring Managers' Attitudes toward African-American Vernacular English. PhD Dissertation, University of Pennsylvania.

Hernández-Chávez, E. (1995). Language Policy in the United States. A History of Cultural Genocide. In: T. Skutnabb-Kangas & R. Phillipson, eds., *Linguistic Human Rights. Overcoming Linguistic Discrimination*. New York, NY: Mouton de Gruyter, 141–158.

Hewitt, R. (1986). *White Talk, Black Talk: Inter-Racial Friendship and Communication amongst Adolescents*. Cambridge, New York, Melbourne: Cambridge University Press.

Hickey, R. (2019). Mining Emigrant Correspondence for Linguistic Insights. In: R. Hickey, ed., *Keeping in Touch: Emigrant Letters across the English-Speaking World*. Amsterdam and Philadelphia, PA: John Benjamins Publishing Company, 1–24.

Hodges, A. (2015). Ideologies of Language and Race in US Media Discourse about the Trayvon Martin Shooting. *Language in Society*, 44(3), 401–423.

Holmes, J. (2006). *Gendered Talk at Work: Constructing Social Identity through Workplace Interaction*. Oxford: Wiley-Blackwell.

Holmes, J. & Stubbe, M. (2003). *Power and Politeness in the Workplace*. London: Longman.

Hornberger, N. H. (2006). Frameworks and Models in Language Policy and Planning. In: T. Ricento, ed., *An Introduction to Language Policy*. Malden, Oxford, Carlton: Blackwell Publising, 24–41.

Horobin, S. (2015). *How English Became English*. Oxford: Oxford University Press.

Hurst, E. & Mona, M. (2017). "Translanguaging" as a socially just pedagogy. *Education as Change*, 21(2), 126–148.

Hymes, D. (1974). *Foundations of Sociolinguistics: An Ethnographic Approach*. Philadelphia: University of Pennsylvania Press.

Ilbury, C. and Kerswill, P. (2023). How Multiethnic is a Multiethnolect? The Recontextualisation of Multicultural London English. In: B. A. Svendsen & R. Jonsson, eds., *Routledge Handbook of Language and Youth Culture*. London: Routledge, 362–376.

Jaspers, J. (2011). Interactional Sociolinguistics and Discourse Analysis. In: J. P. Gee & M. Handford, eds., *The Routledge Handbook of Discourse Analysis*. Abingdon: Routledge, 135–146.

Jaworski, A. & Thurlow, C., eds. (2010). *Semiotic Landscapes: Language, Image, Space*. London & New York: Continuum.

Johnstone, B. (2009). Stance, Style, and the Linguistic Individual. In: A. Jaffe, ed., *Stance: Sociolinguistic Perspectives*. New York: Oxford University Press, 29–52.

Johnstone, B. (2016). Enregisterment: How linguistic items become linked with ways of speaking. *Language and Linguistics Compass*, 10, 632–643.

Johnstone, B., Andrus, J. & Danielson, A. E. (2006). Mobility, Indexicality, and the Enregisterment of 'Pittsburghese'. *Journal of English Linguistics*, 34(2), 77–104.

Jones, T., Kalbfeld, J., Hancock, R. & Clark, R. (2019). Testifying while Black: An experimental study of court reporter accuracy in transcription of African American English. *Language*, online edition for Public Policy.

Jones, W. (1807). The Third Anniversary Discourse, Delivered February 2, 1786. In: *The Works of Sir William Jones*, vol. 3. London: Printed for John Stockdale & John Walker, 34–37.

Joseph, J. (2004). *Language and Identity: National, Ethnic, Religious*. New York: Palgrave Macmillan.

Jucker, A. H. (2015). Pragmatics of fiction: Literary uses of uh and um. *Journal of Pragmatics*, 86, 63–67.

Jupp, J., ed., (2001). *The Australian People*. Cambridge: Cambridge University Press.

Kachru, B. B. (1985). Standards, Codification and Sociolinguistic Realism: English Language in the Outer Circle. In: R. Quirk & H. Widdowson, eds., *English in the World: Teaching and Learning the Language and Literatures*. Cambridge: Cambridge University Press, 11–36.

Kachru, B. B. (1988). The Spread of English and Sacred Linguistic Cows. In: P. H. Lowenberg, ed., *Language Spread and Language Policy: Issues, Implications, and Case Studies*. Washington D.C.: Georgetown Press, 207–228.

Kachru, B. B. (1996). World Englishes: Agony and ecstasy. *Journal of Aesthetic Education*, 30, 135–155, https://doi.org/10.2307/3333196.

Kachru, Y. (2008). Language variation and corpus linguistics. *World Englishes*, 27(1), 1–8.

Kaislaniemi, S. (2018). The Corpus of Early English Correspondence Extension (CEECE). In: T. Nevalainen, M. Palander-Collin & T. Säily, eds., *Patterns of Change in Eighteenth-Century English: A Sociolinguistic Approach*. Amsterdam, Philadelphia, PA: John Benjamins Publishing Company, 45–59.

Kerswill, P. (2003). Dialect Levelling and Geographical Diffusion in British English. In: D. Britain & J. Cheshire, eds., *Social Dialectology: In Honour of Peter Trudgill*. Amsterdam: John Benjamins Publishing Company, 223–243.

Kerswill, P., Cheshire, J., Fox, S. & Torgersen, E. (2013). English as a Contact Language: The Role of Children and Adolescents. In: D. Schreier & M. Hundt, eds., *English as a Contact Language* (Studies in English Language). Cambridge: Cambridge University Press, 258–282.

Kiesling, S. F. (2019). *Language, Gender, and Sexuality: An Introduction*. Abington, New York: Routledge.

King, S. & Rickford, J. R. (2023). Language on trial. *Daedalus*, 152(3), Summer, 178–193.

King's English Society (2022). Welcome to the King's English Society, founded in 1972 as the Queen's English Society. https://kingsenglishsociety.org.

Kircher, R. & Fox, S. (2019). Attitudes towards Multicultural London English: Implications for attitude theory and language planning. *Journal of Multilingual and Multicultural Development*, 40(10), 847–864.

Labov, W. (1963). The social motivation of a sound change. *Word*, 19(3), 273–309.

Labov, W. (1966). *The Social Stratification of English in New York City*. Washington DC: Center for Applied Linguistics.

Labov, W. (1970). The Logic of Non-Standard English. In: F. Williams, ed., *Language and Poverty*. New York: Academic Press, 153–189.

Labov, W. (1972a) *Sociolinguistic Patterns*. Philadelphia: University of Pennsylvania Press.

Labov, W. (1972b). Some principles of linguistic methodology. *Language in Society*, 1(1), 97–120.

Labov, W. (1982). Objectivity and commitment in linguistic science. *Language in Society*, 11, 165–201.

Labov, W. (1988). The Judicial Testing of Linguistic Theory. In: D. Tannen, ed., *Linguistics in Context: Connecting Observation and Understanding*. Norwood, NJ: Ablex.

Labov, W. (1994). *Principles of Linguistic Change. Vol. 1: Internal Factors*. Oxford: Blackwell Publishing.

Labov, W. (1995). Can Reading Failure Be Reversed? A Linguistic Approach to the Question. In: V. Gadsden & D. Wagner, eds., *Literacy among African American Youth: Issues in Learning, Teaching and Schooling*. Cresskill, NJ: Hampton. 39–68.

Labov, W. (1997). "How I got into linguistics, and what I got out of it". http://www.ling.upenn.edu/~wlabov/HowIgot.html

Labov, W. (2001). *Principles of Linguistic Change 2: Social Factors*. Oxford: Blackwell Publishing.

Labov, W. (2003). Uncovering the Event Structure of Narrative. In: D. Tannen & J. E. Alatis, eds., *Round Table on Language and Linguistics*. Washington: Georgetown University Press, 63–83.

Labov, W. (exact date unknown). How I got into linguistics, and what I got out of it. *University of Pennsylvania.* www.ling.upenn.edu/~wlabov/HowIgot.html.

Ladegaard, H. J. & Jenks, C. J. (2015). Language and Intercultural Communication in the Workplace: Critical Approaches to Theory and Practice. *Language and Intercultural Communication,* 15, 1–12. https://doi.org/10.1080/14708477.2014.985302.

Laitinen, M. & Auer, A. (2014). Letters of Artisans and the Labouring Poor (England, c. 1750–1835): Approaching Linguistic Diversity in Late Modern English. In: S. E. Pfenninger, O. Timofeeva, A. Gardner, A. Honkapohja, M. Hundt & D. Schreier, eds., *Contact, Variation, and Change in the History of English.* Amsterdam: John Benjamins Publishing Company, 187–212.

Lanehart, S. (2015). African American Language and Identity: Contradictions and Conundrums. In: S. Lanehard, ed., *The Oxford Handbook of African American Language.* New York: Oxford University Press, 863–880.

Lawson, R. & Sayers, D. (2016). *Sociolinguistic Research: Application and Impact.* London: Routledge.

Leemann, A., Kolly, M.-J. & Britain, D. (2018). The English Dialects App: The creation of a crowdsourced dialect corpus. *Ampersand,* 5, 1–17.

Leith, D. (1997). *A Social History of English* (2nd ed.). London: Routledge.

Le Page, R. B. (1968). Problems to Be Faced in the Use of English as the Medium of Education in Four West Indian Territories. In: C. A. Ferguson, J.A. Fishman & J. Das Gupta, eds., *Language Problems of Developing Nations.* New York: Wiley & Sons, 431–442.

Lim, L. & Foley, J. A. (2004). English in Singapore and Singapore English. In: L. Lim, ed., *Singapore English: A Grammatical Description.* Amsterdam and Philadelphia, PA: John Benjamins Publishing Company, 1–18.

Lippi-Green, R. (1997). *English with an Accent: Language, Ideology and Discrimination in the United States.* London and New York: Routledge.

Lowth, R. (1762). *A Short Introduction to English Grammar: With Critical Notes.* London: J. Hughs.

McArthur, T. (2005). *Concise Oxford Companion to the English Language.* Oxford: Oxford University Press.

McColl Millar, R. (2005). *Language, Nation and Power.* New York: Palgrave Macmillan.

McColl Millar, R. (2012). *English Historical Sociolinguistics.* Edinburgh: Edinburgh University Press.

MacGregor-Mendoza, P. (1998). The Criminalization of Spanish in the United States. In: D. A. Kibbee, ed., *Language Legislation and Linguistic Rights.* Amsterdam and Philadelphia, PA: John Benjamins Publishing Company, 55–67.

McKenzie, R. (2010). *The Social Psychology of English as a Global Language. Attitudes, Awareness and Identity in the Japanese Context.* Dordrecht, Heidelberg, London and New York: Springer.

McWhorter, J. (1998). *The Word on the Street: Debunking the Myth of a "Pure" Standard English.* New York: Plenum Trade.

McWhorter, J. H. (2000). *Spreading the Word: Language and Dialect in America.* Portsmouth, NH: Heinemann.

Madsen, L. M. (2013). "High" and "low" in urban Danish speech styles. *Language in Society*, 42, 115–138.

Mair, C. (2013). The world system of Englishes: accounting for the transnational importance of mobile and mediated vernaculars. *English World-Wide*, 34(3), 253–278.

Makalela, L. (2015). Translanguaging as a vehicle for epistemic access: Cases for reading comprehension and multilingual interactions. *Per Linguam: A Journal of Language Learning = Per Linguam: Tydskrif vir Taalaanleer*, 31(1), 15–29.

Malcolm, I. G. (2018). *Australian Aboriginal English*. Boston and Berlin: Mouton De Gruyter.

Mattheier, K. J. (2010). Is there a Europa language history? *Multilingua*, 29(3/4), 353–360.

Matras, Y. (2020). *Language Contact* (2nd ed.). Cambridge: Cambridge University Press.

Merrison, A. J., Bloomer, A., Griffiths, P. & Hall, C. J. (2014). *Introducing Language in Use*. Abingdon and New York: Routledge.

Mesthrie, R. (2002). South Africa: A Sociolinguistic Overview. In: R. Mesthrie, ed., *Language in South Africa*. Cambridge: Cambridge University Press, 11–26.

Mesthrie, R. & Bhatt, R. M. (2008). *World Englishes: The Study of New Linguistic Varieties*. Cambridge: Cambridge University Press.

Milroy, J. (1992). *Linguistic Variation and Change: On the Historical Sociolinguistics of English*. Oxford: Blackwell.

Milroy, L. (2002). Introduction: Mobility, contact and language change – working with contemporary speech communities. *Journal of Sociolinguistics*, 6, 3–15.

Milroy, Lesley 2002. Social networks. In Chambers, Jack, Trudgill, Peter and Schilling-Estes, Natalie eds., Handbook of Language Variation and Change. Oxford: Blackwell, 549–572.

Milroy, J. & Milroy, L. (1985). Linguistic change, social network and speaker innovation. *Journal of Linguistics*, 21, 339–384.

Milroy, L. (1980). *Language and Social Networks* (1st ed.). Oxford: Blackwell.

Milroy, L. (1987). *Language and Social Networks* (2nd ed.). Oxford: Blackwell.

Milroy, L. & Gordon, M. (2003). *Sociolinguistics: Method and Interpretation* (2nd ed.). Oxford: Blackwell Publishing. doi:10.1002/9780470758359.

Montgomery, C. (2017). Maps and Mapping in (Perceptual) Dialect Geography. In: C. Montgomery & E. Moore, eds., *A Sense of Place: Studies in Language & Region*. Cambridge: Cambridge University Press.

Montgomery, C., & Beal, J. (2011). Perceptual Dialectology. In: W. Maguire & A. McMahon, eds., *Analysing Variation in English*. Cambridge: Cambridge University Press, 121–150.

Montgomery, M. (1989). Exploring the roots of Appalachian English. *English World-Wide*, 10(2), 227–278.

Montgomery, M. (1989). Exploring the roots of Appalachian English. *English World-Wide*, 10, 2, 227–278.

Mufwene, S. S. (2001). What is African American English? In: S. Lanehart, ed., *Sociocultural and Historical Contexts of African American English*. Amsterdam and Philadelphia, PA: John Benjamins Publishing, 21–52.

Mühlenbernd, R. & Quinley, J. (2017). Language change and network games. *Language and Linguistics Compass*, 11(2), e12235.

Mühlhäusler, P. (1986). Bonnet Blanc and Blanc Bonnet: Adjective-Noun Order, Substratum and Language Universals. In: P. Muysken & N. Smith, eds., *Substrata Versus Universals in Creole Genesis*. Amsterdam and Philadelphia: John Benjamins Publishing, 41–56.

Munro, M. J. (2003). A primer on accent discrimination in the Canadian context. *TESL Canada Journal*, 20(2), 38–51.

The Nation's Report Card (2022). NAEP Report Card: 2022 NAEP Reading Assessment. www.nationsreportcard.gov/highlights/reading/2022/.

Nevalainen, T. (2006). Historical Sociolinguistics and Language Change. In: A. Kemenade & B. Los, eds., *The Handbook of the History of English*. Malden, MA and Oxford: Blackwell, 558–588.

Nevalainen, T. (2010). Theory and practice in English historical sociolinguistics. *Kindai Eigo Kenkyuu*, 26, 1–24.

Nevalainen, T. (2015). What are historical sociolinguistics? *Journal of Historical Sociolinguistics*, 1(2), 243–269.

Nevalainen, T. & Raumolin-Brunberg, H. (2003). *Historical Sociolinguistics: Language Change in Tudor and Stuart England* (1st ed.). Harlow: Longman.

Niedzielski, N. A. & Preston, D. R. (2000). *Folk Linguistics*. Berlin/New York: Mouton de Gruyter.

Olsson, J. (2009). *Wordcrime: Solving Crime through Forensic Linguistics*. London: Bloomsbury Publishing.

Orton, H. & Dieth, E. (1962) *Survey of English Dialects (SED), Part I: Introduction*. Leeds: E. J. Arnold & Son.

Pedulla, D. S. & Pager, D. (2019). Race and networks in the job search process. *American Sociological Review*, 84(6), 983–1012. https://doi.org/10.1177/0003122419883255.

Philipson, R. (1992). *Linguistic Imperialism*. Oxford: Oxford University Press.

Piller, I. (2020). Language and Social Justice. In: J. Stanlaw, ed., *The International Encyclopedia of Linguistic Anthropology*. Oxford: John Wiley & Sons, 1–7.

Preston, D. R. (1993). Folk Dialectology. In: D. R. Preston, ed., *American Dialect Research*. Amsterdam and Philadelphia, PA: John Benjamins Publishing, 333–378.

Preston, D. R. (1999). *Handbook of Perceptual Dialectology*. Amsterdam and Philadelphia, PA: John Benjamins Publishing.

Purnell, T., Idsardi, W. & Baugh, J. (1999). Perceptual and phonetic experiments on American English dialect identification. *Journal of Language and Social Psychology*, 18(1), 10–30. https://doi.org/10.1177/0261927X99018001002.

Puttenham, G. (1598). *The Arte of English Poesie*. London: Richard Field.

Queensland (Dept. of Justice and Attorney General). (2001). Aboriginal English in the courts: a handbook.

Quirk, R. (1990). Language Varieties and Standard Language. *English Today*, 6(1), 3–10.

Rampton, B. (1995). Language crossing and the problematisation of ethnicity and socialisation. *Pragmatics. Quarterly Publication of the International Pragmatics Association (IPrA)*, 5(4), 485–513.

Reaser, J. & Wolfram, W. (2007). Voices of North Carolina: Language and life from the Atlantic to the Appalachians. https://cdn.chass.ncsu.edu/sites/linguistics.chass.ncsu.edu/documents/teacher_hi-res.pdf.

Rickford, J. R. (1979). Variation in a Creole Continuum: Quantitative and Implicational Approaches. PhD dissertation: University of Pennsylvania.

Rickford, J. R. (1985). Ethnicity as a sociolinguistic boundary. *American Speech*, 60(2), 99–125.

Rickford, J. R. (1987). *Dimensions of a Creole Continuum: History, Texts and Linguistic Analysis of Guyanese Creole*. Stanford, CA: Stanford University Press.

Rickford, J. R. (1999). *African American Vernacular English: Features, Evolution, Educational Implications*. Oxford: Blackwell.

Rickford, J. R. & King, S. (2016). Language and linguistics on trial: Hearing Rachel Jeantel (and other vernacular speakers) in the courtroom and beyond. *Language*, 92(4), 948–988.

Rickford, J. R. (2019). *Variation, versatility and change in sociolinguistics and creole studies*. Cambridge: Cambridge University Press.

Rickford, J., & King, S. (2019). Language and Linguistics on Trial: Hearing Rachel Jeantel (and Other Vernacular Speakers) in the Courtroom and Beyond. In: J. Rickford & G. Sankoff. *Variation, Versatility and Change in Sociolinguistics and Creole Studies*. Cambridge: Cambridge University Press, 245–300. doi:10.1017/9781316091142.

Rickford, J. R., Sweetland, J., Rickford, A. E. & Grano, T. (2013). *African American, Creole and Other Vernacular Englishes in Education: A Bibliographic Resource*. New York: Routledge; and Urbana, IL: National Council of Teachers of English.

Romaine, S. (1988). Historical Sociolinguistics: Problems and Methodology. In: K. J. Mattheier, ed., *Handbook of Sociolinguistics*. Berlin: Walter de Gruyter, 1452–1469.

Rubdy, R. (2001). Creative destruction: Singapore's Speak Good English movement. *World Englishes*, 20(3), 341–355.

Samuels, M. L. (1963). Some applications of Middle English dialectology. *English Studies*, 44(1–6), 81–94.

Sapir, E. (1921). *Language. An Introduction to the Study of Speech*. New York: Harcourt Brace.

Schendl, H. (2002). Code-choice and code-switching in some early fifteenth-century letters. In: P. J. Lucas & A. M. Lucas, eds., *Middle English from Tongue to Text*. Peter Lang, 247–262.

Schiffrin, D. (1995). Interactional Sociolinguistics. In: S. McKay & N. Hornberger, eds., *Sociolinguistics and Language Teaching* (Cambridge Applied Linguistics). Cambridge: Cambridge University Press, 307–328.

Schleef, E. & Flynn, N. (2015). Ageing meanings of (ing): Age and indexicality in Manchester, England. *English World-Wide*, 36(1), 48–90.

Schneider, E. W. (2007). *Postcolonial English: Varieties Around the World*. Cambridge: Cambridge University Press.

Schneider, E. W. (2016). Grassroots Englishes in tourism interactions: How many speakers acquire "grassroots English" in direct interactions, and what this may mean to them, and perhaps to linguists. *English Today*, 32(3), 2–10.

Schneider, E. W. (2020). *English around the World: An Introduction* (2nd ed.). Cambridge: Cambridge University Press.

Schneider, K. P. (2005). "No Problem, You're Welcome, Anytime": Responding to Thanks in Ireland, England, and the U.S.A. In: A. Barron & K. P. Schneider, eds., *The Pragmatics of Irish English*. Berlin and New York: Mouton de Gruyter, 101–139.

Schneider, K. P. & Barron, A. (2008). Where Pragmatics and Dialectology Meet: Introducing Variational Pragmatics. In: K. P. Schneider & A. Barron, eds., *Variational Pragmatics*. Amsterdam and Philadelphia, PA: John Benjamins Publishing, 1–32.

Schreier, D. (2003). *Isolation and Language Change: Contemporary and Sociohistorical Evidence from Tristan da Cunha English* (Palgrave Studies in Language Variation 1). Houndmills/Basingstoke, and New York: Palgrave Macmillan.

Schreier, D. (2013). Collecting Ethnographic and Sociolinguistic Data. In: J. Schlüter & M. Krug, eds., *Research Methods in Language Variation and Change*. Cambridge: Cambridge University Press, 17–39.

Schreier, D. (2020). World Englishes and Their Dialect Roots. In: D. Schreier, M. Hundt & E. W. Schneider, eds., *The Cambridge Handbook of World Englishes* (Cambridge Handbooks in Language and Linguistics). Cambridge: Cambridge University Press, 384–407.

Sharma, D., Levon, E. & Ye, Y. (2022). 50 years of British accent bias: Stability and lifespan change in attitudes to accents. *English World-Wide*, 43(2), 135–166.

Shuy, R. W. (1968). Detroit speech: Careless, awkward, and inconsistent, or systematic, graceful, and regular? *Elementary English*, 45(5), 565–569.

Shuy, R. W. (1998). *The Language of Confession, Interrogation and Deception*. Thousand Oaks, CA: Sage Publications.

Siebers, L. (2015). Assessing Heterogeneity. In: A. Auer, D. Schreier & R. J. Watts, eds., *Letter Writing and Language Change*. Studies in English Language. Cambridge: Cambridge University Press, 240–263.

Siegel, J. (2006). Language ideologies and the education of speakers of marginalized language varieties: Adopting a critical awareness approach. *Linguistics and Education*, 17(2), 157–174.

Singler, J. V. (2004). The linguistic asylum interview and the linguist's evaluation of it, with special reference to Liberian political asylum applicants in Switzerland. *International Journal of Speech, Language and the Law*, 11, 222–239.

Smith, G. P. (2008). Tok Pisin in Papua New Guinea: Phonology. In: B. Kortmann, E. W. Schneider & K. Burridge, eds., *3 The Pacific and Australasia*. Berlin and New York: De Gruyter Mouton, 188–209. https://doi.org/10.1515/9783110208412.1.188.

Smith, G. (2020). Tok Pisin. In: B. Kortmann, K. Lunkenheimer & K. Ehret, eds., *The Electronic World Atlas of Varieties of English*. (Available online at http://ewave-atlas.org/languages/70, Accessed on 2025-01-30).

Spence, J. L., Hornsey, M. J., Stephenson, E. M. & Imuta, K. (2024). Is your accent right for the job? A meta-analysis on accent bias in hiring decisions. *Personality and Social Psychology Bulletin*, 50(3), 371–386. https://doi.org/10.1177/01461672221130595.

Spolsky, B. (2009). *Language Management*. Cambridge: Cambridge University Press.

Staley, L. & Jucker, A. H. (2021). "The uh deconstructed pumpkin pie": the use of uh and um in Los Angeles restaurant server talk. *Journal of Pragmatics*, 172, 21–34. doi:10.1016/j.pragma.2020.11.004.8.

Stevens, D. (1998). Finding the perfect balance. *English in Education*, 32, 1, 38–44.

Swann, J., Deumert. A., Lillis, T. & Mesthrie, R. (2004). *A Dictionary of Sociolinguistics*. Edinburgh: Edinburgh University Press, x, 368.

Tagliamonte, S. A. (2012). *Variationist Sociolinguistics: Change, Observation, Interpretation*. Oxford: Wiley-Blackwell.

Tagliamonte, S. A. (2015). *Making Waves: The Story of Variationist Sociolinguistics*. Oxford: Wiley-Blackwell.

Thomason, S. G. (2001) *Language Contact: An Introduction*. Edinburgh: Edinburgh University Press. https://doi.org/10.1515/9781474473125.

Ting-Toomey, S. & Oetzel, J. G. (2001). *Managing Intercultural Conflict Effectively*. Thousand Oaks, CA, London, New Delhi: Sage Publications, Inc.

Tottie, G. (2011). Uh and um as sociolinguistic markers in British English. *International Journal of Corpus Linguistics*, 16, 173–197. https://doi.org/10.1075/ijcl.16.2.02tot.

Tracy, K. (1990). The Many Faces of Facework. In: H. Giles & W. P. Robinson, eds., *Handbook of Language and Social Psychology*. Chichester: John Wiley & Sons, 209–226.

Trousdale, G. (2010). *An Introduction to English Sociolinguistics*. Edinburgh: Edinburgh University Press.

Trudgill, P. (1974). *The Social Differentiation of English in Norwich*. Cambridge: Cambridge University Press.

Trudgill, P. (1983). *On Dialect*. Oxford: Blackwell.

Trudgill, P. (1986). *Dialects in Contact*. Oxford: Blackwell.

Trudgill, P. (2003). *A Glossary of Sociolinguistics*. New York: Oxford University Press.

Trudgill, P. (2004). *New-Dialect Formation: The Inevitability of Colonial Englishes*. Edinburgh: Edinburgh University Press. www.jstor.org/stable/10.3366/j.ctv2f4vkzd.

Tse, L. (1996). Language brokering in linguistic minority communities: The case of Chinese- and Vietnamese-American students. *Bilingual Research Journal*, 20(3/4), 485–498.

Vertovec, S. (2006). The Emergence of Super-Diversity in Britain. *Centre on Migration, Policy and Society*, Working Paper No. 25. University of Oxford.

Vertovec, S. (2007). Super-diversity and its implications. *Ethnic and Racial Studies*, 30(6), 1024–1054. doi:10.1080/01419870701599465.

Vincent, D. (1989). *Literacy and Popular Culture: England, 1750–1914*. Cambridge: Cambridge University Press.

Voigt, R., Camp, N. P., Prabhakaran, V., et al. (2017). Language from police body camera footage shows racial disparities in officer respect. *Proceedings of the National Academy of Sciences*, 114(25), 6521–6526.

Wardhaugh, R. (2002). *Understanding English Grammar: A Linguistic Approach*. Oxford UK and Cambridge, MA: Wiley-Blackwell.

Watson, I. (2007). Identity, Language and Nationality. In: S. O'Sullivan, ed., *Contemporary Ireland: A Sociological Map*. Dublin: University College Dublin Press, 351–369.

Watts, R. (2012). Language Myths. In: J. M. Hernández-Campoy & J. M. Conde-Silvestre, eds., *The Handbook of Historical Sociolinguistics*. Chichester: Wiley-Blackwell, 585–606.

Watts, R. & Trudgill, P., eds. (2002). *Alternative Histories of English*. London and New York: Routledge.

Watts, R. J. (2011). *Language Myths and the History of English*. Oxford: Oxford University Press.

Wee, L. (2004). Singapore English: Morphology and Syntax. In: R. Mesthrie. *Varieties or English 4: Africa, South and Southeast Asia*. Berlin and New York: Mouton de Gruyter, 593–609.

Wei, L. (2018). Translanguaging as a practical theory of language. *Applied Linguistics*, 39(1), 9–30.

Wee, L. (2018). World Englishes, second language acquisition, and the linguistic system conundrum. *World Englishes*, 37(1), 51–63.

Weinreich, U., Labov, W. & Herzog, M. I. (1968). Empirical Foundations for a Theory of Language Change. In: E. W. Lehman & Y. Malkiel, eds., *Directions for Historical Linguistics*. Austin, TX: University of Texas, 95–195.

Wells, J. C. (1982). *Accents of English: Volume 1*. Cambridge: Cambridge University Press.

Wieling, M., Grieve, J., Bouma, G., Fruehwald, J., Coleman, J. & Liberman, M. (2016). Variation and change in the use of hesitation markers in Germanic languages. *Language Dynamics and Change*, 6(2), 199–234.

Wiley, T. G. (2003). Language Planning and Policy. In: S. McKay & N. H. Horberger, eds., *Sociolinguistics and Language Teaching*. Cambridge: Cambridge University Press, 103–147.

Wolfram, W. (1993). Ethical considerations in language awareness programs. *Issues in Applied Linguistics*, 4, 225–55.

Wright, K. M. (2023). Housing policy and linguistic profiling: An audit study of three American dialects. *Language*, 99(2), e58–e85.

Index

#BlackLivesMatter xvi, 215–216, 219

accent xv, 2–4, 7–8, 15, 18, 52–53, 133–134, 190, 193, 200, 203, 207, 211, 217, 226, 232, 254–255, 294
acceptance 79, 129, 131, 150, 152, 192, 247
action, affirmative 229
adjacency pairs 156, 185
adstrate 98, 117
African American Vernacular English (AAVE) 6–8, 13, 18, 145, 216, 245, 270, 292, 294
age grading 121, 152
apparent time principle 60, 121, 150, 152
assimilation, linguistic 244, 247, 250
audience design 62–63, 82–83

bad-data problem 136, 152
bilingualism xiii, xv, xvii, 4, 84, 87, 91, 97, 99, 101, 109, 112–114, 117, 175–176, 178, 180–182, 184, 190, 208, 210, 220–221, 223–224, 228–232, 235–238, 242, 245–247, 263, 275, 290
bilingualism, English-knowing 242, 250
Blommaert, Jan xvii, 253, 256–258, 263, 265–268, 271

Chancery Standard 132
Cockney 13–14, 93, 96, 254–255, 271
code
  elaborate 204, 218–219
  restricted 204–205, 219
code-switching xvi, 63, 84, 88, 90, 97, 114–115, 117, 163–165, 168, 179, 181
codification 114, 129–131, 135, 150, 152, 226, 240, 247–248
colonies
  settlement 98, 117
  trade 99, 117
community of practice (CofP) xiii–xiv, 20, 38–39, 52, 71, 73, 80–82, 113, 179, 254, 262, 274
complaint tradition 9, 18, 144
consistency 200, 218–219
contextualization cues 164–165, 167, 172, 179, 182, 184–185
continuum, stylistic 61, 63, 82
Conversation Analysis 156, 185
Corpus of Early English Correspondence (CEEC) 137, 145–146

creoles xv, 11, 84, 96–97, 101–105, 113–114, 116–117, 179, 197, 205, 207–210, 212, 214, 219, 270, 288, 292–293
crossing xvi, 154, 178–180, 182–185

deficit hypothesis 205, 219
Department Store Study 43, 45, 50
descriptivism 11, 18, 288, 293, 295, 303–304
Devonish, Hubert 208, 219
dialect xiii–xvi, xviii, 1, 3–5, 7–9, 11, 13–18, 20–36, 39, 42–44, 47–50, 53–54, 58–59, 62–63, 65, 70, 73–74, 77, 82, 84, 87, 91–97, 99–100, 103, 112–114, 116–117, 121, 125, 127–130, 132–134, 136, 141, 144, 162–163, 165, 178–179, 187–189, 192–195, 197–198, 203, 205–212, 214–218, 232, 240, 242, 245, 250, 253, 255, 269–270, 273–275, 278–279, 282–283, 288, 293–294, 296–298, 302, 304–305
dialectology, perceptual 1, 15, 18, 196–197, 291–292
diglossia 90–91, 114, 117, 207, 300
discrimination, linguistic 192, 194, 215–216, 219
distinctiveness 200–201, 218–219
Dunbar's number 269, 271

early adopters 75–76, 81–82, 146
elaboration 129–131, 150, 152, 247
emigrant letters 141–143, 152
English
  as a Foreign Language (EFL) 88, 96, 110–111, 114, 134
  as a Native Language (ENL) 110–111, 114, 117
  as a Second Language (ESL) 88, 94–95, 109–111, 114, 125, 196
English Only Movement 231, 250
enregisterment 39, 73, 81–82, 262

face xvi, 154, 157, 168–173, 178, 183–185
face-threatening act (FTA) 170–172, 185, 213
face-work 169, 185
feature pool 92, 94, 117, 125
features
  off the shelf 78–79, 82
  under the counter 78, 82
floor 156–159, 161–162, 183–185
frame 166–168, 185

genre 56, 58, 63, 141, 150, 161, 165–166, 168, 183, 185, 199–200, 258
Global Englishes 84, 105–107, 109, 112–113, 117, 221

heterogeneity, orderly 79, 81–82
hypercorrection 95, 117, 136

imperialism, linguistic 225, 250, 266, 269, 271
indexicality xv, 17, 39, 50, 73, 82, 154, 163, 179, 258, 262
innovators 71, 75–76, 80–81
interaction order 165, 169, 185
International Phonetic Alphabet (IPA) xiii, 27–28, 50
internationalization 223, 250

jargons xv, 84, 97, 99–104, 114, 117, 177, 181, 185, 191

Labov, William xiv, 20, 34–38, 40–46, 48–50, 59, 61, 63–66, 71, 74, 76, 79, 81, 122, 140, 146, 165, 188, 190, 192, 196, 203, 205, 254, 273, 280, 293
language analysis for the determination of origin (LADO) 203
language brokering 174–175, 180, 186
language contact xv, 84–86, 88, 97–98, 104, 113–114, 117, 125, 226, 237, 241, 263, 266, 275, 279, 287, 290
language histories from below 123, 137, 140, 152
language hybridization 90, 117
language planning xvii, 160, 174, 189, 220–221, 225–226, 240, 245, 247–248, 250
language proscription 226, 250
language reclamation 235, 250
language survival 220, 239, 244, 250
language vitality 233, 249–250
lingua franca 86, 91, 97, 99–101, 105, 117, 134, 176, 222, 240, 243, 263, 266
linguicism *See* discrimination, linguistic
Linguistic Atlas of New England (LANE) 23, 28, 31, 36
linguistics, forensic 187, 189, 192, 198, 216, 218–219

Māori Language Act 237, 250
marché linguistique 262, 264, 268–269, 271
marketplace, linguistic *See marché linguistique*
Martha's Vineyard xiv, 20, 41–42, 49–51
matched/verbal guise techniques 196–197, 216
mobility xvii, 9, 28, 31–33, 48, 71, 81, 92, 124–126, 128, 137, 146, 180, 238, 252–254, 256–259, 263–265, 268–269, 271, 275, 278, 287–288
Multicultural London English 96, 117, 279–280, 282
multiethnolectalization xv, 95, 117
multilingualism xiii, xv–xviii, 4, 17–18, 58, 65, 84, 87–88, 90–91, 95, 97, 99–101, 103, 105, 109, 112, 114, 117, 127, 154, 165, 174–175, 178, 180–182, 184, 220, 224–225, 231–232, 239, 241–243, 245, 255–256, 262, 268, 271, 282–284, 286–289

nativization 95, 101, 112, 117, 300
networks
 multiplex 67, 70, 72, 75, 82
 social xiv, xvi, 20, 39, 47, 50, 52, 58, 67–69, 71, 75–76, 81–82, 93, 95, 113, 121, 126, 137, 166, 252, 269, 278
 uniplex 67, 72
new-dialect formation 92, 95, 117–118
norm, linguistic 59, 82, 127, 174
NORMs 27, 33–34, 39, 50

observer's paradox 44, 46, 49–50
official language
 de facto 225, 250
 de jure 224–225, 250
Old Bailey Corpus (OBC) 137–138, 152

pidgins xv, 13, 84, 88, 97, 99–105, 113–114, 117, 207, 225–226, 270, 292
planning
 acquisition 226, 244, 248
 corpus 226, 248
 form 250
 function 250
 status 225, 248, 250
Post-Colonial Englishes (PCEs) 112, 117
pragmatics, variationist 186
prejudice, linguistic 53, 193, 219, 291
prescriptivism 12, 18, 53, 132, 144, 146, 188
prestige
 covert 70, 80–82, 264
 overt 70, 80–82, 134, 262
profiling, linguistic 7, 18, 215–216

quotative "like" 55, 78, 82

real-time principle 60, 121, 150, 152
reanalysis 102, 117
Received Pronunciation (RP) 8, 43, 54, 96, 133–134, 152, 207, 211, 306
relexification 103, 117
repertoire, sociolinguistic 4, 18, 57, 67, 71, 73, 75, 102, 109, 159, 168, 176, 182, 209, 217, 232, 252, 262

S-curve 75–76, 82
selection 92–93, 129, 131, 135, 150, 152, 205, 223, 226, 247–249
signs, indexical 165, 167, 182, 184–185
Singlish 13, 18, 241, 243, 250
Social Connotation Hypothesis 14, 18
sociolect 4, 6, 14, 18, 63, 77, 129
sociolinguistics, interactional 155, 158, 165, 173–174, 177, 183–185
Speak Good English Movement xvii, 14, 18, 220, 243, 250

SPEAKING model 55, 58, 65, 72, 81–82
Standard English 9, 14, 18, 89, 102, 115, 127, 132–133, 135, 152, 187, 193, 196–197, 204–208, 210–211, 216, 218, 226, 274
Standard Language ideology 134, 192, 217, 219
stereotypes 5, 7, 15, 44, 74–75, 195
stratification, social 17, 31, 38, 47, 52, 62, 65–66, 70, 80, 82, 122, 137, 146, 149, 188, 253, 258, 262, 280, 282, 291, 302
style xv, 37–38, 40–41, 44, 46–47, 58–59, 61–65, 72, 74, 79, 82, 130, 156, 160, 163–164, 168, 172, 199–201, 205–206, 270, 280, 292
substrate 98, 102, 104, 117, 125
superdiversity 125, 152, 252–253, 256–257, 268, 271
superstrate 97, 100–101, 104–105, 117
Survey of English Dialects 22, 27, 50, 278
switching
  metaphorical 90, 117
  situational 90

translanguaging xvi, 17, 154, 180–184, 186, 289
turn 155–159, 185
turn-taking xvi, 57, 154, 157, 186

uniformitarian principle 121–122, 146, 150, 152

validity
  empirical 137, 150, 152
  historical 137, 150, 152
  social 136–137, 150
variable
  linguistic 32, 37, 59, 82, 297
  sociolinguistic xv, 37, 40, 42–43, 45, 50, 52, 59, 64–66, 79–80, 82, 146, 149, 162–163, 178, 182–183, 265
variation, envelope of xv, 82
vernacular 27, 38, 40, 43, 46, 49–50, 63, 68, 81, 97, 116, 128, 143, 160, 178, 207, 210–211, 215–216, 218, 244, 249, 273, 282, 287, 289, 293–294, 297
vernacularization 223, 249–250

Wenker, Georg 21, 23–27, 50, 59
World Language System xvii, 252, 259–260, 263–271

For EU product safety concerns, contact us at Calle de José Abascal, 56–1°, 28003 Madrid, Spain or eugpsr@cambridge.org.

www.ingramcontent.com/pod-product-compliance
Lightning Source LLC
LaVergne TN
LVHW081523060526
838200LV00044B/1984